D0340486

Enhancing Adult Motivation to Learn

Raymond J. Wlodkowski

Enhancing Adult Motivation to Learn

A Comprehensive Guide for Teaching All Adults

Third Edition

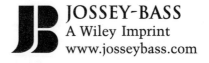

JOSSEY-BASS
A Wiley Imprint
www.josseybass.com

Published by Jossey-Bass
A Wiley Imprint
989 Market Street, San Francisco, CA 94103-1741   www.josseybass.com

Jossey-Bass books and products are available through most bookstores. To contact Jossey-Bass directly call our Customer Care Department within the U.S. at 800-956-7739, outside the U.S. at 317-572-3986, or fax 317-572-4002.

Jossey-Bass also publishes its books in a variety of electronic formats. Some content that appears in print may not be available in electronic books.
Chapter One epigraph from *The Boy Who Would Be a Helicopter* by Vivian G. Paley. Copyright © 1990 by the President and Fellows of Harvard College. Reprinted by permission of Harvard University Press.

Library of Congress Cataloging-in-Publication Data

Wlodkowski, Raymond J.
   Enhancing adult motivation to learn : a comprehensive guide for teaching all adults / Raymond J. Wlodkowski.   —3rd ed.
      p.   cm.   —(The Jossey-Bass higher and adult education series)
   Includes bibliographical references and index.
   ISBN 978-0-7879-9520-1 (cloth)
   1.   Motivation in adult education.   I. Title.
   LC5219.W53 2008
   374.001'9—dc22
                                                                    2007049555

Printed in the United States of America
THIRD EDITION
HB Printing   10 9 8 7 6 5 4 3

The Jossey-Bass
Higher and Adult Education Series

Contents

Preface

When I wrote the last edition of this book, the question that guided its conception was, How can instructors help *all* adults to learn? If we consider only age, income, and ethnicity and race, we have had societal changes in the last ten years that have expanded this challenge significantly. Demographic trends and immigration have increased the diversity of adults throughout postsecondary and workforce education. More adult learners than ever before are English-language learners. The number of younger nontraditional learners and older adult learners in formal educational settings is the highest it has ever been in the history of this country. Among these learners are higher proportions of low-income students as well. Although the enrollment rates for Latino and African American adult learners in two- and four-year colleges have grown, fewer than a quarter of those who enroll complete their degrees.

The increased linguistic and cultural diversity make teaching adults today more exciting than ever before. We have more to learn from each other and more ways to do it better. Our potential as instructors has evolved with greater knowledge in multicultural studies, cognitive and biological sciences, assessment practices, online learning, use of the Internet, and the opportunity to use brain-imaging technology to study learning as it happens.

We continue to have a responsibility to create learning environments that sustain the integrity of all learners as they attain relevant educational success. I am convinced that in conjunction with educational policies that promote the common good, a powerful means to helping all adults learn is to go to the source, to the energy—to human motivation. All adults want to make sense of their world, to find meaning, and to be effective at what they value—this is what fuels their motivation to learn. The key to effective instruction is to evoke and encourage the natural inclination in all adults, whatever their background or socialization, to be competent in matters they hold to be important.

As in the last edition, the model in this book for teaching and planning instruction focuses on how to continually enhance intrinsic motivation among all learners as part of the instructional process. Dr. Margery Ginsberg and I developed the Motivational Framework for Culturally Responsive Teaching in 1994. It is based on the principle that learning and motivation are inseparable from culture. For over a decade, the framework has been applied nationally and internationally with productive learning outcomes.

The Third Edition of *Enhancing Adult Motivation to Learn* is designed to be a practical and immediately usable resource for faculty, trainers, educators, and staff developers whose primary task is instructing adults in universities and community colleges, in professional and industrial settings, and in community organizations. This book will also be very useful to part-time as well as full-time faculty and administrators.

As in the earlier editions, deepening learner motivation and helping adults *want* to learn are the major topics throughout this text. Within the last few years, the number of books about teaching adults seems to have doubled, but this is the only volume focusing on motivation as a constant positive influence during learning. In the chapters that follow, you will learn how to teach or train in ways that make the enhancement of *intrinsic motivation* an essential part of adult learning. Four chapters describe in detail sixty tested strategies for eliciting and encouraging learner motivation. You can choose the strategies that best apply to your content and learning situation.

Among the important additions are insights and examples from the past nine years of application of the motivational framework and the strategies introduced in the previous edition. With applications ranging from postsecondary education to communications technology, in cities from Toronto to Tokyo, ideas advocated in this book have been tried and tested. The results have not been excellent every single time. Through correspondence and on-site visits, I have learned the framework's limitations and advantages and gained a more nuanced understanding of what can be accomplished when teaching is focused on strengthening intrinsic motivation during learning.

What is most exciting to me about this new edition is the integration of a neuroscientific understanding of motivation and learning within an instructional model responsive to linguistically and culturally different adult learners. The research emerging from a biological perspective of learning is used to provide insight and confirm educational practices grounded in knowledge about adult education, the social sciences, and multicultural studies. We are at the beginning of a reciprocal relationship among adult education, biology, and cognitive science, and each has much to learn from the other (Fischer and others, 2007).

This edition has greatly benefited from instructors who use this book as a text for their courses. Their experience and suggestions continue to guide its development. As requested, there are more practical examples and case studies to illustrate the motivational framework and its strategies. In this edition, the sections relating to feedback, self-regulation, and transfer of learning are also more substantive than in earlier editions.

Any instructor who has searched for a straightforward, true-to-life, and useful book on how to enhance adult motivation for learning should find this book helpful. Because the focus of the book is

on motivation and instruction, it does not discuss philosophy, curriculum, or policy in depth. However, there are references to allow
interested readers to pursue further study in most of these areas.
This book is mainly about face-to-face instruction. It can be used
for online learning because the motivational framework and most
of the strategies are applicable to this format. I have worked with
many instructional designers for online learning, and an example
of their instructional plans is included in the Chapter Nine.

Some promises to you the reader:

- A *minimal amount of jargon*. With the growth of technology in adult education and a neuroscientific perspective as part of this edition, I have had to work hard to
  keep this commitment.

- A *little bit of humor*. It's still great to have some fun
  while you're learning.

- *Many examples*. Instructors and learners continue to
  ask for more.

- A *practical and consistent way to design instruction that can
  enhance adult motivation to learn any content or skill*. This
  is my professional raison d'etre. I have co-taught courses
  in disciplines as removed from my background as dye-casting
  and electronics to continue to extend this commitment.

- *Motivation theory and methods positively supported by
  my own experience* Instructors have appreciated this
  characteristic of the book. Nonetheless, please keep
  in mind that my experience is not unlimited.

- A *way to teach that respects the integrity of every learner* This
  promise is a lifelong work in progress. And I do have
  mishaps, faux pas, and mistakes. I continue to videotape my teaching to see if I do as I advocate: to make
  the learner's history, experience, and perspective an

essential consideration that permeates this approach to instruction.

Overview of the Contents

This book focuses on the most important ideas and information to make effective instruction a consistent motivational process that enables optimal learning for culturally diverse adults and their instructors. Chapter One offers a neuroscientific understanding of motivation and learning with discussion and definitions of the physiology of the brain. It also explores the intersection of cultural relevance, adult learning, intrinsic motivation, and neuroscientific understanding, concluding with a view of how instruction can be a path to improving educational success for *all* adults.

Chapter Two addresses the characteristics of adult learners, with particular attention to age, culture, and memory. There are overviews of different orientations to adult intelligences including multiple intelligences, practical intelligence, and emotional intelligence. The last part of the chapter offers a rationale for using a macrocultural approach to adult instruction and learning.

Chapter Three discusses the core characteristics—expertise, empathy, enthusiasm, clarity, and cultural responsiveness—that are necessary for a person to be a motivating instructor. The chapter outlines performance criteria for each characteristic so that you can comprehend, assess, and learn the behaviors that are prerequisites to enhancing learner motivation. It concludes with Paulo Freire's conception of critical consciousness as a guide to creating a learning environment that contributes to the common good of society.

Chapter Four introduces the four conditions—inclusion, attitude, meaning, and competence—that substantially enhance adult motivation to learn. These motivational conditions are dynamically integrated into the Motivational Framework for Culturally Responsive Teaching, a model of motivational theory in action.

This model is also an organizational aid for designing instruction. The framework provides guiding questions for creating instruction that elicits diverse adults' motivation to learn throughout a course or training session.

Chapters Five through Eight provide the central content of this book. Each chapter provides comprehensive treatment of one of the motivational conditions: inclusion is covered in Chapter Five, attitude in Chapter Six, meaning in Chapter Seven, and competence in Chapter Eight. These chapters describe in pragmatic terms how each motivational condition can positively influence learning among culturally diverse adults. They also describe and exemplify a total of sixty specific motivational strategies to engender each of the motivational conditions. Where applicable, I discuss each strategy in terms of its cultural relevance, neuroscientific support, and how it relates to adult learners. In most instances the strategies are referenced to further readings that provide research findings and examples of their use in educational settings.

Chapter Nine summarizes the previous chapters with an outline of all the motivational strategies and their specific purposes. In addition, it explains two ways to use the Motivational Framework for instructional planning, the superimposed method and the source method. The chapter also provides five real-life examples of instructional planning with discussions of how each plan has been designed, using the framework and motivational strategies from the book. With a discussion of the growing literature on self-directed learning and self-regulated learning, this concluding chapter presents useful suggestions for increasing the capacity for lifelong learning among adults. The book ends with an epilogue addressing the ethical responsibility of being an effective instructor of adults.

Acknowledgments

This edition has benefited from the insightful suggestions of instructors, trainers, and students who have read and used this book. Although they have had faith in its merits, they have also spoken to its flaws. I am particularly grateful to David Brightman, senior editor of the Higher and Adult Education Series at Jossey-Bass, for his continuing support of this project and for his enormous patience and guidance. I also want to express my appreciation to Erin Null, editorial assistant at Jossey-Bass, for her responsiveness and care, which contributed to the ease of completing this work. In addition, I want to thank my friends and colleagues at Regis University, George Brown College, and Edgewood College, where I could apply these ideas in earnest and with the benefit of their good will and support. Finally, I wish to thank Margery, Matthew, and Dan for continuing to bring light to my eyes and warmth to my soul throughout this and many other adventures.

Raymond J. Wlodkowski
Seattle, Washington
December 2007

The Author

Raymond J. Wlodkowski is Professor Emeritus at Regis University, Denver, where he was formerly director of the Center for the Study of Accelerated Learning and executive director and founding member of the Commission for Accelerated Programs. He is a licensed psychologist who has taught at universities in Denver, Detroit, Milwaukee, and Seattle. His work encompasses adult motivation and learning, cultural diversity, and professional development. He lives in Seattle and conducts seminars for colleges and organizations throughout North America.

Wlodkowski received his Ph.D. in educational psychology from Wayne State University and has authored numerous articles, chapters, and books. Among them are *Enhancing Adult Motivation to Learn* (Jossey-Bass, 1985), the first edition of which received the Phillip E. Frandson Award for Literature; and *Diversity and Motivation* (Jossey-Bass, 1995), which he coauthored with Margery Ginsberg. Three of his books have been translated into Spanish, Japanese, and Chinese. Wlodkowski has also worked extensively in video production. He is the author of six professional development programs, including *Motivation to Learn*, winner of the Clarion Award from the Association for Women in Communications for the best training and development program in 1991. He has received the Award for Outstanding Research from the Adult Higher Education Alliance, the Award for Teaching Excellence from the University of Wisconsin–Milwaukee, and the Faculty Merit Award for Excellence from Antioch University, Seattle.

Enhancing Adult Motivation to Learn

1

Understanding Motivation
for Adult Learners

*None of us are to be found in sets of tasks or lists of
attributes; we can be known only in the unfolding of
our unique stories within the context of everyday
events.*

Vivian Gussin Paley

Like the national economy, human motivation is a topic that
people know is important, continuously discuss, and would like
to predict. We want to know why people do what they do. But
just as tomorrow's inflationary trend seems beyond our influence
and understanding, so too do the causes of human behavior evade
any simple explanation or prescription. We have invented a word
to label this elusive topic—*motivation*. Its definition varies among
scholars depending on their discipline and orientation. Most social
scientists see motivation as a concept that explains why people
think and behave as they do (Weiner, 1992). Many philosophers
and religious thinkers have a similar understanding of motivation
but use metaphysical assumptions to explain its dynamics.

Today, discoveries in the neurosciences offer a biological basis
for what motivation is. Although this understanding is very far from
complete, what we know about the working of the brain can enrich

and integrate fields as disparate as psychology and philosophy. From a biological perspective, motivation is a process that "determines how much energy and attention the brain and body assign to a given stimulus—whether it's a thought coming in or a situation that confronts one" (Ratey, 2001, p. 247). Motivation binds emotion to action. It creates as well as guides purposeful behavior involving many systems and structures within the brain and body (Ratey, 2001).

Motivation is basic to our survival. It is the natural human process for directing energy to accomplish a goal. What makes motivation somewhat mysterious is that we cannot see it or touch it or precisely measure it. We have to infer it from what people say and do. We look for signs—effort, perseverance, completion—and we listen for words: "I want to . . .," "We will . . .," "You watch, I'll give it my best!" Because perceiving motivation is, at best, uncertain, there are different opinions about what motivation really is.

As educators, we know that understanding why people behave as they do is vitally important to helping them learn. We also know that culture, the deeply learned mix of language, beliefs, values, and behaviors that pervades every aspect of our lives, significantly influences our motivation. What we learn within our cultural groups shapes the physical networks and systems throughout our brains to make us unique individuals and culturally diverse people. Social scientists regard the cognitive processes as inherently cultural (Rogoff and Chavajay, 1995). The language we use to think, the way we travel through our thoughts, and how we communicate cannot be separated from cultural practices and cultural context. Even experiencing a feeling as a particular emotion, such as sadness or joy or jealousy, is likely to have been conceptually learned in the cultural context of our families and peers as we developed during childhood and adolescence (Barret, 2005).

Roland Tharp (Tharp and Gallimore, 1988) tells the story of an adult education English class in which the Hmong students themselves would supply a known personal context for fictional examples. When the teacher used a fictional Hmong name during language practice, the students invariably stopped the lesson to check with one another about who this person might be in the Hmong community. With a sense of humor, these adults brought, as all adults do, their personal experience to the classroom. We are the history of our lives, and our motivation is inseparable from our learning, which is inseparable from our cultural experience.

Being motivated means being purposeful. We use attention, concentration, imagination, passion, and other processes to pursue goals, such as learning a particular subject or completing a degree. How we arrive at our goals and how processes such as our passion for a subject take shape are, to some extent, culturally bound to what we have learned in our families and communities.

Seeing human motivation as purposeful allows us to create a knowledge base about effective ways to help adults begin learning, make choices about and give direction to their learning, sustain learning, and complete learning. Thus, we are dealing with issues of motivation when we as instructors ask such questions as, What can I do to help these learners get started? and, What can I do to encourage them to put more effort into their learning? and, How can I create a relevant learning activity? However, because of the impact of culture on their motivation, the way we answer these questions will likely vary related to the different cultural backgrounds of the learners.

Although there have been attempts to organize and simplify the research knowledge regarding motivation to learn (Brophy, 2004; Stipek, 2002), instructors lack the resources and educational models to consistently and sensitively influence the motivation of linguistically and culturally different adult learners (Guy, 2005). Both culturally responsive teaching (Wlodkowski and Ginsberg, 1995) and neuroscientific understanding of adult learning (Johnson and Taylor, 2006) are recent areas of inquiry and practice in adult education. As a result, instructors still tend to rely on their experience, intuition, common sense, and trial and error. Because intuition and common sense are often based on tacit knowledge, unarticulated understanding, and skills operating at a level below full consciousness and learned within our cultural groups, such knowledge can mislead us. Regrettably, some instructors in culturally diverse settings still grade for participation and believe students should speak directly about personal or uncomfortable topics in front of their peers. These teachers are not mean-spirited or rigid. More likely, they are pragmatic. In general, they believe they get more learner participation by grading for it, and they do not have an effective alternative. And most important, such an approach does not conflict with *their* values.

Without a model of culturally responsive instruction with which to organize and assess their motivational practices, instructors cannot easily refine their teaching. What they learn about motivation from experience on the job and from formal courses is often fragmented and only partially relevant to the increasing diversity in their classrooms and training sessions. However, there are a significant number of well-researched ideas and findings that can be applied to learning situations according to motivation principles. The following chapters thoroughly discuss many of these motivational strategies and present a method to organize and apply them in a manner sensitive to linguistic and cultural differences. As we will see, current neuroscientific principles and research offer considerable support for this model and its related ideas.

Why Motivation Is Important

We know motivation is important because throughout our lives we have all seen the motivated person surpass the less-motivated person in performance and outcome even though both have similar capability and the same opportunity. We know this from our experience and observation. We know this as we know a rock is hard and water is wet. We do not need reams of research findings to establish this reality for us. When we do consult research, we find that it generally supports our life experience regarding motivation. To put it quite simply, when there is no motivation to learn, there is no learning (Walberg and Uguroglu, 1980). In reality, motivation is not an either-or condition, but when motivation to learn is very low, we can generally assume that potential learning will be diminished.

Although there have been research studies of adult motivation to participate in adult education programs (Deshler, 1996; Benseman, 2005), no major research studies thoroughly examine the relationship between adult motivation and learning. If we define *motivation to learn* as the tendency to find learning activities meaningful and worthwhile and to benefit from them—to try to make sense of the information available, relate this information to prior knowledge, and attempt to gain the knowledge and skills the activity develops (Brophy, 2004)—the best analyses of the relationship of motivation to learning continue to be found in youth education. In this field of research, there is substantial evidence that motivation is consistently positively related to educational achievement.

Uguroglu and Walberg (1979) performed a benchmark analysis of 232 correlations of motivation and academic learning reported in forty studies with a combined sample size of approximately 637,000 students in first through twelfth grades. They found that 98 percent of the correlations between motivation and academic achievement were positive. We can reasonably assume that if motivation bears such a consistent relationship to learning for students as old as eighteen years of age, it probably has a similar relationship to adult learning. In support of this assumption, these researchers found that the relationship between motivation and learning increased with the age of the students and the highest correlations were in the twelfth grade.

Perhaps scholars of adult education have been reluctant to examine the relationship between learning and motivation because the bond seems so obvious. As researchers have found (Pintrich, 1991), people motivated to learn are more likely to do things they believe will help them learn. They attend more carefully to instruction. They rehearse material in order to remember it. They take notes to improve their subsequent studying. They reflect on how well they understand what they are learning and are more likely to ask for help when they are uncertain. One needs little understanding of psychology to realize that this array of activities contributes to learning. In a study of adult learners in an urban university, researchers found that when adults perceived their courses as supportive of intrinsic motivation, they were likely to receive higher grades (Wlodkowski, Mauldin, and Gahn, 2001).

Motivation is important not only because it apparently improves learning but also because it mediates learning and is a consequence of learning as well. Psychologically and biologically, motivation and learning are inseparable (Zull, 2002). Instructors have long known that when learners are motivated during the learning process, things go more smoothly, communication flows, anxiety decreases, and creativity and learning are more apparent. Instruction with motivated learners can actually be joyful and exciting, especially for the instructor. Learners who complete a learning experience feeling motivated about what they have learned seem more likely to have a continuing interest in and to use what they have learned. It is also logical to assume that the more numerous their motivating learning experiences in a particular subject, the more probable it is that people will become lifelong learners of that subject.

To maintain a realistic perspective, however, we need to acknowledge that although some degree of motivation is necessary for learning, other factors—personal skill and quality of instruction, for example—are also necessary for learning to occur. If the learning tasks are well beyond their current skills or prior knowledge, people will not be able to accomplish them, no matter how motivated they are. In fact, at a certain point these mandatory learning factors, including motivation, are insufficient. For example, if learners are involved in a genuinely challenging subject for which they have the necessary capabilities, a point will come at which further progress will require effort (motivation), whether in the form of extra practice or increased study time, to make further progress. Conversely, outstanding effort can be limited by the learner's capabilities or by the quality of instruction. Sports are a common example for the limits of capabilities. Many athletes make tremendous strides in a particular sport because of exemplary effort but finally reach a level of competition at which their coordination or speed is insufficient for further progress. An example of the influence of the quality of instruction is a learner who has the capability and motivation to do well in math but is limited by an obtuse textbook with culturally irrelevant examples and an instructor who is unavailable for individual assistance. It is unwise to romanticize or expect too much of motivation. Such a view can limit our resourcefulness and increase our frustration.

One of the indicators of motivation that we most commonly rely on as instructors is effort (Plaut and Markus, 2005). People work longer and with more intensity when they are motivated than when they are not (especially if there are obstacles). Motivated learners care more and concentrate better while they expend effort, and they are more cooperative. They are therefore more psychologically open to the learning material and better able to process information. It is much easier to understand what you want to understand. As Freud (1955, p. 435) said, "One cannot explain things to unfriendly people."

However, it is important to remember that one's cultural background can influence perceptions of effort. For example, when researchers asked what percentage of intelligence is due to natural ability and what percentage to effort, the average percentage due to effort reported by European Americans was 36 percent while Asian Americans reported 45 percent (Heine and others, 2001). Because we may vary to the extent that we recognize effort, as instructors we need to be vigilant about seeing it because motivated learners probably get more spontaneous encouragement and assistance from instructors than unmotivated learners do. We are usually more willing to give our best effort when we know our learners are giving their best effort, an important reciprocity that can affect an entire class.

A Neuroscientific Understanding of Motivation and Learning

What happens biologically when we are motivated to learn? The neurosciences have confronted this question directly and provide remarkable information about what happens within our brains and bodies when we are learning. Although much of this knowledge comes from laboratory studies and work with children (Merriam, Caffarella, and Baumgartner, 2007), much has been learned about the basic structures of the brain and nervous system that provides a biological understanding of motivation and learning. Although this information is not definitive and has not been extensively researched in terms of what happens when adults learn, there is enough agreement in the field of neuroscience about basic structures and processes such as neuronal networks and the function of neurotransmitters to inform teaching in adult education (Johnson and Taylor, 2006).

This book aims to provide a primary understanding of this fundamental research and to use its findings to add support and insight for those ideas that are within the realm of sound adult instructional practice. Ultimately, our ideas about adult learning will need to be considered in terms of their consistency with biological research about learning. We need not make a scientific model preeminent in adult education (Belzer and St. Clair, 2005), but we can use it to strengthen and enrich our work.

An Overview of the Brain

At its most basic level, learning is a biological function, and the brain is most responsible for this process. At this moment your brain is engaged in seeing letters on this page, assembling them into words, connecting those words with meaning, and forming thoughts while it also blocks out distracting sounds like the air conditioning, noises from the outside, and other people talking. Your brain is doing not only all this, but it is also probably suppressing your attention to various odors, sights, and sensations, as well as a few memories and your thoughts about what you might do next after reading this passage. Your brain is also regulating your breathing, blood pressure, and body temperature. And most of the functions just mentioned are happening without any conscious awareness on your part! The brain can do these many different things simultaneously because it is so complex, possibly the most complex object known to us.

Neurons

Recent estimates are that the adult brain has about 100 billion neurons (Bloom, Nelson, and Lazerson, 2001). As illustrated in Figure 1.1, neurons have a cell body, a single long branch known as an *axon*, and multiple shorter branches called *dendrites*. The junction where signals pass from one neuron to another is called a *synapse* (see Figures 1.1 and 1.2). Current brain research supports

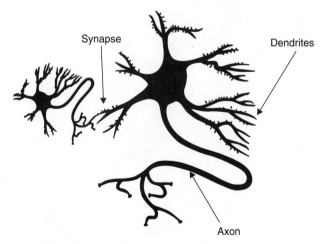

Figure 1.1. Two Neurons Connecting

Source: Jensen, 2005. Used with permission.

the idea that most learning and development occurs in the brain through the process of strengthening and weakening synaptic connections. Because each neuron may have anywhere from one to ten thousand synaptic connections, the number of different patterns of possible connections in the brain is about forty quadrillion, a staggering number, literally beyond my comprehension.

Although there are other cells within the brain, such as glia cells, the neurons are the basic functional cells that appear to control learning. They encode, store, and retrieve information as well as influence all aspects of human behavior (Squire and Kandel, 2000). Neurons act like tiny batteries sending chemical and electrical signals that create processes to integrate and generate information (Jensen, 2005). The threshold for firing at the synapse is determined by the amount of chemicals (called *neurotransmitters*) released onto the receiving neurons (Bloom, Nelson, and Lazerson, 2001). At the synapse, these chemicals either excite the receiving neurons and cause them to fire, or inhibit them from firing, or

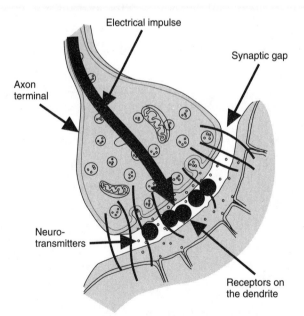

Figure 1.2. The Synapse

Source: Jensen, 2005. Used with permission.

modify their excitability. Examples of common neurotransmitters are dopamine and epinephrine, which are involved in affecting our emotions and mood.

At the most basic level, the extent to which a neuron is active depends on the mass of its dendritic and axonal systems and its overall chemical reactions. The total of all the neurotransmitters arriving from all the dendrites to a neuron's cell body at any moment determines whether it will fire. When we learn something, such as a new word or the name of a new acquaintance, connections containing that information are made between neurons. Through practice and repetition we strengthen the connections and "learn." Neuroscientists have a cliché: "Neurons that fire together wire together." When we learn something, we are building networks of neurons that represent what we are learning. According to Zull (2002, p. 99), "It seems that every fact we know, every idea we understand, and every action we take has the form of a network of neurons in our brain." The brain is constructed so that a smaller unit of knowledge, such as visual recognition of the number 3, is likely to be located in a smaller network of neurons. Small networks are connected with other small and large networks to resemble a forest of neuronal networks with tens of thousands of synaptic connections. Just imagine the possible connections one might have to the number 3! All of these connections are neuronal networks (also called *circuits*) and are apparently dormant before we think of the number 3, but active when we remember it (see Figure 1.3).

From a neuroscientific viewpoint, at the micro level, learning is long-lasting change in existing neuronal networks. When adults learn, they build on or modify networks that have been created through previous learning and experience. These networks are the adult learners' prior knowledge. This is an essential fact that we will return to frequently, both as it pertains to adults' everyday learning and to their cultural perspectives.

An instructor cannot remove the neuronal networks that exist in an adult learner's brain (Zull, 2002). They are a physical entity.

That is why, as instructors, we cannot simply explain something away, especially if it is a deeply held attitude or belief. Literally, another neuronal network has to take the place of the current attitude or belief. That biological development takes repetition, practice, and time. Probably new dendrites must grow and new synaptic connections must form and fire repeatedly. A logical explanation or well-constructed argument usually does not have the biological impact to cause the physical changes in a learner's brain that need to occur for a real alteration in the learner's attitude or belief. If a learner is ready to change a particular belief or attitude, an instructor's explanation may be more persuasive and change can occur. In this case, the learner has developed the neuronal networks through previous learning and experience which need only minimal development or stimulation (our explanation) to

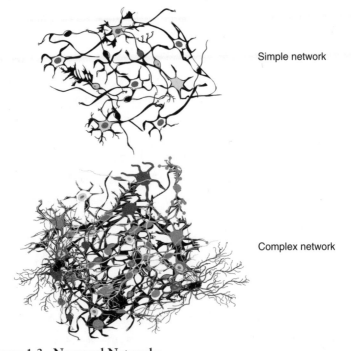

Simple network

Complex network

Figure 1.3. Neuronal Networks

Source: Jensen, 2006. Used with permission.

change the attitude or belief. However, in most instances, Robert Mager's aphorism holds true: "Exhortation is used more and accomplishes less than almost any behavior-changing tool known" (1968, p. 39).

New learning may be able to lessen the use of and even replace particular neuronal networks. Neuronal networks do weaken and die with disuse (Zull, 2002). For all learning, the most pragmatic approach to instruction is to find ways to connect and build on learners' prior knowledge, to begin with what they already know and biologically assemble with them the new knowledge or skill by connecting the established networks and the new networks. A biological approach to learning requires us to find out what adult learners understand and can do, to see such information as a foundation and a map for what we design for the instructional process. The road to masterful teaching takes a compassionate route.

Brain Structures

With the development of neuropsychological tools such as positron-emission tomography (PET) and functional magnetic resonance imaging (fMRI), researchers can study which brain activities are regulated by which brain structures. Both of these instruments are based on the principle that the part of the brain that is most active during a task needs the most oxygen (Bloom, Nelson, and Lazerson, 2001). Although these tools can scan the brain and represent areas high in metabolic activity, they are an indirect assessment of brain structures and their relationship to human action. Based largely on these forms of neuroimaging research and neurosurgery, neuroscientists have categorized areas of the brain and nervous system, aligning them with particular aspects of human functioning and behavior. According to this scheme, the cerebral cortex—the outermost layer of the brain, which is responsible for all forms of conscious activity—can be divided into four lobes that each carry out a set of actions (see Figure 1.4).

- *The frontal lobe.* Located in the area of the forehead; often called the executive; enables us to sustain attention, make plans, solve problems, and form judgments.

- *The parietal lobe.* Located at the top back portion of the head; enables us to locate ourselves in space and process sensory functions, such as messages from the skin and muscles related to movement.

- *The temporal lobes.* Located above and around the ears; enable us to hear, speak, and connect visual areas to language areas, enabling us to see or hear what we read.

- *The occipital lobe.* Located at the back of the head; enables us to see and is involved in the process of attaching emotions to memories and dreams.

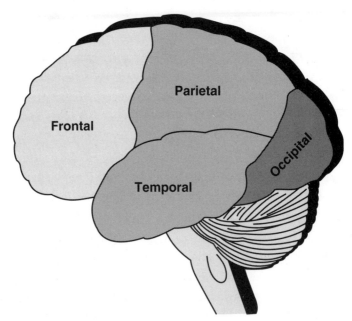

Figure 1.4. Main Areas of the Human Brain

Source: Jensen, 2005. Used with permission.

The middle of the brain, also known as the *limbic system* or *limbic region* (see Figure 1.5), represents about a fifth of the brain, and is extremely important in helping us to feel what we feel about our lives and the world. The limbic system is a group of brain structures that regulate our emotions, those feelings that indicate our motivation about anything. These six are among the most important structures of the limbic system:

- *The amygdala.* A vigilant monitor that gives meaning to human experience on an immediate level. It reacts to experiences before we consciously understand them, especially those that appear threatening or dangerous (LeDoux, 1996). In situations of uncertainty, it primes the brain to be alert and tuned to subtle cues for further possible action (Compton, 2003).

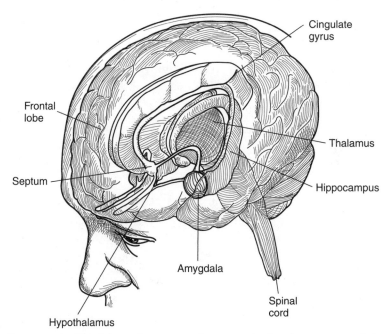

Figure 1.5. The Major Structures Forming the Limbic Region of the Brain

Source: Bloom, Nelson, and Lazerson, 2001. Used with permission.

- *The thalamus.* A relay station for almost all sensory information (Bloom, Nelson, and Lazerson, 2001).

- *The hypothalamus.* Influences and regulates hormone secretion. Because it monitors information from the autonomic nervous system, it affects appetite, sleep, sexuality, and emotions (Bloom, Nelson, and Lazerson, 2001).

- *The hippocampus.* Helps to form long-term explicit (conscious) memories. Although it does not store memories, it integrates new memories with other memories, a function very important to learning (Zull, 2002).

- *The cingulate gyrus.* Encircles the other structures of the limbic system and appears to mediate communication between them and the cerebral cortex (Bloom, Nelson, and Lazerson, 2001).

- *The septum.* Appears to facilitate the release and binding of dopamine, the neurotransmitter primarily involved in creating positive moods and emotions. It plays a role in maintaining and altering motivation (Zull, 2002).

Although identifying these structures of the brain gives us a basic vocabulary for discussing adult learning and motivation, we need to remember that the brain is part of a nervous system that extends to every part of the body. There is strong connectivity within the brain and between the brain and the rest of the nervous system. The brain works so well because its individual structures are so efficiently interdependent.

This broader understanding of the connection between the brain and the central nervous system can lead to some confusion. In conventional usage, the neursoscientific literature does not distinguish between *neuronal networks* and *neural networks*. When it does make a distinction, neuronal networks are usually discussed in relation to brain functioning, whereas neural networks are more often discussed in relation to the central nervous system, which includes the brain, the spinal cord, and the peripheral nervous system. As I use these two similar terms in this book, I will follow this distinction.

Our current knowledge of the central nervous system is still inadequate to explain with specific certainty how the brain operates. The brain's dynamism also makes it an elusive subject for study. As Jensen writes (2005, p. 11), "Whether you are 2 or 92, your brain is a cauldron of changing chemicals, electrical activity, cell growth, cell death, connectivity, and change." For these reasons we need to use our knowledge of the brain judiciously to discuss learning and motivation. Before we carry out any instructional ideas based on neuroscience, we need to understand how well they are integrated and consistent with our current models, research, and practice in adult education.

A Neuroscientific Perspective of Motivation

Merging a neuroscientific understanding of motivation with current knowledge from psychology and education creates ideas that are richer, more nuanced, more complex, and, fortunately, quite promising. The brain has evolved over millions of years as the major organ for ensuring human survival. In evolutionary terms, the neocortex, the part of the brain fundamental to thinking, analyzing, and planning, is considered young because it has evolved within only the last five to ten million years (Zull, 2002). As human beings, we *want to learn* because learning is our means for survival. Knowing what to fear and what to desire is essential to our future. We use cognition to maintain control and to generally navigate away from fear and toward pleasure.

The brain has an inherent inclination for knowing what it wants. In human terms, that means relevance (Ahissar and others, 1992). We are compelled to pay attention to things that matter to us. Every moment of our lives is a competition among our senses to perceive what matters most. Our emotions usually tell us this, often before we can reflect upon the situation and especially when we feel threatened. What matters is defined through our cultural perspectives which carry language, values, norms, and perceptual frameworks to interpret the world we live in.

As we experience our world, events that are accompanied by feelings receive preferential processing in the brain (Christianson, 1992). Because they are salient for survival, emotions add importance to our thoughts and experiences. Structures in the brain and their related neurotransmitters convey these emotions to us moment by moment. For example, the neurotransmitter dopamine is usually connected with feelings of pleasure and elation, and norepinephrine seems to induce a state of arousal.

Although emotions capture our attention, we spend most of our waking hours in mind-body states that are made up of sensations (for example, hunger and fatigue), emotions (joy and anger), and thoughts (optimism and concentration) that combine and recombine simultaneously (Damasio, 1999). These mind-body states are made up of millions of neurons in complex web-like signaling systems that represent our behavior. They are quickly shifting neuronal networks that involve multiple structures of the brain. Jensen (2005) draws an apt analogy when he compares their operation to the dynamic atmospheric patterns we call weather. From a neuroscientific perspective, when we are doing something, these mind-body states represent our motivation. We are likely to identify them by the emotion or mood most obvious to us at the moment, such as "I'm getting *bored* with reading this textbook." Although our mind-body state may seem stable as we proceed with a task, in reality it is in a state of flux, diminishing, strengthening, or changing into another state. On the single page of a book or in the span of five minutes in a course, we may go from feeling inspired, to feeling frustrated, to feeling creative, and then inspired again.

The theories of intrinsic motivation fit very well with a neuroscientific understanding of motivation. As defined by Ryan and Deci (2000, p. 16), "intrinsic motivation is entailed whenever people behave for the satisfaction inherent in the behavior itself." For example, people read a novel because they find it inherently interesting. Behavior that people find intrinsically satisfying probably conforms to what their brains are physiologically disposed to want and induces or is compatible with a positive mind-body state.

We know from psychological research that it is part of human nature to be curious, to be active, to make meaning from experience, and to be effective at what we value (Lambert and McCombs, 1998). These are primary sources of motivation that reside in all of us, across all cultures. When adults can see that what they are learning makes sense and is important according to their values and perspective, their motivation emerges. Such circumstances elicit intrinsic motivation and probably facilitate a mind-body state conducive to learning. Intrinsic motivation is evoked; it is a physical energy aroused by an environment that connects with what is culturally relevant to people.

A neuroscientific understanding of intrinsic motivation confirms that we need to create learning environments that access what biologically motivates adults from within. In addition, intrinsic motivation is probably more emotionally salient and varied than it was originally conceived to be. We feel many different emotions while learning, and they may not all be consistently positive. As instructors, we need to pay close attention to the emotions of adult learners and construct with them a learning environment that supports the optimal expression of their emotions in service of their learning. This topic will be addressed throughout this book.

Although Csikszentmihalyi's theory of intrinsic motivation and flow (1997) directly addresses the importance of feedback in learning, a neuroscientific perspective also emphasizes that feedback is essential to the human need for survival. For how the brain operates, this means the feeling of being in control. Feedback about one's learning and behavior significantly contributes to one's sense of control and is vital to intrinsic motivation and improving learning (Zull, 2002). Extensive coverage of strategies to enhance feedback is found in Chapter Eight.

The Intersection of Cultural Relevance, Intrinsic Motivation, and Neuroscientific Understanding

In 1996, Brookfield emphasized the need for a culturally relevant perspective of adult learning: "The differences of class, culture, ethnicity, personality, cognitive style, learning patterns, life experiences, and gender among adults are far more significant than the fact that they are not children or adolescents" (p. 379). Today, the cultural context is recognized as an essential consideration for defining as well as facilitating adult learning (Merriam, Caffarella, and Baumgartner, 2007). Theories of intrinsic motivation respect the influence of culture on learning. They include the understanding that the learner's perspective, language, values, and ways of knowing must be considered in order to foster adult motivation to learn (Wlodkowski and Ginsberg, 1995). When adults care about what they are learning and know they are becoming more effective at what they value by means of that learning, their intrinsic motivation surfaces like a cork rising through water. The instructor can feel it when the learning environment has stimulated the adults' neurophysiological propensity to provide energy for what matters!

Intrinsic motivation is governed to a large extent by emotions, which in turn are socialized through culture. Emotions influence task engagement, the visible outcome of learner motivation. For example, one person working at a task feels frustrated and stops; a second person working at the task feels joy and continues; and yet another person, with a different set of cultural beliefs, feels frustrated at the task but continues with increased determination. The response to the task—frustration, joy, or determination—may differ across cultures because cultures differ in their definitions of novelty, hazard, opportunity, and gratification and in their definitions of appropriate responses (Kitayama and Markus, 1994). Thus, a person's response to a learning activity reflects his or her culture.

From this viewpoint, culturally responsive teaching is necessary if we are to teach all adults effectively. Even though the learn- ers' internal logic may not coincide with our own, it is present nonetheless. To be effective we must understand that perspective. Rather than trying to figure out what to "do to" learners, we should "work with" them to elicit their intrinsic motivation. Through rela- tionships and teaching strategies, we access their prior knowledge (existing systems of neuronal networks), as expressed through their cultural perspectives, in order to build bridges between what adult learners know and their new learning. Seeing adults as unique and active, we emphasize communication and respect, realizing that through understanding and sharing our resources we create greater energy for learning. When it is working, excellent teaching and learning is like breathing together.

Emotion, Memory, and Intrinsic Motivation

Research in the neurosciences and the field of intrinsic motivation indicates that emotions are critical to learning. Not only do emo- tions largely determine what we pay attention to and help us to be aware of our mind-body states, they also affect what we remem- ber. We are much more likely to remember things that engage us emotionally. It appears that the more powerful the feeling that accompanies an experience, the more lasting the memory.

Long-term memory, durable neuronal networks, seems to be strongly affected by emotions. We know now that long-term memory is not a permanent trace or print of a past event. It works dynamically, reassembling feelings and information from our past into our present understanding. For example, during stressful experiences, hormones such as adrenaline and cortisol are released. They heighten alertness and mobilize parts of the nervous system responsible for movement. They also enhance memory for the experience (LeDoux, 1996; Abercombrie and others, 2003). These hormones are likely to have been present while some of our strongest memories—such as those of births, deaths, and romances—were being made. These chemicals help to create a system of sounds, images, and locations represented by neural networks that are activated and reintegrated among various structures of the brain when they are stimulated by an experience or object such as a question, a person's face, or a particular song (Shimamura, 2002). In the moment, we recall a memory, unaware that thousands of neurons have fired in a particular pattern involving multiple locations in our brain and nervous system.

The biological process of how emotions affect memory is complex and our understanding is incomplete. However, we are reasonably certain that moderate stress and positive emotions such as satisfaction, joy, and feeling creative help us to retain what we are learning and to reassemble what we have learned when we need to recall it (Zull, 2002). Emotions also give texture to events and help us to understand them. Because neurotransmitters such as dopamine that are associated with pleasurable emotions tend to be released in situations of moderate challenge and excitement, we as instructors can create lessons that encourage these emotions and consequently better memory for what is being learned.

In theories of intrinsic motivation, emotions are critical to learning as well. Optimal emotional states for learning, such as flow, have been extensively studied and documented across and within cultures (Csikszentmihalyi and Csikszentmihalyi, 1988). When people are in flow—whether at work, play, or while learning in a course—they feel totally involved, immersed in a seemingly effortless performance, fully alive, and without self-consciousness (Csikszentmihalyi, 1997). Often while being in flow, people report feelings of joy, happiness, creativity, and capability. Emotionally, intrinsic motivation is not static and does not remain constant during learning or work. Flow is one of the most positive states of intrinsic motivation. During this time we are fully absorbed, emotionally positive, and very focused. In other intrinsically motivating situations we may be less consistently involved, only mildly interested, and, at times, feel a bit worn or fatigued. Emotions are labile, neurophysiologically undergoing chemical and biological change. A mere distraction, such as the noise of construction work outside the classroom, can disrupt our concentration. The processes of reading, writing, listening, and problem solving undulate with varying degrees of stimulation and appeal whatever their source.

My experience as a teacher and a learner is that intrinsic motivation often fluctuates during a learning activity. Overall, I may judge my involvement as intrinsically motivated but with periods when I am bored or disinterested. For an entire learning experience, it might be more accurate to gauge my intrinsic motivation along a scale from mildly intrinsically motivated to deeply intrinsically motivated or in flow. However, such a measure does not register all the possible emotions that I may have felt during the learning activity, such as interest, wonder, and worry. Also, I know from experience that the degree of value that adults have for an activity affects their perception of how motivating that activity is. For example, writing, at times, can be frustrating and tedious. My value for it is obviously strong and there are periods when I seem to be anesthetized from the tedium. But moment to moment, it is my emotions that tell me the degree of my intrinsic motivation for the task at hand. Given the physiology and dynamics of brain functioning, an understanding of intrinsic motivation as a supple phenomenon is fitting. Eventually, intrinsic motivation will probably be more accurately measured by an instrument that has the capacity to measure intensity as a thermometer determines temperature. Beyond brain functioning, this instrument will also need to be sensitive to differing emotional states.

Underserved and Diverse Adult Learners in Postsecondary Education

As a field of study and advocacy, adult education has been a force for increasing adults' access to and success in postsecondary education. Through political action, literacy efforts, and program development, adult educators have contributed to increasing the number of adults who have earned professional certification and degrees in two-year and four-year colleges. Partially but significantly due to these efforts, nearly 40 percent of all college students today are adults 25 years and older (National Center for Education Statistics, 2002). Programs responsive to the needs and development of adult learners abound in industry, business, and college. If current trends continue, more than 50 percent of all adults between 25 and 55 will be involved in some form of adult education by 2010 (Cook and King, 2004).

However, success in higher education for historically under-represented groups (African Americans, Latinos, and Native Americans) and low-income adults continues to be a serious concern. In 2002, 29 percent of all 25- to 29-year-olds had completed four or more years of college. For whites, the percentage was nearly 36 percent; for African Americans, 18 percent; and for Latinos, slightly less than 9 percent. Although there has been improvement since 1974 for each racial/ethnic group, the improvement parallels the current disproportionate rates of progress. While the Latinos who completed four or more years of college increased 3 percent and African Americans increased 10 percent, whites increased nearly 14 percent during the same period (Mortenson, 2003).

Research indicates that family income is a major factor affecting college graduation. Forty percent of adult undergraduates, roughly 2.5 million people, have annual incomes less than $25,000 (Cook and King, 2004). In 1995–96, among low-income adults who were pursuing either a bachelor's or associate degree, only 7 percent achieved a bachelor's degree and 8 percent an associate's degree within the next six years. In this same time period, 42 percent of traditional-age students (18- to 24-year-olds) who were pursuing a bachelor's degree accomplished their goal (Cook and King, 2004). The competing demands of family and work as well as educational challenges due to insufficient academic preparation likely combine to lessen the chances of success in college for many low-income adults. With 70 percent of current jobs requiring some form of postsecondary education (Carnevale and Desrochers, 1999), low-income adults are ensnared in low-wage occupations with little prospect of moving themselves or their families out of poverty.

Historically underrepresented groups and low-income adults are underserved students, lacking the accessibility and support, financial as well as academic, to be successful in postsecondary education. This situation is a critical issue for adult educators. In 2002, 50 percent of people living in poverty in the United States were African American or Hispanic (U.S. Department of Labor, 2003). Their economic status is undeniably due to their lack of education beyond high school and their historic underrepresentation in higher education. As adult educators, we have a moral and professional obligation to render postsecondary education accessible and successful for all adults. In my opinion, this mandate applies as well to trainers in business and industry, where educating adults is an enterprise that matches or exceeds postsecondary education in financing and resource allocation.

Improving higher education and making it more equitable is far more than an altruistic venture. The nation needs to remain competitive with skilled and effective workers in a global marketplace (Friedman, 2005). At the time of this writing, we are in the midst of the largest immigration in the history of this country. Between 1991 and 2001 approximately 10.2 million people immigrated to the United States (Constitutional Rights Foundation, 2006). Today, this trend continues. In addition, there is an estimated population of 12 million undocumented workers residing in the United States. Such demographics emphasize the need for adult educators and trainers to make higher education and advanced training accessible and successful for all adults.

Postsecondary education benefits the United States citizenry as well as the individual. Higher levels of education correlate with higher incomes, better health, and lower levels of mortality (Lleras-Muney, 2002). Education is associated with lower rates of crime, fewer illegitimate births, and less dependency on welfare benefits (Lochner and Moretti, 2001; Wolfe and Zuvekas, 1995). According to the U.S. Department of Education (1998), college-educated adults (85 percent) are more likely to vote than high school graduates (72 percent) and high school dropouts (50 percent). From their review of postsecondary education and employment, Anthony Carnevale and Donna Desrochers conclude (2004, p. 33), "Adults who are not equipped with the levels of knowledge and skill necessary to get, and keep, good jobs are denied full inclusion and tend to drop out of the mainstream culture, polity, and economy."

Among the greatest losses for our society when underserved adult students are not present in our college programs are their cultural perspectives and aesthetics. As microcosms of the broader society, college courses often implicitly and explicitly perpetuate stereotypes and larger systems of inequality—for example, conspicuous consumption without consideration of the common good. Adult students from underrepresented economic backgrounds and ethnic or racial groups can offer ideas, language, examples, and frames of reference that can help majority groups examine ways in which they may unknowingly use dominant beliefs and values that inhibit the welfare of others. For example, individual freedoms may favor the more privileged. And how government monies are allocated is a topic likely to be more informed by adults from different income groups.

In general, diversity as a broad category including race, class, gender, ethnicity, sexual orientation, religion, disability, age, and other significant differences is central to education as preparation to live and work within a global economy with many different people. In fact, research with traditional-age college students indicates that when they are exposed in their courses to diverse perspectives through interaction with students different from themselves, they develop more complex thinking skills and learn more (Gurin and others, 2002). My personal experience with adult students supports this finding. For a more equitable and effective pluralistic society, we need to learn with diverse adults. For the future, diversity in adult education is an imperative and an opportunity.

Instruction as a Path to Improving Educational Success among All Adults

Efforts to increase the success of adult learners in higher education offer promising policies and insights. They include financial assistance, especially to low-income adults (Cook and King, 2005; Choitz and Widom, 2003); stronger student support services including academic advising, personal counseling, tutoring, and remediation (Purnell and Blank, 2004; Flint and Associates, 1999); a commitment to adult learners with a focus on meeting their needs (Cook and King, 2005; Flint and Associates, 1999); and faculty and instruction responsive to adult learners (Cook and King, 2005; Flint and Associates, 1999; Grubb and Associates, 1999). Many of the studies cited in this paragraph were conducted at community colleges, where the majority of adult learners in postsecondary education are enrolled. However, the largest number of adult learners, approximately 61 million, participate in work-related courses and training (Paulson and Boeke, 2006). Unless specifically referenced to higher education, all instructional methods, principles, and models suggested in this text apply to this population as well.

No single policy, program, or response significantly raises the persistence and degree completion of adult learners (Cook and King, 2005; Flint and Associates, 1999). What is required is a systemwide effort to improve a range of elements from financial assistance to instruction. Three books and reports that outline, discuss, and offer examples of these elements and how they might be implemented are *Best Practices in Adult Learning: A Self-Evaluation Workbook for Colleges and Universities* (Flint, Zakos, and Frey, 2002), *Improving Lives through Higher Education: Campus Programs and Policies for Low-Income Adults* (Cook and King, 2005), and *Promoting Student Success in Community College and Beyond* (Brock and LeBlanc, 2005).

The focus of this book is on how instructors, teaching, and learning environments can enhance the motivation of all adults to learn. Researchers have found that improvements in instruction can contribute to increased student persistence and success (Grubb and Associates, 1999; Kuh and others, 2005). Their suggestions include more active learning, greater relevance of subject matter to students' lives, and higher levels of student engagement. Best practices for adult learners in postsecondary institutions include the same three suggestions as well as inclusive learning environments, use of the language of learners and their communities, and assessment of learner competence through performance outcomes (Flint, Zakos, and Frey, 2002).

Thus, we can see some convergence between the recommendations from research to improve adult success in college and the literature about best practices for adult learners. This gives us more confidence about what we need to do in the area of instruction to enhance adult learning and motivation. The Motivational Framework for Culturally Responsive Teaching (Wlodkowski and Ginsberg, 1995), which forms the major focus of this book (see Chapter Four), systematically includes these instructional practices as an integral aspect of instructional design and teaching. Factors of this motivational framework have been significantly associated with higher grade point averages (Wlodkowski, Mauldin, and Gahn, 2001) and higher performance (Wlodkowski and Stiller, 2005) among adult learners. This framework can serve as an effective guide for educators and trainers as we plan and carry out our instruction with adult learners. A strength of this model is that it recognizes that human motivation is inseparable from culture and at the same time understandable as energy resulting from biological processes largely within the brain. This approach to teaching allows for a useful integration of these two important sources of pedagogical knowledge. In the next chapter we will deepen our understanding of motivation to learn as it relates to culture and adult development.

2

Understanding How Aging and Culture Affect Motivation to Learn

The afternoon knows what the morning never suspected.

Swedish proverb

Released from comparison with youth, "old" can be hip, powerful, and aesthetic. Old is rhythm and blues. Old is marching with Martin Luther King Jr. Old is hearing a scratchy vinyl record of Edith Piaf singing lyrics of love and loss and knowing from your own life she is telling the truth many times over. Old is Michelangelo's *David*. Old is the Kama Sutra. And old is the Taj Mahal. As James Hillman writes (1999, p. 42), "When 'old' gains its definition only by pairing, it loses its value. In a culture that has only identified with 'new' . . . 'old' gets the short end of the comparative stick, and it becomes ever more difficult to imagine oldness as a phenomenon apart from the lazy simplicities of conventional wisdom."

In fact, the word *old* derives from an Indo-European root that means "to nourish." In medieval times, *old* meant "fully nourished or matured." Not that old is better than young or new; old is its own thing—certain to be humbled by aging and death but also to be affirmed for the character, perspective, and vitality it can offer to life among all ages. Old is the nurturance of grandparents, the guidance of mentors, and the stories carried through our families that give us an identity and a sense of connection with all living things. As we will see in this chapter, older adults are a rapidly growing group among adult learners, and their characteristics and needs enrich and challenge adult education.

Characteristics of Adult Learners

It is a bit frustrating but understandable that in the field of adult education there is no agreement on the definition of *adult* (Paulson and Boeke, 2006). The term is culturally and historically relative. Some cultures regard puberty as entry into adulthood, whereas others use legal codes to permit and promote adult behavior. In the United States, people can vote at eighteen but cannot drink until twenty-one and, in particular instances, can be tried in court as adults at fourteen. In conventional terms, being an adult is often associated with having some kind of major life responsibility, such as full-time work or dependents.

Chronologically, adults can be divided into three groups: younger adults (18 to 24 years old), working-age adults (25 to 64 years old), and older adults (65 and older). Most students attending traditional colleges where they board and are enrolled full time are younger adults. However, most research and theory in the field of adult education pertains to working-age adults, who are assumed to work at least part time while going to school. As the number of older adults continues to grow, they are also of increasing interest in adult education. In the 2000 U.S. Census, older adults accounted for 12 percent of the total population.

Today, 73 percent of all college students can be identified as nontraditional learners (National Center for Education Statistics, 2002). They possess one or more of the following characteristics: delayed enrollment into postsecondary education, part-time attendance, financial independence, full-time job, dependents other than a spouse, being a single parent, and having a nonstandard high school diploma. Most of these nontraditional students are working-age adults, but some are young adults or older adults. Although nontraditional students are considered at greater risk of failing to complete a degree, nearly one-third of them succeed. Maybe what is actually at risk are the generalizations made about them.

The focus of this book is on working-age adults, nontraditional college students, and older adults. Unless specifically stated otherwise, all strategies, principles, and models proposed in this text can be applied to them.

Women make up the majority (approximately 65 percent) of adult college students 25 and older. They compose approximately 65 percent of this population (Aslanian, 2001). Three reasons primarily explain why they outnumber men: (1) there are more women than men in the general U.S. population 25 and older; (2) more women view education as a path to success; and (3) women today have more opportunity to go to college than previous generations due to changes in role expectations and family support.

Among students 25 and older, approximately 12 percent are ethnic or racial minorities (Aslanian, 2001). This adult minority population is much smaller than the overall minority population in higher education (approximately 30 percent), especially in community colleges. According to the National Center for Education Statistics (2001), 39 percent of African American, 54 percent of Hispanic, 47 percent of American Indian, and 38 percent of Asian American and Pacific Islander postsecondary students attend community colleges. In some community colleges in large urban areas and in the West and Southwest United States, minority students have become a majority. As Berta Vigil Laden has observed (2004), "The term *minority* is being replaced with the more descriptive terms *racially diverse* and *emerging majority* to convey more fully these students' presence in institutions of higher education." Many of these community college students are 25 and older or are younger adults with characteristics of working-age adults such as full-time jobs and dependents. We are witnessing a cultural transformation whose beginning is most strongly felt in community colleges. All these groups of adult learners share a common goal: they want to use the knowledge and skills they acquire to enhance their careers or professional opportunities—for better jobs, higher salaries, coveted promotions, or simply staying competitive (Aslanian, 2001).

Another national trend is the increasing number of older adults working full time and participating in adult learning. Over 2 million adults 65 and older participate in work-related courses and training (O'Donnell, 2005). Not only does learning add purpose to life for many older adults, it also appears to improve their health (Campbell, 2006). Researchers from multiple disciplines concur that learning is essential to a satisfying later life (Manheimer, 2002). Learning during older adulthood appears to be related to better physical vitality and cognitive functioning.

Prior postsecondary education may increase older adults' desire for learning. Some scholars believe education is addictive and that the more education people have had, the more they will want, especially in later life (Mehrotra, 2003). Postsecondary education may establish a desire for intellectual activities such as reading, reflecting, and problem solving. Continuing these pursuits sustains brain-cell growth and higher cognitive functioning among older adults (Diamond, 2001). In this respect, college-educated older adults may be more likely to value learning for its own sake (Purdie and Boulton-Lewis, 2003). Because they often are in a position to choose what they learn, older adults are more likely to find learning intrinsically motivating. The Gerontological Society of America has confirmed the understanding that aging is about adding life to years, not years to life. As adult educators, we can help make this self-fulfilling prophecy come true.

Specific Effects of Aging

We have described the benefits of learning for older adults. The potential for a satisfying and vital life seems greater than ever before. But there are also many myths and stereotypes about older people, frequently negative ones. Let's take a closer look.

It was once thought that aging was a barrier to learning. This seems less so than ever before. Improved sanitation, nutrition, hygiene, and advances in medical drugs and treatments have increased life expectancy in most industrialized countries. As of 2006, the average life expectancy in the United States was 77.8 years (U.S. Census Bureau, 2006). Since the early 1990s, it has been documented that people remain more active and feel physically better for longer in their older years (Smolak, 1993). Adults over 85 are the fastest-growing segment of the U.S. population (U.S. Department of Health and Human Services, 2003). With the vitality projected by popular icons like Gloria Steinem and B. B. King, even 70 no longer seems old. (This seems ever so true as I enter my early sixties.)

There are significant culturally related differences as people age. For example, women live longer than men (U.S. Census Bureau, 2006). To put this generalization in perspective, between the ages of 65 and 74, there are 83 men for every 100 women; among people over 85, there are only 46 men for every 100 women. As we grow older, women eventually outnumber men by more than two to one. In addition, there is far less ethnic or racial diversity among older adults. The percentage of the U.S. population that is non-Hispanic White increases with age from 79 percent of people between 55 and 64 years of age to 87 percent of those who are 85 and over. This decrease indicates some of the disparities in income, living environments, disease exposure, and available medical care between the majority population of this country and its racial/ethnic minorities.

Although racial/ethnic inequalities persist, becoming older does not mean automatic physical, emotional, or mental deterioration, and the effects of aging differ from person to person. As people reach their 40s and 50s, they undergo changes in vision, cardiovascular and respiratory functioning, reproductive potential (among women), and muscular and skeletal resilience (Bee and Bjorkland, 2004). Beginning slowly, this decline usually accelerates as people enter their 70s. Compensation can offset this deterioration. Eyeglasses, hearing aids, medications, increased illumination, and increased time for learning are some of the ways to equalize learning opportunities for older adults.

Central Nervous System, Vision, and Hearing

According to longitudinal studies, most normal, healthy adults can be efficient and effective learners well into old age (Schaie, 2005). Although considerable individual differences exist, the intellectual capacity to learn declines only modestly until most people are in their 80s. Variables that reduce the risk of intellectual decline among older adults are absence of chronic diseases, a favorable living environment, an active lifestyle, a partner with high cognitive functioning, satisfaction with one's life, and continued involvement with learning (Merriam, Caffarella, and Baumgartner, 2007; Campbell, 2006).

Because of research on the aging brain, aging is no longer seen as inevitably leading to brain damage and decline. Aging is now seen as a much more complex phenomenon: through reorganization and plasticity the brain can sustain a productive and happy life far into the older years (Reuter-Lorenz and Lustig, 2005). There is evidence that the brains of adults in their 70s and 80s continue to produce new neurons for cognition (Prickaerts and others, 2004). The combination of physical exercise, stimulating environments, and continued learning appears to be able to increase brain cell growth and connections throughout life (Willis, 2006).

Older learners may require more time to learn new things because, on the average, their reaction time is slower than that of younger learners (Schaie and Willis, 2002). This is due to changes in the central nervous system. However, individual older adults differ substantially in this regard, and the type of task makes a significant difference as well. For example, putting a puzzle together or hitting a button to respond to the identification of a symbol is far different from creating an effective business plan or providing legal advice about a real problem. Speed of response by itself should not prevent anyone from learning what he or she wants to learn. Allowing older adults to control the pace of educational experiences and their exposure to educational materials is an excellent strategy to accommodate any decrease in reaction time.

Some people believe that because of the decline in vision, reading is a serious problem for older adults. However, in the absence of disease or serious impairment, the normal physical changes of the eyes can be accommodated through the use of eyeglasses and brighter light. Older adults do have more difficulty rapidly processing visual information and should be allowed more time and control for extracting information from printed materials, computer screens, photographs, films, and other screen projections (Pesce and others, 2005).

The decline in hearing has also been well researched (Bee and Bjorkland, 2004). Hearing difficulty affects more than 25 percent of adults over the age of 65, and more than 50 percent of males over the age of 75. In addition to hearing loss, as people become older they may also develop a "translation" problem. Rapid speech is more difficult for older adults to decipher. In addition, adults over 50 usually have some impairment in discerning very soft sounds and high-pitched sounds. Attending to the acoustic environment and moderating the speed of presentation and verbal delivery can help older adults adjust for this sensory loss.

Intellectual Functioning

As a psychologist, I am among those who no longer regard intelligence as a unitary property. Rather, intelligence seems to make more sense and be a much more useful concept when understood as consisting of multiple factors or a number of different intelligences. Standardized intelligence measures such as the WAIS-III or earlier WAIS-R are very academically oriented rather than being sensitive to an adult's capacity to solve real-life problems. Their narrow framework, cultural bias, and low correlation with work performance caution against using these standardized intelligence tests to make decisions about most adults (Tennant, 2005).

Multiple Intelligences

If we understand intelligence as the ability to solve problems or to fashion products that are valued by one's culture or community, we realize intelligence cannot be conceptualized apart from the context in which people live. There is always an interaction between individuals' biological proclivities and the opportunities in their culture for learning. Thus there exist multiple ways to be capable and to demonstrate intelligence.

According to Howard Gardner (Checkley, 1997) people have the capacity for at least eight intelligences (see Table 2.1). Individuals differ in the strength of these intelligences. Some perform best when asked to manipulate symbols of various sorts (linguistic and logical-mathematical intelligences), whereas others are better able to demonstrate their understanding through a hands-on approach (spatial and bodily-kinesthetic intelligences). Rather than possessing a single intelligence, people have a *profile of intelligences* that combine to complete different tasks. This means that tools and techniques are part of one's intelligence and its use. The Inupiat hunter who must discern sea, stars, and ice from a small boat on the Arctic Ocean meets an intellectual challenge as profound in its own way as that faced by a systems analyst deciphering the federal

Table 2.1. Gardner's Multiple Intelligences

Intelligence	Example	Core Components
Linguistic	Novelist, journalist	Sensitivity to the sounds, rhythms, and meanings of words; sensitivity to the different functions of written and spoken language
Logical-mathematical	Scientist, accountant	Sensitivity to and capacity to discern logical and numerical patterns; ability to handle long chains of inductive and deductive reasoning
Musical	Composer, guitarist	Abilities to produce and appreciate rhythm, tone, pitch, and timbre; appreciation of the forms of musical expressiveness
Spatial	Designer, navigator	Capacities to perceive the visual-spatial world accurately and to perform transformations on one's initial perceptions and mental images
Bodily-kinesthetic	Athlete, actor	Abilities to know and control one's body movements and to handle objects skillfully
Interpersonal	Therapist, politician	Capacities to discern and respond appropriately to the moods, temperaments, motivations, and desires of other people
Intrapersonal	Philosopher, spiritual leader	Access to one's own feelings and inner states of being with the ability to discriminate among them and draw on them to guide behavior; knowledge of one's own strengths, weaknesses, desires, and intelligences
Naturalist	Botanist, Farmer	Capacity to recognize and classify plants, animals, and minerals, including grass, all varieties of flora and fauna, and rocks

Source: Adapted from Viens and Kallenbach, 2004; Checkley, 1997.

budget at a computer terminal. The crucial question, then, is not, How intelligent is one? but, How is one intelligent?

Practical Intelligence

Day in and day out, what is called *practical intelligence* may be for most people the paramount intelligence during the adult years. Tennant and Pogson describe practical intelligence as that which emphasizes "practice as opposed to theory, direct usefulness as opposed to intellectual curiosity, ... and commonplace, everyday action or thought with immediate, visible consequences... it seeks to do, to move, to achieve something outside of itself, and works toward that purpose" (1995, p. 42). When applied in a particular domain, practical intelligence is often referred to as *expertise*. As such, practical intelligence is often based on prior experience. In their particular area of expertise, most experts show quick, economic problem solving and superior memory (Chi, Glaser, and Farr, 1988).

Robert Sternberg (1997) is a leading scholar and researcher in the area of practical intelligence, which he views as what most people call common sense. According to him, being successfully intelligent involves thinking analytically, creatively, and practically and choosing effectively how and when to use these abilities. The main component of practical intelligence is tacit knowledge—"knowledge that reflects the practical ability to learn from experience and to apply that knowledge in the pursuit of personally valued goals" (Sternberg and others, 2000, p. 104). Practical intelligence is a promising area of research for adult education. Understanding this ability may help people to develop greater capacity for effective performance in their careers and avocations.

Emotional Intelligence

In 1995, Daniel Goleman joined the forum about multiple intelligences with his advocacy for emotional intelligence. Although his conceptualization is quite similar to Gardner's descriptions of interpersonal and intrapersonal intelligence (see Table 2.1), it is based on the intellectual model proposed by Salovey and Mayer (1990). According to Goleman (1995), to be successful in life one must sensitively use the five domains of emotional intelligence: knowing one's emotions, managing one's emotions, motivating oneself, recognizing emotions in others, and handling relationships. Recent neuroscientific findings (see pages 17–20 in Chapter One) have given Goleman's ideas additional support. In addition, researchers who have studied emotional intelligence in the workplace have found it to be a promising construct (McEnrue and Groves, 2006).

An integration of current research and theory suggests that intellectual capacity during adulthood is a combination of genetic expression, experience, and knowledge that displays continued growth and highest potential in culturally relevant, real-life situations. As adult educators, we can explore these rich ideas about the human intellect and use them to enhance our educational practices, but with a constant critical understanding. The construct of intelligence has a history of being oversold.

Memory

Memory has received a good deal of attention by researchers in learning. Working memory, the initial processing and storing of information that occurs within approximately five to thirty seconds, becomes more problematic as adults age (Bee and Bjorkland, 2004). A common example is increasing difficulty remembering several new names just after being introduced at a party. Generalizing about long-term memory, the capacity for retaining information for minutes or years, is complicated. As people get older, they have more problems transferring (encoding) information into long-term memory. They also have more difficulty retrieving memories. But storage of encoded memories is fairly constant as people age (Hoyer and Roodin, 2003). Older adults appear to process information more slowly, especially when it is complex.

They also seem less inclined to seriously consider material they see as irrelevant or confusing (Bee and Bjorkland, 2004). When information is learned well, and new material is integrated with prior knowledge, older adults remember and use this knowledge into old age.

Age differences in memory are far less dramatic when material is familiar and meaningful. Retention of factual knowledge such as vocabulary or news events shows little if any decline from young adulthood through old age (Hoyer and Roodin, 2003). Generally, older learners are likely to have the most problems with initial learning and subsequent recall when learning activities are fast paced, complex, or unusual. They usually are not as efficient as younger adults in acquiring, organizing, and recalling new information.

In *Adults as Learners*, Pat Cross (1981) has made several practical suggestions for helping older adults with memorization: (1) present new information in ways that are meaningful and relevant; (2) include aids such as mnemonics, advance organizers, and checklists to help older adults organize and relate new material to prior knowledge; (3) present at a pace that permits mastery in order to strengthen long-term memory; (4) present one idea at a time and minimize competing intellectual demands; and (5) summarize frequently to facilitate organization and retention. To this list I would add (6) encourage taking notes on any items of interest and (7) facilitate the application of the new information to relevant issues and problems as soon as possible.

Many other instructional suggestions can be made in relation to characteristics of adult development. They are distributed throughout this book in relationship to specific motivational strategies.

Participation

Earlier in this book, we indirectly addressed the topic of participation in Chapter One's discussion of the accessibility and retention of underserved adult learners in postsecondary education. In a broader sense, participation—undertaking learning projects, courses, and programs—has a long history of research in adult education. Carol Aslanian's research (2001) provides insights on this topic for both continuing and postsecondary education. Her findings indicate that adult participation is usually due to a *life transition* that motivates the person to want to learn. The decision to participate in learning at a particular time is triggered by a specific life event. Given a choice among seven possible life transitions, 85 percent of the adults in her study named a career transition such as changing or advancing their careers. For 71 percent, the specific triggers also related to career events such as seeing a job downsized or having to use a computer for the first time. In seeking education, adults in her study looked primarily for quality (program, faculty, course, degree) and convenience (location, schedule, length of time to complete program) as criteria for selection. In general, life transitions and triggers vary culturally.

From a sociological viewpoint, unequal access to wealth and power is the foremost explanation for some adults' lower educational aspirations (Deshler, 1996). There is little doubt that such social factors as unemployment, schooling, home background, government support for or neglect of education, and provision of education in languages other than English powerfully affect the consideration of formal learning for adults. The third edition of this book addresses ways to foster inclusion in learning environments and support adult learners' participation, because their motivation is frequently more vulnerable than that of younger learners.

Cultural Diversity and a Macrocultural Perspective

The impact of culture on the human perspective is formed by a complex interaction: we each construct our own reality by interpreting the external world on the basis of our unique experiences with it and our beliefs about those experiences. Neuroscience offers biological support for this remarkable intricacy. As Zull notes, "The diversity of individual brains is infinite" (2002, p. 248). In adult education, research on cultural diversity usually focuses on age, gender, race, ethnicity, and income relative to access to and success in higher education.

As noted earlier, this information is extremely important, especially for program and policy decisions. In the classroom and distance learning we need to go further than statistics and generalizations about cultural groups to respond to cultural diversity; we need to see adults as individuals with complex identities, personal histories, and unique living contexts. For example, a person is not just older *or* just African American *or* just female; she is older, African American, *and* female. This example is still too simple because it does not include her religious/spiritual beliefs, sexual orientation, income status, or profession, among other possible cultural characteristics. Culturally, a person has a variety of identities that are woven into a personal history and lived in an individual context. As Trina Gabriel advises in an article about Gen Xers of color (2003, p. 25), "There is no one way for members of various racial or ethnic groups to view the manner in which race or ethnicity affects their lives." And there is no *one* way for an instructor to view adult learners based on the obvious aspects of their culture.

The foremost challenge of education and training, at every level and in every venue, is to create equitable and successful learning environments for *all* learners. Realistically accomplishing this goal means respecting the cultural integrity of every learner while enhancing every learner's motivation and learning. Responding to the intricacy of every individual's multiple cultural identities and the cultural diversity found throughout education and training, Margery Ginsberg and I developed a macrocultural pedagogical model, the Motivational Framework for Culturally Responsive Teaching (Wlodkowski and Ginsberg, 1995). This framework is fully discussed and exemplified in Chapter Four. It is built on principles that apply within and across cultures. Instead of using a microcultural perspective that, for example, identifies a specific ethnic group and prescribes particular approaches to teaching according to assumed characteristics of that specific ethnic group, our pedagogy emerges from literature on and experience with creating a more pluralistic approach to teaching that can elicit the intrinsic motivation of *all* learners.

Our emphasis is on creating a convergence of multiple ideas and methods from which teachers and learners may choose in order to support the diverse perspectives and values of adult learners. Our reservation about microcultural models is that a pedagogy that may work well with one ethnic or racial group may not be effective with another group. However, microcultural approaches to teaching offer effective complementary models for teaching adults (Guy, 2005). They can be used in tandem with the Motivational Framework for Culturally Responsive Teaching. Culturally responsive teaching is characterized by respect for diversity; engagement of the motivation of all learners; creation of a safe, inclusive, and respectful learning environment; teaching practices that cross disciplines and cultures; integration of culturally responsive practices into all subject areas; and the promotion of justice and equity in society (Wlodkowski and Ginsberg, 1995; Phuntsog, 1999).

Location of Responsibility for Learning

The "carrot and stick" remains the most popular metaphor for motivation in this society. It is constantly used by the media, offered as an analytical tool by political pundits, and referenced by educators. For learning, the emphasis is on the use of extrinsic rewards such as grades, eligibility, and money. When learners do not respond to these incentives, they are often seen as responsible for their lack of motivation. They are likely to be described as lacking ambition, initiative, or self-direction. The question many instructors ask is, How do I motivate them? as though the adult learners are inert. Such a question implies that these learners are inferior, somehow less able and certainly less powerful than the instructor. They need motivation! This attitude dims the instructor's awareness of the learners' own determination and tends to keep them dependent and in need of further help.

Instructors who use an intrinsic and macrocultural approach to motivation consider the learners' perspective fundamental. "Seek first to understand" is our watchword. We can then see that some learners' socialization may not accommodate rewards such as grades and test scores. The question, How might this learning environment and system of incentives diminish the motivation of some learners? is a viable means to finding clues for improving the learning situation. We know there is an interaction between learner motivation and the dynamics of the setting for learning, and we must take the responsibility to foster an optimal environment for everyone. Crucial to educational equity is the understanding that the most favorable conditions for learning vary among people. Because learning is the human act of making meaning from experience, involving all learners requires us to be aware of how they make sense of their world and how they interpret their learning environment.

Two Critical Assumptions for Helping Adults Want to Learn

A construct as broad and as complex as motivation invites controversy and argumentation. One of the most likely causes of misunderstanding is the receiver's uncertainty about the assumptions of the sender of the message. It is this lack of clarity, rather than a lack of logic, that increases the likelihood of disagreement. I offer the following assumptions so that you can better understand why I have chosen the ideas for instruction that follow. These assumptions form a substantial part of the foundation and rationale for the approaches advocated in this book.

The first assumption is that *if something can be learned, it can be learned in a motivating manner*. People must be motivated to some degree to formally learn anything, even if the result of that motivation is merely paying attention. Our brain continuously selects the most relevant information from the enormous amount of stimuli constantly affecting us. Most often our brain is disregarding irrelevant information. In the lower part of the brain, the reticular activating system (RAS) filters all incoming information. Through this process, our brain selects, often without our conscious awareness, what to pay attention to and what to ignore (Willis, 2006). Before adults can learn anything, someone or something has to gain their attention.

As instructors, once we have someone's attention, we can use a myriad of possible influences to sustain that attention and develop interest. In a perverse way, commercial advertising is a testimony to the human ability to make anything attractive and appealing. If something is worth an instructional effort, there should be some degree of worth to the material. It must meet some kind of valid need, or there would be no reason for making it the purpose of instruction. Finding that need, affirming it, and engagingly developing it through instructional processes that are culturally responsive are challenges, without a doubt, but not impossible ones.

The second assumption is that *every instructional plan also needs to be a motivational plan*. More often than not, the variables that interfere with and complicate learning are human variables—people's needs, emotions, impulses, attitudes, expectations, irrationalities, beliefs, and values. Not surprisingly, these are motivational variables as well. Most subject matter is rather stable and controllable. Often it has a logical structure and sequence. Finding an instructional design format for most subject matter is relatively easy (Morrison, Ross, and Kemp, 2006). There are many to choose from, but most do not adequately address the human and cultural variables just mentioned. However, motivational theories are vitally concerned with these variables and offer many methods and principles to deal with them (Elliot and Dweck, 2005). The challenge, then, is to integrate these methods and principles with instruction into a cohesive framework.

Many instructors do try to make their teaching motivationally appealing, but they usually rely on intuition and decisions made while teaching. Their difficulties arise when learner motivation seems to be low or diminishing. They have no formal plan for solving problems and often lack exact methods to revise, refine, or build on (see Chapter Nine). Without such formal plans and methods, instructors may feel helpless, hopeless, and prone to blame the learners themselves. When they turn to books on motivation, the vast array of competing and conflicting theories often leaves them only more confused. There is very little guidance to ensure consistent application, especially in working with diverse adult learners. A plan can remind us of what to do and when to do it and show us where we might possibly flex and adjust along the way. If we have no plan to enhance learner motivation, our efforts too often depend on trial and error and lack cohesion and continuity.

The research and literature on motivation has many constructive suggestions for instructors; however, without a method of planning for those suggestions, instructors will probably apply them inconsistently. This book offers a method of planning so that instructors may be inspired to reflect on and to act on Csikszentmihalyi's challenging realization that "it is how we choose what we do, and how we approach it, that will determine whether the sum of our days adds up to a formless blur, or to something resembling a work of art" (1997, p. 13).

3

Characteristics and Skills of a Motivating Instructor

*Even virtue itself, all perfect as it is, requires to be
enspirited by passion; for duties are coldly performed,
which are but philosophically fulfilled.*

Anna Jameson

Consider for a moment a motivating instructor who helped you as an adult to genuinely want to learn, who was able to influence you to go beyond another course finished, another credit earned. See that person, and remember what learning was like with that individual. Pleasant? Exciting? Startling? Absorbing? There are many possible reactions but seldom the ordinary. Most of us have had at least one such instructor. And every one of us has the potential to be such an instructor to other adults. Let's start with the basics.

Motivating instructors are not entirely magical. They are unique; they do have their own style and strengths. But research, observation, and common sense all point to essential elements that are the foundation of their instruction. These core characteristics can be learned, controlled, and planned for by anyone who instructs adults. I see them as the five pillars on which rests what we as instructors have to offer adults. If we lack any one of them, we will be less capable of responding effectively to the many complexities that can strain an instructional relationship with adults.

These five pillars are *expertise, empathy, enthusiasm, clarity,* and *cultural responsiveness.* Our most advantageous approach as instructors is to see these pillars as skills and not as abstractions or personality traits. They can be learned, and they can be improved upon through practice and effort.

Instruction is a pragmatic art, a craft. We create, compose, and perform for the benefit of learners. Every professional artist has a practice regimen, and fundamentals make up a considerable portion of it. Just as exercise is an inherent part of the lives of fine dancers, and daily practice is a continual ritual for outstanding musicians, so too are these basic elements the foundation for motivating instruction. If we use them steadily and strive always to refine them, they can be developed and enriched. They are achievable.

Expertise: The Power of Knowledge and Preparation

The pillar of expertise has many different names. Some people prefer to call it substance, knowledge, or competence (Shulman, 1987). Expertise has been identified as part of practical intelligence which can be learned (Sternberg and others, 2000; Grotzer and Perkins, 2000). Whatever the name, a useful definition of expertise for those of us who instruct adults boils down to three parts: (1) we know something beneficial for adults, (2) we know it well, and (3) we are prepared to convey or construct it with adults through an instructional process. Adhering to these three criteria will render our expertise most effective.

1. We Know Something Beneficial for Adults

Watch a group of uninterested adults in any kind of learning activity—an in-service training session, a lecture, a business seminar. (You have probably been a participant, at least a few times, in such a dreary experience yourself.) Their voices aren't shouting, but their minds and bodies are: "Don't waste my time." "Who are you kidding?" "I wish I could get out of here!" "I don't need this." It's almost palpable. As learners, adults are demanding, and rightfully so.

An instructor of adults is quite unlike a teacher of children or adolescents. This person is an adult among adults. He or she cannot count on the advantages of age, experience, and size for extra leverage or added influence as an elementary school teacher might. Many adults will have had experiences that far surpass those of their instructor. As a group, they have out-traveled, out-parented, out-worked, and out-lived any of us as individual instructors. Collectively, they have had more lovers, changed more jobs, survived more accidents, moved more households, faced more debts, achieved more successes, and overcome more failures. It is unlikely that we can simply impress them with our title, whether it is trainer or professor.

Also, most adults come to learn for a definite reason. They are pragmatic learners. They want their learning to help them solve problems, build new skills, advance in their jobs, make more friends—in general, to do, produce, or decide something that is of real value to them. The dominant question adult learners have for any instructor is, Can you really help me?

We begin to answer this question by determining whether we indeed have something beneficial to offer adult learners. We have to ask ourselves, What do I know that this group can understand, use, or apply that will help them? Answering this question with *relevant concrete examples* of the knowledge, skills, or awareness that we can offer this group is the first step in avoiding the classic mistake that many so-called experts make when instructing adults—thinking that simply knowing a lot about a subject is enough to teach it effectively. Colleges abound with knowledgeable professors who teach quite poorly. In many instances, they have not considered what students might know and be able to contribute. They have not taken the step of connecting their knowledge to the daily needs and lives of their students. For this reason, there is no bridge to common understanding or means to construct knowledge collectively. As we saw in Chapter One, the neural networks that represent the prior knowledge of the learners remain unstimulated and unavailable for new growth and connection.

When we instruct a group for a lengthy period, we eventually become quite naked: our words and actions peel away the camouflage of our academic degrees and experience to reveal to learners whether what we know really makes a difference. Connecting our expertise to learners' perspectives and prior knowledge, before we begin to instruct, builds our confidence that we do have something of value to share and that time is on our side.

2. We Know Our Subject Well

There is no substitute for thoroughly knowing our topic. Nothing beats it. Whatever experience, reading, reviewing, or practice it takes, its payoff far outweighs its cost.

By asking yourself the questions that follow, you can determine whether you know something well enough to be able to instruct adults.

1. *Do I really understand what I am going to teach?* Can I explain it to myself in my own words?

2. *Can I give more than one good example of what I am teaching?* A story, a joke, a fact, a piece of research, an analogy—there are many types of examples. The main thing is to have more than one. This demonstrates the depth and breadth of your understanding and increases your ability to reach learners for whom a single example would not have enough explanatory power.

3. *Can I personally demonstrate the skill* (if you are teaching a skill)? Being able to do so gives you real credibility, in your

own eyes and in the eyes of others. If you are not able to demonstrate the skill, or if this is inappropriate, are there models, films, or videotapes that can do the job?

4. *Do I know the limits and consequences of what I am teaching?* If, for instance, you are explaining a managerial technique, do you know what types of employees it may not work with or under what conditions it would be unwise to use it? What are its effects on production and morale? Does it entail any personal risk for the manager? Your consideration of possible limits and consequences reveals the sensibility of your expertise.

5. *Do I know how to bridge what I am teaching to the world of the learners—their prior knowledge, experience, interests, and concerns?* Do I know where and how to let what they know inform what I know? If you do not, your knowledge may be irrelevant or misapplied.

6. *Do I know what I don't know?* Where are the boundaries of my own knowledge and skill? How far am I from the cutting edge of my discipline? To be aware of your limits is a very intelligent modesty. Adults don't expect instructors to know everything, but they do want an honest appraisal of the usefulness of what they are learning because they may apply so much of it. Instructors who know their own frontiers can better qualify and temper their instruction. Learners are therefore less likely to become disillusioned or to misapply what they have learned, and instructor and learner alike can better see the direction of future needed learning.

Knowing our subject matter well enhances our confidence, flexibility, and creativity as instructors. We may still have learners who are difficult to reach, but our fund of knowledge will not be what fails us. We can count on it. We can also be more open to questions and new directions that may come from our learners. When a person has really mastered a concept or a skill, he can be playful with it. Spontaneity and improvisation are more possible for the competent. Consummate artists and scientists base their experiments on knowledge. Deep understanding of a subject transforms mere information into useable knowledge (Donovan, Bransford, and Pellegrino, 1999).

3. We Are Prepared to Convey or Construct Knowledge with Adults through an Instructional Process

The emphasis of this criterion is on the *immediate* planning and organization of instruction and materials for a lesson or learning activity—the intensive preparation just before the instructional moment. Brilliant and scholarly people at the zenith of their professions are notorious for poorly prepared instruction. Albert Einstein was known for burying his head in his notes, with his words haltingly emerging in a monotone through his mustache. It is difficult to imagine, but some people actually engaged in small talk while he lectured.

Being well prepared for instruction shows in two essential ways: we have a relaxed familiarity with our materials, and we can look at our learners most of the time. We can actually have a conversation with them. This makes them participants in moment-to-moment communication with us rather than a cardboard audience of faces. If we are tied to our notes, if we cannot put our manuals down, if we do not know what the next step is, our chances of being motivating instructors are nil.

Vital instruction flows. There has to be a union between the instructor and the learners so that both parties feel part of a single process. Effective instructors set the stage for this fluid enterprise by knowing their material well enough to read learner cues and to change qualities of voice, emphasis, and direction in response to signs of interest, insight, and possible boredom. Learners feel that an instructor who does this is talking with them rather than at them, because the instructor's responsiveness to them is so apparent. They can see these reactions in the instructor's eyes and facial expressions. Questions and give-and-take between the instructor and the learners seem integrated into the stream of the lesson. Like an expert navigator on a familiar ship, the instructor who has the touch and feel of the material can sail a steady course in any sea.

The immediate preparation for motivating instruction is whatever it takes for us to feel confident that we will spend most of the instruction time being with the learners and being able to talk with them. For the experienced instructor, this preparation may be a few moments of quiet reflection; for the novice, it may entail hours of review, rehearsal, and organization. The range is wide. Notes, index cards, outlines, textual materials, and PowerPoint are appropriate to use as long as they don't stultify our thinking, reduce complicated ideas to bullet points, or inhibit our interaction with our learners (Keller, 2003). If any section of our material seems insurmountable (occasionally this will happen to even the best of instructors), we can make sure our learners can at least look with us. Visual aids, media technology, and handouts are some possibilities. For online learning, teleconferencing, video streaming, and other rapidly developing communication technologies facilitate face-to-face involvement with the instructor.

Any significant achievement demands readiness. Speakers collect their thoughts. Actors reflect on their roles. Athletes visualize their goals. As motivating instructors, we also need to prepare for our quest to involve learners. The time we spend mobilizing our knowledge and abilities just prior to instruction is probably the final step of our preparation. How we feel about the instruction we are about to begin will carry over to how we feel when we meet our learners. The commitment to readiness enhances our confidence, an emotion that gives us excellent access to our best talents and stored memories (Zull, 2002).

Empathy: The Power of Understanding and Compassion

Blanca, a woman in her mid-thirties, decides to take a communications course in the extension program at her local college. For the last six years she has committed herself to the role of homemaker. Now that her children are older and more independent, she is considering college or full-time employment. This course will be the first step. Her friends have encouraged her to take a basic communications class because it would be a reasonable but not too difficult introduction to current educational practices as well as a means to gain some useful skills for the job market. She is motivated.

The class meets once a week in the evening for two and a half hours. At the first class session, the instructor introduces himself, has the students introduce themselves to one another, and lists the requirements for the course — reading the textbook and four assigned articles, passing a midsemester and a final exam, and writing a term paper. He mentions that he is a tough marker and a real stickler for the use of appropriate English grammar in student papers. After a number of questions from the class regarding these requirements, he dismisses them early so that the students can get a head start on their required reading for the next week. Blanca is a bit intimidated but determined.

At the second class session, the instructor lectures on the history of communications theory and outlines a number of research studies that demonstrate the significant effect of different communication innovations. Blanca is impressed by her instructor's knowledge but finds her interest waning. The third class session is a lecture on postmodernism and the politics of media influence.

Blanca decides to drop the course and get a percentage of her tuition back before it's too late for any compensation. When her friends ask her why she didn't finish the course, she looks at them with a perplexed expression and replies, "It just didn't seem like something I needed right now. The course was about communication, but it wasn't what I expected."

There are a number of different ways to look at this scenario. One way might be to consider what Blanca could have done to have helped herself in the course or to have avoided this particular course altogether. Perhaps she should have been more careful in selecting the class; she should have found out more about both the instructor and the course content before she signed up for it. She also might have talked with the instructor and made her needs and expectations clearer to him.

From another vantage point, we could say that the instructor should have taken some time to get to know his students, to gauge their feelings, and to find out what their personal goals and expectations were. Then he could have modified his course objectives and content accordingly. No matter where we place the responsibility, the same core issue remains: adults' goals and expectations for what they are taught will powerfully influence how they motivationally respond to what they are taught. In general, the better their goals and expectations are met by what and how they learn, the more likely they are to be motivated to learn.

As mentioned earlier, most adults come to learning activities for specific reasons. These reasons are based on what they think they need or want. These desires translate into *personally relevant goals* (Ford, 1992). These goals may be more knowledge, new skills, certification of some type, social interaction, or simply relief from boredom. However, if the content or process of instruction does not in some way meet these goals, the learning will have very little meaning for adults. If the learning process does not seem to fulfill any of their personal goals, adults will eventually and inevitably conclude: "This is a waste of time."

In this book I often use the terms *goals* and *personal goals* for what is sometimes referred to as *needs*. This choice of words reflects most motivational theorists' shift away from need as a productive explanation of human behavior (Brophy, 2004). Biologically, human beings are naturally active. They will explore their environment without an unmet need to drive their behavior. Need theory provides only limited understanding of motivation to learn. There is little empirical support for Abraham Maslow's hierarchy of needs (1970), other than physiological and safety needs, across different cultures (Whaba and Bridwell, 1976; Pintrich and Schunk, 1996). People do need to feel physically well and personally safe before they can commit to learning. From an evolutionary and a biological view, these human reactions are facts of life. The language of goals allows us to see adults as active agents responsible for fulfilling their lives based on the interaction of their biology and the purposes and values learned through their culture.

Instructors of adults face the challenge of seeing the learners' world and what they want from it as the learners see it. Adults learn largely in response to their own goals and perceptions, not those of their instructors. Empathy is the skill that allows instructors to meet this formidable requirement for motivating instruction. As a discipline, adult education seems to universally recognize the importance of empathy in teaching adults (Rossiter, 2006).

For centuries, writers and spiritual leaders across the world have used words like *compassion, consideration,* and *understanding* to convey how essential empathy is for life on earth (Goleman, 2007; Hays, 2001). Carl Rogers, an advocate for empathy in teaching, defined *empathy* as "the ability to understand the student's reactions from the inside, a sensitive awareness of the way the process of education and learning seem to the student" (1969, p. 111). Daniel Goleman describes empathy as "the ability to know how another feels" (1995, p. 96). He believes it is the essential people skill.

As instructors we are wise not to confuse empathy with projection. Alfie Kohn explains the distinction: "There is a world of difference—the difference between your world and my world to be exact—between imagining yourself in someone else's situation and imagining *her* in her situation. It is the difference between asking what it is like to be in someone else's shoes and what it is like to have that person's feet" (1990, p. 112).

For instructors of adults, the pillar of empathy has three parts: (1) we have a realistic understanding of the learners' goals, perspectives, and expectations for what is being learned; (2) we have adapted our instruction to the learners' levels of experience and skill development; and (3) we continuously consider the learners' perspectives and feelings. These three criteria will help us know when we have reached the level of empathy necessary for motivating instruction.

1. We Have a Realistic Understanding of the Learners' Goals, Perspectives, and Expectations for What Is Being Learned

As a process, comprehending the learners' goals, perspectives, and expectations involves an, swering two important questions: How do I best find out what the learners' goals, perspectives, and expectations are? and, When do I know I realistically understand the learners' goals, perspectives, and expectations?

Rosemary Caffarella (2002) describes widely used methods for gathering information about adult learners and generating ideas for their educational programs. Table 3.1 summarizes these methods for finding out about learners prior to the learning experience.

In recent years, Appreciative Inquiry (Watkins and Mohr, 2001) has emerged as a counterparadigm to conventional ideas for initiating change and learning. Rather than identifying problems and using a critical perspective to understand what to change in an organization, Appreciative Inquiry (AI) focuses on the generative forces in a system and asks, What are the things we appreciate and want to increase? David Cooperrider (1990) proposes that positive concepts such as ideals and vision have a heliotropic effect. They energize and guide people toward the realization of an ideal, just as plants grow in the direction of a light source. A clear common

Table 3.1. Methods for Gathering Information about Learners' Goals, Perspectives, and Expectations

Method	Description	Guideline
1. Experience or observation	Spending time with learners in their community, work, or learning settings—if possible, during activities related to the learning experience.	Learners observed should represent the gender and ethnic or racial composition of the learning group. Focus on critical activities or events.
2. Written surveys	Using paper-and-pencil and online formats to gather opinions, attitudes, needs, goals, strengths, preferences, concerns, and perceptions.	Consider the potentially limited reading and writing proficiencies of learners. Some English-language learners may have difficulty with this format.
3. Interviews	Talking with people in person, by phone, or online.	Pretest interview questions with a representative group. Use random sampling or a focus group of people who represent the larger group and are knowledgeable and forthcoming about issues and goals.
4. Group sessions and forums	Identifying, analyzing, and using narratives—stories and folklore as well as stated problems—to understand learners' ideas, concerns, issues, and goals.	Group members should represent the larger group. Sessions can include brainstorming, focus group, and general group discussion.

Table 3.1. (*Continued*)

Method	Description	Guideline
5. Job and task analysis (probably most applicable in workshops and training)	Analyzing and assessing the tasks, activities, and procedures related to the learning goals as performed on the job or in professional settings.	Relevance of information and prerequisite skills is essential for training. Collected information has to be valid. A variety of data-collecting methods can be used: checklists, observation, work records, interviews, and reviews of technical assessments and publications.
6. Tests	Assessing learners' knowledge, skills, attitudes, and values significantly related to the learning goals.	Measures should be valid, reliable, and relevant; should be conducted long enough before the learning experience so that instruction plans can be adjusted.
7. Printed and computer-generated materials	Analyzing information from reports, manuals, newsletters, media, Web sites, and evaluation studies to better understand the learning group's context and proficiencies.	Documents and media should be up-to-date and relevant.
8. Conversations with colleagues, friends, or family	Engaging in informal discussions to gain insights and ideas about how to design your course or training.	Record ideas and check them regularly to expand the creativity and effectiveness of the learning experience.

Table 3.1.   (Continued)

Method	Description	Guideline
9. Performance and product reviews	Assessing relevance of skills, processes, and products of the learning group.	Use credible assessment sources such as subject experts, competent professionals, and valid rating scales.

Source: Adapted from Caffarella, 2002, pp. 120–121.

image within an organization can generate substantial energy and guidance for focused, creative action.

An AI perspective is based on these assumptions (Watkins and Mohr, 2001):

- In an organization, the way things are is a social construction that can be changed.

- In any situation, a group can find seeds of excellence to build on.

- Excellence is found through looking for examples and sharing stories by members within an organization.

- As an organization creates images of excellence, its system will move toward that image.

The basic AI process for solving problems, creating change, and realizing what to learn may be outlined this way (Watkins and Mohr, 2001):

- The group looks at their experience in the area in which they want to improve by exploring (telling stories about) the times when things were going well— when members of the group felt joyful, excited, and successful.

- As these stories are told and recorded, the group collectively creates a description for what it wants, an image of its ideal.

- The group can go out and ask others how they have effectively dealt with a similar situation.

- The group shares its images, discovers the images that others hold, and "re-creates" a more successful and creative future throughout the organization.

At this time AI is a philosophy, a process, and a movement in organizational development and education. I have participated in the AI process only once. I was involved because of my role as research faculty in an undergraduate program responsible for about six thousand working-adult students. The initial sessions of the AI process were very enjoyable and productive—story telling and images of our desired goals and relationships were very motivating. Eventually, as we continued over three semesters to work toward the goals that resulted from the AI process, political will and perseverance emerged as necessary for real change to occur. Because our work was voluntary, these qualities became difficult to sustain over time. Although most of our goals were not accomplished, we did establish an online tutoring program for the entire undergraduate program, a significant achievement within our school. *AI Practitioner*, a newsletter available online, can provide much more detail about this approach to organizational change and adult learning.

However you find out what the learners' goals, perspectives, and expectations are, it is usually a good idea to talk with the learners about the information you have collected. This is probably best done at the beginning of the learning experience when attitudes are most likely to be developing. Such commentary and related dialogue can enhance your communication with the learners and give them a deeper understanding of the care that is going into the creation of their learning experience.

There is no final answer to the second question, When do I know I realistically understand the learners' goals, perspectives, and expectations? In my experience as a teacher, instruction is nearly always a work in progress, a living composition. The learning objectives we take into a classroom are our vision of what we wish to accomplish. But the learners in that room have their own vision and related goals. Remaining flexible, being open to learners' input, and in some instances, creating learning goals with them are ways to keep our composition vital and relevant. This approach is especially important when the learning group is culturally different from us. Taking some time in the beginning of a course to hear comments and suggestions from learners regarding the course objectives shows our respect for the learners and their experience and perspective. However, unless this is an exceptional situation—for example, a visiting teaching assignment, a crisis workshop, or a Freirean problem-posing—the objectives we have set for our course or module should include most of the goals and concerns that our learners bring with them to the first meeting. By making the effort to understand learners prior to the first instructional meeting, we are more likely to face only moderately refining our instructional plan rather than seriously revising it.

Another type of expectation that is crucial for us to understand is what the adult learner anticipates in the way of course requirements. Learners bring strongly felt expectations with them about what and how much we ask them to do. In our learners' eyes, our fairness and our humanity will significantly depend on how our requirements measure up against their expectations. Usually, the issue for adult learners is time. All course and training requirements take some time to do, whether they involve reading, writing, practice, or problem solving. Many studies have found time constraints to be a major obstacle to participation in adult education (Wlodkowski, Mauldin, and Campbell, 2002). Sometimes instructors think that learners want fewer requirements because they want the easy way out. I think it is much more helpful to see requirements in terms of the time they demand and to recognize that adult learners want to make sure they have enough time to fully demonstrate their real capabilities. The issue is not "give me a break." It's "let's make sure I really have a chance to learn and to become good at what I know." We need to understand the type of learners we have and the amount of time they can realistically afford before we create our course and training requirements.

2. We Have Adapted Our Instruction to the Learners' Levels of Experience and Skill Development

Have you ever been in a course or training program where you didn't have the skills or background necessary to do what you were asked to do? Were you ever in such a program and couldn't leave it? Maybe it was in the military, in secondary school, or worse yet, in something you volunteered for. It's a special kind of misery—a mixture of fear, embarrassment, and infuriation. If there's no hope of learning, we usually try to get out of the situation. Our motivation is to escape, and when that's not possible, at best to endure and to avoid becoming depressed.

As instructors, we don't want to make people fail. In terms of empathy, this means *giving learners things to do that are within their reach.* If we give them assignments that are too easy or for which they have had too much experience, they will be bored and disinterested. We must strike a delicate balance. The instructional goal is to match the learning process, whether it be materials, activities, assignments, or discussions, to the abilities and experience of our learners. We don't want to assign books our learners cannot read or to expect them to be very interested in things they have done many times.

If we are unfamiliar with our learners or if our subject matter is rapidly changing, we may want to use diagnostic or formative evaluation procedures to better understand their capabilities and experiences related to our subject area. We can use interviews, paper-and-pencil tests, simulations, exercises, or whatever helps us know what our learners can or cannot do relative to what we are offering them. The purpose of these assignments is not to categorize learners but to help us create instructional procedures for better adult motivation and learning. Even among professional athletes, coaches begin training camps with exercises and tests that are basically diagnostic. They know from years of hard-earned experience that you cannot take anyone from anywhere unless you start somewhere near where they are. Scaffolding (see Strategy 15 in Chapter Six) is an excellent method for adapting instruction to learners' levels of experience and skill development.

3. We Continuously Consider the Learners' Perspectives and Feelings

More than ever before, technology and the media are bringing education across vast distances and to widely different cultures. Online learning, accelerated courses, and teleconferencing are common delivery systems in training and postsecondary education. Paradoxically, the technology and efficiency of these learning formats only deepens our awareness of how important it is for adult learners to know we instructors care about them and understand them as individual human beings (Wlodkowski and Kasworm, 2003).

Hand in hand with this sensibility is Saint-Exupéry's marvelous maxim, "What is essential is invisible to the eye" (1943, p. 70). Countless important things go on between an instructor and a learner during instruction that no single human sense, no global standardized test, no amazing electronic equipment will ever pick up. In some ways, I wish this were not so. To some extent, this "invisibility" makes incomplete all the ideas and strategies found in this book. And yet anyone who has ever really been an instructor knows that Saint-Exupéry's maxim is true. That is why empathy is as much an attitude as a skill. It is a constant desire to know what our learners are living and experiencing with us as they know and feel it.

Of the skills necessary for empathy, listening is most important. It is the single most powerful transaction that occurs between us and another person that conveys our acceptance of his humanity. The way we listen tells the learner more than anything else does how much consideration we are really giving him. Do we understand? Do we cut him off? Do we look over his shoulder? Do we change the subject? Do we really know what he is feeling?

When we *listen for understanding*, learners are more likely to feel understood and respected, making it safer for them to listen to us (Mills, 1995). Listening for understanding is valuable in teaching because it avoids judging people according to a conceptual framework of our own devising and allows us to become fascinated with how things look to learners. We can be genuinely intrigued by how learners make meaning out of ideas and experience. Such respectful interest can elicit deeper dialogue and mutual understanding.

If we can also *attune our responses* to learners, we have a chance to connect with them emotionally (Goleman, 1995). Attunement occurs tacitly and involves tone of voice, body language, and words conveying to the listener a reciprocal understanding of his or her feelings. A mother does this with an infant when she responds to the child's squeals of delight with a gentle shake, a smile, and a higher-pitched voice expressing glee. An instructor does this with a learner when she responds to a student's frustration with a knowing nod, a furrowed brow, and words communicating a willingness to listen further.

Validation may also be important. Sometimes learners need to know that we can accept how they are feeling given what they have experienced or how they understand the world: "I see you're upset; having lived through the kind of discrimination you've just described probably doesn't leave much choice in the matter. I appreciate the conviction it took to tell us about this. Thank you."

Listening for understanding, attunement, and validation are skills that help convey empathy. To use these skills effectively takes practice. They can best be learned and rehearsed during encounters that are not stressful; they will then be more accessible to you during the emotional heat of conflict or controversy.

Empathy is not simply an altruistic notion. It's a dynamic process, involving people's ability to express their thoughts and feelings to each other in ways that often change the relationship and, most important, continue the relationship. Combined with expertise, empathy makes the instructor a more caring person in the eyes of the learner.

Whenever an instructor can contribute to fulfilling the goals of a learner, especially in a compassionate manner, the learner can identify with the instructor. The learner may begin to take on some of the attitudes and behaviors of the instructor, literally to act in some ways like the instructor. We identify to some degree with almost any leader who significantly meets our needs, whether it is a parent, a political figure, or an instructor. This process is part of the reason we often feel a profound sorrow when such a person dies. A neighborhood organizer, a former coach—any leader important to us can have this effect on us. We have not just lost someone who meant something to us; we have lost a part of ourselves as well.

Identification allows each of us as motivating instructors to leave a legacy. And enthusiasm for our subject can be a noble inheritance.

Enthusiasm: The Power of Commitment and Expressiveness

To instill an awareness of the importance of enthusiasm in an instructor, I often ask people in my courses and workshops to remember a motivating teacher they have had as an adult: someone who taught in a way that evoked their passion for what they were learning and gave value to it. (You may wish to follow along with me.) I ask them to say the teacher's name; to see the teacher's face; to remember what it was like to be in that course, workshop, or seminar; and to remember the feeling they would have as they came into the class and as they left it. After they have had a chance to share their recollections among themselves, I ask them to raise their hands if the teacher they remembered was enthusiastic about what she was teaching them. If I were to count all the people who did not raise their hands in the thirty years I've done this activity, there would be less than forty individuals. With groups as large as five hundred people, it is the norm to have a unanimous show of hands.

I think I inadvertently realized the importance of enthusiasm as a characteristic of teachers when I was a sophomore in high school. Struggling to learn geometry and feeling the steady diminishment of my will and effort, I remember the day the teacher came in with a cart full of plastic circles, squares, and triangles. As usual, she looked listless, dispirited, and withdrawn, qualities her teaching reflected as constants. Bob, the boy next to me whose career in geometry was headed in the same direction as mine, dryly observed as he nodded toward her, "See what geometry can do to you." That was it! To my fifteen-year-old brain, he was right. We could suffer the same fate. Though we both did poorly in geometry, we never felt bad about it. It's unavoidable: we are what we teach. And every learner knows it.

The word *enthusiasm* originates from the Greek noun *enthousiasmos*, which in turn comes from the Greek verb *enthousiazein*, meaning "to be inspired or possessed by a god." Other dictionary meanings include "strong excitement" and "feeling on behalf of a cause or subject." In discussing instruction, I prefer a definition that includes the person's inner feelings as they are expressed in outward behavior.

Enthusiastic instructors are people who care about and value their subject matter. They teach it in a manner that expresses those feelings with the intent to encourage similar feelings in the learner.

Emotion, energy, and expressiveness are outwardly visible in their instruction.

If we care about our instructional topic, we will be naturally inclined to be expressive about it. If we do not care about our subject, we will find it more difficult to produce feelings and gestures. We might be able to act out or invent such expressions for a particular occasion but to maintain such zeal would be laborious. Without a source of inspiration, it is difficult to be inspirational. The goal of encouraging in the learner our value for our subject matter is important as well. This goal motivates us to have rapport with our students and to express our feelings in a way that engages our learners to share in our enthusiasm. Otherwise, we could become so involved in our own emotions that we might teach for our own benefit rather than for the benefit of our learners. Arrogant instructors often display this shortsightedness.

In educational research, enthusiasm has long been linked to increased learner motivation and achievement. According to Cruickshank and his associates (1980), all other things being equal, a teacher who presents materials with appropriate gestures and expressiveness will have students who achieve better on tests than will the teacher who does not gesture, reads in a monotone, and generally behaves in an unenthusiastic manner. The eminent researcher Nathaniel Gage (1979) has suggested that enthusiasm is a "generic" teaching behavior that is useful at all levels of education, in all subject areas, and for all types of students.

Enthusiastic instruction has a powerful influence on the motivation of learners for reasons both psychological and biological. One of the foremost psychological reasons is that instructors are advocates. We are "pleading the cause" of our subject to adults. Some of us lobby for math or technical skills, others for training programs or general education. Whatever the subject, the message is basically the same: "Learn it. It's worth it." Whenever adults are urged to believe something, they perform a keen intuitive scan of the advocate, asking in effect, "What will believing in this do for me?" If we cannot show by our presence, energy, and conviction that this subject has made a positive difference for us, the learner is forewarned. If we appear bored, listless, and uninvolved with what we are asking the adult to learn, his response will be, "If that's what knowing this does for you, by all means, keep it away from me." That is survival. No one wants to invest in something that has not done its own advocate any good. This inherent wisdom makes enthusiasm a necessity for motivating instruction. For adult learners, *how* instructors say it will take priority over *what* instructors say.

Enthusiastic instructors are potent models (Feldman, 1997). Numerous studies have demonstrated that when we focus on other people, we embody their emotions (Niedenthal and others, 2005). As a result, the emotional states of observers correspond to those of the people they are watching. For example, in one study (Hsee and others, 1990) as students watched another student describe one of the happiest or saddest events in her life, they embodied the emotional expressions of the student they viewed and felt similar feelings. Related research indicates that when people feel pain, the same pain-related neurons are activated in observers of the painful condition (Hutchinson and others, 1999). From an evolutionary perspective, human beings are likely to feel the emotions of other human beings because it enhances their communication with them and therefore their survival in a social world.

When adults see an instructor as expert and empathic, they tend to imitate the instructor's emotions and attitudes toward the subject. If expertise is missing, the spirited instructor can simply be dismissed as foolish. Without personal proficiency and compassion for learners, the zealous instructor may appear more a person to be avoided than a person to be admired. Learners can see that a knowledgeable, caring instructor's enthusiasm about the subject is the natural emotional outcome of justified commitment. Because of their biology and pragmatism, adult learners can be inspired by such instructors.

In addition, enthusiastic instructors are constantly producing stimulation by the way they act. They tend to be authentically engaged and may often use exclamations like "Wow!" "Cool!" "Incredible!" "Who could imagine?" They may be corny sometimes, but learners are more likely to pay attention to and understand what enthusiastic instructors say and demonstrate. Greater alertness produces better learning, which makes future stimulation more likely and rewarding. And on it goes. Thus a constant self-perpetuating chain of events is established. It is no wonder learners "can't wait" for the next course session with an inspiring instructor.

The pillar of enthusiasm has two basic criteria: (1) we value what we teach for ourselves as well as for the learner, and (2) we display our commitment with appropriate degrees of emotion and expressiveness. Attending to these two criteria will not only give us some indication of our enthusiasm but also help us sustain it in our instruction.

1. We Value What We Teach for Ourselves as Well as for the Learner

Our own interest in our subject is probably the surest indicator that we value it. Do we devote time to understanding it better? Are we active members of organizations that specialize in our discipline? Do we follow and learn from the best practitioners in our field? Do we read the magazines, journals, and newsletters in our subject area?

What is our area of specialty? Almost every artist, professional, and scholar has one, unique thing she knows or does better than most others in her field—a genuine source of pride. Be it the local chef who creates a celebrated entrée or the Nobel laureate who engages in esoteric research, people who value their work usually develop a particular aspect of their skill or knowledge. It's our way of personalizing and showing appreciation for what we do. Our specialty transforms us: we are not merely an ordinary practitioner in the field but a vital contributor to our subject—a person who adds a singular insight or style to the realm of our work. Enthusiastic instructors distinguish themselves by knowing they possess such exceptional pursuits. Just as we might know of some exotic faraway island, we have discovered something out of the ordinary to share with our learners.

Understanding the effects of what we teach helps us care about our subject area. Knowing that our learners will experience a "first" with us can be a powerful influence on our enthusiasm. The first time I ever read one of Shakespeare's sonnets was with a teacher. The first time I ever used a computer was at a workshop under the guidance of an instructor. The first time I ever learned how to prepare my own media displays was with a trainer. The list is very long and very important to me. Please consider the first-time experiences and skills you bring to learners. They form an inventory to be savored.

2. We Display Our Commitment with Appropriate Degrees of Emotion and Expressiveness

Displaying our commitment to our subject matter is the exhilarating quality that makes instruction enthusiastic. In some ways, we are like cheerleaders. We root for what we believe in.

Allowing ourselves to have feelings about what we teach is the key. Here are some examples: getting excited about new concepts, skills, materials, and future events related to our subject; showing wonder about discoveries and insights that emerge from learners; and sincerely expressing emotions as we are learning with our students: "I feel frustrated by these problems myself," "I became sad as I read this essay," or "I'm happy to see the progress you're making."

A little bit of dramatization may help as well. Whatever the actor in us will allow is a good rule of thumb. We can tell interesting stories about what we teach; role-play our subject matter (by becoming historical figures, delivering quotations and speeches, simulating characters in problems, and so forth); and use the arts and media, such as music, slide shows, and film excerpts, to demonstrate and accentuate our subject matter.

Showing our interest in the world as it relates to what we teach is another attractive way to display our enthusiasm. It not only vividly demonstrates our commitment but also broadens the importance of our subject matter. We can bring in articles and newspaper clippings about current events that relate to what we teach; take field trips; invite guest speakers who work in areas related to our subject matter; self-disclose interesting personal experiences we have had as we learn about our field; and share new learning that we might be carrying on at the moment. Be cautious about using these last two ideas, however. Being too extreme with them could be interpreted as being self-centered, which would be more harmful than helpful with adult learners.

Although emotional involvement, dramatization, and showing interest are ways to display our enthusiasm, how do we really know if our instruction expresses this quality? The following are five indicators commonly found in instruments designed to measure teacher enthusiasm (Larkins and others, 1985):

1. Speaking with some variation in tone, pitch, volume, and speed

2. Gesturing with arms and hands

3. Moving about the room to illustrate points and to respond to questions

4. Making varied, emotive facial expressions as called for

5. Displaying energy and vitality

How people express and perceive enthusiasm varies across cultures. Currently, there is no instrument to measure teacher enthusiasm that is both precise and culturally sensitive. Nor is there an ideal model for enthusiastic teaching. A flamboyant, dynamic speaker who might do well at a corporate training seminar might be stylistically ill suited for a rural school board meeting.

However, the five behaviors in the preceding list are excellent indicators to consider when assessing your enthusiasm while teaching. If possible, you might videotape a few of your instructional experiences and evaluate your use of the five behaviors, taking into account your subject area, the learners you normally teach, and the behaviors of an instructor who successfully enhances the motivation of similar learners. That would provide a sensitive context for your self-assessment and a model for comparison. If you prefer, you might ask a respected colleague to observe you teaching and to give you feedback about your enthusiasm using the five categories as focal points for discussion. I favor the latter approach, especially if it is reciprocal, because I have found the discussion that results from these observations to be enormously informative.

As instructors, we are sometimes faced with solving the problem of *loss of enthusiasm*. Over the years I have found six potential destroyers of enthusiasm. Whether you are a novice or a more experienced instructor of adults, you may find the following descriptions of these hazards beneficial.

1. *Satiation.* You seem to be doing the same thing over and over again. The feeling is one of boredom. There is nothing fresh or new in your instruction. You feel you may be in a rut, and B. B. King's anthem is far too clear to you: "The thrill is gone." One of the best antidotes for this condition is change. Change the content, process, environment, or population of your instructional situation. Ask yourself which aspect of your instruction would benefit from an alteration and take the necessary steps. We know from systems theory that one significant change in a system can change everything else. This principle may be positively applicable to your situation. However, in more extreme situations, satiation can be the signal for the need to consider another work setting or another job.

2. *Stress.* You feel burned out, psychologically drained, and physically near exhaustion. Perhaps you are somewhat depressed as well. Instruction is taking too much out of you. If this is the case, make up your mind to control the stress and not let it control you. Stress does kill. There are myriad books and programs that offer realistic assistance. Contact your professional organization, local health department, or physician for appropriate references.

3. *Lack of success.* You are just not getting the job done. You feel some degree of incompetence. Maybe your learners are not learning well enough, or they seem poorly motivated, or they are not applying what they learn. There may even be discipline problems and personality conflicts between you and the learners. To a large extent, this book is devoted to resolving these issues. An additional intervention would be to discuss the matter with a respected and trusted colleague. Consult with someone. Almost all professionals do so when problems come up in their work. Doctors, lawyers, therapists, and managers readily and wisely seek the counsel of fellow practitioners to resolve the many dilemmas common to anyone who provides a service to human beings.

4. *Loss of purpose.* The ultimate values for which you instruct adults seem vague and distant, possibly forgotten. You no longer feel the pride you once had in your craft. Instruction has become an ordinary, mundane task. You're surviving but not feeling pride in your work. This malady is familiar to almost everyone who does something frequently for long periods of time. It is often a form of taking one's occupation for granted. Some combination of distance, reflection, and the company of other enthusiastic practitioners can often be helpful. Vacations, conferences, conventions, and retreats are some means for self-renewal.

5. *Living in the past.* You are having an attack of the good-old-days bug. The learners aren't as good as they used to be. The instructional conditions have deteriorated. You see things as they

once were. You see things as they are now. You feel depressed. You tell yourself things will not get better. You feel even more depressed. This can lead to cynicism. And if you associate with other cynics, feeding off one another's hopelessness can produce an endless cycle. Break this pattern by seeing your situation as you would like it to be. Allow yourself to imagine how it can happen. Begin to take the necessary steps. Associate with others who are willing to work toward these goals with you. Using processes from Appreciative Inquiry described earlier in this chapter may be quite helpful in this situation.

6. *Plateauing.* Your instruction may be effective, but you no longer believe you can get better. You feel stagnant. Personal and professional growth on the job seems dead-ended. There is very little challenge to your work. You feel resigned rather than committed. If you cannot leave this situation, you may feel trapped. Whether you go or not, the more beneficial alternative is the same: create another challenge for yourself. This means setting a concrete goal in your professional life for which the outcome is not certain. There will be some risk of failure, but that is where the exhilaration comes from. Your challenge could be to raise your instructional goals, try a new training process, or become a mentor to a less experienced instructor. Whatever it is, make it only a moderate risk, meaning that the odds for success are clearly in your favor. Then plan for the challenge and act on it. The results will speak for themselves.

Clarity: The Power of Organization and Language

You are a trainee in a special program your employer has developed. You are attending your first training seminar to gain the appropriate skills for your new position. It is the first hour of the session, and things seem to be going smoothly. Materials have been passed out. The leader has introduced himself. He seems well qualified, experienced, and enthusiastic. In fact, he has just told you that one of the most important prerequisites for success in your new job will be a positive attitude toward your colleagues.

A trainee raises her hand and asks, "I've often heard how important a positive attitude is. But what does that really mean? I think where I get confused is just understanding what an attitude is. Could you tell me what that word means?"

You had not considered it before, but you now realize you are not too sure what an attitude is either. The instructor waits a moment and begins his answer. "Well, ah . . . an attitude is, um . . . sort of like a way of looking at something or maybe thinking about what you see, or feeling a certain way, so that you end up . . . no, let me say, act, uh . . . better yet . . . judge the situation and that makes you behave in a certain way. Like, if you don't like someone, you won't talk to them. Or . . . if you respect something, you'll take better care of it."

The instructor moves on. You are confused, and you notice by the expressions on their faces that most of your peers seem to be feeling the same way, too. Trainee motivation has seriously slipped in the seminar. You feel a bit worried that you will not be able to understand this instructor.

Adult learners endure this situation all too frequently. They have expert, well-intentioned, enthusiastic instructors who do not communicate clearly. In the example just cited, the instructor could have said, "An attitude is the combination of a perception with a judgment that results in an emotion that influences our behavior. For example, you see a neighbor at a party. You like this person. You feel happy to see him. You decide to walk over and say hello." At the very least, the instructor should have asked the trainee if she needed more explanation or examples. This would have allowed for further clarification and might have saved the day.

No matter how expert, empathic, and enthusiastic an instructor is, the fourth pillar—instructional clarity—is still necessary for motivating instruction. People seldom learn what they cannot understand. Worse yet is to have an instructor who seems to know and care about the subject but cannot explain it.

Instructional clarity is teaching something in a manner that is easy for learners to understand and that is organized so that they can smoothly follow and participate in the intended lesson or program. But there is a catch—what may be easy for one person to understand may not be so for another. There is a dynamic between what the instructor does and what the learner brings to the instructional situation. This is the inter-action between the instructor's language and teaching format and the learner's language and experience. Neuroscientifically, we are talking about the bridge from what the instructor knows to the prior knowledge of the learners. Clarity is achieved when the instructor provides a way for the flow of his knowledge to firmly connect with the neuronal networks of the learners. Like cars rolling along a suspension bridge to a network of highways on the other side of a river, the instructor's information rapidly moves into and connects with the stored memories of the learners (Willis, 2006).

For an illustration of how easily this interaction can break down, suppose that an instructor uses an example with which some learners are unfamiliar. Perhaps he refers to a hat trick in the sport of hockey. One learner in the group has never seen a hockey game, and another is learning English and cannot make sense of the phrase. Rather than being enlightened, both learners are confused by the example. Adult learners can become frustrated when they know from their experience that they have the capability to learn but find the instructor's language or methods vague and confusing. Often increasing this tension is their real need for new learning to perform their jobs or advance in their careers.

Many studies confirm that instructional clarity is positively associated with learning (Land, 1987; McKeachie, 1997). Berliner (1988) found that *expert teachers*, effective teachers who have

developed fluid and often masterful solutions to common classroom problems, are extremely well organized and thoughtful
about teaching procedures. Instructional designers have focused
on how instructors can organize knowledge so that learners acquire it and integrate it with their prior knowledge
(Morrison, Ross, and Kemp, 2006). Educators in multicultural
and linguistic studies have also researched how instructors can use
communication skills to promote the learning and participation
of English-language learners (Kinsella, 1993; Samovar, Porter, and
McDaniel, 2005).

It is difficult to prescribe what an instructor should do to
guarantee instructional clarity. Significant research continues in
this area, and much evidence is still coming in. However, two
performance standards are worth considering: (1) we plan and
conduct instruction so that all learners can follow and understand,
and (2) we provide a way for learners to comprehend what has
been taught if it is not initially clear. Using these two guidelines can help us establish and develop instructional clarity for
learners.

1. We Plan and Conduct Instruction So That All Learners Can Follow and Understand

This guideline emphasizes organization and language. Organization
is the logical connection and orderly relationship between each
part of our instructional process. Do we provide a good map—that
is, can learners follow us from one learning destination to the next?
Do we emphasize the most important concepts and skills, just as a
road map highlights the larger cities?

Beyond good outlining, planning for instructional clarity includes the following:

- Anticipating problems learners will have with the
  material and having relevant examples and activities ready to deepen their understanding.

- Creating the best graphics, examples, analogies, and stories to make ideas easier to understand. (Much more information about this idea is found in Chapters Six and Seven.)

- Including checkpoints in the form of questions or problems to make sure learners are understanding and following the lesson.

- Knowing the learning objective and preparing a clear introduction to the lesson so that students know what they will be learning.

- Considering the use of *advance organizers* and *visual tools*. These are graphics, examples, questions, activities, and diagrams that support understanding of new information. They direct learners' attention to what is important in the coming material, highlight the relationships of the ideas to be presented, and remind learners of relevant information or experience. (For extensive discussion and examples, see Chapter Seven.)

- Rehearsing directions for such learning activities as simulations, case studies, and role playing so that learners will be clear about how to do the activities and can experience their maximum benefits.

During instruction, we can also enhance clarity by using explanatory links—such words as *if*, *then*, *because*, and *therefore*—that tie ideas together and make them easier to learn (Berliner, 1987). Consider the difference in clarity when an instructor says, "Thomas Jefferson owned slaves. Some historians question his greatness as a president," as opposed to, "Some historians question Thomas Jefferson's greatness as a president because he owned slaves."

When we signal transitions from one major topic to another, we help learners follow along. Such phrases as *the next step*, *the second phase*, and *now we turn to* ... tell learners that we are changing the focus of our discussion.

Most important is to use words, descriptions, and examples that are familiar to learners. If we are talking about a *pattern* and refer to it as a *configuration*, we are more likely to be understood than if we call it a *gestalt* or a *harmonic*. In general, the main goal is to avoid being obscure.

Obvious from this discussion is the importance of language. Comprehension for English-language learners can be extremely challenging because so much advanced learning is abstract and context-reduced, lacking real objects, visual images, and the social clues (such as facial expressions and feedback from others) one might have during a conversation. Kinsella (1993) offers helpful suggestions for increasing clarity for English-language learners during instruction:

- Pair less proficient English users with sensitive peers who can clarify concepts, vocabulary, and instructions in the primary language.

- Increase wait time (by three to nine seconds) after posing a question to allow adequate time for the learner to process the question effectively and formulate a thoughtful response.

- Make corrections indirectly by mirroring in correct form what the learner has said. For example, suppose a student says, "Many immigrants in Seattle from Southeast Asia." You can repeat, "Yes, many of the immigrants in Seattle *come* from Southeast Asia."

- Use these conversational checks regularly in class discussions, lectures, and small-group work:

Confirmation checks	"Is this what you are saying?" "So you believe that ..."
Clarification requests	"Will you explain your viewpoint so that I can be sure I understand?"
Comprehension checks	"Is my use of language understandable to you?"
Interrupting	"Excuse me, ..." "Sorry for interrupting. . ."

- Write as legibly as possible on the board or media, keeping in mind that students from some countries may be unfamiliar with cursive writing.

- Allow students to record classes for repeated listening to comprehend and retain information.

- Modify your normal conversational style to make your delivery as comprehensible as possible: speak slightly slower, enunciate clearly, limit idiomatic expressions, and pause adequately at the end of statements to allow time for learners to clarify their thoughts and to take notes.

- Relate information to assigned readings whenever possible and give the precise place (page numbers) in the text or selection so that learners can later find the information for study and review.

- Allow learners to compare notes near the end of class or training and to ask you any questions they could not answer among themselves.

2. We Provide a Way for Learners to Comprehend What Has Been Taught if It Is Not Initially Clear

We can meet this criterion in many different ways, depending on how and what we teach. The range of possibilities spans reviewing difficult material to announcing office hours for learners who want personal help.

The Instructional Clarity Checklist in Exhibit 3.1 is a way of surveying these many options. It is also a means of obtaining learner feedback to tell us how clearly learners understand us. Statements that relate directly to guideline 2 ("We provide a way for learners to comprehend what has been taught if it is not initially clear") are preceded by an X. Statements relating to guideline 1 ("We plan and conduct instruction so that all learners can follow and understand") are preceded by an O. The Instructional Clarity Checklist is a concrete way to better understand how clear our instruction really is. If we videotape ourselves during instruction, we can use this checklist to assess the clarity of our instruction while we actually see and hear ourselves interact with learners.

Cultural Responsiveness: The Power of Respect and Social Responsibility

Think of someone who respects you, someone who easily comes to mind and about whose respect you have little doubt. I have two notions about this person. The first is that he or she very seldom, if ever, threatens you in order to make you do something. The second is that your opinion matters to this person. Your way of understanding things can influence this person, especially the way he or she treats you. These two notions do not amount to a philosophical treatise on respect, but to most of us in our daily lives, they are how we know whether or not we are respected. They are particularly valid in a learning environment, and they demonstrate why respect is essential to the motivation of adults. Without respect, the reason someone does something for another is fear, obedience, ignorance, lust, or love; with the possible exception of love, these causes are best avoided in most adult learning environments.

Exhibit 3.1   Instructional Clarity Checklist

This checklist is designed primarily for learners to complete, but it can also be adapted to become a self-informing survey. In its present form, it can be given to learners for their feedback on your instruction. This will tell you from their point of view what you do well and what you may need to do to improve the clarity of your instruction.

Instructions: after each statement, place a check mark under the category that most accurately applies to it.

As our instructor, you:	All of the time	Most of the time	Some of the time	Never	Doesn't apply
○ 1. Explain things simply.					
○ 2. Give explanations we understand.					
○ 3. Teach at a pace that is not too fast and not too slow.					
○ 4. Stay with the topic until we understand.					
✕ 5. Try to find out when we don't understand and then repeat things.					
○ 6. Show graphics, diagrams, and examples to help us understand.					
○ 7. Describe the work to be done and how to do it.					
✕ 8. Ask if we know what to do and how to do it.					
✕ 9. Repeat things when we don't understand.					

○ 10. Explain something and then use an example to illustrate it.					
× 11. Explain something and then stop so we can ask questions.					
○ 12. Prepare us for what we will be doing next.					
○ 13. Use words and examples familiar to us.					
× 14. Repeat things that are hard to understand.					
○ 15. Use examples and explain them until we understand.					
○ 16. Explain something and then stop so we can think about it.					
○ 17. Show us how to do the work.					
○ 18. Explain the assignment and the materials we need to do it.					
○ 19. Stress difficult points.					
○ 20. Show examples of how to do course work and assignments.					
× 21. Give us enough time for practice.					
× 22. Answer our questions.					
× 23. Ask questions to find out if we understand.					
× 24. Go over difficult assignments until we understand how to do them.					

Source: Adapted from Gephart, Strother, and Duckett, 1981, p. 4.

As part of the fifth pillar—cultural responsiveness—I stress *respect for diversity*, an understanding that people are different as a result of history, socialization, and experience as well as biology. Thus, it is normal for learners to have different perspectives, and all of them have a right to instruction that accommodates their diversity.

Social responsibility, the second essential quality of cultural responsiveness, emerges from this respect for diversity. If we agree that all people matter, we must ask the question, What is my teaching ultimately connected to beyond myself and my students? I vitally believe in the interdependence of all people and things. Motivation does not occur in a vacuum. It is energy with a consequence. This understanding obliges me to see my work in the context of an ideal for social justice, because I know better than most that people's motivation to learn is released by a vision of a hopeful future. That means I seek to foster effective learning for all learners with attention to the collective good of society. How I do this may differ or at times conflict with others who have the same intent, whether they are learners, colleagues, or people I do not personally know. Therefore, the following guidelines for cultural responsiveness are both necessary and relevant: (1) we create a safe, inclusive, and respectful learning environment; (2) we engage the motivation of all learners; and (3) we relate course content and learning to the social concerns of learners and the broader concerns of society.

1. We Create a Safe, Inclusive, and Respectful Learning Environment

In a safe learning environment, there is little risk of learners' suffering any form of personal embarrassment because of self-disclosure, lack of knowledge, a personal opinion, or a hostile or arrogant social environment. We can go a long way toward developing this kind of security by assuming a nonblameful and realistically hopeful view of people and their capacity to change.

Blame is a classic trap, one in which our normal instincts disable us. When a problem or disagreement emerges, we often seek to assign responsibility. In so doing, we may find fault or label a person, often without validity or empathy. Blaming can create a cycle of reciprocally hostile attitudes and actions that damages relationships among people, especially culturally different people (Wlodkowski and Ginsberg, 1995). As ugly as it is to say it, blaming is usually some version of, "Oh, since that's the way you see it, your welfare no longer matters to me."

Rather than blame, we instructors can model and support increased understanding and mutual problem solving and exploit these opportunities for further learning. Beverly Daniel Tatum (1992) offered an excellent example of doing this in her course the Psychology of Racism. She explicitly taught with the assumption that because prejudice was inherent in her students' environments when they were children, they could not be blamed for what they had intentionally or unintentionally been taught. Nonetheless, they all had a responsibility to interrupt the cycle of oppression and needed to realize that understanding and unlearning prejudice may be a lifelong process. She acknowledged that students may not all be at the same point in the process and should have mutual respect for each other, regardless of where they perceive each other to be. Her excellent book, *Why Are All the Black Kids Sitting Together in the Cafeteria?* (2003), extends this understanding to people's identity and personal development, offering constructive ways to talk about race and difference that are applicable not only to adolescents but to adults as well.

Ridding a learning environment of blame does not mean that we give up our critical reasoning or avoid facing the truth as we understand it. It does mean realizing that a different viewpoint can give us information that leads to shared understanding and a clearer path for communication; that although I may see things differently than you do, I do not withdraw my respect for you. A realistically hopeful view of people is not a mask to cover problems or difficulties. We do not ignore human suffering. But we do pay attention to opportunity, give the benefit of the doubt, expect learners to do well, and allow ourselves to find joy in the process of working toward the solutions to problems.

The modus operandi of an instructor who wants to foster a safe, inclusive, and respectful learning environment is to share the construction of knowledge. This is not a method as much as it is a value and a way of being. It means encouraging all learners to understand their own creation of meaning and to accept the integrity of their own thinking (Oldfather, 1992; Rogoff and Chavajay, 1995). From history to physics, knowledge changes and varies. This realization requires us to be responsive to each learner's oral, written, and artistic self-expression. Accordingly, we invite the ideas, feelings, and concerns of every learner in the community, placing exploration of differences at center stage rather than in the shadows.

From this perspective, the learner's voice is critical (Lather, 1991). Truth is a process of construction in which the learner participates (Gilligan, 1982; Belenky and others, 1986). A learner must trust her own thinking if she is to be intrinsically motivated. How many times have we heard an instructor say, "Those people just don't like to think"? Well, if we are the learners and it isn't our own thinking, and if we can't say that we see things differently without fear of rejection or threat, then such thinking is unlikely to be very appealing. Telling and hearing *our* stories is essential to human nature. Stories are compelling because they are one of the foremost ways our brains make sense of things (Cozolino and Sprokay, 2006). To know we are using our own minds to transcend what we know, to play with ideas, and to realize clearly what was once vastly incommunicable can be ecstasy.

When learners know that the having and sharing of ideas is a sincerely respected norm in the learning environment, they will be more likely to expose their thinking. In fact, it is one of the few ways they can come to realize that there are multiple viewpoints on any issue and to appreciate how others also use the process of construction for their own learning and grasp of truth. Nevertheless, under the safest of circumstances, because of prior learning and experience, adults from dominant groups are more likely to feel safer than adults from marginalized groups. As instructors we still need to ask who is probably going to feel safer or less safe and what are the contexts we need to develop and shift so that everyone has an opportunity to express themselves (Tisdell, 1998; Sinacore and Enns, 2005).

2. We Engage the Motivation of All Learners

In any course or training, it's pretty easy to absolve ourselves of responsibility for the lack of motivation of some students. Now and then I even hear the excuse, "They have a right to fail." This implies that strenuous efforts to encourage learning among resistant students may deny them their freedom of choice and constitutional legacy. However, my most common experience has been that most instructors of adults are sometimes frustrated, confused, or at a loss as to what to do about learners who seem reluctant to learn or, more often, reluctant to do enough to learn what the instructor would consider satisfactory. Some of us resolve this issue by teaching to a certain segment of the class: those adults who most easily learn with us, leaving the rest to the hands of fate. Yet we need to be aware there is clear evidence that those learners left at the roadside of adult education are generally culturally different from their instructors, income level being one of the most dominant dissimilarities (Cook and King, 2004).

If we accept that students become intrinsically motivated when they can see that what they are learning makes sense and is important to them, we are required as instructors to be respectful of our students' culture, perspectives, concerns, and interests. Our finding salient ways to include these compelling aspects of their lives in the creation of a learning environment or a lesson is essential to engaging the motivation of all learners. With this awareness, we strive to create the educational experience with our learners, interpreting and deepening the meaning we share together. I understand this goal to be an ideal and possibly a never-ending, unfulfilled challenge. But I also believe that to act as though I can reach this ideal is both responsible and wise. I offer the Motivational Framework for Culturally Responsive Teaching (introduced in Chapter Four) as the most realistic means I have found to consistently meet this challenge.

3. We Relate Course Content and Learning to the Social Concerns of Learners and the Broader Concerns of Society

Education is inextricably connected to society. It directly contributes to the construction of the individual and society. We are what we learn to be. People and society are developed in one direction or another through education (Shor, 1993). Ethics and politics are inherent in the instructor-learner relationship (authoritarian or democratic), in readings chosen for the syllabus (those left in and those left out), and in the process of learning (for example, which questions get asked and answered, and how deeply are they probed). Because people cannot escape the pervasive human need to invest meaning in their world and must have a hopeful future to feel a deep motivation to learn (Courtney, 1991), the connection of our instruction to broader social concerns that affect how people live, work, and survive is inescapable. As instructors we have a social responsibility to promote equity and justice.

With the growth of cultural diversity and the numbers of historically underrepresented students in adult education, the model of *cultural competence* has emerged. This set of processes may enable instructors to be more equitable and effective with students from a variety of cultures. Practitioners from a variety of fields including medicine, counseling, and education believe that cultural competence includes the following three critical elements (Chiu and Hong, 2005):

1. Self-understanding and awareness of one's own cultural values and biases

2. Specific knowledge about the history, perspectives, and values of the various cultural groups one is working with

3. Adapting one's behaviors and skills to conduct appropriate and successful interactions with culturally different people

Although these competencies make sense and are desirable, cultures are so complex and interactions so nuanced that being competent to teach culturally different adults is not a static set of skills that one can master, but an evolving process of learning, a fine goal to continuously strive toward and one that needs to be accompanied by an awareness of one's own limitations. Substantial research supports this generalization (Chiu and Hong, 2005), but my life as a teacher is the strongest voice for this caution.

Living authentic experiences with culturally different groups, participating in events that take us into culturally diverse homes and neighborhoods, and being open to encounters that allow us to learn the values and practices of other people promote intercultural understanding and empathy, qualities that contribute to cultural competence (Ancis and Ali, 2005). Chapter Nine focuses on the first element of cultural competence, *self-understanding*, as a self-assessment for applying the Motivational Framework for Culturally Responsive Teaching. The second element, *specific knowledge about the culturally different group*, is generally addressed in this chapter under the section discussing empathy. Ideas for the third element, *adapting one's behavior and skills for successful interactions*, are found in this chapter in the discussions of clarity and cultural responsiveness and in all the sections of this book that address the essential condition of inclusion.

I have found Paulo Freire's conception of a *critical consciousness* (1970) to be an invaluable guide to creating a learning environment in which the integrity of all learners is effectively supported and where learning seems likely to contribute to the common good of society—to inform as well as to transform us. Instructors with a critical consciousness reflect the following qualities (Shor, 1993):

- *Power awareness.* Approaching our instruction and content with an understanding that society is constructed by organized groups; realizing who has power and how power is structured and used in society, especially as it influences learners in the course. Closely related is *positionality*, sensitivity to how qualities of identity such as privilege, class, and gender of both instructors and learners can affect the learning process and whose world views and "truths" dominate the learning environment (Sinacore and Enns, 2005).

- *Critical literacy.* Using analytic habits of thinking, reading, writing, and discussing that go beneath surface impressions, traditional myths, opinions, and clichés; understanding the social contexts and consequences of any subject matter; being willing to probe for the deeper meaning of an event, reading, statement, image, or situation, and applying the meaning found to one's own as well as the learners' situation.

- *Desocialization.* Recognizing and challenging prejudicial myths, values, behaviors, and language, especially those learned in mass culture, such as class bias and excessive consumerism.

- *Self-education.* Using learning opportunities to initiate constructive social change, ideas, and projects; for example, using action research in a course to inform a local paper, corporation, or community organization about discovered abuses or inequities.

In this chapter, we examined and discussed the five pillars of motivating instruction—expertise, empathy, enthusiasm, clarity, and cultural responsiveness. They are five necessary, interdependent, and vital building blocks. They form a strong foundation, but they are not a complete structure. We could not consider the material that follows in this book without first acknowledging these core characteristics. In presenting the motivational strategies in this book, I am strongly urging the instructor who uses them to do so in a manner that is expert, empathic, enthusiastic, clear, and culturally responsive. Under these circumstances, the strategies are more likely to be both respectful and effective with adult learners.

4

What Motivates Adults to Learn

What sets the world in motion is the interplay of
differences, their attraction and repulsion. Life is
plurality, death is uniformity.

Octavio Paz

As a discipline, motivation is a teeming ocean. A powerfully influential and wide-ranging area of study in the social sciences, motivation at its core deals with *why people behave as they do*. But in terms of scholarly agreement and tightly controlled boundaries of application, motivation swarms with abundant and rich and often dissimilar ideas. Theoretical assumptions that human beings are rational, materialistic, pragmatic, individualistic, and self-directed coexist with views of human beings as irrational, spiritual, altruistic, communal, and other-directed (Gergen and others, 1996).

This state of affairs has been brought about by the complexity of human behavior, our awareness of the influence of biological and social processes on any human endeavor, and the realization that claims for knowledge in the human domain are relative to the culture in which they are spawned. Regarding motivation, learning, and instruction, the ideas in this book are largely *constructivist* and linked to evolving neuroscientific research. From the constructivist viewpoint, people actively construct their own knowledge and learn through their interaction with and support from other people and objects in the world (Bruning and others, 2004). Underlying this interaction are the processes of the brain and central nervous system. To better understand motivation and learning requires us to perceive a person's thinking and emotions as inseparable from each other and from the social context in which the activity takes place. For example, would I have these thoughts (writing clearly about adult motivation) and feelings (mild anxiety—maybe I won't) if I were not in front of a personal computer swamped by research journals and texts and aware of my history as a teacher of adults? It seems unlikely that I would. However, I am still an individual with my own thoughts, guided by personal interests and goals. I live as a socially and culturally constructed being with an individual identity in a biologically functioning body. Amazingly, these ways of being human exist at the same time.

In general, ideas from neuroscience and constructivism are compatible with intrinsic motivation's tenets that human beings are curious and active, make meaning from experience, and desire to be effective at what they value (McCombs and Whisler, 1997). For example, what adults find relevant, that which interests them and matters most to their brains, is directly related to their individual values, which are social constructions. As we proceed to describe the Motivational Framework for Culturally Responsive Teaching (Wlodkowski and Ginsberg, 1995) and its related conditions and strategies, I will weave these congruent ideas throughout the discussion, based largely on their salience and most often from the perspective of intrinsic motivation.

What Is Adult about Adult Motivation to Learn

Responsibility is the cornerstone of adult motivation. Almost all cultures hold adults more responsible for their actions than they do children. For adults this is an inescapable fact. This deep social value for responsibility is why competence, being effective at what one values, looms so large and so consistently as a force for learning among adults.

Although there is no unified comprehensive theory of adult learning, certain concepts are especially insightful for teaching adults. In his discussion of andragogy (adult learning as it differs from how children and adolescents learn), Malcolm Knowles provided two assumptions that add to our understanding of adult motivation: (1) "Adults have a self-concept of being responsible for their own lives . . . [and] develop a deep psychological need to be seen and treated by others as being capable of self-direction" and (2) "Adults become ready to learn those things they need to know or . . . to cope effectively with their real-life situations" (1989, pp. 83–84). These two assumptions continue to reflect the social norms of the majority society in the United States, a largely individualistic and pragmatic culture. Most employers and educational institutions value and reward self-directed competence. Most adults are socialized with these values. These cultural conventions account for one of the most widely accepted generalizations in adult education: *adults are highly pragmatic learners.*

Research consistently supports Knowles's second assumption: adults choose vocational and practical education that leads to knowledge about how to do something more often than they choose any other form of learning (Aslanian, 2001). The largest category of continuing education globally is directed toward upgrading job-related knowledge and skills (Mott, 2006; Schied, 2006). Adults have a strong need to apply what they have learned and to be competent in that application, and institutions and employers have a pressing need for more knowledgeable and skilled workers. The reciprocal needs of adults and employers interact with economics to produce a powerful demand for learning that increases personal and professional competence.

Adults by social definition, economic need, and institutional expectation are responsible people who seek to enhance their lives through learning that develops their competence. The usefulness of what is learned generally is a greater influence on adults' motivation to learn than its intellectual value. The second major characteristic that distinguishes adults' motivation to learn is *their accumulated experience and learning*. The sum of adults' personal knowledge and acculturation influences what they regard as useful, relevant, and interesting to learn. Neuroscientifically, prior knowledge determines what matters and to what adult brains are attuned to pay attention to and concentrate on (Zull, 2006).

One might say that prior knowledge and experience are equally important influences for the motivation of children and it's true. However, *how* previous experience and learning affect what adults and children find interesting to learn and *how* they act with that information differs. Maturity of brain development makes the difference. Neurologist and middle school teacher Judy Willis explains, "The prefrontal cortex is the last part of the brain to mature. This brain region is the center for emotional stability, moral reasoning, judgment, and executive functions such as concentration, planning, delayed gratification, and prioritizing. Because of fluctuations in the developing prefrontal cortex, teens might have difficulty communicating ideas and feelings, making wise decisions, or establishing consistent self identities" (2006, p. 67).

The prefrontal cortex may not be completely developed until a person is between 25 and 30 years old (Gogtay and others, 2004). The neurons in the frontal lobe form rules from learned experiences (Wallis, Anderson, and Miller, 2001); this is where we create large holistic views of what the world is, what we want to do about it, and in what direction we want to go (Zull, 2002). A fully developed prefrontal cortex with a well-integrated set of life experiences probably contributes to what is conventionally described as maturity—the ability to make responsible decisions on a regular basis with consideration of their consequences for the welfare of others as well as oneself.

Experientially, adults generally differ from children quantitatively; they have more experience by virtue of being older. Qualitatively, adults have had more time and seen the benefits and outcomes of a greater variety of experiences. Neurologically, their brains are more developed and capable of judging, planning, and making decisions about their experiences in a manner that is more integrated, stable, reflective, and future oriented. This constellation of characteristics probably makes the *value* of what adults learn more important to them. Recent research indicates that adult college students (28 and older) have a greater intrinsic goal orientation academically than college students 21 or younger (Bye, Pushkar, and Conway, 2007). This finding may reflect adults' greater desire to learn for a sense of accomplishment, effectiveness, and value for what is being learned. It may be that the *worth* of what is learned is more important to fostering their intrinsic motivation than it is for younger students. What these differences in experience mean motivationally is that adults are more likely than children to have these characteristics:

- To use relevance (what matters rather than what is playful or stimulating) as the ultimate criteria for sustaining their interest

- To be more critical and more self-assured about their judgment of the value of what they are learning

- To be reluctant to learn what they cannot endorse by virtue of its value, usefulness, or contribution to their goals

- To be sensitive to and require respect from their teachers as a condition for learning

- To want to actively test what they are learning in real work and life settings

- To want to use their experience and prior learning as consciously and as directly as possible while learning

- To want to integrate new learning with their life roles as parents, workers, and so forth

There are other differences between children and adults in terms of their motivation to learn, but research, theory, and my own history as a teacher confirm that the influences of responsibility and experience are the most notable. Like the roots of a tree, they may not always be obvious, but when it comes to enhancing adult motivation, they are needed to sustain and support everything we do as instructors.

Integrated Levels of Adult Motivation

Adults want to be successful learners. This goal is a constant influence on them, because success directly or indirectly indicates their competence. *If adults have a problem experiencing success or even expecting success, their motivation for learning will usually decline.* Although the meaning of success for adults may vary depending on socialization (for example, success may be individual recognition or collective family pride), adults pay keen attention to indicators of success while they are learning (Mordkowitz and Ginsburg, 1987).

Adult motivation can operate on integrated levels, with multiple feelings and thoughts occurring simultaneously. The most basic integrated level for instructors to take notice of is *success + volition.* For their motivation to be sustained, adults need to feel willing as well as successful in the learning activity. There is almost no limit to the number of specific reasons why an adult might want to learn something, but unless there is a willful intention to learn, motivation is likely to wane as time goes on. That is because it is difficult for an adult to feel responsible unless she has willingly done something to be accountable for. There will be more discussion about volition when we focus on attitude later in this chapter. At the very minimum, instructors who want to enhance adult motivation need to plan how to help adults to be successful and willing learners.

A higher level of motivational integration is *success + volition + value*. At this level, the adult learner does not necessarily find the learning activity pleasurable or exciting but does take the activity seriously, finds it meaningful and worthwhile, and tries to get the intended benefit from it (Brophy, 2004). Adults feel much better when they have successfully learned something they wanted to learn and that they value. This separates superficial learning from relevant learning and provides the learning process with the potential to be intrinsically motivating.

The highest level of this progression is *success + volition + value + enjoyment*. Simply put, at this level the adult has experienced learning as pleasurable and intrinsically motivating. To help adults successfully learn what they value and want to learn in an enjoyable manner is the sine qua non of adult instruction and neurological access. I have never found an adult to be dissatisfied with instruction that engenders this level of emotional integration. It is the kind of teaching that receives awards and is long remembered and appreciated. I do not state this as an incentive for you but as the exposition of a reality. Instructors who teach in this manner are truly masterful because they have made the difficult desirable. Adults want to be joyful in the pursuit of valued learning, especially in the realms of life where competence is cherished but formidable to obtain. And for instructors who want adults to successfully learn with a reasonable amount of effort, such teaching is the most challenging and rewarding route to follow.

In order to accomplish this kind of teaching or training, Dr. Margery Ginsberg and I developed the Motivational Framework for Culturally Responsive Teaching (Wlodkowski and Ginsberg, 1995) to guide instructional planning as well as to provide a way to instruct that is intrinsically motivating for diverse adults in formal learning situations. The rest of this chapter describes the essential conditions that make up the framework, offers an overview of the framework, and concludes by applying this model to an actual instructional situation.

Theories and research in the social sciences and multicultural studies, and more recently in the neurosciences, have indicated at least four motivational conditions that can substantially enhance adult motivation to learn—inclusion, attitude, meaning, and competence.

How Inclusion Fosters Involvement

Inclusion is the awareness of adults that they are part of a learning environment in which they and their instructor are respected by and connected to one another. Social climate creates a sense of inclusion. Ideally, learners realize that they can consider different, possibly opposing, perspectives as part of their learning experience. At the same time, there is a mutually accepted, common culture within the learning group and some degree of harmony or community. The atmosphere encourages learners to feel safe, capable, and accepted.

Mentioned but rarely defined, respect seldom appears in the indexes of most psychology and adult education textbooks. Nonetheless, its importance to human beings is irrefutable. *To be free of undue threat and to have our perspective matter in issues of social exchange are critical to our well-being and learning.* Pam Hays (2001) notes that in helping interactions, respect is as or more important than rapport in many cultures, including Latino, African American, Asian, Arab, and European American. Fear of threat or humiliation hinders adults from being forthcoming with their perceptions of their own reality. Neuroscientists recognize fear as a universal emotion and as a response that is deeply ingrained in the human brain (Perry, 2006; Ratey, 2001). Threat of any kind causes people to focus on ways to be safe. We look for information and behavior to respond to the threat. We are not interested in the new or nuanced. We want the familiar and comforting. In such circumstances, an instructor does not find out learners' understanding of the world or their true ideas. If there is no meaningful dialogue and if no relevant action is possible, learners become less motivated, as well they must.

Connectedness in a learning group is perceived as a sense of belonging for each individual and an awareness that each one cares for others and is cared for. There is a shared understanding among group members that they will support each other's well-being. In such an environment, people feel trust and an emotional bond with at least a few others; because of this, there exists a spirit of tolerance and loyalty that allows for a measure of uncertainty and dissent. When the attribute of connectedness is joined with respect, it creates a climate in a learning group that invites adults to access their experience, to reflect, to engage in dialogue, and to allow their histories to give meaning to particular academic or professional knowledge—all of which enhance motivation to learn.

With a sense of inclusion, most adults can publicly bring their narratives to their learning experiences. Telling and hearing our stories is essential to human nature. It is the way we make sense of things and carry our knowledge forward. Sharing stories is truth telling across generations. When stories are well told they contain unpredictability and engender emotions in the teller and the listener. These qualities enhance neuronal network integration and long-term memory (Cozolino and Sprokay, 2006). Like music, stories can seamlessly carry us into different cultures where we can identify and empathize with people who initially may seem quite different.

With stories, adults can personalize knowledge—use their own language, metaphors, experiences, or history to make sense of what they are learning (Belenky and others, 1986). When adults are encouraged by the learning atmosphere to use their own social and cultural consciousness, they can construct the cognitive connections that make knowledge relevant and under their personal control (Vygotsky, 1978).

Aside from research (Poplin and Weeres, 1992) and our common sense, which both tell us that learners who feel alienated achieve less than those who do not, consider your own experience of being a minority. On those infrequent occasions when I have been, even if it's not a matter of ethnicity but simply having a different point of view, I remember struggling to make myself heard and understood as I wanted to be understood. My anxiety was usually palpable. I also remember those occasions when the instructor created an atmosphere that allowed my differences to be respectfully heard. I spoke more easily, learned more, and was certainly more open to learning more. Unless we are the ones discounted, we are often unaware of how motivationally debilitating feeling excluded can be. Ask any group of adults about their motivation in a course where they felt excluded. Their answers are searing.

The foundation of any learning experience resides in the nature of the instructor and learner relationships. On a moment-to-moment basis, probably nothing is quite as powerful. We are social beings, and our feelings of inclusion or exclusion are enduring and irrepressible.

How Attitudes Influence Behavior

In general, an attitude is a combination of information, beliefs, values, and emotions that results in a learned tendency to respond favorably or unfavorably toward particular people, groups, ideas, events, or objects (Samovar and Porter, 2005; Scherer, 2005). For example, an accountant is required by her company to take an in-service training course. A colleague who has already taken the training tells her that the instructor is authoritarian and arrogant. The accountant believes her friend and finds herself a little anxious as she anticipates the new training. At her first training session, the instructor matter-of-factly discusses the course and its requirements. The accountant judges the instructor's neutral style to be cold and hostile. She now resents the mandatory training. This accountant has combined information and emotions into a predisposition to respond unfavorably to a person and an event. If the accountant's colleague had told her the instructor was helpful and caring, her response might have been different.

Attitudes powerfully affect human behavior and learning because they help people make sense of their world and give cues as to what behavior will be most helpful in dealing with that world. If someone is going to be hostile toward us, it is in our best interest to be careful of that person. Attitudes help us feel safe around things that are initially unknown to us. Attitudes also help us anticipate and cope with recurrent events. They give us guidelines and allow us to make our actions more automatic, making life simpler and freeing us to cope with the unexpected and more stressful elements of daily living.

Although attitudes can be influenced by a variety of situational factors such as strong needs, drugs, or illness, they are largely learned, frequently in a cultural context. Culture helps to shape our attitudes through such processes as experience, direct instruction, identification, and role behavior, as in parent-child communications. Because attitudes are learned, they can also be modified and changed. New experiences constantly affect our attitudes, making them shift, intensify, weaken, or reverse. As with any concept, the brain eliminates or prunes the neurons that represent the diminishing attitude by secreting an enzyme, calpain, that causes the neurons to self-destruct (Willis, 2006). Unless deeply ingrained and very well learned, attitudes may fade or seemingly disappear because they have not been used or supported through further learning. People, the media, and life in general constantly impinge on them. Attitudes can be personally helpful, as in the case of a positive expectancy for success, or they can be personally harmful, as in the case of an intense fear of failure. Our attitudes constantly influence our behavior and learning.

In unpredictable situations, our attitudes are very active, because they help us feel more secure. As an instructor of adults, you can be assured that students' attitudes will be an active influence on their motivation to learn from the moment instruction begins. Adult learners will immediately make judgments about you, the particular subject, the learning situation, and their personal expectancy for success. They really can't do otherwise. Beyond knowing that their attitudes are a constant influence on their motivation and learning, we cannot make broad generalizations about particular groups of adults with respect to *learning* in formal education and training programs.

However, with respect to *participating* in adult education programs, there has been considerable research on attitudes in the last four decades. According to these studies, women, and people with more education, and people with moderate to high incomes tend to hold positive attitudes toward adult education (Blunt, 2005). However, their attitudes are, at best, only moderate predictors of their decision to participate.

Two of the most important criteria for developing a positive attitude among adult learners are *relevance* and *volition*. Irrelevant learning is likely to annoy or frustrate us. We not only find such learning unimportant or strange but also implicitly know we are probably doing it because of someone else's domination or control. Our brains resist adaptation to senseless tasks (Ahissar and others, 1992), and this knowledge tends to trigger or foster a negative attitude that is sustained both psychologically and biologically. If we had some degree of choice or more input in the learning situation, we would alter its irrelevant aspects to better accommodate our perspectives and values.

Personal relevance is not simply familiarity with learning based on the learners' prior experience. Because of media saturation, people can be familiar with a particular television program or magazine yet find it totally irrelevant. People perceive personal relevance when learning is connected to who they are, what they care about, and how they perceive and know.

In an inclusive and relevant learning environment, learners can act from their most vital selves and their curiosity can emerge. They want to make sense of things and seek out challenges that are appropriate to their capacities and values. This leads to what human beings experience as interest, the emotional nutrient for a continuing positive attitude toward learning. When we feel interested, we have to make choices about what to do to follow that interest. Such volition may be willed by the learner or determined in collaboration with the instructor. Or it may be suggested or directed by the instructor but *endorsed* by the learner because such guidance adheres to socially approved standards. For example, in some East Asian societies people frequently identify with choices made for them by significant others (Chirkov and others, 2003). This orientation may come from familial, religious, or other cultural beliefs about collective values.

For the processes of learning—thinking, practicing, reading, revising, studying, and other similar activities—to be desirable and genuinely enjoyable, adults must see themselves as personally endorsing their learning because they have chosen it or they see themselves as pursuing a valued or collective goal. Global history and social science merge to support this observation: people always struggle against oppressive control and strive to determine their own lives in order to express their deepest beliefs and values. Learning is no exception.

How Meaning Sustains Involvement

According to Jack Mezirow, "a defining condition of being human is that we have to understand the meaning of our experience" (1997, p. 5). Making, understanding, and changing meaning are fundamental aspects of adult development that continuously take place in a sociocultural context (Gilligan, 1982; Tennant and Pogson, 1995). But what is meaning from a motivational perspective? In relationship to learning, what is the meaning of meaning itself?

There are a number of ways to unravel this concept. From a neurological perspective, when the brain receives new information, it searches existing neural networks to find a place for the information to "fit." If there is a connection, the new information makes sense. Prior knowledge, what we already know, allows us to *understand* the new information. However, to have *meaning* the new information has to be relevant, somehow connected to something that matters to us (Sousa, 2006). For example, if an adolescent received information about early retirement planning, it might make sense but not matter. To a working adult the same information would be more likely to be important and, therefore, not only make sense but be meaningful as well.

Another way to understand meaning is to see it as an increase in the complexity of an experience as that experience relates to our values or purposes. Adults create meaning through "their cultural, symbolic, and spiritual experience, as well as through the cognitive" (Tisdell, 2003, p. 42). This meaning may be beyond articulation. Emotion, art, and spirituality are essential to human experience and incontestably have meaning but it may not be expressible in words. For example, as I grow older, the meaning of friendship increases in conceptual complexity (different types and qualities of friendship) as well as in emotional and spiritual impressions I cannot easily describe in words.

Deep meaning implies that the experience or idea that is increasing in complexity is connected to an important goal or ultimate purpose, such as insuring the safety of one's family or finding a vocation in life. As the philosopher Susanne Langer (1942) posited, there is a human need to find significance. Across many cultures, achieving purpose appears fundamental to a satisfying life (Csikszentmihalyi and Csikszentmihalyi, 1988). When we assist learners in the realization of what is truly important in their world, they access more passionate feelings and can become absorbed in learning. Emotions both give meaning and influence behavior. If, for example, learners become troubled when they discover that certain tax laws create economic inequities, the complexity of their understanding has increased, and they may now find their agitation propelling them toward further reading about tax laws and legislation.

We can also understand *meaning* as the ordering of information that gives identity and clarity, as when we say that the word *castle* means "a large fortified residence" or when we recognize our telephone number in a listing. This kind of meaning embraces facts, procedures, and behaviors and contributes to our awareness of how things relate, operate, or are defined, but it doesn't deeply touch our psyche. A good deal of professional information falls under this description. Such information builds on prior knowledge and we can make sense of it, but it seems only slightly relevant and easily can become boring and unavailable for long-term memory. By recasting this information in a context of goals, concerns, and problems relevant to adults, instructors can infuse it with deeper meaning. Even the word *castle* takes on deeper meaning when adults can relate it to personal travel, memorable films and literature, and possible archetypes from fantasy and history. Fortunately, a number of motivational strategies can enhance the meaning of less relevant information by stimulating the memory, curiosity, and insight of learners. We will discuss these at length in Chapter Seven.

Though adults may feel included and have a positive attitude, their involvement will diminish if they cannot find learning meaningful. By making the learners' goals, interests, and cultural perspectives the context of challenging and engaging learning experiences, instructors can secure their continuing participation. If they are challenged, adults will learn more about something they care about. If they are engaged, they will actively pursue this knowledge. A challenging learning experience in an engaging format about a relevant topic is intrinsically motivating because it increases conscious (and neural) connections to important adult purposes. Meaning is at the core of motivation and learning for adults because it is where their ideas and emotions join to fulfill their personal, cultural, and spiritual commitments.

How Competence Builds Confidence

Competence theory (White, 1959) assumes people naturally strive for effective interactions with their world. We are genetically predisposed to explore, perceive, think about, manipulate, and change our surroundings to promote an effective interaction with our environment. Practicing newly developing skills and mastering challenging tasks engender positive emotions, feelings of efficacy that are evident even in early infancy. Researchers have demonstrated that babies as young as eight weeks old can learn particular responses to manipulate their environment. In one such study (Watson and Ramey, 1972), infants were placed in cribs with a mobile above their heads. By turning their heads to the right, they activated an electrical apparatus in their pillows, causing the mobile to move. These children not only learned to "move" the mobile but also displayed more positive emotions (smiling, cooing) than did the infants for whom the mobile's movement was controlled by the experimenter.

This innate disposition to be competent is so strong that we will risk danger and pain to accomplish a more able relationship with our environment. Consider the one-year-old who repeatedly falls while attempting to walk and, although still crying from a recent tumble, strives to get up and go at it again. Or the adult who, on gaining proficiency at one level of skiing, swimming, climbing, or running, "naturally" moves on to the next level, often putting body or being in jeopardy. The history of the human race is a continuous catalogue of bold scientists and adventurers who have relentlessly reached out to explore their world. We humans are active creatures who want to have a part in shaping the course of our lives.

As adults, we most frequently view competence as the desire to be *effective at what we value*. Our socialization and culture largely determine what we think is worth accomplishing (Plaut and Markus, 2005). As we move from childhood to adulthood, our feeling competent increasingly involves social input. Parents and teachers and schools and jobs, the unavoidable stuff of growing up, increasingly replace independent play and toys.

Because awareness of competence is such a powerful influence on human behavior, adults who are learning and can feel their progress are usually well motivated to continue their efforts in a similar direction. Because adults enter educational programs with a strong need to apply what they have learned to the real world, they are continually attentive to how effectively they are learning. They know their families, jobs, and communities will be the arenas in which they test this new learning. Therefore, they are more motivated when the circumstances under which they assess their competence are authentic and reflect their actual lives.

In formal learning situations, adults feel competent when they know they have attained a specified degree of knowledge or a level of performance that is acceptable by personal standards, social standards, or both. This sense of competence usually comes when adults have had a chance to apply or practice what they are learning. When they have evidence through *feedback* of how well they are learning and can make internal statements such as "I really understand this" or "I am doing this proficiently," adults experience feelings of efficacy and intrinsic motivation because they are competently performing an activity that leads to a valued goal. This experience of effectiveness affirms their innate need to relate adequately to their environment. Biologically, active testing of learning increases neural activity across the brain. This trial-and-error process includes our prediction of the expected outcome which is confirmed or disconfirmed through feedback and drives the learning process forward, activating pleasure structures in the brain as we proceed (Schultz and Dickinson, 2000; Poldrack and others, 2001).

The process and the goal are reciprocal—one gives meaning to the other. If someone wants to learn how to use a computer because it is a valued skill, his awareness of how valuable computer skills are will evoke his motivation as he makes progress in learning computer skills. However, the gained competence, the progress itself, is likely to increase the value of the goal, making computer skills more valuable; the person could eventually enter a career that was before unimaginable (perhaps prompting that common existential question, How did I get here?).

When people know with some degree of certainty that they are adept at what they are learning, they feel confident. This confidence comes from knowing that they have intentionally become proficient. Their self-confidence emanates from such internal statements as "I know this well" or "I will be able to do this again."

The relationship between competence and self-confidence is mutually enhancing. Competence allows a person to become more confident, which provides emotional support for an effort to learn new skills and knowledge. Competent achievement of this new learning further buttresses confidence, which again supports and motivates more extensive learning. This can result in a spiraling dynamic of competence and confidence growing in continued support of each other. To feel assured that one's talents and effort can lead to new learning and achievement is a powerful and lasting motivational resource. It is also the mark of a true expert or champion in any field. Instructors can help adults learn to be confident by establishing conditions that engender competence. It is a wonderful gift.

The Motivational Framework for Culturally Responsive Teaching

We have seen how important and complex the relationship of motivation and culture is to adult learning. Instructors need a model of teaching and learning that respects the inseparability of

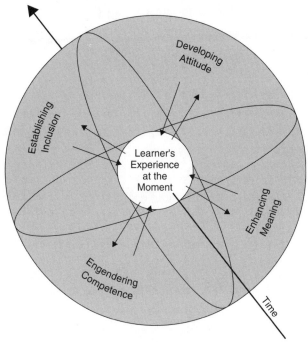

Figure 4.1. The Motivational Framework for Culturally Responsive Teaching

Source: Wlodkowski and Ginsberg, 1995, p. 29. Used with permission.

motivation and culture and integrates the emerging knowledge from neuroscience. The Motivational Framework for Culturally Responsive Teaching provides this understanding (Wlodkowski and Ginsberg, 1995). It dynamically combines the essential motivational conditions that are intrinsically motivating for diverse adults (see Figure 4.1). It provides a structure for planning and applying a rich array of motivational strategies. Each of its major conditions is supported by theories aligned with intrinsic motivation. Each condition's powerful influence on learner motivation is also substantiated by research from the social sciences and neurosciences.

The Motivational Framework for Culturally Responsive Teaching is respectful of different cultures and capable of creating a common culture that all learners in the learning situation can accept. It is a holistic and systemic representation of four intersecting motivational conditions that teachers and learners can create or enhance. The four essential conditions are these:

1. *Establishing inclusion*: creating a learning atmosphere in which learners and teachers feel respected and connected to one another

2. *Developing attitude*: creating a favorable disposition toward the learning experience through personal relevance and volition

3. *Enhancing meaning*: creating challenging and engaging learning experiences that include learners' perspectives and values

4. *Engendering competence*: creating an understanding that learners are effective in learning something they value

People experience emotions and motivational influences as a very rapid (in milliseconds) integration of intersecting processes occurring both consciously and unconsciously (Winkielman, Berridge, and Wilbarger, 2005). You meet a friend you have not seen for many years. As you embrace your friend, many emotions rush through you—joy, sorrow, love, perhaps regret. In that moment, your perceptions of your friend intersect with a history of past events recalled in your mind. A number of feelings arise from this dynamic network. How many of them affect you at this or any given moment? No one really knows.

From Buddha to Bateson, scholars and thinkers have understood life and learning to be multidetermined. As we have discussed earlier, researchers view cognition and emotion as neurophysiologic processes, occurring either individually or socially, that integrate the mind, the body, the activity, and the ingredients of the setting in a complex interactive manner (Lave, 1997; Scherer, 2005). Meeting your friend alone in an airport might be a very different emotional experience from meeting her in her home with her family present. Human beings frequently act without deliberation. Our perception and action arise together, each contributing to the co-construction of the other. *Much of the time we compose our lives in the moment.*

Realizing how complex adult motivation and learning are requires us to plan carefully for instruction. Because the four motivational conditions work in concert and exert their influence on adult learning in the moment as well as over time, we need to be intentional about how we establish and coordinate these conditions when we plan or design a lesson.

Motivational planning works best when it is integrated throughout the entire lesson. All the examples of instructional design or planning are anchored in theories and strategies that support adult intrinsic motivation to learn. Planning carefully with adult motivation in mind not only helps us to be more effective instructors, it avoids a serious pitfall common to teaching: blaming learners for being unresponsive to instruction. When instructors design a lesson without the enhancement of learner motivation as a consideration threaded throughout its composition, they do not have a motivationally based plan to analyze for possible solutions to motivational difficulties that arise during instruction. Without a motivationally oriented instructional plan, the problem may seem unsolvable. As instructors, we are likely to become frustrated and more prone to place responsibility for this state of affairs on the learners themselves. Speaking from my own experience, I know how difficult it is to be openly self-critical. Defense mechanisms like rationalization and projection act to protect our egos. Planning instruction with motivation in mind helps us to keep our attention on the emotions of adults while they are learning, on how we are proceeding through the designed lesson, on how we instruct, and what we can do about that instruction when it is not as vital as we would like it to be. This kind of focusing diminishes our tendency to blame, which is a common reaction to problems that seem unsolvable.

Applying the Motivational Framework for Culturally Responsive Teaching

Let us take a look at the Motivational Framework for Culturally Responsive Teaching in terms of the teaching-learning process. Because most instructional plans have specific learning objectives, they tend to be linear and prescriptive: instructors sequence learning events over time and predetermine the order in which concepts and skills are taught and when they are practiced and applied. Although human motivation does not always follow an orderly path, we can plan ways to evoke it throughout a learning sequence. In fact, because of motivation's emotional base and natural instability, we need to painstakingly plan the milieu and learning activities to enhance adult motivation, especially when we face a time-limited learning period. For projects, self-directed learning, and situational learning (as in the case of problem posing), we may not be so bound to a formal plan.

The most basic way to begin is to transform the framework's four motivational conditions into questions to use as guidelines for selecting motivational strategies and related learning activities to include in the design of your instructional plan:

1. *Establishing inclusion*: How do we create or affirm a learning atmosphere in which we feel respected by and connected to one another? (Best to plan for the *beginning* of the lesson.)

2. *Developing attitude*: How do we create or affirm a favorable disposition toward learning through personal relevance and learner volition? (Best to plan for the *beginning* of the lesson.)

3. *Enhancing meaning*: How do we create engaging and challenging learning experiences that include learners' perspectives and values? (Best to plan *throughout* the lesson.)

4. *Engendering competence*: How do we create or affirm an understanding that learners have effectively learned something they
value and perceive as authentic to their real world? (Best to
plan, when possible, *throughout* the lesson and, in general, at
the *ending* of the lesson.)

Let us look at an actual episode of teaching in which the
instructor uses the motivational framework and these questions
to compose an instructional plan. In this example, the teacher is
conducting the first two-hour session of an introductory course in
research.

The class takes place on Saturday morning. There are twenty adult
learners ranging in age from twenty-five to fifty-five. Most hold full-time
jobs. Most are women. Most are first-generation college students.
A few are students of color. The instructor knows from previous
experience that many of these students view research as abstract,
irrelevant, and oppressive learning. Her instructional objective is as
follows: *students will devise an in-class investigation and develop
their own positive perspectives toward active research*. Using the
four motivational conditions and their related questions, the instructor
creates the sequence of learning activities found in Table 4.1.

Let's look at the narrative for this teaching episode.

The teacher explains that much research is conducted collaboratively. The course will model this approach as well. For a beginning
activity, she randomly assigns learners to small groups and encourages them to discuss any previous experiences they may have had
doing research and their expectations and concerns for the course
(strategy: collaborative learning). Each group then shares its experiences, expectations, and concerns as the teacher records them on
the overhead. In this manner, she is able to understand her students'
perspectives and to increase their connection to one another and
herself (motivational condition: establishing inclusion).

Table 4.1. Instructional Plan Based on the Motivational Framework for Culturally Responsive Teaching

Motivational Condition and Question	Motivational Strategy	Learning Activity
Establishing inclusion: How do we create or affirm a learning atmosphere in which we feel respected by and connected to one another? (beginning)	Collaborative learning	Randomly form small groups in which learners exchange concerns, experiences, and expectations they have about research. List them.
Developing attitude: How do we create or affirm a favorable disposition toward learning through personal relevance and volition? (beginning)	Relevant learning goals	Ask learners to choose something they want to research among themselves.
Enhancing meaning: How do we create engaging and challenging learning experiences that include learner perspectives and values? (throughout)	Critical questioning and predicting	Form research teams to devise a set of questions to ask in order to make predictions. Record questions and predictions.
Engendering competence: How do we create or affirm an understanding that learners have effectively learned something they value and perceive as authentic to their real world? (ending)	Self-assessment	After the predictions have been verified, ask learners to create their own statements about what they learned about research from this process.

The teacher explains that most people are researchers much of the time. She asks the students what they would like to research among themselves (strategy: relevant learning goal). After a lively discussion, the class decides to investigate and predict the amount of sleep some members of the class had the previous night. By having students choose the research topic, this strategy engages adult volition, increases the relevance of the activity, and contributes to the emergence of a favorable disposition toward the course (motivational condition: developing attitude). The students are learning in a way that includes their experiences and perspectives.

Five students volunteer to serve as subjects, and the other students form research teams. Each team develops a set of observations and a set of questions to ask the volunteers, but no one may ask them how many hours of sleep they had the night before. After they ask their questions, team members confer and each team ranks the five volunteers in order of the amount of sleep each had, from the most to the least (strategy: critical questioning and predicting). When the volunteers reveal the amount of time they slept, the students discover that no research team was correct in ranking more than three volunteers. The students discuss why this outcome may have occurred and consider questions that might have increased their accuracy, such as, "How much coffee did you drink before you came to class?" The questioning, testing of ideas, feedback, and predicting heighten the engagement, challenge, and complexity of this learning for the students (motivational condition: enhancing meaning).

After the discussion, the teacher asks the students to write a series of statements about what this activity has taught them about research (strategy: self-assessment). Students then break into small groups to exchange their insights. Their comments include such statements as, "Research is more a method than an answer," and, "Thus far, I enjoy research more than I thought I would." Self-assessment helps the students extract from this experience a new understanding they value (motivational condition: engendering competence).

This snapshot of teaching illustrates how the four motivational conditions constantly influence and interact with one another. Without establishing inclusion (small groups to discuss concerns and experiences) and developing attitude (students choosing a relevant research goal), the enhancement of meaning (research teams devising questions and predictions) might not occur with equal ease and energy, and the self-assessment to engender competence (what students learned from their perspective) might have a dismal outcome. Overall, the total learning experience encourages equitable participation, provides the beginning of an inclusive history for the students, and enhances their learning about research.

In this class session, the strategies and their related activities work together holistically as well as systemically. Removing any one of the four strategies and the motivational condition it evokes would likely affect the entire experience. For example, would the students' attitude be as positive if the teacher arbitrarily gave them the task of researching sleep among themselves? Probably not, and this mistake would likely decrease the research teams' efforts to devise questions.

From a neurophysiological view, when the instructor establishes inclusion by having small groups of students discuss their experiences with research, she is facilitating a safe and relaxed climate, an optimal situation for brain functioning. In such a comfortable atmosphere, the amygdala can enhance the passage of information through the students' limbic systems and into their brain centers for higher cognition and executive processing. When she asks the students to choose a relevant research topic to develop attitude, she positively heightens their emotional state by stimulating their interest. Feelings of interest improve their brains' active processing and memory for the events and ideas that are occurring. When she enhances meaning by challenging the students to make predictions, she further stimulates their positive emotional state. Feelings of involvement and playfulness deepen the students' neural transport of information and their complex thinking. This processing is more likely to lead to both retention and new learning. The opportunity for self-assessment to engender competence promotes feedback and reflection activating the frontal lobe of the brain and the cingulate gyrus. These structures promote emotion and more complex neural connections across the brain. This activity drives the learning process to further test student predictions, resulting in more feedback, more pleasurable neural stimulation, and the greater possibility of long-term memory for what has occurred.

One of the values of the Motivational Framework for Culturally Responsive Teaching is that it is not only a model of motivation in action but also an organizational aid for designing instruction. By continually attending to the four motivational conditions and their related questions, the instructor can select motivational strategies from a wide array of theories and literature to apply throughout a learning unit. The teacher translates these strategies into a set of sequenced learning activities that continuously evoke adult motivation and facilitate learning.

Table 4.1 is an example of a fully planned lesson in which the learning activities are derived from and aligned with motivational strategies. To use this framework, pedagogical alignment—the coordination of approaches to teaching that ensures maximum consistent effect—is critical. The more harmonious the elements of the instructional design, the more likely they are to sustain intrinsic motivation. That's why a single strategy—collaborative learning or self-assessment, for example—is unlikely to evoke intrinsic motivation. It is the mutual influence of a *combination* of strategies based on the motivational conditions that elicits intrinsic motivation.

As Table 4.1 shows, there are four sequenced motivational strategies, each based on one of the four motivational condi-tions. Each strategy has been translated into a learning activity. The Motivational Framework for Culturally Responsive Teaching allows for as many strategies as the instructor believes are needed to complete an instructional plan. The instructor's knowledge of the learners' motivation and culture, the subject matter, the setting, the technology available, and the time constraints will determine the nature of and quantity of the motivational strategies. This motivational framework provides a holistic design that uses a psychological and neuroscientific understanding of learning, a time orientation for planning, and a culturally responsive approach to teaching to foster intrinsic motivation from the beginning to the end of an instructional unit.

For projects and extended learning sessions, such as problem solving or self-directed learning, the sequence of strategies may not include all four motivational conditions. For example, inclusion and attitude may have been established earlier through previous work, advising, or prerequisite classes. These conditions may need less cultivation, and the conditions of meaning and competence may be most important to foster. Chapter Nine specifically deals with how to compose motivating lessons and uses five extensive case examples to illustrate effective instructional designs.

———————

The Motivational Framework for Culturally Responsive Teaching is the foundation for a pedagogy that crosses disciplines and cultures to respectfully engage *all* learners. Its purpose is to foster intrinsic motivation with the understanding that human motivation is inseparable from culture. The four motivational conditions of the framework are congruent with recent neuroscientific studies indicating how people are motivated to learn. The framework is a means to create compelling learning experiences in which adults can maintain their integrity as they attain relevant educational success.

Each of the next four chapters focuses on an essential motivational condition and its specific motivational strategies, including examples of related learning activities. These strategies are realistic teaching methods. They are deliberate instructor actions that enhance a person's motivation to learn. *The strategy contributes to stimulating or creating a motivational condition: a mental and emotional state* in which the learner desires knowledge and skill and puts forth energy to engage learning—the thinking, practicing, and so forth.

Your understanding of these strategies and how to use them can significantly increase the creativity, skill, and impact of your instructional planning. That the strategies primarily stress what you can do does not mean that adult learners bear no responsibility for their own motivation or are dependent on you for feeling motivated while learning. The purpose of this book is to respectfully evoke, support, and enhance the motivation to learn that all adults possess by virtue of their own humanity and to make you a valuable resource and vital partner in their realization of a motivating learning experience.

5

Establishing Inclusion among
Adult Learners

*When a system of oppression has become
institutionalized it is unnecessary for individuals to be
oppressive.*

Florynce Kennedy

When we are teaching, exclusion is usually an indirect act, an omission of opportunity or of someone's voice. We're usually not mean-spirited but, more likely, unaware that a perspective is missing, that a biased myth has been perpetuated, or that we aren't covering topics of concern to certain adults. In fact, most adult learners, usually those who have been socialized to accommodate our method of instruction, may like our course or training. Things seem pretty pleasant. Why go looking for trouble?

We need to be mindful about our instruction because, as Adrienne Rich has so eloquently said, "There is no way of measuring the damage to a society when a whole texture of humanity is kept from realizing its own power" (1984). When it comes to the perspective of this book, I believe that enabling people to realize their own power relates to our obligation to create an equitable opportunity to be motivated to learn as well as to have the right to an equitable education. The two are inseparable. To begin, I believe we have to be vigilant about the patterns we see in our courses and training. Are some people left out? Do particular income groups or ethnic groups do less well than others? Who among the adults we teach or train are the people whose motivation to learn is not emerging or seems diminished? How might we be responsible for or contribute to these trends?

My experience is that teaching or training begins with relationships, respectful relationships. For most adults, the first sense of the quality of the teacher-student relationship is a feeling, sometimes quite vague, of inclusion or exclusion. Upon awareness of exclusion, adult learners will begin to lose their enthusiasm and motivation. If you'd like to appreciate this tendency by working directly with adults themselves, try the exercise called "Marginality and Mattering" (Frederick, 1997). Ask adults to remember a moment in the recent past (a week to a month) when they felt marginal, excluded, or discounted—"the only one like me in a group, not understood or, perhaps, unaccepted." Ask them to reflect on this and then to pair off and discuss the following questions: How did you know? How did you feel? How did you behave? Then ask them to remember a moment when they felt that they mattered, were included, or were regarded as important to a group. Ask them to pair off again to discuss the same three questions. Ask the adults to reflect on both situations and to discuss the patterns of thinking, feeling, and behaving that emerged, the influence of those patterns on their motivation and enthusiasm, and how the changes in motivation and enthusiasm might relate to learning and teaching. As this exercise will demonstrate, our motivation is constantly influenced by our acute awareness of the degree of our inclusion in a learning environment. When we don't feel safe, complex information is often blocked from passage to higher cortical functioning and memory storage, which slows learning and increases our frustration, aggression, or withdrawal.

Feelings of cultural isolation often cause adult motivation to learn to deteriorate. In a course or training seminar, a sense of community with which all learners can identify establishes the foundation for inclusion. Our challenge as instructors is to create a successful learning environment for all learners that (1) respects different cultures and (2) maintains a common culture that all learners can accept. We are fortunate, because adults are community-forming beings. Our capacity to create social coherence is always there (Gardner, 1990). We need community to find security, identity, shared values, and people who care about us and about whom we care. As more and more adults sandwich their education between work and family, an adult education setting may provide one of the few opportunities to experience community and a sense of belonging. But mere contact with those different from us does little to enhance intercultural appreciation. Mutual respect and appreciation evolve from the nature of our contact. The norms we set as instructors and the strategies we use to teach will largely determine the quality of social exchange among our learners. Those norms should be supportive of equity, collaboration, and the expression of each learner's perspective (Wlodkowski and Ginsberg, 1995). It simply makes sense to set a tone in which learners can come together in friendly, caring, and respectful ways.

The strategies that follow contribute to establishing a *climate of respect*. In this atmosphere, intrinsic motivation is more likely to emerge because learners can voice the things that matter to them. Their well-being is more assured. They can begin to develop trust. Neurologically, we have prepared for a relaxed and alert social environment. Relevant learning is possible.

These strategies also enable learners to *feel connected* to one another. This feeling of connection draws forth learners' motivation because their social needs are met. Feeling included, people are freer to risk the mistakes true learning involves as well as to share their resources and strengths. Before we discuss these strategies, we need to look at some of the dimensions of nonverbal communication across cultures that are often critical to effective intercultural

communication. Your understanding of these important and extensively researched dimensions should increase your capacity to
sensitively apply the strategies to establish inclusion. To describe
these dimensions, I have followed the approach of Peter Andersen
and Hua Wang (2006, pp. 250–266) that addresses this topic.

Understanding Dimensions of Intercultural Nonverbal Communication

Today contact between people from various cultures continues
to increase. International migration is at an all-time high. The
amount of intercultural contact in today's world is unprecedented,
making the study of intercultural communication more important
than ever.

Two of the most fundamental nonverbal differences in intercultural communication involve space and time. Time frames of
cultures may differ so dramatically that if only these differences
existed, intercultural misunderstandings could still be considerable. In general, time tends to be viewed in the United States
as a commodity that can be wasted, spent, saved, managed, and
used wisely (Andersen, 1999). Other cultures may have a more
relational understanding of time. In traditional cultures and in
many cultures in developing countries, time moves to the rhythms
of nature, the day, the seasons, the year. Human inventions like
seconds, minutes, and hours may have no real meaning.

Research has documented that cultures differ substantially in
their use of personal space, the distances they maintain, and their
regard for territory (Gudykunst and Kim, 1992). Considerable
intercultural differences have been reported in people's kinesic
behavior (Goldin-Meadow, 2003), including their facial expressions, body movements, gestures, and conversational regulators.
Stories abound in the intercultural literature of gestures that signal
endearment or warmth in one culture but are obscene or insulting
in another. Differences in kinesic behavior come into play in a

learning environment; they can determine how one gets the floor in conversation, shows deference or respect, indicates agreement or disagreement and approval or disapproval. For the teacher, these norms of participation may seem obvious and their derivation from European American norms of conduct unimportant, but to a learner from another culture, such expectations may be alienating or exhausting (because of the relentless anxiety of determining how to behave appropriately), especially if learners are directly called on to recite and are graded for oral participation in class.

Along with genetics, culture is the most enduring, powerful, and invisible shaper of our communication behavior. Research has shown that cultures can be located along several dimensions that help explain intercultural differences in nonverbal communication. Most of the adult learners we teach will probably not be international students; however, they will often have ethnic backgrounds and histories of immigration that make the dimensions discussed in the sections that follow informative for our work.

Immediacy

Immediacy behaviors are actions that simultaneously communicate warmth, closeness, and availability for communication and approach rather than avoidance (Andersen, 1998). Examples of immediacy behaviors are smiling, touching, making eye contact, being at closer distances, and using more vocal animation. Some scholars have labeled these behaviors *expressive* (Patterson, 1983). Cultures that display considerable interpersonal closeness or immediacy have been labeled *contact cultures*, because people in these cultures stand closer and touch more (Hall, 1966). People in *low-contact cultures* tend to stand farther apart and touch less.

It is interesting that high-contact cultures are generally located in warmer countries, and low-contact cultures in cooler climates. Considerable research has shown that high-contact (more expressive and immediate) cultures are found in most Arab countries, the Mediterranean region, the Middle East, Eastern Europe, Russia, and virtually all of Latin America (Jones, 1994). Moderate- to low-contact (less expressive and immediate) cultures are found in much of Northern Europe and among white Anglo-Saxons in the United States (Remland, 2000). Compared to the rest of the world, East Asia and countries such as China, Japan, and Korea are low-contact cultures that rarely touch in public (McDaniel and Andersen, 1998). In general, these findings are painted with a fairly broad brush and subject to a wide span of individual variation.

Individualism–Collectivism

One of the most fundamental dimensions along which cultures differ is their degree of individualism or collectivism. The main cultures of Europe, Australia, and North America north of the Rio Grande tend to be individualistic. The main cultures of Latin America, Africa, Asia, and the Pacific Islands tend to be collectivist. Individualists are oriented toward achieving personal goals, by themselves, for purposes of pleasure, autonomy, and self-fulfillment. Collectivists are oriented toward achieving group goals, by the group, for the purposes of group well-being, relationships, togetherness, and the common good. Collectivist cultures from Asia are likely to emphasize harmony among people and between people and nature (Andersen and others, 2002).

The United States is considered to be a highly individualistic country (Hofstede, 1980). Although written more than twenty years ago, the outlook described in *Habits of the Heart* appears to remain dominant: "Anything that would violate our right to think for ourselves, judge for ourselves, make our own decisions, live our lives as we see fit, is not only morally wrong, it is sacrilegious" (Bellah and others, 1985, p. 142). Many people in the United States find it difficult to relate to cultures in which interdependence may be the basis of a sense of self. Although individualism has been argued to be the backbone of democracy, it has also been considered to contribute to crime, alienation, loneliness, and narcissism in U.S. society.

Different ethnic groups in the United States vary along the dimensions of individualism and collectivism. For example, African Americans tend to be more individualistic, whereas Mexican Americans tend to place more emphasis on group and relational solidarity (Hecht, Andersen, and Ribeau, 1989).

The degree to which a culture is individualistic or collectivistic affects adult communication and nonverbal behavior. People from individualistic cultures are more remote and distant proximally. People from collectivist cultures tend to work, play, live, and sleep in closer proximity to one another. Lustig and Koester maintain that "people from individualistic cultures are more likely than those from collectivist cultures to use confrontational strategies when dealing with interpersonal problems; those with a collectivist orientation are likely to use avoidance, third party intermediaries, or other face saving techniques" (1999, p. 123). People in collectivist cultures may suppress both positive and negative emotional displays that are contrary to the mood of the group, because maintaining the group is a primary value (Andersen, 1999). Individualistic cultures encourage people to express emotions because individual freedom is a paramount value. In the United States, flirting, small talk, smiling, and initial acquaintance appear to be more important than in collectivist countries, where the social network is more fixed and less reliant on individual initiative. Collectively oriented people tend to value compliance with social norms above the individual pursuit of happiness.

Gender

The gender orientation of a culture has a major impact on role and communication behavior, including occupational status, dress codes, the types of expressions permitted to each sex, the interactions permitted with strangers or acquaintances of the opposite sex, and all aspects of interpersonal relationship between men and women. As conceptualized here, the gender dimension refers to the rigidity of gender rules (Hofstede, 1980). In less rigid cultures, both men and women can express more diverse, less stereotyped sex-role behaviors. Today, Saudi Arabia would be an example of a country with more rigid gender roles, and the United States a country with less rigid gender rules. Research suggests that less rigid cultures evoke patterns of behavior that result in more social competence, success, and intellectual development for both men and women (Andersen, 1999).

Power Distance

Another fundamental dimension of intercultural communication is power distance. Power distance, the degree to which power, prestige, and wealth are unequally distributed in a culture, has been measured in a number of cultures using the Power Distance Index (PDI), developed by Hofstede (1980). In cultures with high PDI scores, power and influence are concentrated in the hands of a few rather than more distributed throughout the population. Most African, Asian, and Latin American countries have high PDI scores. The United States is lower than the median in power distance. Cultures differ in terms of how status is acquired. In many countries, such as India, class or caste determines one's status. In the United States, power and status are typically determined by money and material acquisition (Andersen and Bowman, 1999).

Emotional displays tend to be related to status in cultures with high power distance: for example, in high power-distance cultures, people are usually expected to show only positive emotions to high-status others. The relatively easy smiles of many Asians may be a culturally inculcated effort to lessen tension with those perceived as higher-status individuals; efforts to smooth social relations are considered appropriate to a culture with a high PDI. For many Asian students, modesty and deference in the presence of their instructors are what their culture expects. Vocal cues are also affected by power distance. A loud voice in a high-PDI culture may be offensive to higher-status members.

Context

The last dimension of intercultural communication that we will discuss is context. A high-context (HC) communication is a message in which most of the information is either in the physical context or internalized in the person. Very little is in the coded, explicit part of the message (Hall, 1976). Lifelong friends often use HC messages that can be nearly impossible for an outsider to understand. A gesture, a smile, or a glance provides meaning that doesn't need to be articulated. Low-context (LC) messages, such as a legal brief or a computer language, are just the opposite. Most of the information is in explicit code and must be elaborated and highly specific. Very little of the communication is taken for granted (Hall, 1984; Andersen, 1999).

The lower-context cultures are found in Switzerland, Germany, Scandinavia, Canada, and the United States (Gudykunst and Kim, 1992). These cultures are highly verbal and pay much attention to specifics and details. The higher-context cultures are found in Asia, notably China, Japan, and Korea (Hall, 1984; Lustig and Koester, 1999). Strongly influenced by Zen Buddhism, these cultures place a high value on silence, on less emotional expression, and on unspoken, nonverbal parts of communication (McDaniel and Andersen, 1998). American Indian cultures with migratory roots in East Asia are like these cultures in their use of HC communication.

Communication is quite different in HC and LC cultures, and frequently people from one culture will misattribute the causes for the behavior of people from the other group (Andersen and others, 2002). People from LC cultures may be perceived as excessively talkative, belaboring the obvious, and redundant. People from HC cultures may be perceived as secretive, sneaky, and mysterious. People from HC cultures are particularly affected by contextual cues. Facial expressions, tensions, movements, speed of interaction, location of interaction, and other "subtleties" may have meaning for people from HC cultures but not be noticed by people from LC cultures.

Perhaps, like me, you appreciate how daunting it is to understand someone from another culture. You may also be joyful about the number of possible ways there are to be human. I benefit (not without anxiety) from knowing that my teaching is shaded by a persona that is more rigidly masculine than I like, fairly expressive with a median PDI, analytically low context, and leaning leftward toward collectivism. This kind of self-awareness makes me more mindful of nonverbal communication and gives me a better chance to provide instruction compatible with the norms of learners from other cultures. By being conscious of these tendencies, I believe I'm less likely to impose them on others as expected behaviors. Continuing to be sensitive to cultural differences helps me to select educational practices that accommodate the communication styles of those adults whose socialization has been unlike my own. The following discussion of the motivational strategies will continue to emphasize intercultural understanding as a means for effective instruction.

Engendering a Feeling of Connection among Adults

As discussed in Chapter Three, the core characteristics of empathy and cultural responsiveness significantly influence the degree to which we engender a feeling of connection among adults. Increasing our awareness of what we have in common and instilling a sense of mutual care are essential. A good place to begin preparing ourselves is to consider the learners we expect to be teaching and our own *positionality* in the group—that is, the cultural group identities we have that may influence our own outlook as well as how these learners will look upon us (Johnson-Bailey and Cervero, 1997). The more visible identities are race, gender, age, and physical ability or disability, but our identities also include ethnicity, class, and sexual orientation as well as the cultural variations discussed in the preceding sections.

For example, when I teach an extension course, I need to realize that being an older male, middle-class, Polish-American academic gives me a certain perspective that may be quite different from that of the younger African American, working-class women who are some of the students in my course. I have had very different experiences regarding such issues as health, education, safety, and economic security. If I merely follow personal opinions and familiar routines, I may give an advantage to one group of students over another in the topics I choose, in the time or opportunity students have to speak, and in the feedback I give. Indeed, for certain groups of students, I may not have the "expertise" in matters of personal psychology and social relations I think I have. Yet if I think only of these sorts of things or believe that I must know every detail, I can feel overwhelmed and immobilized. I want also to hold in my mind the large strands of life that I and all my students share: the mutual desire for good health, education, and security; the emotions of sorrow, joy, and love; the experiences of family, death, birth, and illness; and the reason we all came together—to learn. That desire, my awareness of difference and common ground, and the knowledge that I can flex and plan make me realistically enthusiastic. And I know where I can begin. I like to start with introductions. This is the time to positively engage the adult learners' limbic systems, to create a relaxed and alert emotional state where prior knowledge is readily available, and people are open to learning and connecting with each other.

Here and in the following chapters are motivational strategies that embody the Motivational Framework for Culturally Responsive Teaching. A motivational strategy is a deliberate teacher action or instructional process that is likely to enhance motivation to learn among adults. Please note that I have numbered the strategies consecutively for organizational purposes, not to indicate an order of preference or a particular sequence to follow. The selection of each strategy you use will depend on your philosophy, situation, and goals.

Strategy 1: Allow for Introductions

Introduce yourself. This is definitely for the first meeting of the group and seems quite obvious, but it is amazing how many instructors fail to extend this common courtesy. Say a few things about who you are, where you're from, why you're conducting the course or training session, and by all means, welcome the group. I find it particularly beneficial when I can mention something I sincerely appreciate. It could be about the group, its history or locale, our purpose, or other possibilities that make the situation distinct or special. This really shouldn't take more than five to ten minutes.

It is also a good idea to give the learners a chance to introduce themselves as well. This emphasizes their importance and your interest in them as people. It also helps people start to learn each other's names (name tents are a valuable supplement to this strategy) and significantly reduces the tension so often present at the beginning of courses and training sessions. Scores of books have been written describing different exercises for helping people get acquainted in new social situations (Johnson and Johnson, 2006). My particular favorite among such methods is multidimensional sharing, the next strategy I describe.

Strategy 2: Provide an Opportunity for Multidimensional Sharing

Although similar in style, introductory course activities for multidimensional sharing differ from most icebreakers. They tend to be less game-like and intrusive. They also provide insight or new learning relevant to the topic or subject being taught. For example, "Decades and Diversity," an activity described later in this section, is used to demonstrate the influence of age and popular culture on adult norms and perspectives for an adult development course that I teach.

For adults from cultures that value modesty, introductory activities that require self-disclosure or the sharing of deeper emotions may seem contrived and psychologically invasive. I remember a teaching workshop where a well-meaning trainer asked us as part of the introductory activity to "share about one person who loves us." Rather than encouraging connection, this request tended to stall the development of mutual care among us.

Opportunities for multidimensional sharing are those occasions —ranging from introductory exercises to personal anecdotes to classroom celebrations—when people have a better chance to see one another as complete, evolving human beings who have mutual needs, emotions, and experiences (Wlodkowski and Ginsberg, 1995). These opportunities give a human face to a course or training, break down biases and stereotypes, and provide experiences in which we may see ourselves in another person's world.

There are many ways to provide opportunities for multidimensional sharing, depending on the history, makeup, and purpose of the group. Informal ways include potluck meals, recreational activities, drinks after class, and picnics. For introductory course activities, anything that gets people to relax and to laugh together or helps them learn each other's names deserves our serious attention. Here are two introductory activities I have often used.

Learners usually need some time to think before they begin this activity, which can be a small- or large-group process. The group members each introduce themselves and recommend one thing they have read (such as an article, story, or book) or seen (such as a TV program, film, video, or real-life experience) or heard (such as a speech, CD, or song) that has had a strong and positive influence on them. They each conclude by stating the reasons for recommending their choice. After everyone has made a recommendation, the instructor leads a whole-group discussion of the relationship of culture to the group's recommendations as well as their rationales.

The second activity, which I learned from Margery Ginsberg, is called "Decades and Diversity." People in the group divide themselves into smaller groups according to the decade in which they graduated (or would have) from high school (the sixties, seventies, eighties, and so on). Each decade group brainstorms a list of items in three to five areas of experience at that time: popular music, clothing styles, major historical events, weekend social opportunities (What did you usually do on a Saturday night?), and standards (What was considered significant immoral behavior for you as an adolescent—something forbidden by your family?). Then each group reports on its list. The activity concludes with a discussion by the members of the entire group about their insights, the possible meanings of the lists, and the process they engaged in. These discussions illuminate the powerful influence of age and the accompanying culture at the time of adolescent socialization.

These activities are most inclusive and motivating when they validate the experiences of the adults involved and establish feelings of affiliation with you and with other learners. The more natural and appropriate such opportunities feel, the more likely a genuine sense of community can evolve.

Strategy 3: Concretely Indicate Your Cooperative Intentions to Help Adults Learn

Almost everyone who has something new to learn is vulnerable to a nagging fear—what if I really try and I can't learn it? Adults commonly experience this fear, because so much of what they must learn will directly influence their job performance or family relations. For instructors to let learners know at the outset that there is a concrete means of assistance available will help learners reduce their fear and save face. Be it announcing our availability during office hours or at breaks in a workshop, arranging online tutorial assistance, or creating a procedure whereby learners who are having difficulty can use special materials or aids—essentially, our message is, "As instructor and learner, we are partners in solving your learning problems. I want to help you, and it's OK to seek help." We are telling the learners that their vulnerability will be safeguarded and that they will have a nonjudgmental and interested response to their requests for assistance (Hill, 2004). With this strategy, we offer immediate evidence that we do care about the people who learn with us.

Strategy 4: Share Something of Value with Your Adult Learners

The next time you hear a professional speaker, whether it is at a banquet or a conference, keep track of how much time elapses before that person tells a joke or a humorous anecdote. It will probably be less than three minutes, and it will happen about four out of every five times. Professional speakers know the value of *sharing humor*. It does far more than break the tension between speaker and audience. It says: If you can laugh with me, you can listen to me. You can identify with me. You can see I am a human being and that I have emotions too. All sharing has this potential—to break down stereotypes and to allow the learners to experience our common humanity without self-consciousness. Humor is a very efficient means to this end. It also tells the learners that there are at least times when we do not take ourselves too seriously, that we have some perspective on life, and that the way we teach will allow for the vitality of laughter in the learning process.

Another type of effective sharing is to relate a *credible intense experience*. This may be trouble we have had on the job, a difficult learning experience, a crisis within our family, an unexpected surprise, an accident—something that tells the learners that we have mutual concerns and a shared reality. This form of sharing should relate to the topic at hand, or it will seem forced. I sometimes tell about problems I have had with apathetic learners. I know most of my audience has had similar problems, and this gives me a chance to share what I have learned from these dilemmas. This type of sharing is also a two-way street. Seeing the concerned faces in the audience increases my identification with them as well.

Sharing *your involvement with the subject matter*—problems, discoveries, research, or new learning—is a way to show your enthusiasm as well as your humanity. Adults are interested in seeing how their investment in the subject they are studying might pay off for them. When we share our involvement with the topic, we model this potential for them and reveal something about our real selves as well.

Another powerful form of sharing is to give adult learners *our individual attention*. When we do, we are committing one of our most valuable assets as instructors to our learners—our time. Being available to learners before, during, and after class directly tells them we care about them. Also, one-to-one contact creates a more personal and spontaneous interaction.

In general, sharing *something about our real selves*, when done tactfully and appropriately, gives adult learners a chance to see us beyond the image of an instructor. Most people are a bit surprised when they see their teachers in everyday settings like supermarkets, shopping centers, and theaters. Part of this surprise is due to novelty, but part is also due to how dramatically set apart most learning environments seem from the real world. By judiciously self-disclosing our reactions to common experiences—television shows, sporting events, travel, maybe even a little trouble we've had with life along the way—we give adult learners a chance to identify positively with us and become more receptive to our instruction (Jourard, 1964; Hill, 2004).

Strategy 5: Use Collaborative and Cooperative Learning

Although there are a wide variety of *collaborative learning methods*, most emphasize the learners' exploration and interpretation of course material to an equal or greater extent than the instructor's explication of it. When everyone participates, working with a partner or in small groups, generating questions and facing challenges together, collaborative processes energize group activity. Instructors who use these procedures tend to think of themselves less as singular transmitters of knowledge and more as co-learners and co-constructers of knowledge. Humans are highly evolved social beings, so we naturally want to know what other people are thinking and feeling (Brothers, 2000). These tendencies enhance our emotional and motivational involvement in learning. Through collaborative learning we are also more active learners, making both social and synaptic connections (Cross, 1999).

From their review of the research on collaborative and cooperative learning in higher education, Elizabeth Barkley, Patricia Cross, and Claire Major (2005) have found abundant evidence that collaborative learning is an effective and motivating format for nontraditional students—underrepresented racial and ethnic groups, working-adult students, commuters, and re-entry students. They note that "almost everyone" (p. 22) seems to benefit from group learning situations. In their estimation, collaborative learning is also an instructional method where all students can learn *from diversity*, benefiting from the linguistic and cultural perspectives that can be experienced in this format. Among their conclusions, the following sums up one of my own beliefs: "The evidence... is so strong that collaborative learning has multiple advantages if done well, that it would be folly not to learn how to operate collaborative learning groups productively" (p. 24).

Among the many collaborative learning possibilities, *cooperative learning* represents the most carefully organized and researched approach (Cranton, 1996). Although some scholars see cooperative learning as more teacher-centered and discouraging of individual dissent (Bruffee, 1995), I think most instructors of adults will use the level of authority that feels comfortable for them and can implement cooperative learning in a manner that respects individual differences in perceptions and construction of knowledge (Barkley, Cross, and Major, 2005). My treatment of cooperative learning in this book serves the latter purpose.

More than one-third of all studies comparing cooperative, competitive, and individualistic learning have been conducted with college and adult learners. In an analysis of 120 of these investigations, David Johnson and Roger Johnson (1995) found that cooperative learning promotes individual achievement significantly more than do competitive or individualistic efforts. A meta-analysis of 375 relevant experimental studies in which research participants varied in age, economic class, and cultural background also supported this finding (Johnson, 2003). When adults learn cooperatively, they tend to develop supportive relationships across sociocultural and linguistic groups. Cooperative learning groups give learners the following opportunities:

- To construct and extend their understanding of what is being learned through explanation and discussion of multiple perspectives

- To use the shared mental models learned in flexible ways to solve problems jointly

- To receive interpersonal feedback about how well they are performing procedures

- To receive social support and encouragement to take risks in increasing their competencies

- To be held accountable by their peers to practice and learn procedures and skills

- To acquire new attitudes

- To establish a shared identity with other group members

- To find effective peers to emulate

- To discover a "voice" to validate their own learning [Rendon, 1994]

As its practitioners and researchers strenuously emphasize, cooperative learning is more than placing learners in groups and telling them to work together. According to Johnson and Johnson (2006), cooperative learning is a rigorous procedure whose fundamental components are (1) positive interdependence, (2) individual accountability, (3) promotive interaction, (4) social skills, and (5) group processing. To organize lessons so that learners do work cooperatively requires an understanding of these five basic components and their conscientious implementation in the group and in the lesson. A significant amount of cooperative learning also needs to take place within the learning environment to permit monitoring by the instructor and to allow groups to initially establish themselves while they can receive needed support.

1. *Positive interdependence* occurs when learners perceive that they are linked with group members in such a way that they cannot succeed unless their group members do (and vice versa) or that they must coordinate their efforts with the efforts of their partners to complete a task (Johnson and Johnson, 2006). They sink or swim together. Each group member has a unique contribution to make to the group because of resources, role, or responsibilities. For example, in the popular *jigsaw procedure*, a reading assignment is divided among the group, with each member responsible for comprehending a separate part and explaining or teaching that part to all other members of the group until the entire group understands the total reading assignment. The following are three additional ways to create positive interdependence in a cooperative learning group.

- *Positive goal interdependence.* The group is united around a common goal, a concrete reason for being. It could be to create a product, report, or answer, or it could be general improvement on a task so that all members do better this week than they did last week. Outcomes might include a skill demonstration, a media product, an evaluation summary, a problem solution, an action plan, or just about anything that leads to greater learning and that the group members can produce and hold each other responsible for.

- *Positive resource interdependence*. Each group member has only a portion of the resources, information, or materials necessary for the task to be accomplished, and the members have to combine resources in order for the group to achieve its goals. The metaphor for this approach is a puzzle, and each group member has a unique and necessary piece to contribute to the puzzle's solution. For example, for an upcoming exam, each member of a group might be responsible for a different study question; when the group convenes, members share their knowledge of the question and check to make sure all groupmates have satisfactorily comprehended this knowledge.

- *Positive role interdependence*. Each member of the group selects a particular role that is complementary, interconnected, and essential to the roles of the other group members. Suppose, for example, that the learning goal is the development of some skill, such as interviewing. One group member is the person practicing the skill (the interviewer), another person is the recipient of the skill (the interviewee), and a third person is the observer-evaluator. In this manner, each person has an essential contribution to make in terms of either skill practice or feedback. Roles can easily be rotated as well.

In all cooperative learning groups, it is extremely important that the learners are very clear about the assignment, the goal, and their role. Especially with diverse learners, checking for thorough understanding can make the difference between a satisfying and a confusing learning experience. Positive interdependence works best when all group members understand that each person has a part to do, that all members are counting on each other, and that all members want to help each other do better.

2. *Individual accountability* occurs when each individual's learning is assessed, the results are shared with the learner and the group, and each learner is responsible to the other group members for contributing a fair share to the group's success (Johnson and Johnson, 2006). One of the main purposes of cooperative learning is to support each member as a vital, competent individual. Individual accountability ensures that all group members will be strengthened by learning cooperatively and that they will have a good chance of effectively transferring what they have learned to situations where they are without group support.

Some texts emphasize individual accountability as a means to prevent *hitchhiking*, or contributing little to the group's success but reaping large benefits from the contributions of other group members. My experience is that this seldom occurs when cooperative norms are well in place and competitive assessment or grading procedures are eliminated.

Individual accountability can be enhanced in the following ways:

- Keep the size of the groups small. Typical size is two to four members.

- Keep the role of each learner distinct.

- Assess learners individually as well as collectively.

- Observe groups while they are working.

- Randomly request individuals to present what they are learning, either to you or another group.

- Request periodic self-assessments and outlines of responsibilities from individual group members.

- Randomly or systematically ask learners to teach someone else or you what they have learned.

- If grading, assess and assign a grade for individual contributions to the group's performance or product.

A simple and positive way to support individual accountability and prevent related conflict among group members is to brainstorm answers to the question, How would we like to find out whether someone in our cooperative learning group thought we were not doing enough to contribute to the benefit of the total group? Then write the possible actions for all to see and discuss them. Such a procedure can go a long way to avoid unnecessary suspicion or shame.

3. *Promotive interaction* occurs when group members encourage and assist each other to reach the group's goals (Johnson and Johnson, 2006). This includes sharing information, resources, and emotional support as well as challenges and discussions to achieve the relevant goals. Mutual care should permeate this interaction, as it does, for example, when someone in a cooperative writing group reads something she has written and a fellow member offers sincere and helpful suggestions to improve the manuscript. This sort of interaction allows different perspectives and commitments to take hold.

4. *Social skills* facilitate communication that enables group members to reach goals, get to know and trust each other, communicate accurately, accept and support each other, and resolve conflicts constructively (Johnson and Johnson, 2006). Even though adults want to cooperate, they may not be able to do so effectively if they lack conventional social skills.

My experience with diverse adults is that when the norms of collaboration and "no blame" are discussed and made explicit, they (along with participation guidelines, discussed later in this chapter) create a learning climate that significantly reduces aggressive conflict. There is then less need for direct training in conventional interpersonal skills, such as *active listening*, which can seem contrived and strange, especially to people who do not identify with the dominant culture.

It is appropriate for an instructor to intervene in a group, when necessary, to suggest more effective procedures for working together. Yet instructors should not rush to intervene. I often find that if everyone exercises a little patience, cooperative groups work their way through their own problems and construct not only timely solutions but also methods for solving similar problems in the future. Sometimes, simply asking group members to temporarily set aside their task, describe the problem as they see it, come up with a few solutions, and decide which one to try first is enough to get things moving along satisfactorily.

5. *Group processing* occurs when members reflect on their group experience to identify actions that were helpful and unhelpful and to decide what actions to continue or change (Johnson and Johnson, 2006). For groups that continue over longer periods (more than a few hours) or that are significantly diverse, discussing group functioning is essential (Adams and Marchesani, 1992). Adults need time to have a dialogue about the quality of their cooperation, to reflect on their interactions, and to learn from how they work together. This *processing time* gives learners a chance to receive feedback on their participation, understand how their actions can be more effective and cohesive, plan for more helpful and skillful interaction for the next group session, and celebrate mutual success. As instructors, we need to allow time for this activity and to provide some basic structure for it—for example, by suggesting the group discuss a few things it is doing well and one thing it could improve. Early group processing significantly reduces the chances for aggressive conflict to emerge in a group.

In general, heterogeneous groups work well. Unless projects or special reasons require members to stay together, remixing groups at the beginning of new activities can have a revitalizing effect and makes working with different people a course norm. However, practical reasons may sometimes override the benefits of heterogeneity. Students' interest in a specific topic, accessibility for meetings outside of class, very limited skills, or language acquisition issues might predicate more homogeneous groups. For projects or activities with significant assessment consequences (for example, if they represent a large proportion of a course grade), I usually accept individual completion as an option. I do this to respect the more individualistic as well as other possible cultural orientations that may exist among class members. In addition, for some activities (usually quite informal), I find that letting students form their own groups (ranging from two to four members) allows a greater comfort level for those adults less at ease with cooperative learning.

Once cooperative learning groups start working, our role as instructor is that of colearner, observer, adviser, and consultant. Without being obtrusive, we should watch cooperative groups, especially as they *begin* their tasks. Sometimes we can see that certain groups will need clarification or guidance. Otherwise we remain available, always keeping in mind that it is the learners themselves who are the major resources for support and assistance to one another.

Exhibit 5.1 is an outline for planning cooperative learning activities. It is adapted from the Cooperative Lesson Planning Guide from *Active Learning* (Johnson, Johnson, and Smith, 1991).

Exhibit 5.1   Cooperative Lesson Planning Guide

Step 1. Select an activity and desired outcome(s).

Step 2. Make decisions.

   a. Group size:_____

   b. Assignment to groups:_____

   c. Room arrangement:_____

   d. Materials needed for each group:_____

   e. Roles:_____

Step 3. State the activity in language your students understand.

     a. Task:_____

     b. Positive interdependence:_____

     c. Individual accountability:_____

     d. Criteria for success:_____

     e. Specific behaviors to encourage:_____

Step 4. Monitor.

     a. Evidence of cooperative and encouraged behaviors:_____

     b. Task assistance needed:_____

Step 5. Evaluate outcomes.

     a. Task achievement:_____

     b. Group functioning:_____

     c. Notes on individuals:_____

     d. Feedback to give:_____

     e. Suggestions for next time:_____

Source: Adapted from Johnson, Johnson, and Smith, 1991, pp. 35–36.

Many different types of groups can be structured as cooperative learning groups. The following list shows some of the possibilities.

- *Special interest groups* are organized according to categories of participants' interests for the purposes of sharing information and experiences and exploring common concerns.

- *Problem-solving groups* are organized to develop solutions to substantive problems of any nature.

- *Planning groups* are organized to develop plans for activities, such as field trips, guest speakers, or resource use.

- *Instructional groups* are organized to receive specialized instruction in areas of knowledge or skill. The instructional task cannot be taught in a large-group setting, such as in a science laboratory, human relations seminar, or machine-operation training course.

- *Investigation or inquiry groups* are organized to search out information and report their findings to the entire learning group.

- *Evaluation groups* are organized for the purpose of evaluating learning activities, learner behavior, or any issue that requires feedback or decision making on the part of the learning group or instructor.

- *Skill practice and writing groups* are organized for the purpose of practicing a set of specified skills. Often group members share feedback and critique each other's work.

- *Tutoring or consultative groups* are organized for the purpose of tutoring, consulting, or giving assistance to members of other groups.

- *Operational groups* are organized for the purpose of taking responsibility for activities important to the learning group, such as room arrangements, refreshments, preparation of materials, operation of equipment, and the like.

- *Learning-instruction and reciprocal teaching groups* take responsibility for learning about a particular subject and instructing themselves, the rest of the learning group, or both. In the process of helping each other to learn, students deepen their knowledge of the topic they teach. Examples include jigsaw procedures and exam preparation teams.

- *Simulation groups* are organized to conduct an intergroup exercise, such as role playing, a game, or a case study review, to increase knowledge or build skills.

- *Learning achievement groups* are organized to produce a learning product that develops the members' knowledge, skills, or creativity, such as designing a research project.

- *Cooperative base groups* are cooperative learning groups that remain together for a long period, such as a course or term, have a stable membership, and foster individual accountability as they provide personal support, encouragement, and assistance in completing course responsibilities, reaching team goals, and making academic progress (Johnson and Johnson, 2006).

- *Learning communities* are a form of block scheduling that enables college students to take more than one course together and work as a study team over a semester or longer (Tinto, 1998). These groups, which often involve integration of curricula (such as psychology and English literature or math and economics) and team teaching, have demonstrated positive effects on the persistence and graduation rates of community college students including working-age adults (Bailey and Alfonso, 2005).

Considering the length of this section on cooperative learning, you might infer that I think competitive and individualistic learning should be abandoned in adult education and training. On the contrary, I like competitive activities *when my peers and I can freely choose to participate or not to participate.* I fondly remember those movies of the fifties in which the Step Brothers or Fred Astaire and Gene Kelly would engage in a friendly rivalry of dancing, each person topping the other only to see the other person dance with even more fantastic choreography. That's what good competition is about: choosing to elevate others and oneself to a higher plane of performance, whether it is in dancing, basketball, debate, or making wine—knowing you need each other because achieving your very best vitally depends on someone else accomplishing her very best.

Also, for less consequential learning, for drill practice, and for enjoyment, when the stakes are not very high (the most you can win is a round of applause), individual and intergroup competition can be quite effective. For any learning task where students' differences and capabilities are significant, as in math or writing, an individualized approach may be more helpful to some learners. Also, there are occasions when organizing coopera-tive learning can take too much time. What matters most is that cooperation is the norm for learning, that we are a community of learners who care about the learning of our peers as we do about our own learning. The more intellectually and socially connected adult learners feel—to one another and their instructors—the more they will persist in their education (Tinto, 1998; New England Adult Research Network, 1999). A good resource for collaborative and cooperative learning with specific subject-related examples is *Collaborative Learning Techniques: A Handbook for College Faculty* (Barkley, Cross, and Major, 2005).

Life's most important goals demand cooperation. The nurturing of our children, the quest for peace, and the safeguarding of the environment rely on mutual goodwill. Whether or not these aspirations are ever met relates profoundly to the way we learn in groups.

Strategy 6: Clearly Identify the Learning Objectives and Goals for Instruction

As soon as adults know the objectives of an instructional unit, they begin to form a personal theory about the choices and competencies necessary for accomplishing those tasks. They ask themselves such questions as, Where do I begin? Am I able to do this? What do the other people in this course seem to know about these objectives? These reflections influence their attitude as well as their sense of inclusion. Academically, the objectives have a unifying force. These goals set the purpose for which the learners are there and show them, at the very least, what they presently hold in common, no matter their background. Objectives provide the mutual bond for learning and are why cooperation makes sense. Learners can more clearly understand and discuss their expectations. For English-language learners, clear objectives are even more critical.

Entire books have been written about how to construct learning objectives. I understand them to have at least three possible forms: (1) clearly defined goals, (2) problem-solving goals, and (3) expressive outcomes.

1. *Clearly defined goals.* When specific objectives, skills, or competencies are appropriate and meaningful, especially in technical areas such as medicine and engineering, clearly defined goals can heighten learners' sense of control and capability. These goals let learners know what skills and knowledge they need to acquire and inform them about what may be necessary to achieve those skills and knowledge. For instructors, they provide a focus for designing instruction, guide the choice of lesson content, and give an appreciation of what assessment is needed for understanding if learning has occurred (Smith and Ragan, 2004). The three essential elements for constructing a learning objective are *who* (the learners), *how* (the action verb), and *what* (the contents) (Caffarella, 2002)—for example, "As a result of this workshop, participants [the learners] will create [the action verb] a résumé containing their professional achievements [the contents]." Adults studying to be medical technicians are likely to appreciate knowing that they (the learners) are going to take (the action verb) blood samples indicating blood type and Rh factor (the contents). Performance or product learning goals are often more clear when demonstrated with examples, models, or films: a dance routine, a

graphic design, or an experimental procedure—whatever it takes so that confusion does not detract from learners' expectation to succeed.

Walter Dick, Lou Carey, and James Carey (2004) suggest two more elements of specific learning objectives: conditions under which the learning is to be demonstrated and the standards or criteria for acceptable performance. The following clauses are examples of given conditions in learning objectives:

With the following problem . . .

Using this software . . .

When a patient declines assistance . . .

Without help from the emergency unit . . .

Criteria for acceptable performance include examples like these:

. . . with 80 percent correct

. . . with three or fewer errors

. . . with completion in thirty minutes

. . . with all patients

In 1956, Benjamin Bloom and his colleagues developed a classification system of educational objectives that has affected education on a global scale. Now known as Bloom's Taxonomy, the six basic cognitive objectives underwent a major revision by educational researchers (Anderson and Krathwohl, 2001) to recognize and reorder them as cognitive processes that more accurately represent recent research on how the brain functions. Very briefly, in this revision the names of all levels were changed to verb forms to make them more useful for constructing learning objectives. In addition, the original objective *Synthesis* became *Create* and replaced *Evaluate* (originally *Evaluation*) as the cognitive process representing highest complexity. Exhibit 5.2 summarizes these changes.

Exhibit 5.2   Revised Levels of Bloom's Taxonomy

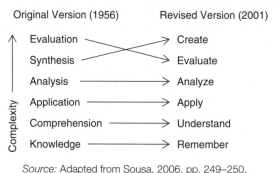

Source: Adapted from Sousa, 2006, pp. 249–250.

In the examples in Table 5.1, the affective process "Influence Attitudes, Values, and Beliefs" is added to Bloom's Taxonomy of cognitive processes to stress the need for learning objectives that are important but often overlooked when using only conventional cognitive processes as a guide. These examples include action words and a learning objective for each process for a course in adult development. In each objective, the learner is inferred.

2. *Problem-solving goals.* Much of what we aspire to and cherish as human beings is not amenable to uniform and specific description. How could one convincingly define integrity or describe how water tastes? As Eisner states, "To expect all of our educational aspirations to be either verbally describable or measurable is to expect too little" (1985, p. 115).

The problem-solving goal differs in a significant way from the conventional instructional objective (Schön, 1987). In working on a problem-solving goal, the learners formulate or are given a problem to solve. *Although the goal is clear* (solve the problem), *the learning is not definite or known beforehand.* For example, in a social science course, learners might be asked how to reduce crime in a particular area, or in a design seminar, learners might be asked to create a paper structure that will hold two bricks sixteen inches above a table. In both situations, there is a range of possible solutions and learning. Problem-solving goals place a premium on intellectual exploration and the higher mental processes while

Table 5.1.   Action Words and Learning Objective Examples

Process	Action Words	Objective
Create	Imagine, pretend, design, invent, envision	Taking into account the characteristics of older adults, design an urban park in which they could be physically and artistically engaged.
Evaluate	Judge, critique, assess, recommend, appraise	Given this case study of a working adult, recommend in order of priority and with accompanying rationales four actions he might take to improve his chances of attaining his bachelor's degree within three years.
Analyze	Distinguish, compare, organize, modify, refine	Using your own timeline of significant life events, compare the insights provided by Perry's *Forms of Ethical and Intellectual Development* with those provided by Belenky, Clinchy, Goldberger, and Tarule's *Women's Ways of Knowing* for three events that altered your life profoundly.
Apply	Practice, use, demonstrate, employ, complete	After reading a relevant biography of your choice, use at least four central concepts from our course to demonstrate your own adult developmental understanding of this person's life.
Understand	Explain, discuss, outline, summarize, teach	Choose an economic or political problem facing low-income adults in your community and outline a research study that could provide findings or data to more effectively address this.

Table 5.1.   *(Continued)*

Process	Action Words	Objective
Remember	Recognize, recall, define, describe, identify	Without using your text, describe Paulo Freire's emancipatory philosophy and one place or situation in which it has been effectively applied.
Influence attitudes, values, and beliefs	Challenge, defend, justify, resolve, dispute	After reviewing relevant research, write an essay to challenge or defend the generalization that accelerated learning is an effective learning format for working adults. Use at least three documented studies to support your argument.

supporting different cultural perspectives and values. Students' alternative solutions offer explicit evidence of the benefit of diverse talents and viewpoints. Relevant and genuine problems are most likely to elicit learner motivation.

3. *Expressive outcomes.* Another type of educational goal identified by Eisner (1985, 1999) focuses on expressive outcomes, learning objectives that emerge as the result of an intentionally planned activity. In these instances, learning goals do not precede an educational activity; they occur in the process of the activity itself. They are what we and the learners construct after some form of engagement. How many times have we read a book, seen a film, or had a conversation with learners whose resonance gives rise to so many questions and inspirations that to limit learners to our educational intention is a confinement of imagination? Encouraging expressive outcomes allows us to share reciprocally with learners various media or experiences derived from our lives, such as critical incidents and critical conversations (Brookfield

and Preskill, 2005). Afterward, through dialogue, we can mutually decide what direction learning should take.

Problem-solving goals and expressive outcomes support the preeminence of adult self-determination and perspective in defining relevant learning goals. These forms of establishing a learning purpose are an excellent means to initiate transformative learning (Mezirow, 2000) and critical teaching (Freire, 1970). They more readily allow knowledge to be examined and constructed rather than prescribed. I once began a course in adolescent psychology by watching with the class a few excellent films in which adolescents were the main characters. After this viewing and through the compelling dialogue that evolved, we constructed the course topics, reading list, and projects to facilitate our learning. The resulting course proved so powerfully informative that it was expanded the next semester to include two seniors from the local high school as co-teachers.

Strategy 7: Emphasize the Human Purpose of What Is Being Learned and Its Relationship to the Learners' Personal Lives and Current Situations

Because relevance is so neurophysiologically compelling (Ahissar and others, 1992), adults feel a pull to belong to a group that meets their personal needs and aspirations. Finding a purpose in what they are learning that is connected to their real world gives adult learners something to care deeply about and to work in common to achieve. This purpose has the potential to be a shared vision, one that inspires cohesion, participation, and action.

This strategy is based on the assumption that *anything* worth teaching matters to adults. If it does not bear a relationship to a human need, feeling, or interest, why would we instruct or train for it? For us as instructors the question is, What are the human ramifications of what we are helping learners know or do? Once we have an answer to this question, the relevance of what we instruct will be clearer, and we can think of ideas to make this meaning part of the learning process. Whether we are teaching people how to wire a circuit, how to speak another language, or how to write a complete sentence, these skills and knowledge serve human purposes. If we can understand these qualities, especially as they may relate to the daily lives of our learners, we have some guidance in selecting which social aspects of the learning experience we may wish to emphasize.

Giving a human or social perspective to a learning experience infuses it with value beyond the technical requirements of the task and changes it from an expendable, isolated activity into a potentially valued source of personal satisfaction for the learner (Kitayama and Markus, 1994); for example, an instructor might say, "We are not just studying how to use a new telecommunications system, we are learning a more effective and efficient way to communicate that benefits ourselves and our clients." If this viewpoint is sincerely portrayed by the instructor and embraced by the learner, the instructional activity has acquired a transcendent meaning. In plain words, this makes learning special. In fact, the structure of the previous quotation can be used to express the human ramifications for any specific learning objective: "We are not just studying [a specific topic or skill]; we are learning [human purpose]."

When human beings are in any way the topic of study, do their morals, values, decisions, problems, feelings, and behavior resemble similar qualities in our learners? If so, it may be worth the time to ask them to deal with these aspects of human existence through reflection, discussion, or writing. When our topics are in the realm of the physical and natural sciences, such as biology, chemistry, physics, and geology, showing how this knowledge relates to understanding challenges faced by humanity or how it can make life saner and more peaceful bonds learners in common cause. For skills from math to medicine, there is evidence that using human problems to learn them can stimulate teamwork as well as self-direction in adult learners (Hmelo-Silver, 2004). In technological fields such as computer programming and systems engineering, accentuating their contributions to human endeavors can diffuse their mechanistic isolation and humanize the learning process.

In the previous examples, we discussed emphasizing the human dimension of what is being learned so that learners can more easily identify with the topic. Probably more emotionally relevant is any learning situation in which the topic has an immediate relationship to the learners' personal daily lives (Freire, 1970). If an instructor is conducting a seminar on substance abuse as a community problem, what are the implications of the information for the communities of the participants and, more important, for their own families? In a similar vein, when an instructor is demonstrating a sales technique, why not demonstrate it with the typical client encountered by the sales personnel who are learning the technique? Consider a basic education instructor teaching the difference between a circle and a square. This may seem a highly abstract concept, but if, as a point of discussion, the instructor asks the learners to think of important circles and squares in their own lives, something abstract instantly becomes relevant. The closer we bring our topics and skills to the personal lives of our learners in the here and now, the more available will be their emotional involvement and sense of common purpose.

Creating a Climate of Respect among Adults

Across most cultures, to be respected in a group means, at the minimum, that you have the freedom to express yourself with integrity and without fear of threat or blame and that you know your opinion matters. When mutual respect is present in a learning environment, adults normally feel safe, accepted, and able to influence the situation when appropriate or necessary. Misunderstanding may be the least obvious, but the most common enemy of respect. The first recommended strategy is meant to help all members of a learning group avoid misapprehending their situation at the most vulnerable time in their tenure, the beginning.

Strategy 8: Assess Learners' Current Expectations, Needs, Goals, and Previous Experience as It Relates to Your Course or Training

Although we may have conducted a needs assessment of the learners, they may still have perspectives they haven't voiced or important interim experiences of which we are not aware. A number of years ago, I conducted a morning workshop on motivation for a group of teachers who were going to strike that afternoon. I did not know this. Needless to say, things weren't going very splendidly, and I hadn't a clue why. Until I asked the participants what was going on, no self-talk, including "Carpe diem!" made a difference.

We can confirm or alter our expectations or prior assessments with information gathered face-to-face during the opening segment of the lesson. Using this strategy as part of the introductions, we can say, "When you are introducing yourself, please include your expectations for the course." Asking learners to fill out a short questionnaire or to answer a few questions projected on a screen is also a possibility. Giving learners the chance to describe worries or concerns can often provide insight into their perspectives regarding the course or training.

For learning experiences during which there is likely to be controversy, we may want to provide a private way for learners to convey their expectations and needs. Maurianne Adams (Adams, Jones, and Tatum, 2007, pp. 401–402), who teaches courses in social justice, offers a good example of this approach:

> At the end of the first class, I give students time to write to me, telling me whatever they want me to know about themselves, such as their background or preparation

for the class, their goals for themselves in this class, any worries they may have about the class, or any physical or other disabilities they want me to know about so I can adjust assignments and activities. These are confidential. Then during the semester, I ask them to write again, telling me how they are doing, what they are struggling with, what questions or problems they have, what aspects of my teaching they find helpful, and what they wish I would change.

Adams's description emphasizes the importance of *checking in* with learners during a course or training. My experience has been that the more diverse the group, the more important it is to check in early and often to see how successfully the course and I are meeting expectations. For example, for a three-day workshop, I will check in every day no matter how well things seem to be going. When we are working with diverse learners, it is often easy to leave people out in terms of their goals and experiences without realizing it. Unless respectfully invited, people from cultures with high power distance usually are not forthcoming with this kind of information. Frequent checking in helps us adjust our instruction with minimum difficulty for learners and for us. My experience is that most adults see checking in as a caring and respectful thing to do.

Strategy 9: Explicitly Introduce Important Norms and Participation Guidelines

Every learning group is unique. It develops its own internal procedures, patterns of interaction, and limits. To some extent, it is as if imaginary lines guide and control the behavior of learners in a group. These are norms, "the group's common belief regarding appropriate behavior, attitudes, and perceptions for its members" (Johnson and Johnson, 2006, p. 17). These *shared expectations* guide the perceptions, thinking, feeling, and behavior of group participants and help group interaction by specifying the kinds of responses that are expected and acceptable in particular situations. All learning groups have norms, set either formally or informally. For a group norm to influence members' behavior, members must recognize that it exists, be aware that other group members accept and follow it, and feel some internal commitment to it.

Norms are the core constructs held in common that can ensure safety and build community among learners. Norms can create the kind of atmosphere that allows charged feelings and disagreements to be buffered as well as respectfully considered. The norms of collaboration, sharing the ownership of knowing, and a nonblameful view (see Chapter Three) are critical to fostering inclusion among diverse adult learners (Wlodkowski and Ginsberg, 1995). However, a norm can be confusing to people whose culture has not socialized them for it. People who are more oriented toward individualism or high power distance may feel perplexed or even distressed by the norms just mentioned. That's why these and all important norms should be made explicit. Knowing the boundaries in a group helps members immensely in guiding their behavior.

There are several ways to implement norms (and participation guidelines) in a group. One common method is simply to state them as the rules that govern the behavior of the group. Certainly, we want to offer a rationale for them and an opportunity for discussion, remaining flexible when appropriate. We can support norms through modeling. Our formal and informal behavior toward learners has a powerful effect on the norms of the learning group. Another method is to incorporate the institutional norms of group members into the learning group. This is a common method in business settings. Learners often assume that the norms that govern their behavior in a particular institution will transfer to learning events sponsored by that institution.

Norms can also be established through consensus. Learners might suggest which norms are needed or which need editing or specific discussion. This is an opportunity for other norms to be added as well. The instructor can then lead the group through a decision-making process to gain the group's consent for acceptable recommendations. Two group skills extremely important for appropriately handling this process are conflict management and consensus decision making (Johnson and Johnson, 2006). Generally, adults will more actively accept norms they have helped establish. Ownership gives them a sense of personal choice, an understanding that the norms reflect their values, and a better awareness of the need for their support to maintain the norms. Finally, the more clearly they see how a norm aids in the accomplishment of a goal to which they are committed, the more readily adults will accept and internalize the norm.

When course or training content is challenging and the learning process is experiential and interactive, adults appreciate *participation guidelines*. By clearly identifying the kinds of interactions and discussion that will be encouraged and discouraged, the instructor and learners create a climate of safety, ensuring that everyone will be respected.

The first meeting is an appropriate time to establish these guidelines and to request cooperation in implementing them. Through fifteen years of experience and at least a few abrasive moments, I have found the following rules to be generally acceptable as well as extremely beneficial for establishing inclusion (Wlodkowski and Ginsberg, 1995; Griffin, 1997b):

- Listen carefully, especially to different perspectives.

- Keep personal information shared in the group confidential.

- Speak from your own experience, saying, for example, "I think..." or "In my experience I have found..." rather than generalizing your experience to others by saying, for example, "People say..." or "We believe..."

- Express perspectives without blaming or scapegoating.

- Avoid generalizing about groups of people.

- Share airtime.

- Focus on your own learning.

I have found that instructors who use participation guidelines usually have a few that are nonnegotiable (Tatum, 1992). This makes sense because everyone is safer when we as instructors know what our professional limits are. Although their list may be longer or shorter, most adults accept and generate these guidelines because they reduce feelings of fear, awkwardness, embarrassment, and shame. They also provide a safety net for critical discourse. Leaving participation guidelines open to further additions and referring to them when necessary keeps the boundaries of the learning environment clear and dynamic.

Nonetheless, there are times when course content or student and teacher comments addressing inequity or controversial social issues can challenge student beliefs or raise intense emotions such as fear, guilt, or anger. As instructors at such times, we need to "stand outside the classroom experience and anticipate such dynamics," relieving some of the pressure, as Johnella Butler advises, by being the teacher who, "directly acknowledges and calls attention to the tension in the classroom" (1985, p. 236). When we initiate or allow a discussion that directly addresses tensions and fears, adults have a chance to engage in their learning more completely, with their emotions and their thoughts. We also must keep in mind that these discussions contain contradictions and dilemmas that may remain unresolved when the discussion has ended (Butler, 2000), possibly providing information and insight, but not a neatly packaged resolution.

On some occasions, I have alerted students that the content or experience that I have planned or suggested may leave some of us quite uncomfortable and indicate a few of the reasons that reaction might be expected. In general, this has usually relieved some anxiety and allowed some students to be more patient and open to learning that challenges their personal beliefs and experience.

Strategy 10: When Issuing Mandatory Assignments or Training Requirements, Give Your Rationale for Them

Adults hate busywork. Many of them have had teachers who handed out assignments without rhyme or reason. Because requirements demand time, energy, and responsibility, even the most motivated adult learner will feel apprehensive when the assignments are handed out. (Notice how quiet it gets!)

When we state the rationale for requirements, learners will more likely accept that we have carefully considered them; that we realize the obligations, benefits, and results of the requirements; and most important, that we respect learners and want to share this information. It is also no small advantage to us that by offering the rationale, we are more likely to ensure that learners will understand the purpose of the assignment.

As in most matters of communication, difficult news is best received when it is delivered directly and concisely. Here are two examples.

> An instructor might say: "At the end of this unit, I will ask each of you to role-play a conflict-management situation in a small-group setting. Each of you will be asked to resolve this problem by applying the suggestions for conflict management that are most relevant to a collectivist culture. This will give me the opportunity to give each of you guided practice and feedback so that you can refine your skills and have a chance to test this approach under simulated conditions."

> Or an instructor might say: "In addition to the readings in your textbook, I've assigned three outside articles and put them on reserve at the local library. I realize this may be somewhat of an inconvenience for you. However, each of

these articles contains a case study that is far more realistic and comprehensive than any of those found in your text. These case studies will provide much better examples of the principles you are studying and give you a chance to explore the benefits of these theories in situations much closer to your own real-life experiences."

Even with the clearest rationale for them, assignments are assignments, and usually no one applauds after they are given. This silence may simply reflect the realistic concern of adult learners who are accepting a new responsibility.

Strategy 11: Acknowledge Different Ways of Knowing, Different Languages, and Different Levels of Knowledge or Skill among Learners

One of the myths perpetuated about adults is that if you're older, you know more. This fiction doesn't account for all we have learned that is wrong, incorrect, unethical, or misleading. It also doesn't cover for what we have forgotten and confused, not to mention those vast stores of irrelevance attached to our dendrites. (Does anyone really care that I can name every U.S. capital that begins with the letters *A*, *B*, or *C*?) We may certainly know more about some things, but we do have our limits. At best, aging and wisdom are dubious partners. Nonetheless, the myth is an intimidating one, and many adults feel uncomfortable when they realize they may know less than other participants in a course or training. Often it's more a case of knowing things differently or with a different language. In teaching about research, for example, with its buckets of jargon, I have found that adults are openly relieved to know *reliability* means something as straightforward as "consistency."

To relax things a bit as well as make them more equitable, we can acknowledge to learners that we would appreciate knowing when there's a different way they understand something or a different language they might use. We need also to acknowledge that for adults who are English-language learners, the language they most readily speak may be from a culture that defines certain aspects of reality differently from the conventions of our course or setting (Fong, 2006). As an example, in Cantonese the words for *heat* and *cool* usually do not refer to the *temperature* of food and drink but to the *nature* of food that produces a cool or warm effect on your body. In this Chinese culture, these words are used in relation to balancing one's consumption of *warm* and *cool* foods. In the United States, balancing one's diet is related to consumption of the four main food groups: fruits and vegetables, meat and poultry, breads and grains, and dairy products.

For many courses, from child psychology to computer science, adults in attendance also may differ greatly from one another in their experience and knowledge, some people being novices and others having more experience than the instructor. After we perform some form of assessment to understand these disparities and acknowledge that the disparities are OK, we need to find a way to move forward together. We may do this using special project work, peer tutoring, cooperative learning (Strategy 5), or differentiated instruction (Strategy 14), where students work at different paces with varied learning options based on learner readiness and prerequisite skills—whatever allows us to learn most effectively and remain a mutually respectful community.

As I close this chapter, it is probably a good time to say a few words about resistance in a learning group when it occurs in the *beginning* of a course or training. Resistance often comes up because the learning experience is required or because people believe they have been unfairly mandated to attend. The group feeling tends to be some version of "we don't need this" or "this is going to be a waste of time." In these circumstances, it is usually best to openly acknowledge the situation and the possible feelings that may be occurring in the group. If appropriate, we can attempt to better understand the situation from the learners' perspective, listening well and gaining a fuller understanding. Then being realistically compassionate, we can plan or engage in learning that emphasizes immediate relevance and choice for them (discussed in Chapter Six). These procedures have a good chance of moving the group forward.

The challenge of inclusion is to find ways for adults to know they are respected and part of a learning community, genuinely engaging their spirit, their experience, and their perspective. A mere strategy does not create such a milieu. Inclusion is the result of a determined living harmony, a constancy of practices blended with ideals from the beginning to the end of every lesson of every session of every course.

6

Helping Adults Develop Positive Attitudes toward Learning

Exhortation is used more and accomplishes less than almost any behavior-changing tool known.

Robert F. Mager

We all spend a great deal of our time trying to influence other people's attitudes, especially the attitudes of those for whose work or effort we have some responsibility. We talk, show evidence, list logical reasons, and in some instances, actually give personal testimony to the positive results of this desired attitude. We are trying to be persuasive. Intuitively, we know it is best for people to like what they must do. Instructors want learners to feel positively toward learning and the effort it takes to accomplish it. However, exhorting, arguing, explaining, and cajoling are usually very inefficient means of helping someone develop a positive attitude toward learning. All these methods have a glaring weakness: they are simply words—"talk," if you will—that have nowhere near the impact of the consequences, conditions, and people involved in the learning task itself. When persuasion is successful, the *process* and *outcomes* of learning are what tell the story for the learner. When unsuccessful, persuasion becomes a form of linguistic static, badgering, or nagging that undermines the development of a positive attitude in the adult learner.

In general, it is probably best not to try to talk adults into learning. There are far more powerful things we can do in the presentation of the subject matter as well as in our treatment of adults to help them build positive attitudes toward their learning and themselves as learners. This chapter will examine a number of strategies that encourage adults to look forward to learning and, perhaps most important, feel eager to learn more.

Four Important Attitudinal Directions

As stated in Chapter Four, attitudes predispose adults to respond favorably or unfavorably toward particular people, groups, ideas, events, or objects. From a cultural and a neuropsychological view, in order for adults to have a positive attitude toward learning, they have to see it as *relevant.* They also have to see it as an activity to which they are responding with *volition*, free choice, self-determination, or compliance with something they endorse. When relevance and volition are present at the beginning of a learning activity, most adults initially find learning appealing, something they want to do.

Adults' attitudes usually focus on one or more of four directions: (1) toward the instructor, (2) toward the subject, (3) toward their self-efficacy for learning, and (4) toward the specific learning goal or performance. Together, these attitudes influence adult intentions to learn.

Theoretically, these four adult attitudinal directions integrate the self-motivation processes of self-regulation theory (Zimmerman and Kitsantas, 2005)—self-efficacy, outcome expectations, task interest or value, and goal orientation—with the cultural beliefs, values, and norms that adults bring to a learning situation. Because of its usefulness for teaching, I've retained the very basic

Table 6.1.   Attitudinal Directions

Perception +	Judgment →	Emotion →	Behavior
I see my instructor.	He seems helpful.	I feel appreciative.	I cooperate.
The instructor announces the beginning of a new unit on family relations. (subject)	Learning more about being an effective parent is relevant to me.	I feel interested.	I pay attention.
It is my turn to present my project to the seminar. (self-efficacy)	I am knowledgeable and well prepared for this task.	I feel confident.	I give a smooth and articulate presentation.
The instructor is giving a surprise quiz. (learning goal or performance)	I haven't studied. I'm not prepared for this quiz.	I feel anxious and frustrated.	I can't think well. I do poorly on the quiz.

interpretation of an attitude as a combination of a perception with a judgment that often results in an emotion that influences behavior (Ellis, 1989). The examples in Table 6.1 illustrate the possible influences that attitudes can have on behavior and performance in learning tasks.

Whenever we instruct, we want to establish a learning environment in which these four attitudinal directions are positive and unified for the learner. *We want adults to respect us, to find the subject appealing, and to feel confident that they can successfully learn the specific task before them.*

If any one of these four attitudinal directions becomes seriously negative, the adult's motivation to learn can be impaired. For example, he might respect the instructor, feel confident as a learner, and objectively expect to do well but still intensely dislike the subject area. This sometimes happens with required courses or training; competent instructors find capable adults disinterested and apathetic. In a similar vein, an adult could like the instructor and the subject and be confident as a learner but realize he lacks the time or the proper materials to be successful in the learning task. It is quite likely that this person's overall motivation to learn will be significantly reduced, and trying hard will probably lead only to frustration. This situation often arises when one learner has to compete against another learner whose preparation and material advantages seem far superior to his own.

In most instances, adults experience their attitudes immediately, without premeditation or serious reflection. They hear or see something, and the attitude begins to run its course. The instructor introduces the topic, and the learner's attitude toward that topic emerges. The instructor assigns homework, and the learner quickly has an attitude toward the assignment. Once an adult has had an experience, the attitude will occur, like it or not. It may be only a vague feeling, but it is still an influence on behavior. In my work as a teacher, the immediacy of adult attitudes toward new learning experiences is a *truism*.

As instructors we have to be aware of what can be done to influence learner attitudes positively at the *beginning* of any learning experience. The attitudes will be there from the very start. Having them *work for* learners and us offers the best chance for motivated learning to occur. Although most of the following strategies can be implemented throughout the learning experience, the discussion here will stress their use at the beginning of learning and training activities.

Creating a Positive Attitude toward the Instructor

Ask any adult learner—a negative attitude toward an instructor, whether online or face to face, makes that instructor a barrier between the material to be learned and the learner. Instead of feeling at ease because a respected instructor is offering an attractive lesson, the learner may feel tense because of the dissonance of a disliked instructor offering an attractive lesson. We have all experienced this discomfort in everyday life: we feel uneasy purchasing a car from a salesperson we don't like or accepting a gift from someone we disrespect. In those instances, it seems better not to buy the car or accept the gift, because then our actions are consistent with how we feel toward the person. In learning situations, adults are more open and responsive to tasks they receive from an instructor they like and respect. They are quite the opposite with an instructor they don't like or respect. Optimal motivation for learning will diminish.

As discussed in Chapter Three, the core characteristics of expertise, empathy, and cultural responsiveness are major influences in establishing a positive attitude toward the instructor. Because the learners' relationship to the instructor bears strongly on learners' feelings of inclusion, the strategies for creating a positive attitude toward the instructor were presented in Chapter Five. The strategies in that chapter that are especially relevant to learners' attitude toward the instructor are the following:

- Allow for introductions. (Strategy 1)

- Concretely indicate your cooperative intentions to help adults learn. (Strategy 3)

- Share something of value with your adult learners. (Strategy 4)

- When issuing mandatory assignments or training requirements, give your rationale for them. (Strategy 10)

- To engender a safe learning environment, acknowledge different ways of knowing, different languages, and different levels of knowledge or skill. (Strategy 11)

Building a Positive Attitude toward the Subject

Please read the following words out loud:

English	Psychology	History
Technology	Math	Geology
Biology	Research	Economics
Writing	Algebra	Chemistry

Which word evoked the strongest emotional response? Was it a positive or a negative feeling? Most of the listed subject areas are common to the educational experience of adults. They have taken such courses, and they usually have distinct attitudes toward them. Any new learning that involves elements from past courses will cause immediate attitudinal reactions on the part of adults. That is why adults so often ask questions like these at the beginning of new courses and training sessions: How much writing will I have to do? What kind of math does this training require? What will I have to research? Adults have strong opinions about both their capabilities and their feelings toward such requirements. They carry attitudes toward them that often are decades old and very entrenched (Smith, 1982). New learning often causes mixed reactions in adults. They might want to learn about innovative uses of technology but honestly have real fears if any math is involved in the training.

To some extent, new learning goes against the grain of the personal autonomy and security of adults. Older adults have usually found a way to cope with life and have formulated a set of convictions (Schaie and Willis, 2002). New learning often asks them to become temporarily dependent, to open their minds to new ideas, to rethink certain beliefs, and to try different ways of doing things. This may be threatening or difficult for them, and their attitudes can easily lock in to support their resistance. For some adults, speaking in front of the group is an ordeal. Specific learning techniques, such as role playing and videotaping, can also make some adults quite anxious.

As we know from Chapter Two, such stress can overstimulate the limbic system, particularly the amygdala, and impede reasoning and long-term memory. For tense adults, real learning is a struggle. As instructors, we want to create with learners a positive emotional state where they have an intentional bias toward learning. Whatever we can do as instructors to minimize adults' negative attitudes and to foster positive attitudes toward the entire instructional process will improve their motivation and their chances for learning. Invigorated by our enthusiasm, the following strategies are a means to this end.

Strategy 12: Eliminate or Minimize Any Negative Conditions That Surround the Subject

Robert Mager (1968) once wrote that people learn to avoid the things they are hit with. It is a common fact of learning that when a person is presented with an item or subject and is at the same time in the presence of negative (unpleasant) conditions, that item or subject becomes a stimulus for avoidance behavior. Things or subjects that frighten adults are often associated with antagonists and situations that make them uncomfortable, tense, or scared. Therefore, it is best not to associate the subject with any of the following conditions. These tend to support negative learner attitudes and repel adult interest:

- *Pain*: acute physical or psychological discomfort, such as continuous failure (where learner effort makes no difference), poorly fitting equipment, or uncomfortable room temperature

- *Fear and anxiety*: distress and tension resulting from anticipation of the unpleasant or dangerous, such as threat of failure or punishment, public exposure of

ignorance, or unpredictability of potential negative
consequences

- *Frustration:* an emotional reaction to an obstacle to
  purposeful behavior, such as information presented
  too quickly or too slowly, tests that are unannounced
  (euphemistically called *pop quizzes*), or inadequate feedback on performance

- *Humiliation:* an emotional reaction to being shamed,
  disrespected, or degraded by sarcasm, insults, sexist
  comments, or public comparison of learners' efforts

- *Boredom:* a cognitive and emotional reaction to weak,
  repetitive, or infrequent stimuli, as in learning situations that lack variety, cover material already known,
  or are monopolized by the same people talking over and
  over again

This list is quite dismal. However, just as a slate must be wiped
clean before clear and lucid new writing can be set down, learning
environments must have these negative conditions removed before
positive conditions can effectively occur. Otherwise, the best efforts
of motivating instructors can be contaminated and diffused by the
mere presence of such oppressive elements.

*Strategy 13: Positively Confront the Erroneous Beliefs, Expectations,
and Assumptions That May Underlie a Negative Learner Attitude*

Some learners have mistaken beliefs that support their negative
attitudes. For example, learners may think, "If I have to do any math
in this course, I won't do well in it," or "Communications training
has never helped anyone I know," or "If I make a mistake, I'll
really look bad." Assumptions of this sort can cause learners to fear
and resist a subject (Ellis, 1989). People maintain their negative
attitudes by repeating such beliefs to themselves. If you think an

individual learner (or the group) holds such beliefs, you can use the following guidelines to help reduce the negative attitude:

1. Tactfully find out what the learner might be telling herself that leads to the negative attitude. ("You seem somewhat discouraged. Could you tell me what might be happening or what you might be thinking that's leading to such feelings?")

2. If the learner appears to have a self-defeating belief, point out how negative feelings naturally follow from such a belief. ("If you believe making a mistake will really make you look foolish in front of your peers, you probably feel fearful and anxious about trying some of the group exercises.")

3. Suggest other assumptions that might be more helpful to the learner. ("You might tell yourself that this is guided practice, where everyone including your instructor expects some mistakes, and that the purpose of the exercises is to refine skills, not to demonstrate them at a level of complete proficiency.")

4. Encourage the learner to develop beliefs, based on present reality, that promote well-being. ("When you start to feel discouraged or negative, check out what you are telling yourself and see if it really helps you. Consider whether some other beliefs or expectancies would be more helpful. You might want to discuss this with me so that I can give you feedback and suggest other ways of looking at the situation.")

Sometimes it's useful to ask the learner, "What might have to happen for you to believe you could do well or to change your attitude in a positive direction?" This question may help the learner describe relevant examples of evidence that will fit her perspective and produce a shift in attitude. At a workshop, I once asked this question of a group of reluctant college faculty. They anonymously wrote their answers on cards, which I read back to them. Midway through the deck I found myself reading the answer,

"A public hanging of the dean." Fortunately, the dean graciously laughed. Her sense of humor and compassion took us to another level of discourse, and the workshop progressed with much more effectiveness.

Strategy 14: Use Differentiated Instruction to Enhance Successful Learning of New Content

It is difficult for anyone to dislike a subject in which they are successful. Conversely, it is rare to find anyone who really likes a subject in which they are unsuccessful. We know that adults come into courses with varying levels of academic readiness, especially in institutions with open enrollment policies such as community colleges. Adults are likely to be discouraged if they lack the academic skills or experience to make successful progress in their courses. They may also feel disheartened when they realize how much extra time and effort they will need to expend in order to learn. Also, there is the age-old problem of some students speeding ahead while others learn more slowly. (As an older learner, I hasten to add, more slowly does not mean less well.)

Although differentiated instruction has focused mainly on learning among elementary and secondary students (Tomlinson, 2005), it can be adapted to teaching adult learners. Seeing diversity as an array of strengths on which to build, it is a flexible form of instruction that matches content, process, and outcomes to students' differences in readiness, interests, and needs. I have found that its suggestions for making content more flexible (Tomlinson, 2001) encourage adult learners' attitudes and efforts. Following are some ideas you may find helpful as well. These ideas have worked much better when I have added two conditions: (1) evidence that effort makes a difference and (2) continual feedback regarding progress of learning.

• In addition to the main instructional techniques (such as experiential learning, discussion, and the course textbook), it is advantageous to have a number of alternative texts, resource materials, and instructional processes available to accommodate differences in academic readiness and learning needs among adult learners. The following are some alternatives:

Collaborative and cooperative group study procedures can be available to learners as they need them. Small groups of learners (two or three) could meet regularly to go over points of difficulty in the learning process. (See Strategy 5 in Chapter Five for additional specific ideas.)

Multiple texts and supplemental materials including journals, magazines, and downloads from the Internet increase the probability of reaching *all* adult learners with content that is meaningful and relevant. Textbooks with many pictures, diagrams, and graphic organizers can offer a clearer examples for some learners who are having difficulty with the main textbook. For English-language learners, reading main ideas and principles in their native language and then in English may be an avenue to deeper learning.

Media, films, and the Internet often provide additional illustrations, explanations, and greater breadth and depth than print materials for both more advanced and less advanced students.

Digests of key ideas are one- to two-page summarizations of the key concepts and principles in a learning unit. They help learners to identify what is important to understand, integrate, and remember. They can be organized as a flow chart or a concept map highlighting essential vocabulary and questions. These digests also clarify for us, as instructors, what the core ideas are for a given unit or topic of study. Table 9.1, Summary of Motivational Strategies, in Chapter Nine is an example of such a digest for this book.

- *Concept-based teaching* can provide an in-depth understanding of a discipline because it emphasizes the thorough use of main ideas and principles over superficial facts (Donovan, Bransford, and Pellegrino, 1999). This approach, rather than memorization, helps all students to develop understanding and to create networks of meaning for future use and long-term memory. For example, a major concept and competency in history is to understand how evidence from primary and secondary sources becomes historical knowledge. This process is what historians do, and understanding it well transfers to the critical reading of print and electronic journalism. This type of learning is more valuable than memorizing the dates of battles or the names of explorers, and other facts so common to history exams. In addition, knowing how to gather and integrate evidence from primary and secondary sources applies to the social sciences, humanities, and law as well as history. Concept-based teaching reduces time spent on inconsequential information, allowing more time to learn and integrate principles that cross disciplines and build neural networks to enhance future learning.

- *Tutorial assistance* is helpful for many learners. Few of us are excellent across all disciplines. (I did pretty well with the social sciences but I needed a tutor to pass French in college.) Peers can be excellent tutors, especially for time-limited assignments and projects, when the speed of their mastery exceeds others and they are available for temporary support. For long-term support, in addition to tutoring the institution may offer, there are a number of 24/7 online tutoring services available.

- *Learning contracts* are excellent for students who differ in readiness, interest, and needs because contracts offer flexibility for each of these variables. They encourage relevant learning tailored for every student. Strategy 24 later in this chapter provides a detailed discussion of learning contracts.

- *Time* to complete tests and in-class assignments reduces anxiety and allows every adult a chance to do well.

• *Formative assessments* are ongoing assessments designed to make an individual's thinking and learning visible to him and his instructor (Donovan, Bransford, and Pellegrino, 1999). These measures provide opportunities for the learner to improve his learning and for the instructor to improve her teaching. Strategy 50 in Chapter Eight discusses this approach to assessment.

Most of the ideas from differentiated instruction are not new. Tutoring and formative assessment, two obvious examples, have longstanding support for their effectiveness. However, it is the systematic use and combination of these methods that make them powerful, especially for learners who vary in academic readiness. An important strategy that is frequently identified with differentiated instruction, but can stand alone because of its usefulness in many educational areas, is *scaffolding complex learning.*

Strategy 15: Use Assisted Learning to Scaffold Complex Learning

Lev Vygotsky (1978), a pioneer in social constructivist theory, realized that a person could solve or master certain problems and skills when given appropriate help and support. Such learning, often called "assisted learning," provides *scaffolding*—giving clues, information, prompts, reminders, and encouragement at the appropriate time and in the appropriate amounts and then gradually allowing the learner to do more and more independently. Most of us naturally scaffold when we teach someone to drive a car or play a card game. The *zone of proximal development* (ZPD) is the phase in a learning task when a learner can benefit from assistance (Wertsch, 1991). The upper limit of the zone is the place where the learner can perform the task independently; the lower limit is the place where the learner can perform the task but needs assistance.

Most of us learned to drive a car with someone in the seat next to us who prompted and reminded us of what to do and when to do it as we navigated a road. In the beginning, this "coach" usually had to scaffold pretty intensely: "Check your speedometer"; "I think you're speeding"; "Watch out for that car"; "If you don't stop, we are going to have an accident." We were obviously in the lower limit of our zone of proximal development for driving.

From a neurological perspective, scaffolding, the practicing and being coached to drive a car, resulted in new dendrites growing along the axons of thousands of neurons. Over time, with more practice and coaching, these new dendrites and their axons formed branches that created strong neural pathways and networks resulting in a speedy and efficient circuitry with multiple pathways. Now, biologically in the upper limit of the ZPD, we can drive independently.

Myriad other learning tasks strongly benefit from scaffolding. Whether adults are learning to solve math problems, conduct experiments, or use a personal computer, our assessing their zone of proximal development and structuring the appropriate scaffold can lead to their success. Adults deeply appreciate the support that assisted learning offers because it tends to be concrete, immediate, and tailored to their obvious needs. The following are some of the assisted-learning methods that can be used to scaffold more complex learning (Association for Supervision and Curriculum Development, 1990; Tappan, 1998). The description of each method includes an example in which I model assisting students to learn to write a research report.

- *Modeling.* The instructor carries out the skill while the learners observe, or the instructor offers actual examples of learning outcomes, such as finished papers or solved problems. (I ask the learners to read two previously completed reports. One is excellent; the other is satisfactory.)

- *Thinking out loud.* The instructor states actual thought processes in carrying out the learning task. (I talk about some of the goals and criteria I would consider before writing the report. I ask the learners why one report was considered excellent and the other only satisfactory. I supplement the learners' perceptions with my own.)

- *Anticipating difficulties.* As the learning proceeds, the instructor and learners discuss areas where support is needed and mistakes are more likely to occur. (Because the sections of the report that discuss findings and statistical analyses seem most challenging to the learners, we discuss how these sections were done in the two reports and arrange for prompt feedback on the learners' initial drafts of these sections in their own reports.)

- *Providing prompts and cues.* The instructor highlights, emphasizes, or structures procedural steps and important responses to help learners clearly recognize their place and their importance to the learning task. (I provide an outline for writing a research report with exemplars from previous reports.)

- *Using dialogue and discussion.* The instructor engages the learners in a conversation where the understanding of concepts and procedures of the learning task deepens and becomes more organized. The give and take of these mutual explorations includes critique but in a way that alternates between serious and playful discussion (Brookfield and Preskill, 2005). (I talk with the learners about the research they consider relevant and would like to know more about, sometimes lightly joking with them about the omnipotence and unlimited time needed to do such research. Nonetheless we earnestly discuss what hypotheses and data such reports should include.)

- *Regulating the difficulty.* The instructor introduces a more complex task with simpler tasks and may offer some practice with these. (Using the previous discussion as a context, I give the learners a basic research scenario, a hypothesis, data, and an analysis scheme and ask them each to write a brief research report with this information.)

- *Using reciprocal teaching and practice.* The instructor and the learners rotate the role of instructor; in that role, each learner provides guidance and suggestions to others. (While I monitor, each learner presents his or her brief research report to a learning partner who acts as the instructor and gives supportive feedback. Then they reverse roles. The same process will be carried out with the first draft of their actual research report.)

- *Providing a checklist.* Learners use self-checking procedures to monitor the quality of their learning. (I give the learners a checklist of questions and quality criteria to consider as they write their reports.)

Possible metaphors for the provider of assisted learning are "sensitive tutor," "seasoned coach," "wise parent"—all people who tell us just enough, what we need to know when we need to know it, and trust us to chart the rest of our journey to learning. Assisted learning conveys an underlying message: "You may stray, but you will not be lost. In this endeavor, you are not alone." The image is not of the learner as rugged individualist or solitary explorer. Rather, assisted learning embraces a vision of remarkable possibility nurtured by a caring community.

Developing Self-Efficacy for Learning

Goethe believed that the greatest evil that can befall a person is that he should come to think ill of himself. When it comes to learning, this aphorism is most relevant to the adult's perception of self-efficacy. Some learners may not have a negative attitude toward their instructor or the subject, but they may judge that they lack the capability to successfully learn in the task at hand. Learners holding such perceptions have low self-efficacy for the learning goal and their motivation to learn is usually diminished for the activity or course. A learner with low self-efficacy might think, "I'd like to learn Spanish. The teacher seems great. But I just have never been good at learning other languages. I don't think I'm going to do well in this course." This learner is likely to give up easily when he encounters frustration or failure during the learning process: "I got a C minus on the first test. Maybe I should drop this course while I can get most of my money back and before I really do poorly."

Albert Bandura defined *self-efficacy* as "beliefs in one's capabilities to organize and execute the courses of action required to produce given achievements" (1997, p. 3). Self-efficacy is a personal assessment of one's capability to perform a specific task. (Because I have written two editions of this book, my self-efficacy for writing a third is relatively high. However, my self-efficacy for playing well in a pick-up football game is extremely low. In fact, my self-efficacy for throwing a football well is quite low.)

Adult self-efficacy is situation specific and, although future oriented, it is largely based on performance in past experiences. Self-efficacy beliefs are stronger predictors of adult behavior than are other self-perceptions such as self-concept and self-esteem, which are more global and have less specific meaning (Bandura, 1997; Bong and Skaalvik, 2003). Bandura's ideas about self-efficacy and learning are relevant to understanding the motivation of adults because they account for the reciprocal influence of the learner and the environment on each other (Merriam, Caffarella, and Baumgartner, 2007). As an example, consider an instructor whose self-efficacy for effectively discussing United States foreign policy with learners is high. Although the learners respond tentatively, their feedback indicates they want to talk further about important global issues. The instructor is encouraged and adds a discussion of recent events in the Middle East to the syllabus, knowing this topic will probably invite controversial opinions from the learners. This interaction reflects how an individual's self-efficacy produces behavior and how the environment is affected by that behavior and how its response alters the future behavior of that individual. This kind of interaction reflects adult reality. Such interactions are also the basis for pragmatic strategies that can enhance adult perceptions of their self-efficacy in learning situations.

As instructors, we need to remember that adult perceptions of self-efficacy are always situation specific. A person might feel quite physically adept but very incompetent in academic situations. This kind of variation exists for academic subjects as well. A learner might feel quite superior in English and very inferior in math. Adults constantly modify their self-efficacy beliefs in specific areas of learning. This malleability means that during classes or training sessions instructors have an opportunity to influence learners' self-estimation.

Many adults harbor doubts about their learning capabilities. They often underestimate and underuse their capacities (Knox, 1977). Their family members may reinforce their self-doubts by questioning their talent or the need for certain learning. Later adulthood and old age are periods when many learners are especially vulnerable to these sources of anxiety.

When adults begin courses or new learning activities, we can provide experiences from which they can derive higher self-efficacy and, consequently, greater self-confidence as learners. Bandura (1997) found that self-efficacy expectations are generally acquired through four sources. (1) *Mastery experiences* are direct experiences of success and failure in given tasks over a lifetime. These are probably the most powerful influences on adult self-efficacy beliefs and are stored as prior knowledge in our long-term memories. (2) *Vicarious experiences* are situations in which we watch the learning task successfully performed by someone whom we view as similar to ourselves. The more closely we identify with the model, the more likely the greater will be that model's influence on our self-efficacy expectations for the task. (3) We also acquire self-efficacy through *social persuasion*, when someone we trust encourages us to believe that we can, usually with greater effort, accomplish the task at hand. (4) Self-efficacy is promoted in situations where our *level of arousal* is supportive for effective action, such as when our limbic system processes feelings of relaxation, alertness, and enthusiasm for the task ahead.

Mastery experiences, vicarious experiences, and social persuasion will provide basic theoretical underpinnings for the strategies offered in this text to enhance adult self-efficacy for learning. Any strategy that supports a positive emotion for learning also supports a positive level of arousal. Unless stated otherwise, all the strategies in this book are oriented in this direction, especially those in Chapter Five, "Establishing Inclusion among Adult Learners."

Before we move to particular strategies related to self-efficacy, I want to emphasize again the strategies of *differentiated instruction* and *scaffolding* (Strategies 14 and 15, respectively). Although presented in the section about attitudes toward the subject, these strategies also strongly influence self-efficacy expectations for the learning task. Differentiated instruction and scaffolding can be combined with the strategies that follow to foster beliefs among adults that they are, indeed, capable learners.

Strategy 16: Promote Learners' Personal Control of Learning

For people to build self-efficacy from past or present mastery experiences, they usually need to realize that they are most responsible for their learning. They need to feel a sense of personal causation in the process of learning—that they *control* how, what, and when they learn (Plaut and Markus, 2005). At first, this may seem obvious: if a person pays attention, studies, and practices, of course the person will feel responsible for any successful achievement. However, when we remember that instructors usually establish requirements, issue assignments, give tests, generally set the standards for achievement, often control the learning environment, and sometimes require learner participation, it is not difficult to understand how learners could come to believe that instructors are more responsible for their achievement than they are. Even when a person is successful, he or she may feel very dependent as a learner and consequently bound to the demands and directions of the instructor for future learning. In this way, a learner can feel like a pawn and not develop self-efficacy.

Adults are inclined toward autonomy in many aspects of their daily lives. The following methods to increase their sense of personal causation while learning should effectively complement this tendency.

- *The learner plans and sets goals for learning.* Planning validates the individual as the originator and guide of the learning process. The next section, "Establishing Challenging and Attainable Learning Goals," offers specific strategies for how to do this.

- *To the extent appropriate, the learner makes choices about what, how, with whom, where, and when to learn something.* Choice permits the learners to feel greater ownership of the learning experience. They can choose topics, assignments, when to be evaluated, how to be evaluated, and so forth.

- *The learner uses self-assessment procedures.* When learners can appraise mistakes and successes while learning, they experience a concrete sense of participation in the learning act. Sometimes learners can get the feeling that more mistakes are created by the instructor than are committed by the learners. Self-assessment procedures can prevent this misperception and give the learners a sense of control from the beginning to the end of the learning experience. When people can determine for themselves whether they are really learning something, they feel more responsible for that learning. See Strategy 54 for an elaboration of this method.

- *The instructor helps the learner to identify personal strengths while learning.* For example, "You have a number of assignments to choose from, but you seem to have a real talent for explaining things well and could probably give a very interesting oral presentation. What do you think?" Learners who know and take advantage of personal assets while learning are likely to feel greater self-efficacy.

• *The learner logs personal progress while learning.* This allows learners to recognize personal growth and learning as they take place.

• *The learner participates in analyzing potential barriers to progress in learning.* For example, the instructor might ask, "What do you think the difficulty might be?" or "In your estimation, where do you think the confusion begins?" By participating in solving their learning problems, learners feel more commitment to their resolution and are more aware of their role in the learning process. An added plus for instructors is that adult learners frequently know better than we do where problems in learning are occurring.

• *When advisable, the learner makes a commitment to the learning task.* This accentuates the learner's volition. It prevents denial or withdrawal of personal responsibility for learning. When we ask a learner, "Are you sure you're going to do it?" or "Can I feel certain that you're going to try?" and we receive a sincere affirmative answer, we are helping to amplify the learner's sense of self-determination. When people make commitments and *follow through on them*, these assertions enhance their effort for learning (Harkins, White, and Utman, 2000). However, as instructors, we should use this technique sparingly and with careful forethought. If it lacks integrity, it becomes a mere manipulation and an insult to the learner.

• *The learner has access to prompt feedback.* Prompt feedback during learning leads to stronger feelings of personal control and self-efficacy. This is one of the main reasons some online instruction programs can be so powerful for increasing motivation. The computer program can give immediate feedback so that the learner has moment-to-moment awareness of progress in learning. This constant back-and-forth *dialogue* between software program and the learner gives the learner a strong sense of control in the learning process. In many ways, the computer tells the learner it will not respond until the learner responds first. The learner's personal control is undeniable.

In contrast, the slower the feedback, the more difficult it is to know whether a response has had any effect at all. Imagine having a conversation with someone who waited a minute or longer to answer a question. You would probably wonder if you were actually being heard. Anything an instructor can do to ensure the quickest possible pace of accurate feedback will concretely help emphasize learner responsibility. See Chapter Eight for a comprehensive discussion of the appropriate use of feedback.

The purpose of these methods is to emphasize that the *majority* of responsibility for learning is under the control of the learner. As we have learned earlier in this book, personal control is one of the main ways that our brains know to survive (Zull, 2002). Neurologically, feeling in control while learning is very motivating.

Strategy 17: Help Learners Effectively Attribute Success to Their Capability, Effort, and Knowledge

This strategy focuses on the outcome of learning when it is successful. *Success* in a broad sense can mean passing a test, receiving an excellent grade, completing a fine project, satisfactorily demonstrating a new skill, finding an answer to a problem—*any achievement that turns out well in the eyes of the learner.*

Adults frequently think about the consequences of their behavior. If they have an important success, they will often reflect on a reason or a cause for that success. Some educational psychologists call these inferred causes *attributions* and have created a theory and body of research to demonstrate the significant effects of attributions on human behavior (Weiner, 2000). For instructors, the important understanding is this: when people have a successful learning experience, it will probably enhance their self-efficacy and their motivation to believe that the major causes for that success are their capability, effort, and knowledge. Because learners internally control those causes, they can feel genuine pride. In addition, capability is stable (it lasts), so learners who see themselves as capable can feel more confident when similar learning tasks arise. Even though effort and knowledge are less stable (sometimes it's difficult to persevere or remember), it is probably these aspects of behavior over which learners feel the most control.

Differences in success in many academic subjects are largely due to differences in experience. Those learners who have had more experience with a particular learning task—through previous education, training, work, or travel—have more knowledge explicitly and tacitly for the task at hand. They are likely to be more successful performing the task than learners who are less experienced with the task (Brophy, 2004; Sternberg, 1997). Examples of tasks that come to mind from my own experience are writing reports, comparing ideas, making calculations, and designing lessons. With patience, persistence (effort), and help (knowledge) from instructors, less successful learners gain the learning necessary to achieve in the domain that the task represents. Having taught research and introductory statistics, I have seen how acquiring domain-specific knowledge, such as basic algebra, during the course can cause adult learners who initially doubted their capability in these subjects to thrive.

Effort attributions are a bit tricky. We want adults to know that learning may take perseverance and patience, but we don't want them to think it is "all hard work." Such an attribution could discourage them or make them less confident about their capabilities. Gaining experience to learn something does take tolerance of mistakes and patient persistence. Knowing that knowledge can be gained through study and practice and that effort is often a matter of will reduces learners' feelings of helplessness. Understanding that reasonable but not overwhelming effort is necessary provides realistic hope for learners. For example, an instructor might say, "Learning how to solve differential equations will take practice and time. However, we'll be able to help each other each step of the way. We'll chart our progress to show how this persistence and support pays off."

Knowledge attributions, especially when offered as *strategy*, can be very effective for promoting self-efficacy. We want learners to believe there is a "way" to learn or perform a task. If so, (1) we can help them help themselves, (2) learning is possible and not restricted to ability, and (3) reasonable effort makes sense and will pay off. The best part of this attribution is that it's true! In fact, a sensitive use of strategy for planning and carrying out lessons is the main attribution offered in this book to enhance adult motivation.

Here are some ways to help learners attribute their success to capability, effort, and knowledge:

- Provide learners with learning tasks suitable to their capabilities. "Just within reach" is a good rule of thumb. These kinds of tasks challenge learners' capabilities and require knowledge and moderate effort for success.

- Before initiating a learning task, stress the importance of learners' persistence and knowledge for success. This should be a reminder and not a threat: for example, "Considering the challenge of this task, we'll have to practice and become proficient before we apply what we know." This alerts the learners to their responsibility and increases the likelihood that they will attribute their success to effort and knowledge.

- Send verbal and written messages to accentuate learners' perceptions of capability, effort, and knowledge in relation to their success. To reinforce capability, you might say: "That's a talented performance" or "You seem to be a natural at doing this." To acknowledge effort: "Great to see your dedication to this work pay off" or "I know a lot of perseverance went into this

project." To highlight knowledge or strategy: "Your
skills made a real difference" or "Your experience with
outlining is apparent in your writing." The great thing
about such statements is that they can be distributed all
the time.

Certain subjects, such as math, writing, and art, are conventionally understood to be ability-driven when in reality they greatly
benefit from effort and strategy. For example, knowing there are
five interesting ways to begin an essay (with a statistic, quotation,
question, anecdote, or revelation) is a strategy that can make
starting a new paper an enjoyable challenge rather than an oppressive frustration. When we attribute effective learning to attainable
knowledge or strategy, we can build learners' self-efficacy as well as
increase their personal value for these goals.

*Strategy 18: Help Learners Understand That Reasonable Effort and
Knowledge Can Help Them Avoid Failure at Learning Tasks That Suit
Their Capability*

The term *failure* is used here in its broadest sense to encompass
mistakes, errors, lack of completion, poor test results, low grades,
or unskilled performance. Learners who experience an unsuccessful
learning outcome can do little to improve unless they believe
further effort or knowledge can make a difference. To paraphrase
Martin Seligman (1975), intelligence, no matter how high, cannot
manifest itself if the person believes that his own actions will have
no effect. For people who believe their failure is due to lack of
aptitude, more effort will make little difference if they share the
common belief that ability is very difficult to change. The result will
be discouragement. Bad luck, too difficult a task, and poor materials
are all attributions learners might make if they believe that personal
effort will only have a small impact on their future performance.
Sometimes these attributions are correct, but sometimes they are
rationalizations that ease adult learners' guilt and frustration.

If we have honest reasons to believe greater effort will improve performance, we need to let the learner know. Strategic knowledge can also be extremely encouraging. The idea of "working smarter" rather than just harder has its appeal. A number of studies have indicated that when learners see themselves as performing poorly, strategy attributions may be better than effort attributions because strategy attributions sustain self-efficacy beliefs longer (Zimmerman and Kitsantis, 1999). When instructors give learners an outline or show them how to use the Internet for conducting research, they can readily see how these strategies make learning easier as well as more informative.

In general, when adults see their learning as unsuccessful, attributions of effort and knowledge (or strategy) can give them hope for improving future performance. The ability to tactfully reveal these attributions to learners is an immeasurable asset: for example, "I realize you might be feeling quite bad about how this assignment turned out, but my honest estimation of your performance is that with continued effort you can definitely improve. Here are the units that seem to need further review." What seemed like defeat can actually lead to a higher level of creativity and learning.

Strategy 19: Use Relevant Models to Demonstrate Expected Learning

As Albert Bandura (1997) points out, perceptions of self-efficacy can also be acquired through vicarious learning. Observing similar adults successfully perform a learning task can be a powerful positive influence on adults' performance expectations. A number of years ago I had a short break with reality and thought that rock climbing could be fun. I actually took a course entitled Rock 101. The instructor was at least 15 years younger than I and was quite lean and muscular. He showed us the proper technique for climbing as he scrambled up a vertical cliff like a spider on a web. When he asked for the first volunteer, I found my eyes locked on the ground below my shoes and I could hear my mind saying, "No way." But my friend David, older than I and a bit portly, did volunteer. And he made it to the top of the cliff on his first try. I was the second volunteer. What seemed impossible was the beginning of a 17-year avocation for which I am still grateful.

Because many adults often find learning unfamiliar as well as abstract, they honestly wonder if they can do it. Unlike many young children, most adults are not enthusiastic volunteers for a public attempt at a new learning task. Any time we can provide examples of people who are similar to the learners and are successfully performing the expected learning activity, we have taken a significant step toward enhancing their self-efficacy. This strategy is originally derived from the research of Albert Bandura: "Seeing similar others perform successfully can raise efficacy expectations in observers who then judge that they too possess the capabilities to master comparable activities. . . . Vicariously derived information alters perceived self-efficacy through ways other than social comparison. . . . Modeling displays convey information about the nature and predictability of environmental events. Competent models also teach observers effective strategies for dealing with challenging or threatening situations" (1982, pp. 126–127).

With adults, modeling is one of the best strategies for enhancing performance in new learning. Once I starting using this strategy in my courses, the quality of work and motivation among adult students rose dramatically. For the research course, I have three to five former students with the same demographics as my current students come to the first class session. All the former students were successful in the course and their reports (graded and with written comments) are duplicated and available for the current students. As a panel, the former students discuss with the current students what their beginning attitudes toward the course were (not always positive), how they worked and cooperated to learn, what challenges they faced and surmounted, and so forth. About halfway through the panel session, I leave so that the entire group can converse without my involvement or monitoring. This modeling process has been so effective in lowering tension, raising learner performance expectations and self-efficacy beliefs, and enhancing the quality of student work that I have never abandoned it. For my other courses, if I do not have former students join us, I have their videos, papers, and projects available for examination and discussion.

Film and video technology provide wonderful ways to organize and demonstrate what we want adult learners to achieve. If a skill, technique, or discussion can be learned and demonstrated, today's technology enables us to bring it to our learners and in a concrete way to raise their expectations for success. Observational learning can be a very specific and structured process that learners use to self-regulate their learning. As such, it has been researched in academics and athletics. These studies offer strong evidence that people who learn vicariously and adapt the model's methods to their own learning are more successful and motivated than people who rely on solely individual means to learn (Zimmerman and Kitsantas, 2005).

Strategy 20: Encourage the Learners

Bandura (1997) sees a useful role for persuasion as a positive influence on self-efficacy. If a trustworthy person can convince us that we can accomplish something with reasonable effort, we may believe that person and make a more sincere and persistent attempt to accomplish the task. Rather than calling such "convincing" persuasion, I prefer the word *encouragement* and what it implies.

Encouragement is any behavior by which we show the learner that (1) we respect the learner as a person, no matter what is learned, (2) we trust and believe in the learner's effort to learn, and (3) the learner *can* learn. An adult who perceives that the instructor's respect is contingent only on learning performance may feel dehumanized. Such a criterion for acceptance by the instructor denies the adult's other worthy qualities and makes the person into a "thing" that learns without feelings or dignity. The primary foundation for encouragement is our caring about and acceptance of the learners. This caring and acceptance creates the context in which we choose ways to show confidence and personal regard for the learners' efforts and achievements. We can encourage learners in the following ways.

• *For each learning task, demonstrating a confident and realistic expectancy that the learner will learn.* Essentially we are conveying the message, "You can do it," but without implying that the task is easy or simple. Whenever we tell learners that something is easy, we have placed them in a lose-lose dilemma. If they successfully do the task, they feel no pride because the task was easy in the first place. If they fail, they feel shame because the task was implied to be simple.

• *Giving recognition for effort.* Any time we seriously attempt to learn something, we are taking a risk. Intentional learning is a courageous act. No one learns 100 percent of the time. Some risk is usually involved. We can help by acknowledging learners' effort and by respecting their persistence. Any comment that expresses the idea "I like the way you try" can help learners understand that we value their effort. When insecure learners know that we honestly esteem their effort as they are working toward achievement, it does a great deal to reduce the debilitating effects of performance anxiety. This acknowledgement of effort need not exclude positive expectations for performance or achievement.

• *Minimizing mistakes while the learner is struggling.* Sometimes learning is like a battle. The critical edge between advancement and withdrawal or between hope and despair is fragile at best. Our emphasis on a learner's mistakes at such a moment will accentuate whatever pessimistic emotions the learner is already feeling and is a way to encourage self-defeat.

• *Emphasizing learning from mistakes.* Help adults see a mistake as a way to improve future learning. When we help them learn from a mistake, we directly show them how thinking and trying are in their best interest and that we have confidence they will learn.

- *Showing faith in the adult's capacity as a learner.* This faith translates into "sometimes it may be difficult, but I believe you can learn, and I will work with you toward that goal." Whenever we give up on a learner, we also give up on ourselves as instructors. Realistically, some of our learners may prefer that we give up because it makes it easier for them to stop trying. By showing consistent trust in the learners' capacity to achieve, we maintain our responsibility as instructors, and we emphasize the learners' responsibility for continued effort.

- *Working with the learner at the beginning of difficult tasks.* It's amazing what can be lifted and moved with just a little help. Sometimes learners are momentarily confused or do not know what to do next. As a form of early scaffolding, our proximity and minimal assistance can be just enough to help a learner find the right direction, continue involvement, and gain the initial confidence to proceed with learning.

- *Affirming the process of learning.* We need to acknowledge all parts of the learning endeavor—the information seeking, the studying, the practicing, the cooperating, and so forth. If we wait for the final product—the test results, the project, or any other final goal—we may be too late. Some learners may have given up along the way. Our delay also may imply that the learners should wait until the end of learning to feel good about learning. Even waiting for some minimal progress can sometimes be a mistake. Learning does not follow a linear progression; there are often wide spaces, deep holes, dead ends, and regressions. Real encouragement says the task of learning is itself important and emphasizes the intrinsic value of the entire process of learning.

Establishing Challenging and Attainable Learning Goals

One of the strongest influences on self-efficacy is how the learner interprets and sets the goal for learning (Bandura, 1997; Brophy, 2004). This process influences expectancy for success in learning and has a strong impact on self-efficacy beliefs. It is possible that a learner could initially like a subject, feel positively toward the instructor, believe she is very effective in the subject, but still not expect to succeed because there is not enough time to study for the particular training or course unit. For adults, the decision to invest time in a learning activity may be as important as the decision to invest money or effort (Lowe, 1996). Sometimes adults do not understand what is necessary to do well in a course, and this confusion leads to discouragement. Establishing challenging and attainable learning goals with adults strongly supports their self-efficacy and reduces confusion and time concerns.

In my experience, this motivational purpose and the strategies that accomplish it are essential to adult self-efficacy in training and courses. Most adults do not use the language of strategies like *goal setting* and *contracting*, but they do, internally and silently, wonder, "Can I do this?" or "Can I do well in this course?" They base their answers on the syllabus, the course or training requirements, the criteria for assessment, and prior experience.

From a neurological perspective, when we anticipate a learning goal we are attempting (1) to reduce uncertainty, (2) to use prior knowledge from previous mastery experiences to estimate how to accomplish the goal, and (3) to understand whether the learning goal represents an accomplishment that we value. If this information "fits," the learning goal makes sense and looks attainable. In that first hour of a new course, when we are looking at course content and requirements, our brains are looking for the *big picture*, for patterns that ideally say, "From this information, I know that I can do this and I want to."

When expectancy for success is high and adults can commit to reaching the given learning goals, there is usually an increase in their performance and motivation (Locke and Latham, 2002). When their expectancy for success is low, adults tend to protect their well-being by remaining withdrawn or negative. Instructors often interpret this as apathy or resistance, but for the learners it is usually self-protection, more to do with realistic doubt than with being irascible. In such instances, clearly demonstrating that the learning goal is concretely possible to achieve can be a significant positive influence on learners' attitudes.

Strategy 21: Make the Criteria of Assessment as Fair and Clear as Possible

Assessment is thoroughly discussed in Chapter Eight. However, because learning goals and assessment procedures go hand in hand in the beginning of most adult education courses and training, we need to pay some attention to assessment as an attitudinal issue. In the view of most adults, how they are assessed will play a crucial role in determining their expectation for success. The outcomes of assessment in the form of grades and quantitative scores can powerfully influence their self-efficacy beliefs as well as their access to careers, further education, and financial aid such as scholarships and grants. Therefore, assessment criteria are extremely relevant to developing or inhibiting a positive attitude toward learning. Whenever we formulate learning goals, we should simultaneously address assessment procedures and criteria.

If learners understand the criteria and agree to them as fair, they know which elements of performance are essential. They can more easily self-assess and self-determine their learning as they proceed (Angelo and Cross, 1993). This should enhance their motivation, because they can anticipate the results of their learning and regulate how they learn (studying, writing, practicing, and so on) with more certainty. Assessment criteria help them to gauge the relationship between their effort and the learning outcomes of that effort. This reflection encourages both strategy and effort attributions that also support their motivation.

In general, we ought to demonstrate how we or the learners can assess the quality of their learning: what is being looked for in the assessment, how it is valued, and how this value will be indicated. This discussion of evaluation usually entails clarifying terms, standards, and calibration of measurement, so that all of us come to a common understanding and agreement about how these indicators of learning are applied, scored, and integrated. As the current cliché in assessment theory goes, "There are no more secrets!" We want learners from day one to know what assessment looks like, how it's done, and by what criteria their work is appraised. If we want learners to succeed, they should not have to guess what is expected of them. We will be more explicit about this with examples in Chapter Eight. A very good text in terms of illustrations and case studies of assessments, many of which are applicable to adults, is *Classroom Assessment Techniques: A Handbook for College Teachers* (Angelo and Cross, 1993).

The less mystery there is surrounding evaluation criteria, the more likely learners are to direct their own learning. We are wise to allow for questions and suggestions about assessment. It is very beneficial to make available some examples of concrete learning outcomes—past tests, papers, projects, and media—that you have already evaluated using the same criteria, thus giving learners realistic illustrations of how you have applied them. There is a direct connection between this strategy and Strategy 19—the use of relevant models to demonstrate expected learning. Personally or through exemplars of their past work, former students can demystify the criteria of assessment and inspire their peers to relevant accomplishments.

Strategy 22: Help Learners Understand and Plan for the Amount of Time Needed for Successful Learning

As we have discussed, time is precious to adults. In a study focused on why adults leave college before completing their degree, lack of time was the dominant theme (Wlodkowski, Mauldin, and Campbell, 2002). Adults in this study repeatedly made reference to competing priorities such as work and family. In general, they did not have enough time to meet the demands of schoolwork and to care for their families and perform their jobs. A quote from a woman in the study amplifies how overwhelming school can be for adults: "I felt like I was going in four directions at the same time and just finding enough time to drive to school was becoming a problem" (p. 7).

It is often very difficult for adult learners to estimate the amount of time a given course, assignment, or practice regimen might take. Some will overestimate. Some will underestimate. Others will procrastinate, as busy people often do. If a learning activity will require a significant amount of time, it is best for learners to know this so that they can plan more effectively, avoid procrastination, and begin to set *proximal goals*—goals that make sense and are achievable in the near future with reasonable effort (Brophy, 2004).

A proximal goal is the motivational premise behind the expression "One day at a time." Often we have to break down or segment an ultimate goal into subgoals in order to have the sense of self-efficacy to achieve it. This approach may be as helpful for successfully completing a course or a project as it is for recovery from an addiction. In education, we may not realize it, but when we outline the steps, responsibilities, and timelines for completing a project, we are often setting proximal goals—and significantly increasing our chances for a successful and motivating accomplishment.

Strategy 23: Use Goal-Setting Methods

This is a more individualized approach to increasing adult learners' expectancy for success and their self-efficacy. Efficacious learners persist longer, especially when they encounter difficulties (Bandura, 1997).

The advantage of goal setting is that it brings the future into the present and allows learners to become aware of what they need to do to have a successful learning experience. Goal setting not only prevents learners from unrealistic expectations but also gives them a chance to plan and self-regulate specifically for obstacles that prevent success (Zimmerman and Kitsantas, 2005). Using the goal-setting model, learners feel more control and can calculate what to do to avoid wasting time or experiencing self-defeat. Thus, before even beginning the learning task, they know that the effort they expend will be worthwhile and that there is a good probability for success. As postsecondary education continues to evolve into a greater number of alternative formats, learning more frequently involves projects and complex tasks (Wlodkowski and Kasworm, 2003). For these forms of performance assessment, goal setting is a real asset to the instructor and the adult learner.

There are many different methods of goal setting (Locke and Latham, 2002). The example that follows is an eclectic adaptation of various models in the literature. If the learner is to have a good chance of accomplishing the learning goal, the instructor and learner should consider the following eight criteria together. In order to take these criteria beyond abstract suggestions, I present an actual case from my experience to exemplify how each of the criteria can be applied.

Yolanda Scott-Machado, whose tribal affiliation is Makah, is an adult learner in a research course. To learn more about a variety of skills and concepts including research design, validity, reliability, sampling procedures, statistical analysis, and operationalization, Yolanda wants to design, conduct, and report a research study in an area of personal interest. She has questions about the concept of learning styles, especially as it is applied to American Indians. She wants to carry out a study to determine if urban Indian high school students, when compared to urban European American high school students, score significantly higher in the field-sensitive mode as measured by Witkin's Group Embedded Figures Test. This is an ambitious study for a beginning research student. We launch the goal-setting process by examining the criterion of achievability.

---

1. *Discuss whether the goal is achievable.* Can the learner accomplish the learning goal with the skills and knowledge at hand? If not, is there any assistance available and how dependable is that assistance? (These questions directly address learner self-efficacy beliefs.)

Yolanda feels confident, and her competent completion of exercises in class substantiates that confidence. She is also a member of a class cooperative learning group and values her peers as knowledgeable resources. We work out a plan that includes a preliminary conference with peers to garner their support, and a follow-up call to me.

Is there enough time to reach the goal? If not, can more time be found, or should the goal be divided into smaller goals? (These questions can help to establish proximal goals.)

This question is a bit tricky. Yolanda will need at least fifty students in each of her comparison groups. At the minimum, she will need to involve two high schools. Can she get the necessary permission? Who will do the testing, and when? The bureaucratic maneuvering and testing could drag on and complicate the study.

---

2. *Determine how progress will be measured.* In what specific ways will the learner be able to gauge progress toward achievement of the goal? In many circumstances, this measure can be something as simple as problems completed, pages read, or exercises finished. To respect learners' different ideas of how to accomplish their long-range goals, you should schedule meetings to talk about their evolving experience.

We decide that the most important "next step" is for Yolanda to write a research proposal and bring it in for a meeting with me. Then she can plan a schedule for completion of the study.

3. *Determine how much the learner desires the goal.* Why is the goal important to the learner? Is the goal something the learner wants to do or values accomplishing? The learner may have to do it or perhaps should do it, but is the goal wanted as well? If it isn't, then the learner's satisfaction level and sense of volition will be less. Goal setting can be used for "must" situations, but it is best handled if you are clear about it and admit to the learner the reality of the situation to avoid any sense of manipulation. When possible, aligning the goal with other, desired outcomes is helpful. This alignment can increase a learner's motivation, much as a railroad engine gains power by hooking up with another moving engine.

Yolanda wants to do this study. She believes that certain teaching practices derived from learning styles research may not apply to some Northwest Indian tribes or urban Indians. Because educators so often advocate these methods for teaching Indians, Yolanda believes more caution about their use may be necessary. In addition, she is considering advanced graduate study in psychology and views research skills as an important addition to her résumé.

4. *Create a consistent way to focus on the goal (optional).* Some learners feel the need for a daily plan that keeps their attention focused on their goal; the plan helps them avoid forgetting or procrastinating. For others, such an idea may seem oppressive. Possible reminders are outlines, chalkboard messages, and daily logs.

Yolanda finds this option unnecessary.

---

5. *Preplan to consider and remove potential obstacles.* The question for the learner is, What do you think might interfere with reaching your goal? Obstacles may range from other obligations to the lack of a quiet place to study. Planning ahead to reduce these barriers should decrease their obstructive force and give the learner a strategy to contend with them.

When I ask Yolanda about potential obstacles, she remarks that her "plate is pretty full" and probably the biggest obstacle would be to take on something else while she is conducting the research project. We joke about practicing to say no and eventually decide to leave this possibility to her best judgment.

---

6. *Identify resources and learning processes with the learner.* Engaging the learner in a dialogue about how she would like to reach the learning goal can be a very creative process. This is the time to consider the learner's various talents, strategies, and preferred ways of knowing. Will accomplishing the learning goal involve media, art, writing, or some other possibility? What form should it take—a story, a research project, or a multimedia presentation? Identifying outside resources—such as library materials, local experts, exemplary models, or films—aids and sometimes inspires the entire learning process.

Yolanda decides to review the literature on learning styles, especially as it refers to American Indians and other native people. She also chooses to interview a professor at another university and an Indian administrator at a local school district. She decides that her format for reporting her study will be the conventional research thesis outline.

---

7. *The learner makes a commitment.* This is a formal or informal gesture that indicates the learner's agreement to accomplish the learning goal. It can range from a shared copy of notes taken at the meeting to a learning contract (Strategy 24). This affirms the learner's determination and acknowledges the shared resolve of the learner and the instructor, building trust, motivation, and cooperation for further work together.

Yolanda composes a contract, which we agree on at our next meeting. (Her contract appears as an example in the discussion of Strategy 24.)

---

8. *Arrange a goal review schedule.* To maintain progress and refine learning procedures, the learner and the instructor may need to stay in contact. Because of the way time varies in its meaning and feeling to different people, contact can occur at regular or irregular intervals. The main idea is that trust, support, and the opportunity for adjusting with new strategies continue.

If progress has deteriorated, reexamine the criteria. Asking, for example, "What did you do instead?" may help uncover hidden distractions or competing goals. Or search for informative feedback (Brophy, 2004) with questions such as, What's working and why? and What needs to change (or improve) and how?

We have three meetings at irregular intervals prior to Yolanda's completion of an excellent study. To find a large enough sample for her research, she eventually involves five high schools. Her research indicates that urban Indian high school students are more field-independent than European American high school students, suggesting the possibility that research conducted on American Indian learning styles may be misleading and is far from conclusive across tribes and regions.

Strategy 24: Use Learning Contracts

Although they can be used independently, learning contracts are an excellent complement to goal setting. Adult educators consider them to be an effective means for fostering self-direction, volition, improvement of learning performance, and expectancy for success among adult learners (Berger, Caffarella, and O'Donnell, 2004). Learning contracts can accommodate individual and cultural differences in experience, perspective, and capabilities (Lemieux, 2001; Tsang, Paterson, and Packer, 2002). They are effective for assisting adults in understanding their learning interests, planning learning activities, identifying relevant resources, and becoming skilled at self-assessment (Brookfield, 1986). The ability to write contracts is a learned skill, and teachers may have to spend considerable time helping learners focus on realistic as well as manageable activities. In my experience as a teacher, I have found Stephen Brookfield's observation to be instructive: "Particularly in institutions where other departments and program areas conform to a more traditional mode, learners will often find it unsettling, inconvenient, and annoying to be asked to work as self-directed learning partners in some kind of negotiated learning project. Notwithstanding the fact that learners may ultimately express satisfaction with this experience, initially, at least, there may be substantial resistance. It is crucial, then, that learners be eased into this mode . . . and faculty must make explicit from the outset the rationale behind the adoption of these techniques" (1986, pp. 82–83).

Learning contracts tailor the learning process to the individual and provide maximum flexibility for content, pace, process, and outcome. They usually detail in writing what will be learned, how the learning will be accomplished, the period of time involved, and the evidence and criteria to be used in assessing the learning. The learner can construct all, most, or part of the contract depending on her and the instructor's knowledge of the subject matter, the resources available, the restrictions of the program, and so on. For example, what is learned (the objective) may not be negotiable, but how it is learned may be wide open to individual discretion.

The contract document usually consists of the categories shown here (Berger, Caffarella, and O'Donnell, 2004):

1. Learning goal or objective. (What are you going to learn?) For further elaboration, see Strategy 6 in Chapter Five.
2. Choice of resources, strategies, and activities for learning. (How are you going to learn it?)
3. Target date or timeline for completion.
4. Evidence of accomplishment. (How are you going to demonstrate your learning?)
5. Evaluation criteria and validation of learning. (What criteria will be used to evaluate the learning, and how and by whom will the evidence of learning be evaluated and confirmed?)

The following are two examples of learning contracts. The first covers a specific skill to be accomplished in a short period of time in an undergraduate communication skills course. The second is the contract submitted by Yolanda Scott-Machado.

Sample Contract: Paraphrasing Skills

Learning goal. To apply and learn paraphrasing skills for actual communication situations.

Learning resources and activities. View videotapes of paraphrasing scenarios. One hour of role playing paraphrasing situations with peers.

Timeline. One week (dates specified).

Evidence of accomplishment. Participate in paraphrasing exercises under instructor's supervision and monitoring.

Evaluation criteria and validation of learning. Contribute appropriate paraphrasing responses to 80 percent of the communications from my peers. Eighty percent of my responses reflect the meaning of these communications as assessed by my instructor.

Sample Contract: Research Project of Yolanda Scott-Machado

Learning goal. To conduct a research study to examine if urban Indian high school students when compared to urban European American high school students have a significant perceptual difference as measured by Witkin's Group Embedded Figures Test.

Learning resources and activities. Conduct a review of the literature on learning styles, especially as this concept relates to American Indians. Interview a professor at the University of Washington who specializes in the relation of learning styles to people of color. Also, interview a local American Indian school administrator who has responsibility for a number of projects involving American Indian students. Carry out the research while remaining in communication with my cooperative learning group and our teacher.

Timeline. Complete study, analyze data, and submit first draft of the research report two weeks before the end of the semester to allow for revisions.

Evidence of accomplishment. Final draft of research study conducted according to the design agreed upon with my teacher.

Evaluation criteria and validation of learning. A self-evaluation indicating what I learned and why it was important to me. Validation by the teacher regarding the quality of my research design and its analysis; also his assessment of the cogency of my discussion and conclusion as drawn from the research evidence. For this validation, he will compare the elements and structure of my research report to the studies offered as excellent models of research on the first day of our course.

Nancy Berger, Rosemary Caffarella, and Judith O'Donnell (2004) have some helpful ideas about the use of learning contracts with learners who are inexperienced or unfamiliar with them.

- Enlist the aid of learners more familiar with designing learning contracts to help those beginning this process.

- Give learners with less experience more time to develop their plans.

- Allow the less-experienced learners to develop a mini-learning plan first and then complete a more thorough one.

- Give learners clear guidelines for developing contracts. Supply a number of diverse samples to encourage a variety of learning processes and outcomes.

- Expect that the *evaluation criteria and validation of learning* is likely to be the most challenging aspect of constructing the learning contract. Adult learners do not usually have much practice in creating criteria to evaluate their own work and will need your support and coaching.

In general, the use of learning contracts is, like good writing, often a process of revision and refinement. Using collaborative groups, remaining open to feedback from learners about their contracts, and staying flexible and ready to make reasonable adjustments are ways to ensure their effective use.

Creating Relevant Learning Experiences

The last section of this chapter focuses on relevance as a means to foster a positive attitude toward learning. The strategies described here could have been placed along with those aligned with *attitude toward the subject* (Strategies 12 through 15). However, the following strategies originate more from literature and research related to a sociocultural perspective, the understanding that culture and a social world mediate learning (Nasir and Hand, 2006). Each strategy creates learning activities that respect the adult learner's perspective and unique capabilities. Also embedded in these strategies is a connection between what is learned and the usefulness of that learning by the learner in the real world (Gardner, 2006).

As discussed in Chapter Four, for adults to see learning as truly relevant it has to be connected to who they are, what they care about, and how they perceive and know. If I were to base this book *only* on personal experience, I would say the quickest path to boredom and resistance among adults is an irrelevant lesson. Conversely, the fastest avenue to their interest and involvement is a relevant lesson. Due to our instinct for survival, evolved over millennia, our brains just do not tolerate what does not seem to matter to us (Ahissar and others, 1992). As soon as we get a blip on our mental radar of something that strikes us as aimless or senseless or insignificant, we are biopsychologically on our way out. Gone. Those eyeballs glazing over are the real thing. The following strategies give us a set of practices to relevantly respond to the learning preferences and differences among diverse adults.

Strategy 25: Use the Entry Points Suggested by Multiple Intelligences Theory as Ways of Learning about a Topic or Concept

When we offer adults only a single way of knowing a concept or problem, they are forced to understand it in a most limited and rigid fashion. By encouraging learners to develop multiple ways to engage a subject and having them relate these representations to one another, we can move away from the tyranny of the "correct answer" so often dominant in education and arrive at a fuller understanding of our world. Most knowledgeable and innovative practitioners of any discipline are characterized precisely by their capacity to access critical concepts through a variety of routes and apply them to a diversity of situations. In addition, this overall approach makes us colearners with our students and more likely to take their views and ideas seriously; all of us can thus develop a more comprehensive understanding.

Howard Gardner (1993) and teacher/researchers in the Adult Multiple Intelligences Study (Viens and Kallenbach, 2004) propose that most concepts and topics can be approached through a variety of "entry points" (engagement activities) that, roughly speaking, map onto the multiple intelligences (listed in Table 2.1) and allow all learners relevant access. Gardner (1993) advocates thinking of any topic as a room with at least five doors or entry points. Awareness of these entry points can help us introduce a topic with materials, formats, and activities that accommodate the wide range of cultural backgrounds and profiles of intelligences found among a group of diverse adults.

Let us look at these five entry points one by one, with one example from the natural sciences (photosynthesis) and one from the social sciences (democracy) to show how each entry point might be used in approaching these concepts.

1. Using the *narrational* entry point, we present a story or narrative account about the concept. In the case of photosynthesis, we might describe with appropriate vocabulary this process as

it occurs in several plants or trees living in our environment, including any differences. In the case of democracy, we could trace its beginnings in ancient history and make comparisons with the early development of constitutional government in a selected nation.

2. Using the *logical-quantitative* entry point, we approach the concept with numerical considerations or deductive and inductive reasoning processes. We could approach photosynthesis by creating a timeline of the steps of photosynthesis and a chemical analysis of the process. In the case of democracy, we could create a timeline of presidential mandates, congressional bills, constitutional amendments, and Supreme Court decisions that broadened democratic principles among people in the United States. Or we could analyze the arguments used for and against democracy by relevant political leaders throughout history.

3. The *foundational* entry point explores the philosophical and terminological facets of a concept. This approach is appropriate for people who like to pose fundamental questions—of the sort that we often associate with young children and with philosophers. A foundational corridor to photosynthesis might be the comparison of a transformative experience of our own or of a relevant individual, family, or institution with the process of photosynthesis, assigning parallel roles as they fit (for example, source of energy, catalyst, and so on). A foundational means of access to democracy could be a discussion of the root meaning of the word, the relationship of democracy to other forms of decision making and government, and the reasons one might prefer or not prefer a democratic rather than a socialist political philosophy.

4. Using the *esthetic* entry point, we emphasize sensory or surface features to appeal to learners who favor an artistic stance toward life. In the case of photosynthesis we could look for visual, musical, or literary transformations that imitate or parallel photosynthesis and represent them in artistic formats such as painting, dance,

mime, video, cartooning, or a dramatic sketch. With reference to democracy, we could experience and consider the variations of artistic performance that are characterized by more individual control as opposed to more collaborative control: an orchestra as compared to a string quartet, ballet compared to experimental modern dance, a stage play compared to improvisational acting, and so on.

5. The last entry point is the *experiential* approach. Some people learn best with a hands-on approach, dealing directly with the materials that embody or convey the concept. In studying photosynthesis, such individuals might carry out a series of experiments involving photosynthesis. Learners dealing with democracy might consider a relevant news issue and "enact" a democratic procedure, whether a legislative, judicial, or executive process. Then they could enact another approach to the same issue, from a less democratic country, and compare their experience of the two diverse processes.

If learning may be deeper and more fully understood through several entry points, we can encourage learners to use a combination of engaging activities for the same concept. This approach is based on the understanding that most intelligences combine to process a domain of learning such as science (Gardner, 2006). Instructors can make available several entry points at the beginning or over time. For example, we might request learners to use the narrational, logical-quantitative, and experiential entry points to learn about photosynthesis. Or we might suggest using two out of three of these entry points. In this way, we also improve the chances that diverse learners with different ways of knowing and differing intelligence profiles can find relevant and engaging ways of learning. Learners may also suggest entry points of their own design. The use of technology, such as films, the Internet, and interactive software, can further enhance these efforts. Exhibit 6.1 presents another example of a concept with five entry points.

Exhibit 6.1   Learning Activities Based on the Five Entry Points from Multiple Intelligences Theory

Concept: All living things are systemically related.
Related principle: All human behaviors affect the earth.

Entry Point	Example
Narrational	Report incidents that show the effects of human behavior on distant places. Identify behaviors according to whether they harm or benefit the planet.
Logical-quantitative	Choose a harmful but inevitable human systemic influence, such as carbon emissions. After finding data that quantify the effects from this systemic influence, search for cultural, economic, and political factors that inhibit or exacerbate this influence.
Foundational	Reflect on your influence on the local environment. Consider which behaviors improve the environment and which pollute it. Examine the beliefs and values that appear critical to each set of behaviors. Create a personal environmental philosophy.
Esthetic	Choose from the following options: create a sketch, a photo journal, a video, a song, or a poem to depict systemic relationships in one's own environment.
Experiential	Create mini-environments in a yard or terrarium. Experiment with such influences as temperature, water, and pollutants. Observe and report effects on various life forms.

For over a decade, in most of the courses I have taught, I have used these five entry points of multiple intelligences theory as an instructional strategy. Because this approach provides relevant learning activities that consistently receive positive and creative responses from learners, I include it in the syllabus for particular courses such as Adult Development and Learning. I also use multiple intelligences theory for creating "exit points," what students can choose to do to demonstrate their learning (Viens and

Kallenbach, 2004). Exhibit 6.2 presents the possible exit points for my Adult Development and Learning course. Students are provided with models for each exit point.

Exhibit 6.2   Five Exit Points Based on Multiple Intelligences Theory to Demonstrate Learning for an Adult Development and Learning Course

Exit Point	Example
Narrational	Keep a record in writing — a journal — of your ideas, questions, and reflections related to the texts, readings, and classes for this course. After completing the reading requirements and the last class, submit your journal and a summary of the key questions, themes, discoveries, and connections and patterns that you became aware of through this process.
Logical-quantitative	Select a major theory of adult learning and a major theory of adult development. Compose a critique of each as it applies to your own work or professional setting. Indicate and exemplify the stated or unstated assumptions, biases, logical inconsistencies, and strengths of argument.
Foundational	Choose yourself, an individual who would reveal an in-depth personal history to you, or a relevant available biography. Plot the person's life according to key transformational events and periods. Explain the revealed pattern according to at least two adult developmental theories and their related principles.
Esthetic	Using various media (sketches, video, photos, and so forth), create a collage or a mixed media project that illustrates your personal theory of adult development and learning.
Experiential	Create a comprehensive instructional design to teach a complex concept or skill to a group of adult learners similar to those you either work with or envision teaching or training. Include strategies for transfer to the workplace in your overall design. Provide a summative rationale describing the important adult learning concepts and theories that have contributed to your design.

Although multiple intelligences theory has been used in adult education, its basic tenets have not been systematically validated (Merriam, Caffarella, and Baumgartner, 2006). Gardner respects this critique and invites further scientific investigation but of the sort that is intelligence-fair and contextualized in real life settings (Gardner and Moran, 2006). My experience with this theory is that it generally provides a more effective instructional approach than any other theory of learning styles for engaging culturally different adult learners. In terms of relevance, it is the most unified and generative strategy I know for responding to both their individual preferences for learning and their unique ways of processing information.

Strategy 26: Make the Learning Activity an Irresistible Invitation to Learn

The first time people experience anything new or in a different setting, they form an impression that will have a lasting impact (Scott, 1969). One of the best things we as instructors can do to secure a positive adult attitude from the very beginning is to make the first learning experience for a new instructional unit or workshop an irresistible invitation to learn. This does not happen because of what we say but because of how it feels to the learners as they do it. We can achieve such an effect when the learning activity meets the following five criteria.

1. *Safe*. There is little risk of the learners suffering any form of personal embarrassment from lack of knowledge, personal self-disclosure, or a hostile or arrogant social environment.

2. *Successful*. There is some form of acknowledgment, conse- quence, or product that shows that the learners are effective or, at the very least, that their effort is a worthwhile invest- ment that is connected to making progress.

3. *Interesting*. The learning activity has some parts that are novel, engaging, challenging, or stimulating.

4. *Personally endorsed.* Learners are encouraged to make choices that significantly affect the learning experience (for example, what they share, how they learn, what they learn, when they learn, with whom they learn, where they learn, or how they are assessed), basing those choices on their values, needs, concerns, or feelings. At the very least, learners have an opportunity to voice their perspectives and they clearly value their compliance.

5. *Personally relevant.* The instructor uses learners' concerns, interests, or prior experiences to create elements of the learning activity or develops the activity in concert with the learners. At the very least, a resource-rich learning environment is available to encourage learners' selections based on personal interest (for example, the library, the Internet, or a community setting).

I vividly remember experiencing these five criteria (for which the acronym is *SSIPP*) in a workshop on adapting to the culture of another country. The initial learning activity focused on learning important expressions in the language of that country. The instructor began by asking the participants which expressions they most wanted to learn and recorded them on a flip chart ("Hello," "Good-bye," "Where is the bathroom?" "How much does this cost?" and the like). The instructor thus met the two criteria of *personally endorsed* and *personally relevant.* After she taught us the expressions, she asked us to pick a partner and practice until we felt proficient. We could then move on to another partner for further practice. The instructor maintained *safety* by keeping the groups small (dyads). *Success* was immediate, and it was *interesting* (and fun) to practice with two different people. From that moment forward, participants used these expressions during breaks and free time.

I have found this strategy so useful that I have made it a mainstay in my lesson planning. Every learning activity I create is assessed according to these five criteria. When an activity does not go well,

I use the criteria to critique, refine, and improve the experience. A prototypical example of this strategy is brainstorming a relevant topic, because such brainstorming is

Safe	All answers are initially acceptable.
Successful	A list is created and acknowledged.
Interesting	Creative answers usually occur.
Personally endorsed	Answers are voluntary and self-chosen.
Personally relevant	The topic was selected because it is relevant.

Strategy 27: Use the K-W-L Strategy to Introduce New Topics and Concepts

Originated by Donna Ogle (1986), the K-W-L strategy is an elegant way to construct meaning for a new topic or concept based on the prior knowledge of adult learners. With three questions—What do I already *know?* What do I *want* to know? and What have I *learned?* —it wonderfully engages their anticipation and curiosity. Adults have a storehouse of experiences that can give extraordinary meaning to novel ideas. The K-W-L strategy offers a simple and direct way to creatively probe their vast reservoir of knowledge.

During the first phase of the strategy, the learners identify what they *know* about the topic. Whether the topic is the gross domestic product, phobias, or acid rain, this is a nonthreatening way to list some of the unique and varied ways adults understand the topic. It allows for multiple perspectives and numerous historical contexts. Just think of what the possibilities might be for a diverse group of adults initiating a unit on immigration law. The discussion of what adults *know* about a topic can involve drawing, storytelling, critical incidents, and predictions.

In the second phase, the learners suggest what they *want* to know about the topic. This information may be listed as questions or subtopics for exploration and research. For example, if the topic were immigration law, questions might include these: Where do most immigrants come from today? Ten years ago? Fifty years ago? What was the last significant immigration law enacted by Congress? Is there evidence that immigrants deny work opportunities to established citizens of the United States? What are some noteworthy contributions of recent immigrants? These questions can serve as ideas for using the five entry points of multiple intelligences theory discussed in Strategy 25. For example, a narrational entry point could be used to look at immigration history, and an experiential and logical-quantitative entry point could be used to conduct research on recent immigration patterns. The K-W-L strategy also meets the five criteria for irresistible learning.

In the last phase, the learners identify what they have *learned*, which may be the answers to their questions, important related information, and new information that counters, confirms, or deepens their prior knowledge.

In this chapter, we have looked at numerous ways to build more positive attitudes toward learning. Which strategies you select will be based on your sensitive awareness of yourself, the adults learning with you, and the learning situation. When your subject is relevant and adults want to learn what is before them, you have an excellent beginning for a successful learning experience. For such a fortunate motivational environment, it is important for the learners' attitudes to be positive—toward you, the subject, their own self-efficacy, and the specific learning goal. In such a situation, you have at the outset a strong motivational state to support instruction and learning. Selecting and carrying out the strategies from this chapter early in your instructional design can benefit the entire learning community.

7

Enhancing Meaning in Learning Activities

*Against boredom even the gods themselves struggle
in vain.*

Friedrich Nietzsche

For centuries, boredom has been a nemesis to the quality of life. Rare is the individual who seems able to continuously escape its oppressive grasp. Work and learning appear to be two areas where people are especially vulnerable to the spontaneous emergence of this vague but powerful emotion. Unlike so many other predicaments of human existence, boredom threatens us not so much with something terrible that may happen but with the realization that *nothing* may happen.

At first glance, boredom seems simple to define and easy to explain. It is often considered to be an individual's emotional response to an environment that is perceived to be monotonous (Davies, Shackleton, and Parasuraman, 1983). However, when adults are interviewed, the reasons they give for feelings of boredom include constraint, meaninglessness, lack of interest and challenge, repetitiveness, and the never-ending nature of a task or job.

From a neuroscientific perspective, when we are bored, environmental complexity is lacking (Jensen, 2006). There is no need for thoughtful decision making to guide us through our physical or social environment. Typically, we are not stimulated and the long-term effect is a decrease in dendritic growth and connectivity. In one study, researchers found that among young adult college students, the less the complexity in their lives, the less the complexity in their brains (Jacobs, Schall, and Scheibel, 1993). Although, we have to be careful about overgeneralization from one study, it does support the numerous animal studies that show that the negative effect from boredom on dendritic growth is greater than the positive effect from enrichment (Diamond and Hopson, 1998). To avoid boredom, we need variety, meaningful challenge, and a certain amount of unpredictability.

Although conventional wisdom would support the idea that boredom directly interferes with learning and performance, the research is far from conclusive on this issue (Renninger, Hidi, and Krapp, 1992). Alertness is reduced, but performance and memory do not appear to readily diminish even in prolonged work situations. Through means of personal will and self-regulation, people seem amazingly capable of continued effort to pay attention when they want to (Tobias, 1994). This is an important insight because the ideas, research, and methods to enhance attention have been more informative for teaching than the exploration of means to reduce boredom has been. The research on gaining, holding, and focusing attention supports the notion that learning is frequently, partly or wholly, work. Intrinsic motivation makes this effort worthwhile, but, more often than not, it does not make arduous persistence unnecessary. However, it can transform tedious perseverance into something more compelling, passionate, and flowing. Let's begin to understand how with a closer look at attention.

Attention is the "preferential processing of sensory information" from the visual, auditory, and other forms of sensory information coming into the brain (Bear, Connors, and Paradiso, 2007, p. 644). When we "pay attention" to something, we simultaneously filter out other information, balance multiple perceptions, and attach emotional significance to perceptions that warrant it.

Imagine yourself driving along a freeway in busy traffic while having a conversation with a friend sitting next to you in the front seat. In the moment you are gauging the speed of the cars in your lane and the next, checking for brake lights ahead, watching road signs for your exit, noticing the music on your sound system, hearing your friend's description of why she's leaving her job, making responsive comments and gestures, and taking note of hunger pangs that are beginning to emerge from your stomach. When suddenly you hear screeching brakes, crushing metal, and an enormous crashing sound just behind you, and you look to see. . . .

This scenario depicts the exquisite neurological juggling act that attention is. In milliseconds we are assigning emotional weight to our level of arousal, our motor orientation, novelty in the environment, our sensations and sensory information, and our memories as well as thoughts (Ratey, 2001). Remarkably, this is an involuntary process. We do not need to think before we focus on an approaching Doberman or take another sip of our flavorful latte.

To say the least, neurophysiologically, the attention system is complex. It starts in the arousal center in the brainstem, connects up through the limbic system, and extends into the cortex, eventually connecting with the frontal and parietal lobes. In *A User's Guide to the Brain*, John Ratey (2001) offers a literate and comprehensive explanation of how attention occurs in the brain and its related systems.

For the sake of instruction, I like to discuss attention in a way that separates it from interest, and involvement. In this respect, the question is, What do we do to gain learner attention? From this perspective we are talking about the earlier period of a lesson or activity, those beginning moments when we want learners to focus on what is important and to attend in the direction most beneficial to their learning. If we see attention as the *first step* in making meaning, we can select strategies that will specifically increase the probability that learners will initially engage what is pertinent to their learning. We will return to this motivational purpose later in this chapter. Now we turn to understanding how attention becomes interest, *the stronger bridge to meaning* in learning.

Engagement, Interest, and Meaning

When we first pay attention to something, it is because its variation, novelty, or relevance has emotional weight or meaning. There is a connection to prior knowledge and emotional experience. Biologically, the information passes through the limbic system to link with existing neural networks. There it activates the executive functions of the parietal and frontal lobes to be interpreted for possible meaning based on previous knowledge. Psychologically, this continuing attention or *engagement* involves more complex thinking to sift through the information and to form more connections to lead to new knowledge or learning.

Focused attention becomes *engagement* when it is persistent and joins with emotion (primarily interest) as well as metacognitive processes, such as learning strategies, to involve the person in learning. This combination of behavioral (persistence), emotional (interest), and cognitive (strategy) processing makes engaged learning an effective means to learning that is more likely to be retained (Woolfolk, 2007). Often there is a social/cultural component because we learn with instructors as well as peers. In a broader sense, socially and academically engaged adult learners are more likely to be successful in higher education (National Survey of Student Engagement, 2007).

Without engagement, learning does not have a chance to have meaning. We need the concentration and time to construct meaning from what we are learning. From my experience, among the components necessary for continuing engagement, interest seems to be the most powerful influence on adult learner engagement.

Interest has numerous definitions but for sake of pragmatism and to hold your interest, I will only discuss three. The first definition is as a basic emotion such as happiness or fear (Silvia, 2001). Due to our curiosity, we feel interested when we find things that are unique or novel or possess elements of unpredictability or surprise. From a walk in the forest to reading a book to hearing a song for the first time, we feel interest because we encounter something different or new. The emotion of interest is always a potential within us, intrinsically motivating and the basis for more enduring forms of interest such as situational interest and individual interest.

Situational Interest

The emotion of interest initiates the development of *situational interest*, a state of interest extending in time and involving focused attention and persistence, which are environmentally sustained by qualities such as surprising information and relevance (Hidi and Renninger, 2006). Unless maintained, situational interest usually has some duration but does not last over time. For example, I am browsing in a bookstore and see a book that has a bright purple cover. It's turned face down, so I can't read the title. I flip it over and in bold black lettering I read *The Many Myths of a Healthy Lifestyle: Bunk, Bull, and Poppycock for the Masses*. Now, I am curious. It wasn't what I expected. I am feeling the emotion of interest. I open the book and browse through chapters with titles like "Godforsaken Gyms and Other Rotting Places," "Accidents Waiting to Happen: Trail Bikes, Skis, and Snowshoes," and "The Hiker from Hell and His Misbegotten Friends." Now my emotion of interest is becoming situational interest. I've been browsing through the book for about twenty minutes. I don't even notice the people around me. My attention is focused and sustained. Some of the excerpts I read have me laughing. The book is a satire with enough evident humor that I purchase it. Will I ever read it? Maybe not. About one out of every five books I buy because of situational interest, I never read.

Often, it is said that children are more curious than adults. I think children are more *obviously* curious than adults. Every day as adults, we are challenged to bring order out of chaos and meaning from paradox. What is puzzling, bizarre, and surprising compels our interest as much through intrigue as through relevance. The same wonder that makes a beach a miracle of small astonishments for a child makes an adult beguiled by a gifted magician. Our beguilement is anchored in our need to remain alive. We anticipate in order to survive, whether to take a step or to enter traffic on a high-speed freeway. We make countless predictions as we live our lives. When the reality turns out to be something unexpected, our reactions can range from a reflexive startle to an enduring fascination. The better we know our learners and their cultural perspectives, the more we can do to stimulate their situational interest and then to attract their individual interest.

Individual Interest

A situational interest can become an *individual interest* when a person sustains involvement and acquires positive feelings, knowledge, and value for the particular content. An individual interest (also known as a personal interest) is "an enduring disposition to engage with particular content or activities whenever opportunities arise" (Brophy, 2004, p. 221).

Let's take the example of the satirical book I purchased. A few weeks later, for a change of pace, I pull it off the shelf and begin to read it. At this point, situational interest is motivating me. I'm looking for a few laughs and not much else. But as I read it, I find myself becoming more and more interested in it as a satire. I remember being fascinated by *Gulliver's Travels* as a college student and later by the caustic wit and irony of James Baldwin's work. I appreciate the author's cleverness and metaphors for some follies of people in pursuit of health. A situational interest (humor) contributes to and melds with my knowledge and value for satire. Through reading this book, I have developed an individual interest.

At my next visit to the bookstore, I ask what other good modern satires the manager might recommend. My individual interest continues and may bring me substantial new learning.

Well-developed individual interest is a *trait* that is relatively stable and enduring (Hidi and Renninger, 2006). We may have an individual interest in the arts, sciences, or sports that has been constant for many years. This kind of personal interest has for decades been used to match adults to educational and occupational activities (Campbell and Hansen, 1981). Individual interest can also occur because of the importance or personal significance of a topic. This latter meaning has more of a cultural bent to it and encompasses the learner's values and concerns. Personal significance is often a bridge to deeper meaning. A relevant problem usually draws out our concerns and experiences. For example, if an instructor asks, "Why is psychology important?" we might be situationally interested in an abstract sort of way. But if the instructor asks, "How has psychology helped or hindered people in your families?" the appeal is to an individual interest of much deeper meaning.

Research indicates that well-developed individual interests as a context for learning have many benefits for the learner:

- Greater resourcefulness while learning (Renninger and Shumar, 2002)

- Longer pursuit of creative endeavors (Izard and Ackerman, 2000)

- Self-regulation while learning (Sansone and Smith, 2000)

- Perseverance to work in the face of frustration (Prenzel, 1992)

Individual interests evolve out of our experience and socialization. Our families, our friends, our culture, and our opportunities contribute to these interests. Although largely about ways to more effectively teach children from working-class Mexican American families, Luis Moll's *funds of knowledge* research identifies creative ways to use culture and family as rich resources for adult individual interests (Moll and others, 1992). *Funds of knowledge* is valued information from the work, home, and spiritual life of family and community members that can be a resource for individual interests. Moll and his colleagues used interviews and home visits to access this knowledge. Here are examples of questions to find out about these funds of knowledge (Ginsberg, 2007):

- Are there topics related to your courses that you tend to talk about when you are with your family or friends? If so, what are they?

- What is important in your culture or family that you would like your instructors to know about?

- How does your life in your community differ from your life in college? (Ask follow-up questions to probe those differences.)

- What are some of the skills or talents in your home or community that you value? That you are proud of?

- What gives your family strength? Your community?

- What interesting or important topics do you talk about at home that you seldom talk about in your courses?

Finding Flow: Enhancing Meaning through Engagement and Challenge

As we have discussed, interest is a natural conduit to engagement. When we find something we value or perceive as appealing, we want to learn about it. We are more likely in such cases to be mentally, emotionally, and physically involved. And engagement is the portal for meaning. Through such total interaction we increase the complexity of an experience, deepening understanding and furthering our values or purposes through learning. All of this can occur in moments, hours, or days.

A major influence motivating this learning is feeling challenged. *Challenge* is an opportunity for engagement that offers the possibilities of deeper understanding, more refined thinking, more complex perceptions, better performance, higher goal attainment, new knowledge, and improved skills. *Challenge occurs when we have to apply current knowledge or skills to situations that require extension or development of them.* Biologically, these situations require prior knowledge and provide conditions for the assembly of new neural networks and the alteration of synaptic structures and their connections (Bear, Connors, and Paradiso, 2007).

Posing problems, conducting authentic research, and using case study methods are strategies that can engage and challenge learners with culturally relevant and therefore interesting content. For these kinds of activities, learners have to clarify distinctions, construct explanations, and create complex understandings. Often a dialogue from multiple perspectives among learners and instructors can result in a new collective understanding. When these processes are relevant, learners cannot help but heighten their own meaning and be involved. They are searching, evaluating, constructing, creating, and organizing the learning material into new or better ideas, memories, skills, understandings, solutions, or decisions. They may create a product or reach a goal. This may be a novel insight they have applied, a new skill learned, a problem solved, or a case completed. In the opinion of many scholars, engaging and challenging learning activities are among the best and most productive ways to learn (Lambert and McCombs, 1998; Donovan, Bransford, and Pellegrino, 1999; Mezirow, 2000; Keeton, Sheckley, and Griggs, 2002; Nakamura and Csikszentmihalyi, 2003).

Engagement ranges from just barely paying attention with low-cognitive and emotional involvement (listening to an important but boring lecture—you have to shift in your seat to stay alert and you need to remind yourself to pay attention and take notes) to deep and total absorption (interviewing a respected and controversial leader in a profession you aspire to—time has flown by and you've been so focused on her responses that you might have forgotten to ask the questions you needed to). Meaning and learning will vary in such situations as well. Jeanne Nakamura and Mihalyi Csikszentmihalyi define *vital engagement* as "characterized both by experiences of flow (enjoyed absorption) and by meaning (subjective significance)" (2003, p. 87). Vital engagement is a valued relationship to learning that stretches a person's capacities and is absorbing over time.

I remember when I first studied boredom. It took me about two weeks to read the initial research, which was done in the Navy during World War II. The studies described how researchers tried to find ways to keep sailors alert as they watched sonar screens for hours; a change on the screen might indicate an approaching submarine. I was fascinated and found to my surprise that boredom was a very interesting topic with insights for maintaining one's attention. Was I vitally engaged? Absolutely. We will further discuss the concept of flow and vital engagement later in this chapter.

The strategies that follow are organized according to the degree of engagement they tend to enhance and therefore the meaning and learning likely to occur. We begin with strategies for times when engagement may be waning, strategies we can use to gain and maintain adult learner attention.

How to Maintain Learners' Attention

"Pay attention or you won't learn anything!" The words have an unsettling effect. They conjure up disquieting, distant images of former teachers, harsh faces, and shrill voices. But whether we liked it or not, they were right. No attention, no engagement, no learning. As instructors we know this dictum only too well. But demanding attention from adults is one of the least effective ways to get it. In fact, pressuring people to watch or listen to us will probably only diminish their willingness to cooperate.

When we want to maintain learners' attention, we are looking for ways to evoke their alertness and to help them engage in the learning activity. Our effort usually involves an arousal of their energy and a refocusing toward the event at hand. By gaining their attention, we also open the way for or restore their interest.

Due to distraction, attention can dissipate in a moment. For adults, who have many responsibilities, mental distraction is an ever-present reality in any learning situation. The following strategies are positive and useful ways to rekindle or sustain attention.

Strategy 28: Provide Frequent Response Opportunities to All Learners on an Equitable Basis

Whenever people are in a learning situation, the amount they will publicly interact with their instructor or peers will generally affect the attention they give to the learning activity (Kerman, 1979). If learners know they are going to respond or perform in a given learning session, they have an incentive for paying attention. Their attention contributes to immediate social consequences. However, if taking notes, monitoring information, or listening to other learners has no imminent effect on their relationship to their instructor or peers, most adults, as social beings, have lost an important reason for focusing on the task at hand. Also, if they see the same few people dominating the response opportunities, they may become discouraged and resentful of the entire process.

Response opportunities are any chances that we or the learning activity provide for learners to participate or perform publicly. These include answering questions, giving opinions, demonstrating skills, and reacting to feedback. As instructors who include adult perspectives and use experiential learning, we want to instill among learners a constant awareness that they will receive opportunities to respond or perform during the learning activity.

When using this strategy for larger group discussions, there are four guidelines for maintaining a caring and respectful atmosphere. *First, we announce to the learning group that we would like to have as many people participating as possible* but that it is always OK to "pass." This gives everyone a choice, keeps the discussion safe, and particularly respects those adults who have not been socialized to respond in front of groups. It also creates an expectancy everyone can use to make sure they are prepared and alert. People do not like to be caught off guard, and many adults have had years of conditioning in situations where if they did not volunteer to respond, they were not required to do so.

Second, we make sure everyone does get an equal chance to respond or perform. Seating charts can be invaluable for this process (and some minor record keeping may be necessary). We can gently revisit those who have passed.

Third, random selection is best on a moment-to-moment basis. The unpredictability gives everyone the feeling that they may be next. However, if the skill or response demands some preparation on the learner's part, a more orderly process of selection may be beneficial. Also, calling only on volunteers can be hazardous unless everyone tends to volunteer. We have all had the experience of seeing the same few people in a group responding or performing over and over again because no one else seems to volunteer. We may find it necessary to call a moratorium on voluntary responding (a few sessions may be all that it takes) so as to give everyone a chance.

Fourth, we respect and affirm each learner's response. For most adults, the real fear of public responding is embarrassment. They need to know they will be treated respectfully for their efforts. By consistently giving learners some degree of credit for their response and by using their responses to move toward further learning, we model respect for everyone. We can respond to almost any response respectfully if we remember that even an answer that is mistaken or not well conceived can be the answer to another question.

For example, if I ask who the president was during World War I and someone responds, "Abraham Lincoln," I can say, "Yes, he was president during a very important war—the Civil War. Now let's find out who was president during World War I." I move on, smoothly and respectfully.

Most mistakes are not random (Gage and Berliner, 1998). They are usually logical and have a pattern. From a biological perspective, making mistakes is critical to new learning (Kopp and Wolff, 2000). In many instances, new information will be more than what our short-term memories can retain and it will fade quickly. Keeping up with taking notes during a lecture is a good example. We often don't get all of what's important to remember. When we discuss what we "think" we know, we need *trial-and-error* processes to make our learning more accurate and to make complex neural connections. That's what feedback during a good deep discussion with our peers and instructors does. Our brain is structured to become active when there is a discrepancy between what we expect and what actually happens. We then have a chance to make stronger and more efficient neural connections, gaining new knowledge that will last. The structure that helps us take advantage of trial-and-error learning is the anterior cingulate, located in the upper front middle of the brain (Kopp and Wolff, 2000).

By encouraging adults to respond and by helping them learn from their answers, we show respect and reduce their fears of participating. Our guiding frame of mind is to let learners know what they can competently do and then, as fluidly as possible, help them take the next possible step. In some cases, this might mean probing further, giving a hint or a second chance, waiting a while longer, soliciting help from another learner, or facilitating another answer for greater insight. As long as we avoid assuming a right-or-wrong attitude toward learning, so much is possible.

The following are some techniques for enhancing learners' reactions to response opportunities:

• When asking a question or announcing an opportunity to perform a task, wait at least three seconds before selecting a respondent (Tobin, 1987). This technique allows everyone to consider the possible answer or skill to be demonstrated. It gives learners a chance to organize themselves mentally and emotionally for their response. Many older adults need a bit more time to locate a response in their long-term memory. It also helps focus everyone's attention on the forthcoming answer or demonstration.

• When you are looking for a volunteer, ask for a show of hands in response to your question or activity and wait three to five seconds after the first indication of a volunteer before selecting a respondent. This technique has the same advantages as the previous one, and it increases the number of possible respondents from which to choose. If we tend to call on the first few volunteers, we often unwittingly "teach" the rest of the learners not to volunteer.

• While pausing before selecting a respondent, look over the entire group. This will tend to increase everyone's attentiveness because your survey encompasses the learners as a unified body.

• For longer responses and demonstrations, alert the rest of the learning community that they will be asked to respond in some fashion to what they have observed; for example: "After Zachary has presented his case study, I'd like to ask a few of you to give him your evaluation of which consultant skills were critical to his success with his client." This method invests the entire learning community in the task at hand and affirms their responsibility to their peers.

• Sometimes use light, humorous, unpredictable methods for selecting a respondent; for example: "The next people to get a chance are all those with birthdays in February," or "Well, let's see who had toast for breakfast. OK, we've got three volunteers." Or ask someone, "What's your favorite color? Blue; that's great. Now check in your group to see who is wearing the most blue, because that's who will begin the next problem for us."

• During any task where learners are working on their own or in small groups, move among them as an available resource and observer. Depending on the situation, you can comment, question, react, advise, or quietly observe. This will prevent learners from being isolated in their work, and let you provide more response opportunities for them.

Strategy 29: Help Learners Realize Their Accountability for What They Are Learning

People tend to take more seriously learning for which they are held accountable (Good and Brophy, 2003). There are times when paying attention takes real effort and determined resolve. Even under conditions that are normally stimulating, fatigue, satiation, and life's everyday problems can take their toll on adults' ability to concentrate. They are more likely to find the will to remain attentive when they clearly know that the knowledge and skills they will eventually demonstrate are directly dependent on their learning experiences.

One sees an almost automatic focusing of attention among learners when an instructor announces, "What we will cover next will be on the final exam." Although testing is a common accountability measure, there are many other possibilities, such as job performance, projects, portfolios, and skill demonstrations. Whatever the form of accountability, adults will usually intensify their concentration on the aspects of their learning experience that directly bear on what they will be held responsible for knowing. However, adults can construe accountability as a coercive force for paying attention. When we mention exams and final projects as being related to their learning tasks, they may feel threatened. Their anxiety is real. We have all felt it. Therefore, we use accountability as a means to enlist learners' attention only when necessary and in an empathic manner, not as a menacing manipulation.

One of the best ways to ensure that accountability is used in an appropriate manner is to be careful that the components of the curriculum or instructional design are interdependent and necessary for achieving and assessing the learning goal. In this way the learners know that *all* the learning activities are valuable and will help them develop the competencies they will need to acquire and exhibit. They will be reassured that there is no busywork and each learning experience contributes to the desired result. A good analogy for this approach is a recipe for a fine soufflé. Every ingredient and every process is necessary to the final outcome. Once we are certain the learning activities are a concise body of requisite experiences geared to reaching the learning goal, the following methods may help to encourage learners' attentiveness.

• Where appropriate, show that your learning program is efficiently designed to build the requisite skills and knowledge for which the learners will be held accountable. Use syllabi, outlines, models, or diagrams to briefly preview the integrated plan and related learning goals. Indicate how you will assess learners (tests, projects, job performance, and so forth) and how the assessment is functionally dependent on the learning process and content. This will help learners understand that their concentration is necessary every step of the way.

• Selectively use *manding stimuli*. Mands are verbal statements that have a highly probable consequence associated with them (Skinner, 1957). When a person yells, "Watch out!" people usually stop what they are doing and quickly check their surroundings. Instructors have available to them many mands that can focus learners' attention: "Please note this"; "Now listen closely"; "It is critical to realize that . . ."; "It will help a great deal in understanding this if you remember that . . ."; "The point that brings this all together is . . ." Wise use of mands is a valuable instructional technique for directing learners' attention to material that will make a difference in their training or education.

• Selectively employ handouts, such as outlines, models, diagrams, advance organizers (Svinicki, 2004), key concepts, and definitions. They help learners follow and focus on your lecture, presentation, or demonstration. Learners are more likely to pay attention to what is important when what is important is concretely noted, well organized, and literally within their grasp. Please be careful with PowerPoint, one of the most pervasive technological tools used today. Although an attractive process for outlines, models, and diagrams, it can reduce complicated, nuanced issues to headings and bullets (Keller, 2003).

• Intersperse lectures and demonstrations with the *think-pair-share* process (Barkley, Cross, and Major, 2005). This is a short processing method to increase attention and involvement in a relevant manner. The instructor asks learners to *think briefly about* what has been stated or observed and then to *pair up* with someone to *share* their reflections for a few minutes. It's a wonderful way to engage students in the middle of any passive learning experience with a thoughtful procedure that invites their perspectives and dialogue. The directions can be focused or general, as the following example illustrates: "Please take a minute to think about how this material relates to your own life. Then turn to a partner and have a brief conversation about your reflections." After completion of this procedure, the instructor can begin a whole-group discussion, solicit comments, list insights, take questions, or move on to the next segment of the lecture or demonstration.

Strategy 30: Provide Variety in Personal Presentation Style, Modes of Instruction, and Learning Materials

Variety has motivational effects (Gage and Berliner, 1998). It is stimulating and draws learners' attention toward its source. People tend to pay more attention to things that are changing than to things that are unchanging. However, to use variety simply for the sake of variety is not a good idea, because learning often requires that a stimulus be held in consciousness for further understanding and retention (Sweller, van Merrienboer, and Paas, 1998). That is why microscopes, photographs, and slides are so valuable to people in the pursuit of knowledge. Whenever we as instructors can change some element of the process of instruction without making that variance so extreme that it distracts learners from the subject at hand, we will probably help them pay attention. Timing variety so that it can serve as a cue to important information or skills is probably one of the best ways to use it to the advantage of motivation and learning.

Let's begin with *variety in personal presentation style* because every instructor is physically an instrument of stimulation. How instructors use their bodies and voices can be a constant source of variety for their learners. The following is a checklist of characteristics that instructors can vary to gain their learners' attention. For each characteristic there are questions that you can use to assess your presentation style during instruction.

• *Body movement.* How often do you move? In what direction? Are you ever among your learners? Are you predictable in your movements? Some movement during instruction is desirable. You can go across the room and along the sides of the room. Now and then "going in" among your learners is another variation. Such movement brings you temporarily closer to all learners and makes them more likely to pay attention to where you will be next.

• *Gestures and facial expressions.* Do you use gestures? If so, what kind? When? How animated is your face? How often do you smile? How does your body language change in relationship to learners' questions, responses, and behavior? Considering the intercultural differences in the meaning of gestures and facial expressions (see Chapter Five), it is difficult to make generalizations about how an instructor should act. In my experience, being energetic and friendly seems appealing to most adult learners.

• *Voice.* What is the tone and pitch of your voice? How often and when do these change? How is your voice used for emphasis, emotion, and support of your topic? If someone could not see you but only hear you, would your voice alone provide sufficient stimulation and variety? Of all the aspects of personal presentation style, the voice is probably the most important yet one of the least studied (Andersen and Wang, 2006). Voice is a *metacommunication*, a communication about communication. It influences everything learners hear their instructors say. Adults tend to accept the vocal quality of a message as the correct cue when a person's words seem to conflict with the way they are spoken (Hurt, Scott, and McCroskey, 1978). For example, "*That* is a good job?" would not be a compliment to adults. Because so much of instruction is talking, creative use and variation of your voice is a major asset to gaining learners' attention. Appropriate pauses can make the voice doubly effective.

• *Pauses.* When and how often do you pause? How long do you remain silent? For what purposes do you use pauses? Like variations in color, pauses are orienting stimuli that arouse our attention (Gage and Berliner, 1998). Pauses can greatly enhance verbal instruction. You can use them to break informational segments into smaller pieces for better understanding, capture attention by contrasting sound with silence, signal learners to listen, emphasize an important point, provide time for reflection, and create suspense or expectation.

The second kind of variety available to instructors is *variety in modes of instruction and in learning materials*. These are the ways in which instructors interact with learners and the activities in which learners can participate while they are learning. Lecturing, discussing, showing a video, and playing a simulation game are four modes of instruction. Learning materials are the physical resources used to instruct, such as films, books, compact discs, and computer software. Variety in instructional modes and materials will usually gain the attention of adults. Some specific guidelines are as follows:

• Vary the modality of learning (usually between auditory, visual, and tactile modes). For example, when you switch the channel of communication from auditory to visual, even momentarily, learners usually become more alert to adjust their attention

(Woolfolk, 2007). By selectively using graphs, storyboards, overhead transparencies, DVDs, and other media, learners can refocus their own attention. Although substantial research has been conducted over the years to determine which media are best for achieving particular learning goals, there are many innovative ideas but no firm conclusions (Aldrich, 2005). When it comes to visual media, it seems that the clearer and simpler the text or diagram, the more effective it is. Selectively using visual aids to draw attention to new or critical information increases their effectiveness (Delahaye and Smith, 1998). Varying the intensity of any stimuli (size, shape, color, loudness, and complexity) has been found to attract learners' attention (Day, 1981).

• Diversify the process of learning, designing interaction so that learners think or act differently from one activity to another. For example, they might move from listening to a CD to solving a problem, or they might watch a video and then discuss its contents, or they might work alone and then in small groups. In each cases, different forms of thinking, acting, and communicating are involved. Every time adults alter the process of learning, they use different mental and physical resources, which prevents fatigue and maintains energy. As the old adage goes, a change is as good as a rest. In addition, the more structures of the brain that are involved in learning, usually the better the learning and recall (Schacter, 1992). People's memory of sporting events and the associated statistics are a good example of this phenomenon.

Strategy 31: Introduce, Connect, and End Learning Activities Attractively and Clearly

Each instructional session usually comprises a number of learning activities. During this time, learners might see a video, engage in a discussion, work on a case study, and complete a self-assessment. A class session is analogous to a sporting event during which each team receives clearly delineated opportunities to exercise its skills.

Baseball gives a team three outs to score; football allows four downs to go ten yards. In sports, these units of participation have obvious beginnings and endings to simplify transitions, to focus spectators' and players' attention, and to keep the game running clearly and smoothly. In a similar manner, a learning activity is enhanced when it is distinctly introduced and clearly connected to previous and future learning activities.

Just as a kickoff tells the crowd, "Pay attention, the action is about to begin," an attractive introduction gives learners the same message. Some stimulating methods of introduction in addition to the use of media and shifts in personal presentation style are as follows:

- *Asking provocative questions:* "How many of you have ever...?" "When was the last time...?" "Did you imagine before you took this training that you were going to...?" "What do you think would happen if...?"

- *Calling on learners to become active:* ask them to help, to move, to observe, to assess, and so on.

- *Creating anticipation:* "I have been looking forward to doing this activity with you since your training session began." "This film will show the concrete advantages of applying the skills you have been learning." "This next set of problems is really tricky; let's see how we do."

- *Relating the learning activity to pop culture and current events:* "You might say the next person we are going to discuss is the Tiger Woods of the computer world." "This case study could provide lyrics for a country western ballad." "What we are going to take a look at next has been organized like an Olympic sporting event."

Connecting learning activities is a real art. Instructors make numerous transitions in any learning session. To segue automatically and fluidly helps maintain learners' attention and maximize instructional impact. The following are some helpful techniques:

- *Using organizational aids:* handouts, outlines, models, and graphs can interrelate concepts, topics, key points, and essential information.

- *Chunking:* working memory is limited to recalling about five to nine unrelated items of information. When we put such information into patterns or chunks, as we do with telephone numbers or under the headings of *what, when,* and *where* for announcements of events, we can more easily remember them (Driscoll, 2005). Looking for commonalities and chunking information into categories such as advantages and disadvantages, similarities and differences, and so on will help adult learners remember information and recall it as they move on to the next part of the lesson.

- *Indicating what the new activity relates to:* this technique involves explaining how the new activity continues the building of a skill or how it further demonstrates a concept or how it may contribute to a future learning goal.

- *Making directions and instructions for the next learning activity as clear as possible:* this technique applies to introducing as well as connecting learning activities. People often stop paying attention because they are confused about what they are supposed to do. By giving accurate directions, we can avoid unnecessary distractions.

- *Checking for understanding:* any time we provide important information, whether it is a concept or a procedure, and especially if what comes next is dependent on this information, we should take a few moments to see if everyone understands. Checking for understanding can be as simple as a question ("Are these directions clear enough?") or as thorough as a formal assessment. Not checking for understanding is one of the most common omissions I see in training and teaching. (Fact is, I *still* have to remind myself to check for understanding.)

Closure refers to how we end a learning activity and help learners feel a sense of completion. Closure not only focuses their attention but also gives them the feeling of satisfaction that naturally arises from having accomplished a learning task. Some helpful means to this end are as follows:

- *Reviewing the basic concepts or skills achieved during the learning activity:* "Before we move on, let us review the main ideas we have discussed thus far."

- *Allowing for clarification at the end of the learning activity:* "Now that we have finished this section, are there any questions about what we have done?"

- *Requesting feedback, opinions, or evaluation:* "Perhaps the best way to end this exercise would be to share with one another what we have learned from cooperating in this task."

- *Being sensitive to the possibilities for spontaneous closure that can arise from any group of learners:* for example, after the training group has voluntarily applauded the response of a colleague, the instructor can say, "I can't think of a better way to end this discussion. Let's take a break."

Strategy 32: Selectively Use Breaks, Settling Time, and Physical Exercises

Sometime learning more only means forgetting more. When learning is substantive, complex, and new, people need time to process and store this information (Stickgold, James, and Hobson, 2000). People need down time, at least a break and sometimes a rest, to connect and consolidate what they are learning (Sanes and Lichtman, 2001). After an activity where considerable new information is considered and new learning takes place, adults often actually say, "My brain is tired." And they are right. They need what Eric Jensen (2005, p. 44) calls *settling time*, a period when there is no new learning, such as a break, a walk, a meal, or relaxing in a pleasant setting. How much time? That's difficult to calibrate. There are a good number of neuroscientists researching this question, and some answers may be available in the near future. From my own experience, I try not to teach anything complex for more than an hour and fifteen minutes without a ten- to fifteen-minute break. I avoid "working lunches," and I try to limit workshops to no more than six contact hours of learning in a single day.

Many adults come to learning activities having already expended large amounts of energy in their family and workplace. Often, they become tired, even in an interesting environment. Once adults become fatigued, their ability to pay attention can readily decline, and the meaning of any activity may diminish.

In general, to provide settling time and to avoid fatigue, *selectively* give breaks or incorporate physical exercise and stretching into your instructional plan. The clock should not automatically determine when breaks are taken. Fatigue is not chronological. Our flexibility about breaks can greatly enhance how well learners feel and the amount of attention they can give. By investing fifteen minutes on a break when it is needed, learners may gain as much as an hour of alertness.

How to Evoke and Sustain Learners' Interest

When learning activities evoke and sustain interest, adults willingly participate. They may not always expend a great deal of effort, but they are learners who want to understand and focus on what they are learning.

At this point, we need to remember that *attention, interest*, and *engagement and challenge* may overlap and can occur simultaneously. What is attention-getting may become interesting, and what is interesting could naturally be a part of an engaging and challenging learning activity. Individually and in combination, they contribute to the motivational condition of *meaning*.

What categorically separates *strategies to evoke and sustain interest* from *strategies to deepen engagement and challenge* is that the latter, such as case studies, are entire methodologies. By their nature they offer considerable challenge, requiring complex and substantive interactions that usually result in a learning product. In contrast, one strategy to evoke interest is to use humor, but it doesn't require a learning product or the extensive involvement that completing a case study does. However, we might use humor to make a case study more interesting. And that's another distinction: we can often use the strategies for attention and interest to deepen engagement and challenge.

This section describes strategies that can make learning more compelling. We begin with two strategies to evoke the individual interests of adult learners.

Strategy 33: Relate Learning to Individual Interests, Concerns, and Values

By embedding the learning activity and what we say and do in current adult interests, concerns, and values, we provide learners a constant stream of *relevant* material. We are exposing them to experiences that will naturally connect to their desire for understanding. In general, the most stirring examples, analogies, supporting evidence, and current events are those that vividly touch on what people already find interesting.

One of the developmental dimensions of maturation during adulthood is a fuller awareness of deep concerns (Knowles, 1980). *Concerns* are especially likely to evoke adults' emotions. They are often more profound and more persistent than are interests because they contain an inner uneasiness. They usually represent a gap between an ideal and reality. They often indicate fear or worry about aspirations. Parents are not only *interested* in their children's health; they are frequently *concerned* about their children's health. In like manner, business owners are not only *interested* in profits but also commonly *concerned* about profits.

If learning is related to adults' concerns, their emotions will be elicited quickly. The question for instructors here is, Does anything about this topic or skill relate to adults' concerns, and if so, can I constructively deal with it? For example, the topic of sexual harassment would likely bring out learners' concerns in a seminar on ethics in the workplace. However, the instructor has to be able to deal constructively with this issue if optimal motivation is to be maintained.

Concerns often relate to human values. *Values* represent the important and stable ideas, beliefs, and assumptions that consistently affect a person's behavior (Taylor, Marienau, and Fiddler, 2000). Someone who values politics does not merely vote; that person probably also joins a political organization, donates money to political causes, writes to political representatives about selected issues, reads about political matters, acts on behalf of political candidates, and frequently talks about politics with friends. Every adult has some strong values. When these are integrated with a learning experience, the adult's interest and other emotions will surface.

When learning events correspond to people's values, people will usually feel reassured. People are pleased to hear their political beliefs supported or to know they are rearing their children soundly and appropriately. But when the instructional content or other learners' perspectives do not mesh with their values, there is a good chance that they will feel tense, threatened, frustrated, and sometimes angry. The following topics are areas with which many adults associate firmly held values (Loden and Rosener, 1991):

Politics	Friends	War, peace
Ethnicity	Money	Authority
Work	Age	Gender
Leisure	Death	Sex
Education	Health	Love
Family	Race	Possessions
Sexual orientation	Religion, spirituality	Culture (art, music, literature)
Clothes	Manners	Personal tastes

When these topics become part of the learning experience, adults' emotional responsiveness is likely to increase. On some occasions there may be disagreement or controversy. Please remember: the degree to which learners generally feel the motivational condition of inclusion does a great deal to maintain mutual respect, as does their understanding of the participation guidelines (see Strategy 9 in Chapter Five). However, this is an appropriate place to discuss instructor leadership and effective communication.

Beyond the instructor's careful attention to the discussion and his skill in exercising the core characteristic of cultural responsiveness (see Chapter Three), the communication roles described below require some experience for proficient use. Practice, feedback, and coaching can improve their effectiveness. The following paragraphs are an adaptation of Pat Griffin's suggestions regarding communication roles instructors can consider using during value-laden discussions (1997a, pp. 286–291).

- *Giving information.* At times, offering factual information in the form of statistics or documented facts is useful. This is often an important way to address misconceptions.

Example: a learner states that gay men are child molesters. The instructor responds, "That's a frequently held notion that's received a lot of attention over the years. However, police records show that over 90 percent of child sexual abuse involves heterosexual men molesting female children." (Notice that the first statement tends to deflect any listener reaction that this idea belongs only to the learner who made the remark. This helps to diminish defensiveness.)

- *Conceptualizing.* Feelings can overwhelm people and cause them to shut down or lose focus. The introduction of useful questions can give people a way to understand their feelings and a means to proceed more productively.

Example: several learners are arguing back and forth about the degree of racism that continues to exist in the United States. The instructor says, "We have some differences of opinion here. What questions might provide insights or clarify the differences between these viewpoints?" (Learners could break into small groups to generate questions, and the instructor could list their questions.)

- *Reflecting.* Sometimes one of the best ways to encourage adults to reconsider their position is to reflect back what they say so that they understand the impact of their words or can begin to identify their underlying assumptions.

Example: the instructor repeats a learner's statement, "So what you're saying is that the Arab population in this city is not really discriminated against because they're financially secure."

- *Working with silence.* Sometimes silence reflects fear or discomfort. Silences can actually provide a powerful learning opportunity and deepen dialogue. On such occasions, we have at least two options. We can ask learners to write down their feelings at that moment or turn to a partner and share their thoughts. Both options give learners a chance to acknowledge and clarify their reactions. Sometimes something as simple as commenting on the silence opens the discussion at a deeper level.

Example: two adults begin to argue vigorously about the role of the federal government in municipal affairs. As their confrontation tails off, silence envelops the learning group. The instructor says, "I'm not sure what this silence means. Can anyone tell us what they're thinking or feeling right now?" Or "Why don't we each take a few minutes to write down what we are thinking or feeling right now. Then, to the degree that you're comfortable, talk about it with a partner before we come back to the entire group."

• *Redistributing.* At times, we need to make space for other adults to participate in a discussion.

Example: "Before we hear from you again, Lynn, I'd like to see if some of the people who haven't had a chance to speak would like to say something." Or "This is great! Everyone wants to talk. Let's try it this way. I'll call three people, and after they've had their turn, I'll call three more, until everyone's had a chance. OK? Let's go."

• *Accepting the expression of feelings.* For some instructors and adult learners, the expression of intense feelings in a learning environment is an unusual experience. At times like this, how we react as instructors will strongly influence all learners' feelings of security and respect. There is no formula. Usually, our reaction is spontaneous. When I look back on my own behavior, it tends to include an acknowledgment and validation of the feeling. Sometimes appreciation is appropriate. Ultimately, we need to guide learners to the next phase of learning.

Example: a learner begins to cry as he tells about the difficulties his mother endured at school because of a severe disability. The instructor says, "Jamal, that's still a painful memory for you (*acknowledgment*). It's difficult to see those we love suffer (*validation*). Thanks for giving us a chance to learn from your own experience (*appreciation*). Now let's take a look at how we might influence a situation like this as administrators (*learning connection*)." (It's never this tidy!)

• *Disclosing personal information*. When we disclose personal information, we need to be clear about the purpose of the disclosure. I agree with Griffin, who states, "It is never appropriate for facilitators to work out their own issues during a class" (1997a, p. 290). If we tell too many personal stories, adults may begin to discount the course as our own "agenda." Personal stories should help learners arrive at a better understanding of a topic or idea.

Example: the instructor says, "I'd like to tell you about something I learned about silence from a Japanese friend. I don't think I could have learned this otherwise." In this case, the personal disclosure is to help learners realize, and recount from their own experience, that different cultural perspectives sometimes give us insights that we cannot gain through our own culture.

• *Addressing conflict*. There are times when we need to encourage the expression of conflicting ideas. (I discuss this further in the section dealing with *critical incidents*.) Learner dialogue about conflicting ideas is an important part of transformative learning. In productive conflict, all learners have a voice, their right to express differing perspectives is assured, respect is maintained, and the participation guidelines (see Chapter Five, Strategy 9) are in effect.

Strategy 34: When Possible, Clearly State or Demonstrate the Benefits That Will Result from the Learning Activity

People usually want to know more about anything that benefits them. They often want to be better, quicker, and more creative in doing what they value. There are many things they want to save and gain, such as time and money. Most adults want to overcome their limitations in health, endurance, and speed. Any learning that offers the possibility of acquiring a desired advantage is not only interesting but can even be alluring.

Many adults value the items in the following list as beneficial to their lives:

Health	Security	Advancement
Intimacy	Friendship	Fitness
Time	Efficiency	Money
Compassion	Wisdom	Patience
Comfort	Popularity	Leisure
Enjoyment	Freedom	Competence
Self-confidence	Respect	Inner peace

If what we offer adults to learn can help them increase or acquire any of these items, many adults will probably consider the learning to be beneficial. This is not an exhaustive list. The most important questions for us are, What real benefits to adults does the planned learning experience offer? and How can I make the benefits apparent and available to them? If we can answer these questions clearly, we have a vital opportunity to increase their interest. For example, what technician could remain indifferent to a trainer who introduced a new tool with the statement, "This instrument can repair 90 percent of all malfunctions in this system."

The remaining strategies in this section offer ways to evoke situational interest. They are probably most applicable to direct instruction, such as presentations and demonstrations, but the first—humor—seems welcome at any time.

Strategy 35: While Instructing, Use Humor Liberally and Frequently

Humor has many qualities—being interesting is one of them. People love to laugh. They will be a little more interested in anyone or anything that provides this possibility. Humor offers enjoyment, a unique perspective, and unpredictability. All these qualities are attractive and stimulating to most human beings. I have yet to hear an adult come out of a training session and say, "I'm not going back. It's too funny in there. All we ever do is laugh."

Biologically, our brains and bodies react to laughter by discharging endorphin, adrenaline, and dopamine (Willis, 2006). We breathe more deeply and get more oxygen. We become more alert. What we learn in the shadow of laughter has a positive association with the people present and the place where it occurs, making both more attractive. Adults who frequently laugh together have good intrinsic reasons for wanting to be a community.

But how does one develop a sense of humor? It still seems to be a bit of a mystery. I've heard Neil Simon say that some words are funny and some are not. For example, *chicken* is funny; *computer* is not. So for years I've challenged computer scientists to tell me a good computer joke. This is the best so far: "Who had the first computer? Adam and Eve. It was an Apple with two megabytes." Maybe Mr. Simon was right.

Well then, how does an instructor successfully incorporate humor into learning activities? There is no guaranteed formula. More than a score of years ago, I heard Joel Goodman (1981) make some helpful suggestions. To this day, I still find them to be a trustworthy guide:

- Remember that people are more humorous when they feel safe and accepted.

- Laugh *with* people (which includes), not *at* them (which excludes).

- Humor is an attitude. Be open to the unexpected, insane, silly, and ridiculous that life daily offers.

- Do not take yourself too seriously. How easily can you laugh at yourself?

- Be spontaneous.

- Don't be a perfectionist with humor. It will intimidate you. No one can be witty or funny 100 percent of the time. (Talk shows are a living testament to this.)

- Have comic vision. If you look for humor, humor will find you.

Strategy 36: Selectively Induce Parapathic Emotions

Parapathic emotions are strong feelings (anger, delight, affection, sorrow) people undergo as they experience something essentially make-believe (Apter, 1982). For example, we can have parapathic emotions while watching a movie or a play. People tend to become interested in anything that can induce such emotions. Excellent speakers often use stories, anecdotes, and quotations to elicit parapathic emotions in their audiences. In colloquial terms, these esthetic renderings act as "hooks" to pull in high levels of audience interest. They are often used in the beginning of speeches and presentations for this very purpose. Adults cannot easily turn their attention away from anything that has made them feel deeply.

As we have stated repeatedly in this book emotions determine what we pay attention to and retain. Emotionally vivid experiences release adrenaline into our systems, making the experience take precedence in our thoughts as well as retrieving associated memories. This process intensifies interest, alertness, and the potential for remembering what occurs (LeDoux, 1996). Whenever we can evoke adults' emotions within the context of learning activities, we will have an excellent means to arouse and sustain their interest. Any medium that can induce powerful emotions, such as literature, drama, and music, is a fertile field to consider as a possible resource.

Strategy 37: Selectively Use Examples, Analogies, Metaphors, and Stories

Examples are the bread and butter of any good instructional effort. They not only stimulate but also, perhaps more than anything else an instructor might easily do, tell learners how well they really comprehend what has preceded those examples (Gage and Berliner, 1998). For learners, examples are the "moment of truth" for personal meaning—when the information, concept, or demonstration is clarified, applied, or accentuated. Good examples give learners a way to focus new learning so that it is concretely illustrated in their own minds. A fine example nurtures learners, enhancing their concentration and mental effort. Most important, it is difficult for learners to remain interested in anything they cannot understand.

Examples are the refueling stations in any learner's journey to new knowledge. Choose them carefully, make them vivid, and use them generously. We must also realize that when learners construct their own good examples, they create meaning that reflects language and imagery more firmly anchored in their world than what we as instructors usually have to offer. When a person can give his own fitting example for something newly learned, deeper learning is at hand.

Analogies and metaphors are examples that enhance interest by colorfully showing new ideas and information in forms and contexts that learners already understand, making a firm connection to prior knowledge. Because adults are experientially rich learners with considerable mental powers of abstraction and deduction, they readily create, use, and appreciate analogies and metaphors (Deshler, 1990). Metaphors allow us to reach meanings not possible with more academic language. For example, to say being the mayor of a large city is enormously challenging is logically clear, but to say being the mayor of a large city sometimes gives you the feeling you might be steering the Titanic adds insight and expands meaning to a deeper and more emotional level. Deshler's method of metaphor analysis (1990) offers rich possibilities for critically reflecting on the values of personal, popular, and organizational cultures.

Stories, especially when they are well told, imaginative, and unpredictable, are extremely interesting. Used wisely and relevantly, they can captivate a group of learners. They are also the way people give meaning to their own lives. Ask anyone to tell their favorite family story or how they celebrated their birthday as a child or an important dream from their past, and you have opened doors to personal understanding in a league with fine literary fiction.

A story well told usually has strong emotional appeal. A good story makes us care about what happens in it. It engages all parts of our brain, including neural networks representing experiences, ideas, actions, and feelings. These form new connections, which are enhanced by the fluid pattern of the story itself. The natural cohesiveness of a story facilitates both retention and recall. If learning is deepest when it engages most parts of the brain, as some scientists claim (Zull, 2002), then sharing a compelling story is a fundamental way of learning, as old as language and as important as fire.

Sometimes it's fun to have a workshop or course storyteller, someone who summarizes the story of the learning group at significant intervals, such as the end of the day or week.

Strategy 38: Use Uncertainty, Anticipation, and Prediction to the Degree That Learners Enjoy Them with a Sense of Security

We don't want to act weird, but we do want how we instruct to have some quality of the unexpected to it. Unpredictability is very stimulating. In fact, the more unexpected the event, the greater the arousal people feel (Apter, 1982). Most of us appreciate a gift, but a gift that comes as a surprise is usually extra special. This same phenomenon has a corollary in learning when we make a true discovery or have a valued unexpected insight. We relish such occasions and are more likely to remember what occurred. I can still remember, as an undergraduate, reading Aristophanes' *The Frogs* and laughing out loud, amazed that people so long ago could be so funny. After I finished the play, ancient history wasn't that ancient any more.

Every form of entertainment, including sports, art, fiction, and humor, makes use of uncertainty and surprise in secure contexts.

When learners do not know exactly what is going to happen next or when it is going to happen, we have usually gained their interest and anticipation. This is the way learning can become an adventure. When adults feel safe and capable, unpredictability breeds a sense of enjoyable excitement. It is exhilarating to be in a course or training session where the possibility for something unexpected occurring is substantial, as long as there is confidence that no one will be hurt. The following are some of the ways we can make instruction unpredictable yet secure:

• We can *plan the unexpected,* diagnosing our materials and methods for patterns of predictability and inserting the unpredictable. For example, in a situation where textual or modular materials have dominated learning, we can choose to depart from them, switching to real-life situations and more individual learner interests. Moment to moment, we might make a mistake on purpose, lecture from a seat among our learners, act a bit out of character, tell a self-deprecating story, or put a great cartoon on the overhead simply because it's a great cartoon. In the context of good taste and proper timing, there are myriad possibilities.

• We can *attempt instructional experiments.* In these instances, we do things that we have carefully considered and that seem effective to us but that we have no certainty about until we actually do them. Every creative instructor has to do a certain amount of experimentation because new methods and materials often can only be tested on the job. Depending on the situation, we may tell our learners that what we are about to do is something quite new and enlist their support and feedback.

• We can *stay aware of the moment and trust our intuition.* Every learning situation is unique, and our next important instructional moment may be entirely dependent on circumstances we could not predict. A question, a cultural or political event, a learner's problem, or the mood of a group can create a learning opportunity where intuition and flexibility may be our only guides.

When I prepared for my first class after 9/11, I was perplexed about what to do. The second meeting of this Adult Learning and Development course was the following Saturday, an intensive format that ran from 9:00 a.m. to 5:00 p.m. I was still sorting out my feelings about what had happened in New York—a roiling mixture of shock, sadness, apprehension, and dread. The voices for retaliation were drowning out other alternatives, where a peaceful process rather than war might be the result. In the university at which I taught, the imperative for aggression dominated discussions. Emotional arguments about the situation were quick to occur, and I had had a few of my own before that Saturday. I knew we had to discuss 9/11 in our course. I had more than a few concerns about the class. Among those that I found most unsettling were war and revenge becoming the most popular themes; arguments getting out of control; my being ineffective in facilitating a respectful discussion; a rift developing between students or between students and me; and a sense that I might not be able to guide us to any redeemable learning outcome.

When I looked over the scheduled topics in our syllabus for that Saturday, they seemed either too superficial or irrelevant for the moment in which we were living. As I scanned ahead, I found Jack Mezirow's chapter "Learning to Think Like an Adult: Core Concepts of Transformation Theory" (2000). It contains a discussion of the phases of human meaning that lead to transformation—from a disorienting dilemma to reintegration with a new perspective. I believed this model offered insight for what was occurring in our society and I decided to use it.

That Saturday morning, with the phases of meaning as a rough outline and the participation guidelines (Chapter Five, Strategy 9) as a set of norms, we talked as a community of learners for four hours. No one wanted a break and it wasn't until lunch time that some growling stomachs ended our discussion. I am not sure what *we* learned. I am confident it was a good experience for just about everyone. Though opinions varied widely, most people spoke respectfully and deeply. After that class, our group took on a special resonance, one that I still remember with appreciation.

Sometimes these learning situations come with considerable risk and do not turn out as positively as the one I've described. Nonetheless, I think we, as instructors, need to remain guided by the consistent observation that adults appreciate relevance and instruction that adjusts to include the important matters that unexpectedly evolve in daily life, whether it's a headline in the morning paper or the fact that someone has just found a new job.

- We can *invite learners to anticipate and predict.* Because of our need to survive, we constantly anticipate and predict. Whether we are attending to the direction another car will take, the number of steps as we go down a stairway, a line continuing on to the next page of a book, or the last glass of milk out of a carton, we regularly assess our environments for what we think will happen next. When what we predict doesn't go as expected, we pay close attention. As stated earlier, these incidents immediately take on emotional significance for potential engagement with our full neuropsychological system. Over millions of years we have evolved to know that when a sight, scent, or sound is something we did not anticipate, we need to become interested because the situation can get risky quickly. We may be more protected from the elements such as wind and rain, but life is still full of possible falls, crashes, and faux pas.

The upside of this phenomenon is that whenever individuals predict or estimate something, they become interested—hooked, you might say—in finding out how it will turn out. For example, there are five capitals in the United States that begin with the letter A. One of them is Atlanta. What are the rest? If you've even thought of a city that begins with the letter A, you're into this. You want to know what the other four capitals are and may even put this book aside to find out. This sort of question is the mainstay of many trivia games but also the stuff of good novels, films, and plays. So when we build anticipation or ask learners to predict an outcome in any subject from accounting to marriage counseling, we have encouraged their interest. Not only that, sometimes it is a delight.

For all four of these suggestions, the guiding rule of thumb is learner security. We may take a chance. We may even make a mistake, but as long as we have maintained the integrity of our learners, we can continue to learn from the process, acting as professionals who know that creativity demands some degree of risk with consequences that are not totally predictable.

Strategy 39: Use Concept Maps to Develop and Link Interesting Ideas and Information

Concept maps are graphic diagrams that represent relationships between concepts and their components. They represent relations between ideas and information with concrete visual connections. They can give us a model for understanding a topic, such as economics (see the mindmap in Figure 7.1) or the process of adult learning (Sheckley and Bell, 2006). They also can be used to visually represent and organize a variety of responses to and ideas about a question that may interest us such as What type of immigration policy should the U.S. adopt?

Any interesting idea or question can be the focus of a concept map. Concept maps can be linear or nonlinear; they can be individually or collaboratively constructed on paper, board, or a computer screen (Hyerle, 1996). They allow adults, especially those more visually oriented, to construct models that reflect the unique set of relationships an idea can generate in their minds. They are particularly effective with English-language learners (Chularut and DeBacker, 2004). From a neurological perspective, concept maps enable adults to see patterns and access existing memory circuitry, structuring transient ideas or information into more enduring memories (Willis, 2006).

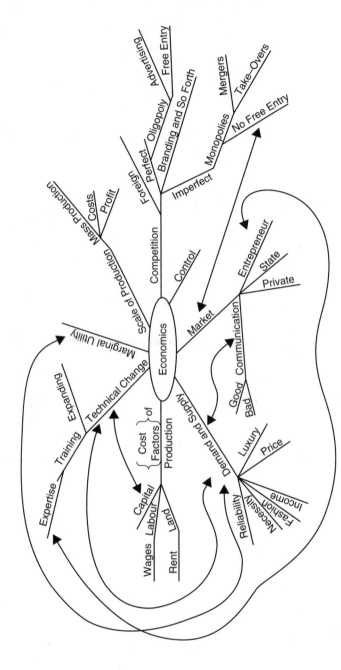

Figure 7.1. An Example of Mindmapping

I often ask adult educators to create a concept map of "Influences on Me as a Teacher." This general topic is in the center of the concept map. Three major influences emanate from the center of the map: (1) former teachers, (2) important knowledge learned on the job, and (3) ideas from reading, courses, and workshops. The educators then add their own major influences. They report that concept mapping allows them to see a web of influences on their teaching and gives them an understanding that is often more profound and insightful than recall alone would have produced.

This map of influences on teaching is an example of mindmapping, one of the most idiosyncratic concept-mapping techniques, which gives adults the freedom to create the form of graphics and the associations themselves (Hyerle, 1996). Mindmapping is a webbing technique popularized by Tony Buzan (1979) that I still find quite useful. His approach begins with a key word (*economics* in the case of Figure 7.1) or an image in the center of the page, followed by extensions expanding outward. Arrows and lines connect secondary ideas to each other; the more important concepts are drawn nearer to the center. Single words are suggested for each line.

Mindmapping and other brainstorming webs can be elaborated with arrows, asterisks, question marks, geometric shapes, three-dimensional drawings, and personal images. Multiple colors can enhance a mindmap as a mnemonic tool. Encouraging learners to create relevant, comprehensive views of connected information can make recall easier and information more accessible (Nesbit and Adesope, 2006). *Visual Tools for Constructing Knowledge* by David Hyerle (1996) remains a valuable resource for a variety of ideas about concept maps and their uses.

How to Deepen Engagement and Challenge with Adult Learners

As we consider the strategies for deepening engagement and challenge, we have to remember that the content of learning is only as important as the learners' interaction with it. These strategies offer ways to learn that acknowledge the multiple perspectives and variety of prior knowledge found among diverse adults. All the strategies are highly interactive processes. Most result in a concrete product created by the learner, using the reflection and dialogue of other learners to construct more complex understanding and knowledge. The challenges generated by these strategies do not compel adults to simply participate; they show why the learning is important and what competent performance looks like (Donovan, Bransford, and Pellegrino, 1999).

In a way, these strategies create a life of their own, a learning narrative to follow. They are composed of procedures that engage the learner with challenging questions, thoughts, and actions to propel learning toward deeper meaning and accomplishment. For example, a case study strategy usually starts with an analysis of the case, which naturally leads to reflection and discussion, followed by an attempt at resolution. The sequence for a research strategy is often to observe, analyze, predict, test, and reflect on results. When the strategies in this section are carried out optimally, learners experience *flow*, the joy of complete engagement.

According to Csikszentmihalyi, when we're in flow, "living becomes its own justification" (1997, p. 32). I agree. I love the feeling of flow—the deeply satisfying experience of an intrinsically motivating activity. We have all had *flow experiences* outside an educational context: the feeling and concentration that sometimes emerge in a closely contested athletic match, in a challenging board game such as chess, or more simply, in reading a book that seems as if it were written just for us or in the spontaneous exhilaration that accompanies a long, deep conversation with an old friend.

In such activities, we feel totally absorbed, with no time to worry about what might happen next and with a sense that we are fully participating with all the skills necessary at the moment. There is often a loss of self-awareness that sometimes results in a feeling of transcendence or a merging with the activity and the environment (Csikszentmihalyi, 1997). Writers, dancers, therapists, surgeons, pilots, and instructors report feelings of flow during engrossing tasks in their repertoire of activities. In fact, when interviewed, they report that flow experiences are among the major reasons why they enjoy and continue to do the work they do.

Learners can have flow experiences as well. If we think of our best courses and finest instructors, we often can remember being captivated by the learning events we shared with them—challenging and creative activities in which we participated at a level where a new depth and extension of our capabilities emerged. Time passed quickly during such experiences, and our desire to return to them was self-evident. They were also not trivial. Effort and concentration were necessary to gain what we did accomplish.

Because flow can be found across cultures, it may be a sense that humans have developed in order to recognize patterns of action that are worth preserving (Massimini, Csikszentmihalyi, and Delle Fave, 1988). Whether we are inspired in a course or in ecstasy in a spiritual ritual, our flow experiences have remarkably similar characteristics (Nakamura and Csikszentmihalyi, 2003):

- *Goals are clear and compatible.* That's why playing games like chess, tennis, and poker induce flow, but so can playing a musical piece or designing computer software. As long as our intentions are clear and our emotions support them, we can concentrate even when the task is difficult. We absorb ourselves in those vivid dreams to which we commit. In such matters, cultural relevance is an inescapable necessity.

- *Feedback is immediate, continuous, and relevant as the activity unfolds.* We are clear about how well we are doing. Each move of a game usually tells us whether we are advancing or retreating from our goal; as we read, we *flow* across lines and paragraphs and pages. In a good conversation, words, facial expressions, and gestures give immediate feedback. In learning situations, there should be distinct information or signals that let us assess our work.

- *The challenge is in balance with our skills or knowledge but stretches existing capacities.* The challenge is manageable but pulls us toward further development of our knowledge or skill (see Figure 7.2). Flow experiences usually occur when our ability to act and the opportunity for action correspond closely. If challenges are significantly beyond our skills, we usually begin to worry; and if they get too far away from what we're capable of doing, fear can emerge. To use a cliché, we're in over our heads, whether it's a project, a job, or a sport. Conversely, when the challenge is minimal, even if we have the skills, we'll feel apathetic. (Busywork comes to mind.) When the challenge is reasonable, but our skills still exceed it, we are likely to become bored. However, if the activity is a *valued* hobby such as crossword puzzles or cooking, we might actually feel relaxed. In general, when desired challenges and personal skills approach harmony, we become energized and stop worrying about control. We're acting instinctively with full concentration, and deep involvement and exhilaration lie ahead. For example, just think of the last time you had a great match in

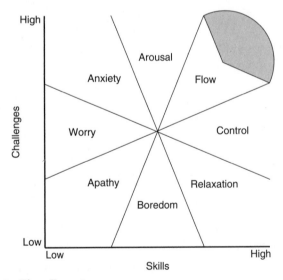

Figure 7.2. Flow Experience
  Source: Csikszentmihalyi, 1997, p. 31. Reprinted by permission of Basic Books, a member of Perseus Book Group.

any game, sport, project, or job-related activity. When I'm with a class and we're really "cooking," I still get goose bumps when it's over and need to find a quiet place just to resonate with my feelings. Remarkable.

• *Vital engagement*, when flow merges with meaning, is one of the pinnacles of what living can be. This phenomenon occurs when there is enjoyable absorption in valued, socially useful tasks such as work, teaching, or learning. A prototypical example would be seeing one's work as a calling and being joyfully immersed in it. Although vital engagement can occur briefly, such as when solving a problem during a course, it is more likely to occur when there is a "felt conviction" that the task is part of something "inherently important" such as art, science, or education (Nakamura and Csikszentmihalyi, 2003, p. 100).

Flow is much more possible than many instructors realize. One in five people experiences flow often, as frequently as several times a day (Csikszentmihalyi, 1997). Generally, it happens when with friends or doing favorite activities.

The purpose of this book is to make learning a lifelong pursuit of vital engagement. Most of us have a favorite subject where we flourish as we learn. As instructors we want to expand the range of those subjects for adults so that there is a consistent conjunction of joy and meaning as they learn across a broader horizon. We reach for this important goal by composing and carrying out learning activities that can flexibly challenge and compellingly engage diverse learners. The genesis of a cherished interest is usually an engrossing and successful learning experience that lasts over time. The following strategies are ideal to help learners find those experiences.

Strategy 40: Use Critical Questions to Stimulate Engaging and Challenging Reflection and Discussion

John Dewey (1933) wrote that thinking itself is questioning. Advocates of transformative learning and culturally responsive teaching urge critical thinking throughout the learning process and, therefore, critical questioning (Mezirow and Associates, 2000; Wlodkowski and Ginsberg, 1995). We should distinguish, however, between a *make-sense orientation* and a *critical orientation*. The make-sense criteria for the validity of a statement are that the statement seems to hang together and fit with one's prior beliefs. If something appears self-evident and makes sense, there is no need to think any more about it (Perkins, Allen, and Hafner, 1983).

With a critical orientation, the data and reasoning are examined for inconsistencies, alternative perspectives are considered, and bias and overgeneralization looked for. A critical orientation is socioculturally constructive and allows us to include a wider human panorama and to consider from different perspectives the social implications of any idea. Critical questioning fosters discussions that are exploratory, unpredictable, risky, and exciting. Such questioning is fundamental to critical reflection and to *democratic discussions* that foster growth in one's capacity for learning and sensitivity to the same capacity in others (Brookfield and Preskill, 2005). Barry Beyer (1987) discerns ten critical thinking skills:

1. Distinguishing between verifiable facts and value claims
2. Distinguishing relevant from irrelevant information, claims, or reasons
3. Determining the factual accuracy of a statement
4. Determining the credibility of a source
5. Identifying ambiguous claims or arguments
6. Identifying unstated assumptions
7. Detecting bias
8. Identifying logical fallacies
9. Recognizing logical inconsistencies in a line of reasoning
10. Determining the strength of an argument or claim

Motivationally speaking, thought-provoking questions make instructors and adults colearners, prompting everyone to make connections between their prior knowledge and what is presented. Such questions are generative, causing us to reflect on our own information and experience and to transform what we know into new meanings.

Critical questioning promotes high-level cognitive processing, stimulating people to analyze, infer, synthesize, apply, evaluate, compare, contrast, verify, substantiate, explain, and hypothesize. However, many adults may not be experienced in posing critical questions in their courses and training. Alison King (1994, 2002) has developed and extensively tested an instructional procedure for teaching postsecondary learners to pose their own thoughtful questions. I have found that adult learners can use this strategy either on their own or in groups.

Using this procedure, the teacher gives the learners a written set of question starters such as "What is the meaning of . . . ?" and "Why is . . . important?" These questions encourage knowledge construction because they serve as prompts to induce more critical thinking on the part of learners and of the instructor as well. Learners use these question starters to guide them in formulating their own specific questions pertaining to the material to be discussed. Table 7.1 includes a list of these thoughtful question stems that can be adapted to any subject when completed with information relevant to that subject. The thinking processes these questions elicit are also listed in Table 7.1. When the instructor offers these question stems to learners for their conversations and dialogue, learners can use their own information and examples to deepen the content of what is to be studied.

As learners read, review, or reflect on course material with these thought-provoking questions in mind, they consider ideas more thoroughly and integrate a wider variety of neural networks. Such cognitive processing connects new ideas for the learners and links them in "different ways to what they already know" (King,

Table 7.1.   Guiding Critical Questioning

Question Starter	Specific Thinking Skill
What is a new example of . . . ?	Application
How would you use . . . to . . . ?	Application
What would happen if . . . ?	Prediction/hypothesizing
What are the implications of . . . ?	Analysis/inference
What are the strengths and weaknesses of . . . ?	Analysis/inference
What is . . . analogous to?	Creation of analogies and metaphors
What do we already know about . . . ?	Activation of prior knowledge
How does . . . affect . . . ?	Analysis of cause-effect
How does . . . tie in with what we learned before?	Activation of prior knowledge
Explain why . . .	Analysis
Explain how . . .	Analysis
What is the meaning of . . . ?	Analysis
Why is . . . important?	Analysis of significance
What is the difference between . . . and . . . ?	Comparison-contrast
How are . . . and . . . similar?	Comparison-contrast
How does . . . apply to everyday life?	Application
What is the counterargument for . . . ?	Rebuttal argument
What is the best . . . and why?	Evaluation and provision of evidence
What are some possible solutions to the problem of . . . ?	Synthesis of ideas
Compare . . . and . . . with regard to . . .	Comparison-contrast
What do you think causes . . . ?	Analysis of cause-effect
Do you agree or disagree with this statement: . . . ? What evidence is there to support your answer?	Evaluation and provision of evidence
How do you think . . . would see the issue of . . . ?	Taking other perspectives

Source: King, 1994, p. 24. Used by permission.

2002, p. 37). In this manner new neural networks are developed, providing more durable connections for memory and better cues for recall.

In addition to King's list in Table 7.1, I like to use the five types of questions Richard Paul (1990) associates with a Socratic dialogue:

Clarification	"What do you mean by … ?"
	Could you give me an example?"
Probing for assumptions	"What are you assuming when you say … ?"
	"What is underlying what you say?"
Probing for reasons and evidence	"How do you know that … ?"
	"What are your reasons for saying … ?"
Other perspectives	"What might someone say who believed that … ?"
	"What is an alternative for … ?"
Probing for implications and consequences	"What are you implying by … ?"
	"Because of …, what might happen?"

Learners can use these question stems to guide them in generating their own critical questions following a presentation, a class, or a reading.

Let us say we have read *Invisible Man*, by Ralph Ellison. We have agreed that we will each bring along two questions, based on the list in Table 7.1, regarding any aspect of the book that we find relevant to our own lives. We break into dyads, and my partner and I share our questions. They read as follows:

1. How does the last line of the book, "Who knows but that, on the lower frequencies, I speak for you?" apply to our everyday lives?

2. What is the Brotherhood analogous to in our own contemporary society?

3. The book has many strengths. It has been heralded as one of the greatest American novels of the second half of the twentieth century. From your perspective, what were its weaknesses?

4. What are examples of invisibility at this institution?

With these queries, we have an opportunity to relate ideas from this novel to our own knowledge and experience. We can have an extensive discussion that may clarify some inadequacies in our comprehension, and each of us has a chance to guide, to some extent, the thinking that will occur. There is opportunity to infer, compare, evaluate, and explain, all of which can lead to better understanding, fuller awareness of social issues, and the possibility of modifying our own thinking.

It may be that on some of these questions we disagree. Conflicting views are usually motivating because there is a social impetus to resolve the dissonance. We will probably have to think more deeply, explain more thoroughly, offer further examples, and negotiate meaning. In an inclusive and respectful learning environment, they offer the circumstances for a passionate discussion—one of the most dynamic pathways to intrinsic motivation and new learning.

Resolution of conflicting viewpoints during a discussion is often facilitated with deft linking questions by a skillful instructor. Being able to ask, "Is there any connection between your conclusion and Terique's last statement?" or "How does that observation fit with Franklin's comment?" may open avenues of new insight or mutual regard. Questions of this sort join the knowledge of learners with other learners, promoting the understanding that discussion is a collaborative process in which each adult can make an important contribution to everyone's learning (Brookfield and Preskill, 2005).

No matter what kinds of questions we as instructors ask, there are a number of questioning practices that can increase learners' responsiveness. The following are suggestions for improving questioning during instruction:

• *Avoid instructor echo*, which is repeating portions of learners' responses to a question. This echoing tends to arbitrarily conclude what the learner has said and dulls further reflection.

• *Avoid pressuring learners to "think" about what has been asked.* Adults usually resent this form of indirect intimidation, which implies they are not motivated or capable in the first place. The question itself should stimulate engagement.

• *Avoid frequent evaluative comments*, such as "That's good," "Excellent," and "Fine answer." Even though these may be positive, they make you the judge and jury, deciding what is better or worse. Acknowledgment, appreciation, and *transition responses* such as "Now I see how you understand it," "Thank you," or "Well, that might mean . . ." (followed by a new question) tend to have greater chances of continuing discussion, interest, and thinking.

• *Avoid "yes . . . but" reactions to learners' answers.* Essentially, this is a rejection of the learner's response. The *but* cancels out what precedes it and affirms what follows it (for example, "Yes, I think that might work, but here is another idea").

• Probe answers to stimulate more thinking and dialogue. Probes are questions or comments that require learners to provide more support, to be clearer or more accurate, and to offer greater specificity or originality. Some examples: "How did you arrive at that conclusion?" "I don't quite understand." "Please explain a bit more." Many of the questions found in Table 7.1 can be used as probes.

Strategy 41: Use Relevant Problems, Research, and Inquiry to Facilitate Learning

A problem can be broadly characterized as any situation in which a person wants to achieve a goal for which an obstacle exists (Voss, 1989). If relevant and within the range of an adult's capabilities, problems, by definition, are engaging and challenging. Processes for solving problems are learned within a cultural context (Gay, 2000). Differences in perspective, communication, and ethical codes may influence how people conceive and approach a problem, from building a home to settling a divorce. This remarkable variety in the ways that diverse adults perceive and resolve a problem can make for a wonderful learning experience.

Adult education has enjoyed a long history in the use of problems as a procedure for learning. Paulo Freire's problem-posing is a distinguished and influential pedagogy throughout the world (Shor, 1993). Ill-structured problems (that is, those not solvable with certainty) have been advocated for transformative learning for over two decades (Mezirow and Associates, 1990). Today, problem-based learning is a general and international approach to learning across multiple disciplines (English, 2005). There are numerous other approaches that use problems and hypotheses as a motivational strategy to deepen engagement, such as critical incidents (Brookfield, 1990) and historical and experimental investigation (Wlodkowski and Ginsberg, 1995). Due to limited space, I will discuss only two forms of practice that are popular in adult education today: *problem-based learning* and *cooperative inquiry*, a form of action research.

The basic steps in problem-based learning may vary, but they generally are based on the assumption that there is no right answer and that learning is a self-directed and constructive process where social context, discovery, and experience lead to new knowledge and skills (Lohman, 2002). Problem-based learning is characterized by the use of real-life problems as a means for people to learn critical thinking, collaboration, and the essential concepts and professional skills of a particular discipline. Professional educators in disciplines such as medicine and nursing use problem-based learning to prepare learners for situations they will face in their work (Murray and Savin-Baden, 2000).

Although the evidence does not support problem-based learning as a superior approach to education, even in its clinical applications

(English, 2005), I have found it to be a useful selective strategy for engaging diverse adults in the pursuit of more substantial knowledge to resolve a relevant problem. Problem-based learning can be an enlightening journey toward the two kinds of objectives advocated by Eliot Eisner (1985) for any educational experience: *instructional* and *expressive*. The instructional objectives are the informational elements or the skills the learner is expected to acquire. The expressive objectives are those that are evoked rather than prescribed. They are usually based on learners' interests and concerns. Expressive objectives can elicit generative themes: substantial, relevant issues affecting the collective good of society, such as health, pollution, or economics.

To explore the possible steps for problem-based learning, I have adapted an example from an inquiry course in arts and sciences at McMaster University taught by P. K. Rangachari (1996). In this unit, learners are exploring the dimensions of health and illness in the modern world, in particular the interaction between providers and recipients of health care.

1. *Brainstorming*. In order to evoke expressive objectives, the first meeting is a brainstorming session during which learners discuss what they believe to be critical issues in health care. Distilled from this effort are such topics as bioethics, alternative medicine, technology in medicine, and funding for health care.

2. *The problems*. Working with the learners' list, the instructor writes the problems, such as the one that follows. This problem is based on the learners' expressed desire to discuss the appropriateness of specific procedures in medicine, specifically surgical rates.

> An article titled "Study Finds Region Surgeons Scalpel-Happy" has appeared in the local tabloid. Naming names, the article identifies the hospital and notes that patients there are twice as likely to undergo

a cholecystectomy, three times as likely to have a mastectomy, and five times as likely to have a hysterectomy compared to other regions in Ontario. The findings implicate the hospital surgeons to be an incompetent, money-grubbing, and misogynistic lot. The president of the hospital has demanded an explanation from the chief of surgery and the chief is livid.

Possible learning issues include (1) a study of variability in the rates of surgical procedures based on demographics and hospital, (2) a profile of a surgeon, (3) an assessment of the surgery and technology identified in the problem, and (4) an examination of how to handle scandal. (Note the variety of entry points for multiple intelligences.)

3. *Definition of learning issues and formation of study groups.* Learners receive the problem. They organize their ideas and previous knowledge related to the problem. They pose questions on aspects of the problem they do not understand or know and wish to learn. These are usually called *learning issues*, and they are often the basis for the learning activities carried out by the students. (In some cases, a problem is so constructed that the essential concepts of the skills of a discipline become intrinsic to the students' learning issues). Learners rank the learning issues they generate in order of importance. Through dialogue and by personal preference, they decide which issues to assign to small groups and which to individuals. In two weeks, learners will teach the findings related to these issues to the rest of the group. The instructor guides the learners toward resources and necessary research.

4. *Preparation for presentations.* During the two weeks prior to their presentations, learners meet, discuss, find and evaluate information, write their reports, and prepare for their presentations. To preserve continuity, the instructor holds an intervening session to discuss any issues that require clarification. Learners also share information and act as resources for one another.

5. *Presentations and assessment.* Learners present the information they have gathered related to their learning issues. The rest of the learners and the instructor grade the presentations and give comments. The instructor provides guidelines for the assessment. In this case, high marks are given for clear and understandable objectives, presentations that communicate the main ideas with specific and logical support, concepts offered with fitting examples that contain rich and vivid details, a narrative and cohesive presentation format, and the exposition of new and relevant information. Along with the marks, each learner receives a typed sheet with the other learners' collated comments. Each presenter (or group) is also required to submit a thousand-word written report of the presentation that the instructor alone grades and comments on.

This example is just one of a number of possible approaches to problem-based learning (Savin-Baden, 2003). You will probably note some similarities between the first three steps of this representation and how our second illustration of this strategy, cooperative inquiry, begins.

Cooperative inquiry is a form of action research. Action research is an approach to empirical research that is undertaken by a group for the purpose of improving a condition or situation in which they are involved (Berg, 2007). In general, it is a rigorous form of investigation but uses consensual and democratic strategies to examine, reflect, and resolve issues affecting the community of participants. It avoids complex statistical techniques and uses language that both lay people and professionals can understand.

In cooperative inquiry, all participants are co-researchers and co-subjects attempting to understand their own as well as each other's lives, agreeing to a set of procedures by which they will observe and record their own and each other's experiences, and learning together how to act to change things and do things better

(Reason, 2000). As Peter Reason notes, there is an agreement among participants to "knowing as a dialogical process" where "collective awareness and thinking transform the sum of their parts" (2000, p. 86). He outlines four phases to conduct cooperative inquiry (the titles are mine). Although he describes his approach as cyclical with the four phases being repeated as needed, for possibly up to a year, I have altered it to exemplify a single cycle. In my own practice, I have not yet found a situation where there has been time for more than three cycles of this process.

> *Phase 1: Exploration and question construction.* Participants explore an area of interest by discussing their concerns and creating a focus for their inquiry. They develop a set of questions and hypotheses. There is mutual agreement to take some action. They decide on the methods of observing and recording their experiences.
>
>> *Example:* In a large, diverse urban community college, eight instructors meet to improve their teaching. There is little funding for professional development. They want to reach beyond a one-day workshop approach to developing their practice. They come from a variety of disciplines ranging from technical to liberal studies. Their common denominator is they all teach large 90-minute sections with 75 or more students. All agree they face the challenge of maintaining student engagement for a full hour and a half.
>>
>> *Question:* How can they more effectively engage the interest of all students during a 90-minute period? This is the question they decide to begin with.
>
> *Phase 2: Gathering information.* Participants observe and record their own and others' experiences related to the research question. They share the information among themselves. They are trying to develop a better understanding of this

experience. New forms of action may come immediately or later depending on the outcomes of their discussion.

> *Example:* Participants pair up and visit each other's classrooms twice. At 10-minute intervals they record the percentage of students engaged in the learning task at hand. They make notes regarding their impressions of what seems to distract students and what seems to sustain their interest.

Phase 3: Analyzing and interpreting the gathered information. Peter Reason calls this phase the "touchstone of the inquiry method" because at this point "the co-researchers become fully immersed in their experience" (2000, p. 87). They may come up with new understandings. They may venture away from their original research question. They may have new creative insights. This is the time when they will act on what they know.

> *Example:* The instructors are fascinated by the similarity of their findings. Although teaching different courses, they see a common pattern: Students seem engaged for the first 15–20 minutes. Then there is a gradual breakdown of interest for about 25 percent of the class. This 25 percent meander in roughly three directions: (1) socializing with peers, (2) doing other school work, and (3) intermittent daydreaming. The instructors' discussion leads to the following generalizations: the disengaged students aren't negative or hostile; they are more interested in doing something else; most of them socialize repeatedly with the same peers; and very few instructors do any collaborative group work in the first half hour of their classes.

Phase 4: Reconsidering the original research question and deciding on further questions and another cycle of research. The group gathers to discuss their original research question in light of their findings, reflection, and experience. They can decide to ask more questions, pursue various actions or interventions, gather more information, begin another cycle of research, or disassemble with new awareness and knowledge resulting from their inquiry.

> *Example:* The eight instructors feel more cohesive as a group. They have come to this answer to their research question: based on our findings, there are two instructional procedures that may increase student interest in our courses; the first is to interrupt the current systems of student disengagement by changing their seating arrangement; and the second is to use collaborative and relevant learning activities within the first twenty minutes of courses to deepen student interest and establish a more active process of learning earlier in the period. Each of the instructors decides to make these changes over the next two weeks. When the two weeks have been completed, they will start another cycle of observation, information gathering, and meeting to discuss the results of their findings.

Epilogue: This was an actual situation where I worked as a consultant. The eight instructors were department heads and program directors. They wanted to try cooperative inquiry before they advocated it to their colleagues. A larger proportion of the college faculty eventually participated in cooperative inquiry. Their major finding was inadequacy of feedback from instructors to students. This awareness resulted in professional development for the college faculty focusing on effective methods for giving students feedback. The following year the institutional research department of the college found that student perceptions of instructor feedback had significantly improved along with student attitudes and climate.

Action research has been found to be a useful means to sustain new learning and transfer among educators (Glanz, 1999).

My own work supports this finding (Wlodkowski, 2003). Action research avoids the jargon of stereotypical research and its veneer of often-alienating statistical banter. As adult learners, educators are motivated by pragmatic, relevant, and accessible knowledge.

Strategy 42: Use Intriguing Problems and Questions to Make Initially Irrelevant Material More Meaningful

Sometimes we have to teach material that learners initially regard as irrelevant. Science and technology are rife with concepts and tools to which people may have had little or no previous exposure. When adults have few links between new information and their experience, we can use intriguing problems and questions to make this material more meaningful.

As these problems engage adults in concrete experience or discourse, they create disequilibrium in their thinking. Things don't quite make sense. This dissonance stimulates intense interest. Like a marvelous magic trick, fascinating problems evoke our speculations, hypotheses, and predictions, often stimulating related prior knowledge. They make us wonder and imagine. We may be guessing, but the neural circuits that are now active are probably closer to a better understanding than the ones available if we were bored. Once that happens, the problems become relevant to us because we cannot easily push aside what we find intriguing.

An example adapted from the work of Jacqueline Grennon Brooks and Martin Brooks (1993) shows how learners can be provocatively invited to better understand the concepts of momentum and energy: The instructor presents a set of five hanging pendula, metal balls of equal size that touch each other in a resting position (see Figure 7.3). The instructor raises one ball and releases it; the learners note that one ball swings out on the other side. The instructor then raises and releases two balls, and the learners observe that two balls swing out on the other side. Raising three balls, the instructor asks the group to predict what will happen when the three balls are let go.

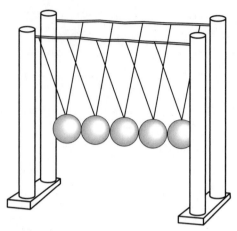

Figure 7.3. A Set of Five Hanging Pendula

Source: Brooks and Brooks, 1993. Used with permission.

Learners usually respond with some or all of the following predictions: (1) one ball will go out, but higher; (2) two balls will go out, but higher; (3) three balls will go out; (4) the balls will "go crazy"; (5) the balls will stop; and (6) the balls will swing together. The learners explain their responses, react to others' responses, and indicate whether they have changed their minds upon hearing others' predictions. Meaning develops through dialogue. Of course, feedback by the apparatus itself will prove or disprove all the ideas, and in fact, within half an hour most groups demand the release of the three balls in order to test their theories. Further activities about momentum and energy are developed based on the learners' emerging interests and understandings.

Presenting learners with discrepant events and contradictory information is a corollary to this strategy. For example, learners may become more interested in the principles of heat transference when they have a chance to think about why the bottom of a paper cup does not burn from the flame of a lighter when the cup is filled with water. Social contradictions can also

stimulate learners' interest. For example, "The world can produce enough food to feed everyone, yet starvation and hunger
run rampant even in countries that have the highest standards of
living." Or "This training method is the most criticized but also
the most widely used in the marketing industry today." In these
instances there must be respect for the learners' contributions, substantive discussion, and social relevance. Otherwise, this method
is little more than an expedient trick to enliven conventional
learning.

Strategy 43: Use Case Study Methods to Enhance Meaning

A case study portrays provocative questions and undercurrents
in a narrative of real events. It requires that learners use their
experience and knowledge to analyze, deliberate, and advance
informed judgments from an array of perspectives and concepts
(Marsick, 2004). The hallmark of cases is their authenticity. With
lifelike, concrete details and characters expressing a personal voice,
they put flesh and blood on otherwise abstract concepts.

Because cases present a dilemma and are open ended, they
tend to stimulate different reactions among members of a group.
Yet they permit learners and instructors to be more open and
less defensive because the situation is someone else's (Hutchings,
1993). We can share our uncertainty as well as our knowledge and
experience because a case presents a knotty problem, not one given
to glib resolution. Dialogue therefore is not limited to the mere
exchange of opinions but rather is imaginative and open to many
ideas.

Having a thorough understanding of the case and its nuances
before teaching it is very important. It should be relevant to
the learners and to the ideas being taught. The facts, context,
and characters in the case should be realistic and pertinent. By
reading the case a few times over, you can begin to see if it meets
such criteria as relevance, authenticity, narrative strength, and

complexity to merit its selection for use. Here are some useful questions to reflect on as you read a case:

What is your first impression?

What are the different ways to interpret this case?

What are the teaching and learning issues?

What is culturally relevant in this case?

Can people construct principles and applications from this case?

Please keep these questions in mind as you read the following scenario, a case composed to stimulate the discussion and application of ideas in this book.

Exhibit 7.1   Issues of Instruction and Diversity

Beverly Hallman is a recently hired instructor at Central College, an urban community college. She is twenty-seven years old and has just completed her master's degree in educational psychology. As a European American woman from a middle-class suburban community, Beverly has very little experience with Latino and immigrant populations. She regards herself as a conscientious instructor with a very challenging job.

Beverly teaches introductory psychology. One-third of her students are learners whose language of origin is Spanish. She is concerned that these students do not participate enough in class but doesn't know what to do about it. She also has a significant number of students who were born in Central and Eastern Europe. Although she would not care to admit it, she finds the male students in this group to be too aggressive in class discussions. The rest of the students are African American and European American. At least a third of the students in her course are over thirty-five years of age.

Beverly's general approach is to be fair to everyone and to try to interest everyone in psychology. The best way she knows to be fair is to treat all students the same way and to try to ignore cultural and ethnic differences as much as possible. There seems to be a tension in the class and no visible attempts to form intercultural friendships.

There are thirty students in Beverly's class. Her teaching approach is to use short lectures followed by short general discussions. Usually the same few students dominate the discussion. Most of them are male and over forty years of age, and none of them are Hispanic. When these students talk about their experiences, the younger students in the class are visibly disengaged and some seem resentful. Beverly administers a weekly quiz that is graded and returned to students. This structure keeps the students focused on note-taking and makes the classroom climate tolerable.

As a new teacher, Beverly feels this is too early to be in a rut. She'd like to spark the class but is afraid of controversy. She believes a psychology course should be more than vocabulary enhancement but is at a loss as to what to do beyond showing a few films. She intuitively knows that some of what she is teaching, especially about social relationships, personality theory, and motivation, is for cultural reasons not realistic or relevant to a good number of her students. But again, she doesn't quite know how to address this issue with them. Also, for Beverly to admit that cultural differences make some aspects of psychology irrelevant and inapplicable might make her quizzes and tests seem unfair.

The worst part is that her students are generally doing poorly. This is most obvious on the summative test she gave at midsemester. Beverly feels responsible. She has half a semester left to go and decides she will ask a more experienced teacher in her department for assistance.

It is a good first step to be sure learners comprehend the goals of a particular case study. For the case study in this example, some goals might be the following:

To increase understanding of how to improve instruction with particular attention to inclusion, motivation, and learning among diverse adult students

To improve understanding of diversity issues—age, ethnicity, bias, fear of conflict, and the like—as they relate to instruction

To analyze and explore multiple perspectives on the issues found in the case

To consider ideas found in this book as they might assist Beverly in the improvement of her instruction

Depending on such factors as the kind of material covered in the case and the experience, trust, and sense of community among the learners, cases can be processed in small groups or as a whole group. It is very important to open the discussion of the case in a manner that invites wide participation and relevant and interested commentary. Here are some suggestions with which to experiment (Hutchings, 1993):

- Ask learners to "free write" (put pencil to paper in a flow of consciousness) for a couple of minutes after reading the case so that they have some reflections to offer.

- Ask each learner to talk with a partner for a few minutes about key issues in the case before you request individual responses.

- Ask a couple of learners to summarize the case before asking others to join in.

- Ask learners to remark about one element they felt was important in the case and record these comments publicly. This lets everyone know there is a range of interpretations before discussion begins.

During the discussion, the kinds of questions we ask can serve different purposes—for example, to encourage further analysis, challenge an idea, mediate between conflicting views, and guide learners to generate principles and concepts and to apply them.

Creating a discussion outline for the case study (see Exhibit 7.2) and being open to addressing questions the learners may have can keep the case study process flowing and relevant.

Exhibit 7.2   A Possible Discussion Outline for a Case Study

1. Which items in this case stand out as significant teaching and learning issues?

   Probes:

   Which of these issues are you familiar with from your own teaching?

   Which of these issues have you had some success in resolving?

   Which of these issues arouse apprehension, and why?

2. What could Beverly do to improve the sense of community among her students?

   Probes:

   What attitudes does Beverly have and what actions has she taken that may increase tension and separation among her students?

   What can Beverly do to increase participation and collaboration among the students?

   What do we know about adult learners that we could apply to make their participation more equitable? More relevant to the rest of the students?

3. How could Beverly be more motivating as an instructor?

   Probes:

   How does Beverly's teaching suppress motivation to learn?

   If you were to transform Beverly's approach to teaching, where would you start? What would you have her learn?

   What in particular have you learned in this book that might be of genuine assistance to Beverly?

At times, it may be very effective to role-play aspects of the case: "What would be your remarks to Beverly if she were to ask you to observe her? Let's hear them, and one of us can react as she might." Other times, it may be beneficial to record key information on the board or a chart. Direct quotes from the case can serve to focus the group.

In general, after students have read the case, the pattern of learning moves from reflection and analysis to the surfacing of concepts and principles, to the development of possible solutions and related hypotheses, and to the application of action strategies to individuals' own practices and purposes. Important to an effective analysis is guiding learners to base their answers on the facts of the case rather than to speculate. Learners should have some practice in planning their solution with attention to timing, strategies, barriers, and consequences, intended or otherwise (Marsick, 2004).

How you close the case discussion is critical. Most cases do not end with "the answer" or in a confident resolution of the problem. Nevertheless, there should be some opportunity for learners to reflect on what they have learned, to privately or publicly identify new understandings, to air unresolved conflicts or questions, and to make plans for making changes or taking action. Some approaches to closing the case study activity are as follows (Hutchings, 1993):

- Ask learners to describe how their understanding of specific principles and concepts were deepened or expanded as a result of doing the case study—and possibly why as well.

- Ask learners to spend some time writing answers to such questions as, What new insights did you gain from this case study and its discussion? What are your lingering questions? What new ideas do you want to try out?

- Ask learners to brainstorm insights, personal changes in thinking or action, or new areas to explore as a result of the case study.

- Go around the group and ask each learner to provide one insight, question, lesson, change, or intuition that has emerged as a result of this process.

Using case studies in technical fields, such as chemistry, may require a more structured approach, but not so structured that the flow of learners' ideas and perspectives would be suppressed. A final note: individually and collaboratively, adults are a great resource for constructing cases.

———————

Much of what we learn as adults is for situations where there is no single best response but multiple better responses with potentially beneficial consequences. Consequently, especially in difficult situations, the less we know the people and the real-life context for applying what we have learned, the more we are likely to fall back upon old habits or ill-formed and incomplete versions of what we have newly learned. I have seen this pattern in myself and I have witnessed it among novice teachers.

As a pre-service teacher educator, I occasionally watched students who were earnest and capable in education courses become confused in their internships and either not apply or misapply what they had learned in their coursework. This often occurred when the student teacher had to manage a disciplinary action, a situation filled with strong emotion, stress, and unpredictability. It was obvious the student teacher was anxious and could apply very little at that moment from what he had heard in class or read in a textbook.

Although this scenario is from a teacher education program, it is analogous to much of college education and employee training, because what we learn in courses and books is so removed from the dynamics and contexts of real life that we are unable to recall or apply our new learning in our work or community. We need to practice new learning in situations that approximate, replicate, or are real life so that we can receive feedback within those situations to deepen and refine our learning, and we need enough time and practice to *embody* this new learning in order to be effective at what we value.

We now come to three motivational strategies that offer the opportunity to practice what we are learning in situations that approximate or are real life; where we can interpret the context, make choices about how we do what we have learned, receive feedback from the consequences of the actions we take, and use in-the-moment judgment to accomplish our goals. For knowledge and skill that are meant to be applied, this is the best way I know to deepen meaning. As we will see in the discussion of simulation, a sea change in teaching and training is ahead of us.

Adaptive Decision Making

For real-life situations that are dynamic and have no clear "correct" answer, where our responses affect the context and the possible choice of responses that follow, we can only learn and retain new knowledge for them *by doing*, by performing it in the real-life situations where it will be used or in contexts that replicate those situations. According to Elkhonon Goldberg (2001), these situations require adaptive decision making. In such situations, there is no clear right answer or response. We do not have a "recipe" for what to do. We have to interpret the situation while it is happening and choose from a number of possible actions. When we drive a car, mediate an argument, or respond to an emergency, we are using adaptive decision making. In such situations, analysis and critical thinking are going on very quickly with responses to feedback firing rapidly and no clear best answer at hand. We have a goal, such as to get to a destination or resolve an argument; we have knowledge and skill to apply; we can make better decisions and actions; but how and what to do are moment-to-moment choices without a complete and final path of action.

Adaptive decision making occurs many times over in our daily lives. When we use knowledge and skill effectively in such situations, we often say we *have a feel for them*. This expression reveals *embodied meaning*, the understanding that the knowledge and skill we apply are available as part of our psychophysiological system (Caine and Caine, 2006). We have learned this knowledge and skill in a way that it is a part of our senses, cognitions, emotions, and physical being, available to us as an actual embodiment of meaning (Damasio, 1999; Varella, Thompson, and Rosch, 1995).

In this regard when we learn something very well and use it, we often say, "It's a part of me." In my case, teaching is a part of me. I have colleagues for whom research and writing is a part of them, instinctual and intuitive. When the young people from information technology come to my aid, I can see that working with computers is part of them. Their quickness with the machine seems reflexive and an extension of their being. Musicians, athletes, artists, and experts offer us countless examples of embodied learning as well. The question then is, How do we get from reading a book about something to having it as embodied knowledge that we can effectively use in situations that require adaptive decisions?

Based on my experience and the research and theory available at this time, we need repeated immersion into real-life situations or their authentic replications, where we can navigate with our new knowledge while we integrate feedback and engage our senses, thoughts, emotions, and actions—our entire psychophysiological system (Caine and Caine, 2006). The next three motivational strategies (44: role playing, 45: simulations, and 46: internships) offer in *ascending order* increasingly realistic contexts for engagement and practice to embody new learning.

Strategy 44: Use Role Playing to Embody Meaning and New Learning within a More Realistic and Dynamic Context

When adults can apply or practice new knowledge while sincerely experiencing people, situations, perspectives, and reactions approximating authentic instances in life, they have an opportunity to embody the meaning of what they are learning and to become more proficient. *Role playing* is the acting out of a possible situation. The learner assumes the identity of a particular person with given characteristics and intentions. Often there is a scenario such as a meeting or a conflict situation.

Because role playing has broad applicability across subject areas and accommodates a variety of perspectives, it is a very useful strategy with diverse adult learners. Role playing gives learners a chance to try out attitudes, ideas, and skills that have been introduced formally by learning materials and less formally by instructors and peers. A realistic situation is established so that learners proceed through the scenario with genuine involvement of their intellect, feelings, and bodily senses.

Role playing gives learners the opportunity to think in the moment, question their perspectives, respond to novel or unexpected circumstances, and consider different ways of knowing (Meyers and Jones, 1993). Role playing can be used to practice a specific skill such as providing an academic progress report in a parent-teacher conference, a collaborative skill such as collective bargaining, a problem-solving skill such as a procedure for a biochemistry experiment, or a synthesizing skill such as organizing an instructional plan using motivational strategies from this book.

Role playing is also excellent for developing empathy and the skill to validate another person. It gives learners and instructors a chance to take on the viewpoints and rationales of people with different perspectives, as might occur, for example, when a lesbian couple and a heterosexual couple discuss the merits of a proposed law concerning domestic partnerships. When there is a chance to reverse roles so that learners act out roles that conflict with their own perspective (for example, when a union member takes on the role of a manager), learners have the opportunity to think and feel from a position they may never have been in. Role playing is an excellent procedure for shifting perspectives, adding insights, and starting conversations that may have been unimaginable before the introduction of this strategy.

The following are some guidelines adapted from the work of Meyers and Jones (1993) for conducting effective role playing:

- *Know where and how the role play conforms to your instructional situation.* Is it a good fit given who your learners are, where the learning is heading, and what learners expect to do? Nothing is worse than a role play that feels contrived or trivializes an important issue.

- *Plan well ahead.* You need to have some degree of confidence that your learners are familiar and proficient enough with the concepts or skills that will be practiced during the activity. Have they seen models or read cases that acquaint them with what they are expected to do? Do they have a fair knowledge of the cultural roles they may assume? If they are uncomfortable, can they excuse themselves or observe until they are more at ease about playing a role?

- *Be relatively sure everyone clearly understands the roles before you begin the role play.* Allow for questions and clarifications. Often it is helpful to write a script, with contributions from learners, describing the attitudes, experiences, and beliefs associated with the role. The learners then study and use the script to deepen their familiarity with the role. For example, an excerpt from a script for a parent may include such statements as "I am a single parent. I work nights in a service job. I often feel exhausted."

- *Set aside enough time for the discussion that follows.* The discussion and analysis are as important as the role play itself. What are the different perspectives, reactions, and insights? What are the learners' concerns? What has not been dealt with that still needs attention? Has the desired learning been accomplished? How? What about the process itself? How can it be improved? This is a good time to raise issues of critical consciousness (see Chapter Three), when impressions are fresh and resonant.

• *When role playing seems potentially embarrassing or threatening, it is often helpful for the instructor to model the first role play and discuss it.* This may alleviate some initial hesitation and allow learners to see our own comfort (we hope) with our imperfections and mistakes.

Freezing the action during a role play can serve many purposes: to critique a perspective, explore learners' reactions to a poignant comment, allow learners to make beneficial suggestions to the actors, and relieve tension. The follow-up activities for a role play are extremely important. Often they can connect what is learned to greater academic and social consequences. For example, a compelling next step could be the creation of an action plan to use what has been practiced and discussed in an actual work or professional setting.

Strategy 45: Use Simulations and Games to Embody the Learning of Multiple Concepts and Skills That Require a Real-Life Context and Practice to Be Learned

Many professions use multiple sets of knowledge and skills over time to effectively reach their goals. Business, health, and educational administrators are obvious examples as they lead their organizations, start new programs, deal with conflicts, and adjust to unpredictable local and global events. For programs that prepare adults for such occupations, simulations may be the only way to embody knowledge and to practice new learning for a reality too distant, too risky, or too expensive for an educational or training environment.

Simulations are constructed environments in which learners assume different roles as they act out a prescribed scenario, a program of action, or the management of a large systemic organi-zation such as a company, hospital, or school. Simulations allow adults to more deeply learn and practice multiple concepts and skills over a shorter time than in real-life experience. For example, six months are shortened to six days. Simulations immerse learners in a reality that mimics real life, allowing them to experience what might remain abstract in textual materials and traditional classes—power, conflict, discrimination, aggression, debt, stress, and expenditure of resources.

Currently, simulations are becoming very popular for training and business education (Aldrich, 2005). As a format for learning, they are vastly improving as rapidly evolving technology makes them more creative and accessible for the classroom and e-learning. A well-designed simulation elicits a variety of feelings in learners, allows for practice of new learning among unpredictable events, replicates the learners' work roles, offers feedback from a variety of sources, supports collaboration, and stimulates decision making with cause-and-effect consequences (Vaughan, 2006).

A complex and highly technical simulation requires a detailed design and developmental guide such as *Flash MX for Interactive Simulation* (Kaye and Castillo, 2003) for its construction. However, the outline by Michael Vaughan (2006) in Exhibit 7.3 for a high-impact business simulation to teach leadership skills would be relevant for simulations in other professional areas such as health and education. The elements in this outline are also instructive for a simpler simulation which an instructor or trainer could construct for a particular course or seminar. Illustrating these elements is a description (Exhibit 7.4) of how Regis University in Denver has used a simulation for the capstone course in its MBA program.

Exhibit 7.3   Elements of a Simulation

Learning to filter information. Success in many professions requires leadership to focus on what's important and to eliminate extraneous information. The simulation should require the learner to discrimi-nate between relevant and irrelevant information in order to make decisions.

Learning to deal with interruptions. Untimely intrusions, from emergency calls to colleagues who "need a moment," are part of every day for a leader. The simulation should entail situations where the learner has to adapt to impositions and to prioritize responsibilities within time constraints.

Implementing clearly defined goals. Leaders are responsible for attaining agreed-upon goals such as market share and enrollment targets. The simulation should challenge the learner to reach a particular goal that is well defined and that can be tracked during the simulation.

Evaluating and reacting to feedback. Effectively responding to feedback is crucial for most leaders. How to assess and react to feedback is a critical skill in any occupation. The simulation should provide several feedback elements that relate to performance and goal achievement.

Exploring options. Trying out different ideas is often not possible in real-life leadership because it's too risky. But a simulation should allow "what if" questions to be played out to realize the consequences of decisions and develop critical thinking.

Practicing collaboration. Leaders have to communicate and collaborate effectively. The simulation should provide opportunities for cooperation, discussion, developing common goals, and responding with mutual support.

Adapting to tension. Things do not always go smoothly for leaders. There are mistakes, conflicts, stress, unmet goals, and so forth. The simulation should offer some demanding and challenging situations where reasonable tension occurs and the learners can accommodate or resolve problems as they progress toward their goal.

Dealing with competition. Leaders often have to compete with other companies, departments, or organizations. The simulation should pro-vide competitive situations. If desirable, these can be made into gaming elements with score keeping and comparisons. They may add fun to the simulation.

Benefiting from acceleration. Leaders can't accelerate time to see how their decisions work out. A simulation affords this opportunity. The simulation should manipulate time so that the learner can have insights about the consequences of her decisions.

Receiving coaching. Most leaders have consultants, coaches, or colleagues to question and probe their decisions. The role of the coach is not to give advice but to stimulate reflection and deeper thinking on the part of the learners. Whether it is the instructor or the simulation itself, there should be processes that stimulate the learners to evaluate their ideas and decisions.

Using a pre-determined guide. The simulation should have a way to guide learner actions. Usually there is an evaluation component or engine in the simulation that electronically or through the instructor assesses the learners' responses and indicates progress and flow. A simple example is a game board which players cross to reach an ultimate goal. Each player's turn determines a variety of possible moves and consequences as they traverse the board. At an elementary level, the game of Monopoly simulates rational investment strategies among mutually respectful real estate brokers. (At least, that's what I told our children until greed and regression emerged to overtake our playful encounters.)

Source: Adapted from Vaughan, 2006, pp. 179–182.

Exhibit 7.4   Description of a Simulation for an MBA Capstone Course

There are 12,000 adult students in the School for Professional Studies at Regis University in Denver. One of its most popular programs is the Master of Business Administration (MBA). Students can take courses that are either in classrooms or online. After interviewing employers who hired its MBA graduates, the program's administrators and faculty decided to make its capstone course more experiential and relevant: to offer students the opportunity to actually lead a business enterprise rather than to learn *about* how it can be done.

To achieve this goal, faculty decided to make the capstone course a simulation that looked and felt like a real company. In collaboration with designers, they created an international shoe company, Mercury Shoes, where students approaching graduation could serve as senior executives. In these roles, the students had a real-life business environment with responsibilities to make decisions about strategic issues based on industry news, market data, stock quotes, quarterly budgets, employment resources, and so forth.

As in the real world, there were news articles, radio reports, and other media that provided valuable as well as distracting information. Students might get a news article about rising wages in an East Asian country or about new technology for inexpensively producing synthetic rubber. Because this information would affect their production and costs, they would have to further study financial and analyst reports, conduct market analyses, and update their knowledge about current company reports in sales, marketing, finance, operations, and human resources. In order to arrive at an effective business strategy, they would also have to be aware of government policies, economics, law, and ethical practices.

Their multibillion-dollar company, including a manufacturing and a service component, reached an international market in at least three continents, so the context and complexity involved in students' decision making was realistic and substantial. Students received feedback from a simulated systemic framework about the intended and unintended consequences of their strategies and actions. In addition, they received coaching to probe their thinking and to facilitate further learning about business executives. At appropriate intervals, faculty provided guidance for students to move forward with plans and strategies. With performance indexes and faculty evaluations as part of the assessment process, learners received further relevant information about their progress toward academic as well as professional goals. With more than 1,500 students successfully completing this course, the capstone simulation continues today with ongoing supplements and refinements to make it an authentic as well as motivating process to embody new learning.

Source: Personal communication from Michael Vaughan, March 6, 2007.

Games can be similar to simulations but they are usually very structured and have a competitive win-lose quality. Video and computer games are currently extremely popular, especially with younger adults. In recent years, they have evolved into multiplayer online games such as Sony's *EverQuest*. Games such as *Lineage* in Korea have hundreds of thousands of players playing at the same time (J. S. Brown, 2002). Similarly, Blizzard's *World of Warcraft* teams up players from all over the world to create war games.

With 3-D graphics, life-like characters, and multidimensional narratives, games can be realistic and engaging. The evolution of *smart models*, whose tactics develop in response to interactions with human players, promises increasing educational and intellectual benefits for challenging people to practice their skills as well as to develop their ingenuity. Haptics, the science of touch, offers the possibility of simulations and games that can be used for learning skills such as surgical procedures and operating dangerous machinery (Vaughan, 2006).

With such advances as artificial life (AL), software agents that possess human characteristics which evolve on the basis of interaction with the environment and people, the possibilities for games and simulations are extraordinary. In the future, learners may be as likely to role play with a machine as with another person. These developments are both fantastic and surreal.

This is new territory for adult education. John Seely Brown offers this insight: "There is something very important happening here. . . . Our goal should be to think carefully about how we can let the virtual augment the physical, and not replace it. . . . None of us know how to navigate this new space flawlessly. We have to listen, experiment, and reflect" (2002, p. 64). In this regard, there is the Serious Games Initiative at the Woodrow Wilson Center for International Scholars in Washington, DC. Its purpose is to "forge productive links between the electronic games industry and projects involving the use of games in education, training, health, and public policy" (Serious Games Initiative Web site, 2007.) Its Web site offers informative opportunities for adult educators.

Strategy 46: Use Visits, Internships, and Service Learning to Raise Awareness, Provide Practice, and Embody the Learning of Concepts and Skills in Authentic Settings

Sometimes there is only the real thing to make learning meaningful and to involve all of our senses and modes of engagement. As sincere as I was as a teacher educator, no role play or classroom simulation ever matched the kind of serious reflection and emotional engagement that working in schools with real teachers and students produced for the learners I worked with in preservice education. Our visit to a high school once a week with assigned responsibilities to assist teachers raised the level of relevance for our course and substantially increased our motivation to learn. Simply put, once we started going to the school, we were "for real."

Most service professions such as teaching, social work, and nursing have clinical practicum and internships. Over the years, the value of practice and learning in authentic settings has become apparent. What I want to emphasize in this strategy is what I would call "connected" visits, relevant real-life situations where adult learners apply and reflect on what they are learning. Here are a few examples of course activities where I have seen learning enter another stratum of meaning and embodiment due to its pertinent use in actual environments:

- Interviewing immigrant families in their homes for courses in education, nursing, and communication

- Tutoring students for courses in numerous disciplines

- Observing and collecting in forests, marshes, and quarries for courses in the earth and environmental sciences

- Visiting auto and other manufacturing plants for courses in numerous disciplines

- Working with politicians and activists for courses in the social and political sciences

- Service learning for courses in social justice

In order to employ this strategy, the questions for us as instructors are the following: Can the learners make a real-life connection to the subject I am teaching? If so, is there any way that I can create a placement or visitation where they can apply what they are learning? If so, can they make that connection in a way that responsibly serves the community they are visiting? An obvious answer to these questions is a course or training that has a service-learning component. However, service learning does not necessarily translate into the embodiment of learning.

Embodiment requires a certain amount of practice, reflection, and refinement over time. Service learning may not be the best opportunity for this regimen. Service learning also needs a critical consciousness (see Chapter Three) for understanding its complexity and possible misapplication. A book that is responsive to these issues is *Service Learning in Higher Education: Critical Issues and Directions* (Butin, 2005). Elise Burton (2003) has written an article that sensitively addresses a transformative service-learning experience for adults engaging their beliefs and knowledge in a powerfully different cultural setting.

Strategy 47: Use Invention, Artistry, Imagination, and Enactment to Render Deeper Meaning and Emotion in Learning

Invention and artistry are ways of creating something with which to express oneself; to respond to a need or desire; to react to an experience; and to make connections between the known and the unknown, the concrete and the abstract, and the worldly and the spiritual and among different people, places, and things. Through art and invention, adults attempt to answer questions such as these: What do I want to express? What do I want to create? What is another way? What is a better way? What do I imagine? What do I wish to render? What does . . . mean to me?

I discuss invention and artistry together because the conceptual and subjective differences between them are difficult to discern and because both ought to be integral to learning and not, as is so often the case with art, separate entities in education. We can consider artistry as an embedding of art in learning rather than as a separate and frequently disenfranchised experience ("Now we are going to do art"). As Jamake Highwater has said, "Knowledge is barren without the capacity for feeling and imagination" (1994). Art is a vivid sensibility within life and learning across all cultures throughout the world. I believe the lack of meaning so frequently attributed to academic learning and professional training may be due to the indirect but nonetheless thorough separation of learning from artistry.

Although invention is more frequently associated with a specific product and technology, it is difficult for us to tell the difference internally between being inventive and being artistic. Both processes can be used in every subject area. Both processes are open ended and entail kindling an awareness of creative possibility while considering educational or training goals. For example, one of my colleagues, Michele Naylor, teaching a course titled Foundations of Education, approached her learners with the question, "What are the things we, as educators in our communities, most deeply want to contribute and accomplish?" The learners were then given an hour to reflect, write, and sketch their reactions to this question. Afterwards they met in small groups to share their responses. This led to the mutual agreement to post their sketches and conduct a large-group dialogue. From this activity the group decided to compose a mural depicting the theme of community and learning. Using poster paints, a large roll of paper, and masking tape, the participants collaborated with their ideas and sketches to create a mural that was six feet high all around the circumference of the classroom. This took about six hours. During the creation of the mural, one of the learners took photographs of the process and created a collage. Each learner also wrote a reflective paper discussing the process of creating the mural and the ideas represented. At the next class session, encircled by the mural they created, the learners summarized their reactions and made connections between this process and the work they did or intended to do in the community.

As an example of invention, I recall a small cadre of adult learners who were struggling to comprehend systems theory and decided to invent a game, played according to systems theory, which could teach the fundamental concepts and principles of this theory in a pleasurable way. The game board was a narrow roll of cloth with simulated steps that when extended created a serpentine figure across the width of a small room. Along its path were stations where players (other learners in the course) were to be interviewed or asked to complete activities and draw graphic models of systemic processes. The game became so popular as a teaching device that the university library acquired it as a resource.

My experience has been that learners across many cultures welcome the invitation to infuse their academic work with artwork, such as sketches and poetry. I have also found that projects that include works of fiction, plays, visual art, musical compositions, songs, and performance art as essential components offer access to some of the most profound understandings adults gain from their learning.

When learners imagine or enact the physical and emotional properties of an idea, the concept becomes more salient, enhancing neural connections and increasing neural growth to deepen learning (Cozolino and Sprokay, 2006). Using images and the physical senses to experience ideas makes them more directly compelling and enhances their emotional associations. For example, it's one thing to say chemotherapy can be devastating. It's quite another to remember accompanying a friend during his sequence of treatments. In quite another direction, suppose the concept under discussion is excellence. Having adults remember what they did and how they felt at a time when they achieved excellence in their lives can enrich and increase the vividness of what the concept of excellence really means.

One of the best ways to use imagination *and* enactment is to create a situation in which learners *become a concept*. They become a representation of an idea and carry out a desired, challenging task. For example, when we learn about feedback, learners and I often create a game analogous to "hot and cold": one of us has to find an object, and the rest of us use tapping as the signal. We become feedback! Afterward we are well prepared to discuss feedback conceptually and to address its nuances concretely. Adventure education and Outward Bound courses do this to the maximum and make a lasting difference, especially with adults (Hattie and others, 1997). If you want to explore the meaning of challenge, crossing raging river rapids attached to a rope with a $4 pulley will give you a memorable opportunity. Or in a more tranquil example, an adult basic education instructor conducting a course in earth science could have the learners physically represent the planets and their movements in order to understand the solar system. There are myriad possibilities with this approach. And it's great for experiencing flow.

When it comes to enhancing meaning with adult learners, it seems important to have a criterion, one measured by feedback, by which we can estimate the motivational quality of our instruction. It's also important to remember that motivation ebbs and flows. Learners are not going to be as active when they are reflecting and contemplating. Sometimes, no matter how much we care, energy drains and dissipates. We also need to keep cultural differences in mind: the person silent and calm may be as intensely motivated as the person with the most bright-eyed expression in the group.

As an instructor, I have found paying attention to alertness in all its manifestations in a learning group is important. Boredom is not always easy to perceive, but sleepiness and what I call the presomnolent stare (eyes glazing over) seem to translate pretty consistently across cultures. If I see more than a few people showing these signs, I find it helpful to assess the learning activity for its qualities of engagement, value, and challenge.

I also want the best learning atmosphere possible. Adult learners have some responsibility for the learning climate. However, as their guide, I want this climate to be optimal. My role is to observe and respectfully orchestrate. If the energy in the group is declining, I may need to do something as simple as suggesting a break or refining the learning activity. The important point is that my observation of the group acts as a motivational altimeter that increases my awareness of learners' responsiveness, so when that responsiveness is falling to a level at which learning is less effective, I can select from among the best motivational strategies I know to stimulate the conditions that evoke motivation. This process is analogous to stoking a fire.

Nurturing an optimal climate for a community of adult learners is a constant challenge, and successfully meeting that challenge increases my feelings of competence and flow. Working in an optimal learning climate is like being in a remarkable conversation. The learning and the relationships are the "gravy" beyond the experience itself. Yet the years have taught me that there is a craft to facilitating these experiences. They are seldom serendipitous. We have to want and plan for an optimal learning climate. But this atmosphere happens only when we are fully present and keenly aware just about 100 percent of the time. It's worth it. Knowing we have helped create a group of vitally active and friendly adults who are enjoying learning can be quite a feeling.

8

Engendering Competence among Adult Learners

That's what reality is.
It's a dream everyone has together.

Jeffrey Eugenides
Middlesex

B eing effective at what we value resonates with something beyond feeling competent. At some level, competence connects with our dreams, with that part of us that yearns for unity with something greater than ourselves. We want to matter. There are many ways to make this so: caring for someone we love, nurturing beauty, living with purpose, finding good in our work, and learning. Although we may do these things day in and day out, we need to believe we do them fairly well. If we do not, we must vaguely realize we are diminishing what makes life worth living and hope a constant in our midst. To be ineffective at what we value is a spiritual dilemma. By being competent we build the bridge that reconciles spiritual satisfaction, a moral life, and altruistic passion. The quest for competence starts with something as simple as a baby looking for a toy behind a pillow and ends in later life with what Erik Erikson called *generativity*, our desire to leave an enduring and beneficent legacy.

The acknowledgment of purposeful agency seems to be universal (Plaut and Markus, 2005), and competence appears to be the most powerful of all the motivational conditions for adults. For people with a European American background, competence usually is perceived as acting as an *independent* self distinct from others. For people from an East Asian background, competence usually is perceived as acting as an *interdependent* self whose actions are conjoint and in relationship with others (Plaut and Markus, 2005).

Across cultures, this human need for competence is not one that is acquired but one that already exists and can be strengthened or weakened through learning experiences. To a certain extent, how adults view the outcome of competent behavior is situationally dependent. In some instances, people may understand competence as an individual proficiency for achieving what is best for one's personal interests. Saving money could be a likely example. In other situations, people may conceive of competence as a collective responsibility, carried out with regard for what is best for others as well as oneself—for example, being environmentally responsible. Individual effectiveness is important, yet it is to be achieved with consideration of our interdependence with all things and our impact on the generations to come.

The quest for a balanced sense of competence is found not only in many native cultures (Michelson, 1997) but also among many workers and employers who actively pursue social and environmental responsibility as an ethical commitment. The emphasis in this book is on finding ways to support adult competence while illuminating the socially redeemable aspects of the individual's increased effectiveness.

Supporting Self-Directed Competence

Because the norm of individual responsibility is very strong in this society, being a self-directed learner is the general expectation for adults. In their everyday lives and when solving personal problems ranging from fixing a leaky faucet to finding a suitable college, most adults are experienced self-directed learners (Merriam, Caffarella, and Baumgartner, 2007). They take primary responsibility for their own learning. Wouldn't it be silly to hear an adult say, "I just don't know how to find a hardware store. And nobody will help me!"

When people can endorse what they are learning and see themselves as volitional and autonomous in their learning, they tend to be intrinsically and positively motivated (Deci and Moller, 2005). This finding is informative for employers (and their trainers), who increasingly require people to capably self-direct their learning in their jobs.

However, sometimes instructors and trainers encounter adults who seem dependent, lacking in self-confidence, or reluctant to take responsibility for their learning. Three of the most common reasons are that (1) these adults have not been socialized to see themselves as in control of their own learning, (2) their experience in school or in the particular domain of learning has been generally negative or unsuccessful, and (3) they do not believe they have a free choice as to whether or not they engage in the learning or training experience. This last reason, very common among adults, is a personal security issue to which adult educators have been sensitive for many years (Brookfield, 1993).

In some instances, adult learners need courses and training not so much because they want them but because they need the jobs, the promotions, and the money for which these learning experiences are basic requirements. This is the reality for many adults, and it may be one about which they feel they have little choice. "Just tell me what to do" is their common refrain. They realize the highly controlling nature of some corporate environments and higher education institutions is beyond their political or personal influence.

Strategies to support adult volition and the self-direction of their learning have been discussed in the previous three chapters. *The strategies that relate to the motivational purposes of respect, self-efficacy, expectancy for success, and deepening engagement and challenge are most effective in this regard.* When combined with the following strategies to engender competence, they create a holistic system in which the competence and the self-direction of adult learners mutually enhance each other. Proficiently applied, the strategies enable adults who feel minimal control of their learning to grow in the realization that they can determine and direct learning they value.

Since these strategies are not culturally neutral, we need to remain sensitive to the different ways that self-directedness may be culturally understood or enacted. For example, one study found that Korean adults who had cultivated self-directedness in their learning without remaining interdependent with their group were seen as immature and self-centered by other group members (Nah, 2000). As with using all of these strategies, cultural responsiveness on the part of the trainer or instructor has to be constant.

Relating Authenticity and Effectiveness to Assessment

In training and more formal learning experiences, assessment exerts a powerful motivational influence on adults because it is the socially sanctioned educational procedure to communicate about their competence. Historically, more than any other action, assessment by the instructor has validated learners' competence. Our comments, scores, grades, and reports affect learners in the present and the future. Assessment often leaves a legacy for adults, directly or indirectly, by having an impact on their careers, vocational opportunities, professional advancement, and acceptance into various schools and programs.

Many adults undergo debilitating stress in testing situations. They often feel awkward and anxious taking exams, especially when there is pressure to perform, a highly competitive environment, or serious consequences for poor performance. Test anxiety has been found to be a widespread problem among adults (Sarason, 1980). As responsible adults with some degree of professional or social standing, we are vulnerable to such uneasiness for valid reasons. Among them may be fears of revelation of ignorance, of negative comparison with peers, and of inability to meet personal standards and goals. I have often thought that one of the great benefits of being an older adult is "No more tests!" However, one does begin to replace those that are academic with those that are medical in this period of life.

In assessment situations, emotion is a double-edged sword that can enhance or diminish performance (LeDoux, 1996). With moderate to mild stress, adrenaline is released. We are more alert. Neural connections are more fluid, and memory systems coordinate to retrieve relevant knowledge. But high anxiety diminishes our capacity to think rationally and the problem-solving part of the brain is less efficient. Our thinking narrows and we react rather than reflect (Sapolsky, 2004). For suggestions to reduce the disabling stress of assessments, please see Strategies 49 and 50.

For assessment to be intrinsically motivating for adults, it has to be *authentic*—connected to adults' life circumstances, frames of reference, and values. For example, a case study could be used as an authentic assessment if it asked learners to respond to a situation that mirrors their work or community life with the resources and conditions normally there. A real-life context for demonstrating learning enhances its relevance for adults, appeals to their pragmatism, and affirms their rich background of experiences (Kasworm and Marienau, 1997). In contrast, an impersonal multiple-choice exam can seem tedious and irrelevant to many adults.

Effectiveness is the learners' awareness of their mastery, command, or accomplishment of something they find to be important

314 ENHANCING ADULT MOTIVATION TO LEARN

in the *process* of learning or as an *outcome* of learning. Therefore, both the processes and the results of learning are significant information for adults. How well am I doing? and How well did this turn out? is a critical pair of questions for adult learning activities. In the example of the case study, to judge the quality of their thinking as they *process* the case, the adults would likely want feedback about how well their responses relate to the issues in the case study. In addition, when they finally resolve the case, they would want to assess the quality of this *outcome* for its merits as well. Motivation is elicited when adults realize they have competently performed an activity that leads to a valued goal. Awareness of competence affirms the need of adults, across cultures, to act purposefully in their world as they understand it.

If we take an institutional perspective, the first aim of assessment is usually to audit adult learning. However, I am in agreement with those scholars (Wiggins, 1998; Taylor, Marienau, and Fiddler, 2000) who have asserted that assessment should primarily be used to enhance learning and motivation. If we truly want *assessment to be a means for learning*, the real question is *How many different ways can we find to help adults become confident that they have learned a topic or a skill proficiently for what matters to them?*

With respect to this question, let's begin with feedback as a motivational strategy, because self-adjustment based on feedback is essential to learning. As James Zull writes, "Testing our (personal) theories is the ultimate step in learning" (2006, p. 7). Adults change or maintain *how* they learn and *how* they perform based on the feedback they receive about their ideas and behavior. Through feedback they *become* more competent—as well as realize they *are* competent.

Strategy 48: Provide Effective Feedback

Feedback is information that learners receive about the quality of their work. Knowledge about the learning process and its results, comments about emerging skills, notes on a written assignment, and graphic records are forms of feedback that instructors and learners use. Feedback appears to enhance the motivation of learners because learners are able to evaluate their progress, locate their performance within a framework of understanding, maintain their efforts toward realistic goals, self-assess, correct their errors efficiently, self-adjust, and receive encouragement from their instructors and peers.

From a neuroscientific perspective, feedback enhances learning and motivational processes within the brain. When we learn, we are anticipating what to do next and making specific predictions based on prior knowledge—for example, in solving a math problem we tell ourselves, "Next I need to multiply 11 times 11 and add that number to my total. That's 122 added to. . . . Oops, or is it 121? I better check my calculator. Glad I did: 11 times 11 is 121." And on we go to solve the rest of the problem. Feedback, in this case via the calculator, informs our predictions and energizes the learning process. Neural activity is initiated by our anticipations and predictions (Schultz and Dickinson, 2000). Feedback evokes signaling among specific neural circuits by confirming or disconfirming our predictions. It also stimulates emotional states (pleasure in being correct, perplexity in being incorrect, and so forth) that provide energy for further neural activity in the learning process. If we're awake and active, feedback is a constant in our lives. It is the essential human process for knowing we're in control. In this way, feedback contributes on a moment-to-moment basis to our need for survival (Zull, 2002).

Feedback is probably the most powerful communication that instructors and peers can regularly use to affect learners' competence. Feedback is as elemental to the sum of a person's knowledge as photosynthesis is to a rainforest. Without it, the benefits of trial-and-error learning would be impossible.

Although most of the research on feedback has been done with youth (Hattie and Timperley, 2007), Morris Keeton and his colleagues emphatically support the finding that feedback is a critical influence for enhancing practice and deepening adult learning (Keeton, Sheckley, and Griggs, 2002). In studies at Harvard, students and alumni overwhelmingly reported that the single most important ingredient for making a course effective is getting rapid instructor response on assignments and exams (Light, 1990). In general feedback is informative when it identifies "what is good and why, as well as what needs to be improved and how" (Brophy, 2004, p.72). However, feedback can be complex and nuance makes a difference. The following paragraphs further describe characteristics of effective feedback:

• Effective feedback *provides evidence of the learner's effect relative to the learner's intent.* This most often is feedback that is based on *agreed-on* criteria, standards, and models (Wiggins, 1998). Learners can compare their work against a standard: a superbly written executive letter, a museum sculpture, a rubric for critical thinking, or a video of a political activist giving a rousing speech. Learners are then in a position to understand what they have done and how it compares to their own goals. They can judge how well they have performed a task or produced a product in terms of a specific target. They are clear about the criteria against which their work is being evaluated and can more explicitly decide what needs to be done for further effective learning.

Such self-assessment leads to self-adjustment. Learners can use this information to guide their effort, practice, and performance more accurately. For example, in a welding course, each learner agrees to produce a ninety-degree corner weld to industry specifications. The standards are written out on paper and available. When the learner makes a weld that she judges to be up to this standard, she comes to a table to compare her weld to welds ranging from excellent to poor. Based on this comparison, the learner adjusts the necessary skills and improves the next weld or, if satisfied, moves on to a more advanced task. The instructor may give guidance if the learner requests it.

- Effective feedback is *informational rather than controlling*. According to the seminal research of Edward Deci and Richard Ryan (1991), feedback is more likely to enhance intrinsically motivated learning when it is *informational*, telling learners about their effectiveness and supporting their self-determination. *Controlling* feedback undermines self-determination and intrinsic motivation by making the adult's behavior seem dependent on forces that demand compliance. For example, for *informational* feedback we might say, "In your paper you've clearly identified three critical areas of concern; your writing is well organized and vivid; I appreciate how well you've supported your rationale with facts and anecdotes." An instructor giving *controlling* feedback for the same behavior might say, "You're making progress and doing as you should be doing, meeting the standards for organization and evidence that I've set for writing in this course." Controlling feedback often contains imperatives such as *should* and *must*. Often the difference between informational and controlling feedback is subtle, but can be extreme in its impact.

- Effective feedback is *specific and constructive*. It is difficult to improve performance when we have only a general sense of how well we have done. Most people prefer specific information and realistic suggestions for how to improve (Brophy, 2004). For example, "I found your insights on government spending compelling. To emphasize your conclusion, you might consider restating your initial premise in your last paragraph." Or "Your ending paragraph is a thorough summarization with well documented facts cohesively organized. However, two of your sentences are in the passive voice. This paragraph might be more powerfully stated with active verbs in those sentences." When you are giving guidance with feedback, it is important to keep in mind how much the learner *wants to* or *ought to* decide on a course of action relative to the feedback. In general, the more that adult learners can confidently self-assess and self-adjust, the more intrinsically motivated they will be.

- Effective feedback can be *quantitative*. In such areas as athletics, quantitative feedback has definite advantages. It is precise and can provide evidence of small improvements. Small improvements can have long-range effects. One way to understand learning is by measuring *rate*, which indicates how often something occurs over a fixed time. For example, a learner is told he completed thirty laps during a one-hour swimming practice. Another way is by measuring the percentage of learning performance that is correct or appropriate. Percentages are calculated by dividing the number of times the learning performance occurs correctly by the total number of times the performance opportunity occurs, as in batting averages and field goal percentages. Another common form of quantitative feedback is duration, which is how long it takes a learning performance to be completed. For example, a lab technician might receive feedback on how long she takes to complete a particular chemical analysis. These are not the only forms of quantitative feedback that are possible, but they are a representative sample. Whenever progress on learning a skill appears to be slow or is difficult to ascertain, quantitative feedback may be an effective means to enhance learner motivation.

- Effective feedback is *prompt*. Promptness characterizes feedback that is quickly given as the situation demands but not necessarily immediately (Hattie and Timperley, 2007). Sometimes a moderate delay in feedback enhances learning because such a delay is simply culturally sensitive or polite. For example, after they perform in public, waiting for learners to reduce their anxiety or talk with peers seems entirely appropriate. In general, it is best to be immediate with feedback but to pay careful attention to whether a delay might be beneficial.

- Effective feedback *should be frequent when practice is vital to the learning goal*. Frequent feedback is probably most helpful when new learning is first being acquired. In general, one can often provide more frequent feedback through technology (such as a radar gun that indicates the speed of baseball pitches) when practice can clearly lead to improvement of skills. Here is an area where neuroscience is providing important insights.

"Practice makes perfect" is an old adage that may be truer than we think. As we have mentioned repeatedly in this book, every skill and bit of knowledge exists as a neural circuit. When we learn, the connecting fibers—the axons and dendrites—join with thousands of other fibers and neurons to create more complex knowledge and skill. These circuits fire signals as we exert this knowledge and skill. Recent neurological studies (Coyle, 2007) indicate that *myelin*, a membranous wrapping around nerve fibers, thickens in response to the frequency of impulses traveling along a particular circuit. "Myelin works like insulation. The thicker it gets, the faster and more accurately signals pass through nerve fibers wrapped within it" (2007, p. 40). Faster impulse speed is crucial to optimal thought and movement. Whether we're reading or playing tennis, the more we practice, the more we myelinate the circuits particular to each skill. This practice allows us to more efficiently and more precisely control signal speed along that circuitry, improving our skill in reading or playing tennis.

K. Anders Ericsson (2006) offers evidence that what people normally call talent is the result of an enormous amount of *deliberate practice*. As described earlier for reading and tennis, deliberate practice enhances the myelination of neural circuitry for these skills and others, such as playing piano or golf. It requires constantly working on technique, requesting continual corrective feedback, and fully concentrating on improving weaknesses. Olympic athletes and other people committed to expert performance in sports spend thousands of hours in deliberate practice. Although the capacity to myelinate exists throughout life, it appears that the greatest capacity for this biological process is during youth and young adulthood (Coyle, 2007).

Myelination would also explain to some extent why once errors have accumulated, improving a skill is more difficult to accomplish. When multiple errors become established, the erroneous techniques have a neural circuitry that is probably well myelinated. The new learning encouraged through feedback may seem too difficult and confusing because of slow signal speed along unmyelinated and undeveloped circuitry, making further progress seem even more remote to an adult learner.

- Effective feedback is *positive*. Positive feedback emphasizes improvements, progress, and correct responses rather than deficiencies and mistakes. It is an excellent form of feedback because it increases learners' intrinsic motivation, feelings of well-being, and sense of competence and helps learners form a positive attitude toward the source of the information. Adults prefer positive feedback because when they are trying to improve, emphasis on errors and deficiencies (negative feedback) can be discouraging. When learners are prone to making mistakes, the instructor's pointing out a decrease in errors may be considered positive feedback. Also, positive feedback can be given with constructive feedback. For example, an instructor might say to a learner, "You've been able to solve most of this problem. Let's take a look at what's left and see if we can understand why you are getting stuck."

- Effective feedback is *related to impact criteria*. Impact criteria are the main reasons a person is learning something, the heart of the individual's learning goal (Wiggins, 1998). Often these are unique or strongly related to a cultural perspective. One person may produce a speech or a piece of writing to inspire, arouse, or provoke. Another may wish to create a design or a performance as a gift for her family or friends. Assessment and feedback should support such individual goals and respectfully deal with what may be ineffable or accomplished only in a realm beyond mechanistic objectivity. We may need to give feedback that is more akin to dialogue or to what many artists do when they respond to how another's work emotionally affects them, rather than "evaluate" that work.

- Effective feedback is usually *personal and differential for skill and procedural learning*. Differential feedback uses self-comparison and focuses on the increment of personal improvement that has occurred since the last time the learning activity was performed. In skill or procedural learning, such as writing, operating a machine, or learning a particular sport, emphasizing small steps of progress can be very encouraging to learner motivation. However, the amount of time that lapses before we *document* such differential feedback can affect its perception. For example, learners may be able to see larger gains and feel a greater sense of accomplishment when their improvement is summarized on a daily or weekly schedule. Portfolios and video are excellent for this type of feedback because each can offer the learner comparisons after significant time and practice.

In addition to the specific characteristics of feedback just listed, some refinements in the composition and delivery of feedback may be helpful. For many skills, *graphing* or *charting* feedback can encourage learner motivation because this visual representation makes progress more concrete and shows a record of increasing improvement.

We should always consider *asking learners what they would like feedback on*, especially when we are working with diverse populations. Their needs and concerns may be different from ours, and the knowledge gained from such discussion can make the feedback more relevant and motivating.

Learners' *readiness to receive feedback* is also important. If people are resistant to feedback, they are not likely to learn or self-adjust. In such cases, it may be advisable to hold off on feedback until a personal conference can be arranged or until learners are more comfortable with the learning situation.

Checking to make sure our feedback was understood can be important for complex feedback or for adults who are English-language learners.

Everything that has been said about feedback thus far also applies to *group feedback.* Whether the group is a team, a collaborative group, or an entire class, feedback on the group's total performance can influence each individual. Because group feedback consolidates members' mutual identification and sense of connection, it helps enhance group cohesiveness and morale.

As a final point, please remember that sometimes the best form of feedback is simply to encourage adults to move forward to the next, more challenging learning opportunity.

Strategy 49: Avoid Cultural Bias and Promote Equity in Assessment Procedures

Probably nothing is more demoralizing to adults than to realize they do not have a fair chance to demonstrate their knowledge or learning. The reality is that it is difficult to avoid bias in any test or assessment procedure that uses language, because the words and examples sway the learner toward a particular cultural perspective. This is especially true for paper-and-pencil tests. A common example of bias is content that favors one frame of reference over another (Kornhaber, 2004). Bias relates not only to ethnicity but also to age and gender. For example, items about sports tend to give males an edge, whereas items of similar difficulty that focus on child care may favor females (Pearlman, 1987). We need always to examine the assumptions embedded in the materials we create or select for assessment. We do not want to penalize anyone for not having been fully socialized in a particular culture or oriented to a dominant perspective (Alfred, 2002). We know adult learning is derived from multiple sources and varied life experiences (Kasworm and Marienau, 1997). So when we are developing our assessment instruments (and all other training and curricular materials as well), it is important to consider the following issues:

- *Invisibility.* Is there a significant absence of women and minority groups in assessment materials? (This implies that certain groups are of less value, importance, and significance in our society.)

- *Stereotyping.* When groups or members of groups are mentioned, are they assigned traditional or rigid roles that deny diversity and complexity within different groups? (When stereotypes occur repeatedly in print and other media, learners' perceptions are gradually distorted, making stereotypes and myths seem more acceptable.)

- *Selectivity.* Does offering or allowing for only one inter-pretation of an issue, situation, or group of people perpetuate bias? (We may fail to tap the varied perspec-tives and knowledge of learners.)

- *Unreality.* Do assessment items lack a historical con-text that acknowledges—when relevant—prejudice and discrimination? (Glossing over painful or contro-versial issues obstructs authenticity and creates a sense of unreality.)

- *Linguistic bias.* Do materials reflect gender bias? For example, are masculine examples, terms, and pronouns dominant? (As in the case of invisibility, this bias devalues the importance and significance of women.)

Even directions for tests can be biased. This is especially true for English-language learners, who benefit from test instructions that are direct and simple. Whenever possible, we want to avoid the passive voice and ambiguous comments. Test instructions should be in short sentences and guidelines should be clear and explicit. We also should allow adequate processing time for questions and directions to be understood.

It is fair and reasonable to provide assessment accommodations for learners with disabilities and for English-language learners (Kornhaber, 2004). For example, they may need to be assessed in a small group or individually. Modifications may include extra time to complete tests, presentation of assessment materials in audio or video, and allowances for different ways of responding, such as dictation or using an interpreter.

Instructors often regard assessments as learning audits to assign grades or evaluation scores. But assessments can also be an excellent instructional method to provide understanding of what adults are learning, how they are thinking, what their progress is, and which learning problems to address. Applied in this manner, they are *formative assessments* that guide instruction and identify areas that learners may need to deepen, improve, practice, revise, or strengthen in terms of their understanding and skill development.

For example, in an accounting course at an urban college, the assessment requires learners to make recommendations based on a cost-volume-profit analysis for the production and sale of a new product for a manufacturing company. Their recommendations and calculations reveal both their conceptual and computational understanding of this analysis. They have had time to practice it and the instructor could easily have chosen to grade their work. However, due to the professional value of this analysis and the linguistic diversity of his students, he prefers to use this assignment as a formative assessment to give each learner feedback about their understanding of this analysis and suggestions for further practice.

With the largest immigrant population in the history of the United States in today's educational and training systems, many adult educators are experiencing greater linguistic diversity among adult learners than ever before. Often there is need for greater practice and feedback during learning for English-language learners to accommodate the linguistic forms, communicative strategies, and Eurocentric context of their courses and training. Formative assessment is one more way for instructors to meet linguistically diverse adults where they are and help them deepen their learning in a way that benefits all learners in the group.

Strategy 50: Make Assessment Tasks and Criteria Clearly Known to Learners prior to Their Use

If we genuinely want self-assessing, self-adjusting, and self-directed learners, we must make sure they comprehend the tasks and criteria by which they are assessed. Trainers in the business world do this frequently, and those of us in higher education must evolve in this direction as well. Adults greatly appreciate clear assessment tasks and criteria because becoming competent is then no longer a guessing game, and they can more clearly assess and guide their own learning. Plainly spoken—no more secrets.

This strategy complements differentiated instruction, scaffolding, and contracting (see Chapter Six). Using it, we make criteria, examples, and models readily available to learners. Where scoring or grades are necessary, we ensure that all learners clearly understand the rationale for their assignment. In fact, one of the issues we need to consider when using this strategy is the degree to which learners participate in the creation and refinement of the assessment criteria. Certainly, we should discuss criteria and assessment procedures at the beginning of a course or training, remaining open to making changes to the process or criteria based on input from the learners. For example, discussion might reveal a lack of time, materials, or opportunities—conditions that may prohibit certain kinds of learning. Therefore, it's quite possible that we could not apply certain criteria fairly.

However, what about revision of criteria or assessment procedures because of differences in the learners' values or perspectives? I don't have an answer that I believe would fit most circumstances, but I do have a procedure that I often find helpful. I offer it not as a formula but as an example of how I have dealt with the complexity of asking adults to participate in shaping assessment criteria.

In a research course, two parts of the assessment process are for students to critique a research article of their choosing and to create a research proposal in an area of interest. The major purpose of the course is for learners to develop an understanding of the primary assumptions, perspectives, and methods that guide research as it can be conducted in the social sciences.

On the first day, I give the learners models of an excellent critique of a research article and an exemplary research proposal that were written by former students in the course. After reading them, the class divides into small groups to discuss why these two examples might be considered commendable. They also reflect on other laudable ways to critique an article or create a proposal that are not mentioned in the examples I offered. During a whole-group discussion, we list both sets of qualities. I then pass out the criteria I normally use, and we see which of their criteria match mine and which do not match. Then we talk further, and after this discussion, I make the agreed-on revisions to the criteria. Often the changes have to do with adding qualitative pieces — sociocultural aspects of research that I may need to consider, such as personal histories and political perspectives.

Transforming training and courses into educational settings where learners share responsibility and authority for their learning is an evolving process for learners as well as for instructors. It may often mean coming to the learning environment with a well-considered plan and set of assessment criteria but being willing to reinvent some of these elements according to the learners and situation. In my experience, both Strategies 49 and 50 markedly reduce adult assessment anxiety, a benefit for which all of us are grateful.

Strategy 51: Use Authentic Performance Tasks to Deepen New Learning and Help Learners Proficiently Apply This Learning to Their Real Lives

Authentic performance tasks are one of the oldest forms of assessment and have been commonly used in training and adult education for many years (Knowles, 1980; Fenwick and Parsons, 2000). Today we have a more sophisticated understanding of these procedures and their central idea: that assessment should resemble as closely as possible the ways adult learners will express in their real lives what they have learned. Thus, for people learning computer programming skills, we would assess their learning by asking them to write and debug source codes of computer programs.

The closer that assessment procedures come to allowing learners to demonstrate what they have learned in the environment where they will eventually use that learning, the greater will be learners' motivation to do well and the more they can understand their competence and feel the self-confidence that emerges from effective performance. From a neuroscientific perspective, authentic assessment contributes to the embodiment of learning, when deeper learning of knowledge and skills occurs as they are used in a real context (Varella, Thompson, and Rosch, 1995). Thus, the neural circuitry and psychophysiological systems throughout our body develop with more capability to apply this learning in future, similar real world situations.

Providing the opportunity for learners to complete an authentic task is one of the best ways to conclude a learning activity because it promotes transfer of learning, enhances motivation for related work, and clarifies learner competence. An authentic task directly meets the adult need to use what has been learned for more effective daily living.

According to Wiggins (1998), an assessment task, problem, or project is authentic if it has the following characteristics:

It is realistic. The task replicates how people's knowledge and capacities are "tested" in their real world.

It requires judgment and innovation. People have to use knowledge wisely to solve unstructured problems, as a carpenter remodeling part of a house must do more than follow a routine procedure.

It asks the learners to "do" the subject. Rather than recite or demonstrate what they have been taught or what is already known, the learners have to explore and work within the discipline, as when they demonstrate their competence for a history course by writing history from the perspective of particular people in an actual historical situation.

It replicates or simulates the contexts that adults find in their workplace, community, or personal life. These contexts involve specific situations and their demands; for example, managers learning conflict resolution skills could apply them to their work situations, with consideration of the actual personalities and responsibilities involved.

It assesses the learners' ability to use an integration of knowledge and skill to negotiate a complex task effectively. Learners have to put their knowledge and skills together to meet real-life challenges. This is analogous to the difference between taking a few shots in a warm-up drill and actually taking shots in a real basketball game, or between writing a paper on a particular law and drafting a bill for a legislator. This assessment criterion involves adaptive decision making, an effective process for the embodiment of knowledge and critical thinking (see Chapter Seven).

It allows appropriate opportunities to rehearse, practice, consult resources, and get feedback on and refine performances and products. These opportunities are so important. Learning and, consequently, assessment are not one-shot enterprises! Almost all learning is formative, whether its purpose is how to repair plumbing, write a publishable article, or bake a pie. We put out our first attempt and see how it works, reads, or tastes. We repeatedly move through a cycle of *perform, get feedback, revise, perform.* That's how most high-quality products and performances are attained—especially in real life. We must use assessment procedures that contribute to the improvement of adult performance and learning over time. Doing so means that assessment is often separated from grading processes to assure learners that their mistakes are not counted against them but are a legitimate part of the learning process.

Table 8.1 contains Grant Wiggins's comparisons of typical tests and authentic tasks.

Strategy 52: Provide Opportunities for Adults to Demonstrate Their Learning in Ways That Reflect Their Strengths and Multiple Sources of Knowing

As adults, most of us are motivated to accomplish assessments in which we can use our strengths to demonstrate the depth and complexity of our learning. Such opportunities cannot use one-dimensional, high-stakes paper-and-pencil testing formats because, by their very structure, tests of this sort reduce and constrict what we can show about what we know. We need either multiple forms of assessment (tests, products, portfolios, and journals) or multidimensional assessment (authentic performance tasks and projects) to adequately reveal the richness of the strengths and sources of our knowing.

At times, the amount of professional time required to accomplish the assessments described here can seem overwhelming. Yet, if we make assessments a partner and part of continuing learning and motivation for adults, rather than merely audits by which to assign grades or scores, assessments themselves become important learning activities, worthy of everyone's time and effort. Nonetheless (I know you are thinking), time constraints will still be a challenge. With this problem in mind, here are some worthwhile assessment activities and methods to support the use of authentic tasks or to be transformed into authentic tasks.

- *Assessment options based on Howard Gardner's multiple intelligences.* Adults have different profiles of intelligences. Their having the opportunity to select an assessment process that reflects their

Table 8.1. Key Differences between Typical Tests and Authentic Tasks

Typical Tests	Authentic Tasks	Indicators of Authenticity
Require correct responses only	Require quality product or performance (or both) and justification	The learner can explain, apply, self-adjust, or justify answers, not just answer correctly using facts.
Must be unknown beforehand to ensure validity	Are known in advance; involve excelling at predictable demanding and core tasks; are not "gotcha!" experiences	The tasks, criteria, and standards by which work will be judged are predictable or known to the learner—as a recital piece, a play, an engine to be fixed, or a proposal to a client can be clearly understood and anticipated prior to assessment.
Are disconnected from a realistic context and realistic constraints	Require real-world use of knowledge; the learner must "do" history, science, and so on in realistic simulations or actual use	The task is a challenge with a related set of constraints that are authentic—likely to be encountered by the professional, citizen, or consumer. Know-how, not plugging in, is required.
Contain isolated items requiring use or recognition of known answers or skills	Are integrated challenges in which knowledge and judgment must be innovatively used to fashion a quality product or performance	The task is multifaceted and nonroutine, even if there is a "right" answer. It thus requires problem clarification, trial and error, adjustments, adapting to the case or facts at hand, and so on.

Table 8.1.   (Continued)

Typical Tests	Authentic Tasks	Indicators of Authenticity
Are simplified for easy and reliable scoring	Involve complex and nonarbitrary tasks, criteria, and standards	The task involves the important aspects of performance or the core challenges of the field of study (or both), not the easily scored; it does not sacrifice validity for reliability.
Are one-shot	Are iterative; contain recurring essential tasks, genres, and standards	The work is designed to reveal whether the learner has achieved real versus pseudo mastery, and understanding versus mere familiarity over time.
Depend on highly technical correlations	Provide direct evidence, involving tasks that have been validated against core adult roles and discipline-based challenges	The task is valid and fair on its face. It thus evokes student interest and persistence and seems apt and challenging to learners and instructors.
Provide a score	Provide usable (sometimes concurrent) feedback; the learner is able to confirm results and self-adjust as needed	The assessment is designed not merely to audit performance but to improve future performance. The learner is seen as the primary beneficiary of information.

Source: Wiggins, 1998, p. 23.

particular intellectual strengths should encourage their parti-
cipation and enthusiasm for demonstrating their competence.
Table 8.2, adapted from *Multiple Intelligences and Adult Literacy*
(Viens and Kallenbach, 2004) and *Teaching and Learning through
Multiple Intelligences* (Campbell, Campbell, and Dickinson, 2004),
is categorized by type of intelligence (see Chapter Two).

The assessment options in Table 8.2 will need criteria for
learners (and instructors) to judge the quality of their learning
and performance. Strategy 53 addresses this need. However, as an
example of the thoroughness that may be needed to meaningfully
assess many of these creative options, consider the criteria below
for assessing an exhibition such as a poster session or the mural
created by Michele Naylor and her students described in Chapter
Seven (Campbell, Campbell, and Dickinson, 2004).

Knowledge of the topic	Supporting evidence
Diversity of perspectives	Organization of format
Communication with visitors	Clarity of materials
Creativity of delivery	Quality of content
Effective use of resources	Overall cohesiveness

In addition to accommodating multiple intelligences, the assessment menu in Table 8.2 offers a range of learning and performance
that require deep understanding—*design, teach, discern, explain,
analyze, write, create,* and the like. For example, a learner in a
science course might design an experiment to analyze the chemicals in the local water supply and write an editorial based on the
results for the local paper. These assessments provide opportunities
for imaginative experiences that allow adults to use their unique
perspectives, preferences, and strengths. Furthermore, with these
assessments adults can develop deeper relationships between new
learning and their cultural backgrounds and values.

Table 8.2.   Assessment Menu for the Multiple Intelligences

Intelligence	Assessment processes
Linguistic	Tell or write a short story to explain . . .
	Keep a journal to illustrate . . .
	Write a poem, myth, play, or editorial about . . .
	Create a debate to discuss . . .
	Create an advertising campaign to depict . . .
	Create a talk show about . . .
	Write a culminating essay to review . . .
Logical-mathematical	Complete a cost-benefit analysis of . . .
	Write a computer program for . . .
	Design and conduct an experiment to . . .
	Create story problems for . . .
	Conduct a mock trial to . . .
	Induce or deduce a set of principles on . . .
	Create a timeline for . . .
	Create a crossword puzzle for . . .
Musical	Create a song that explains or expresses . . .
	Revise lyrics of a known song to . . .
	Collect a collage of music and songs to . . .
	Create a dance to illustrate . . .
	Create a music video to illustrate . . .
	Create an advertisement to . . .
Spatial	Create a piece of art that demonstrates . . .
	Create a poster to . . .
	Create a videotape, collage, photo album of . . .
	Chart, concept map, or graph . . .
	Design a flag or logo to express . . .
	Create a scale model of . . .
	Create a mobile to . . .

(continued)

Table 8.2.   (Continued)

Intelligence	Assessment processes
Bodily-kinesthetic	Perform a play on . . . Invent or revise a game to . . . Role-play or simulate . . . Use puppets to explore . . . Create a sequence of movements to explain . . . Create a scavenger hunt to . . . Create a poster session or exhibition to . . .
Interpersonal	Participate in a service project that will . . . Offer multiple perspectives of . . . Collaborate to resolve a local problem by . . . Teach a group to . . . Use what you've learned to change or influence . . . Conduct an interview and/or a discussion to . . .
Intrapersonal	Create a personal philosophy about . . . Discern what is essential in . . . Explain your intuitive hunches about . . . Explain your emotions about . . . Explain your assumptions in a critical incident . . . Keep a reflective journal to . . .
Naturalist	Discover and describe the patterns in . . . Create a typology for . . . Relate and describe the interdependence of . . . Observe and describe . . . Use a field trip to analyze . . . Based on observation and field notes describe your learning about . . .

• *Portfolios and process folios.* Regardless of its purpose, a portfolio is a sample of a person's work or learning. It can provide more diverse examples created over a longer time than a single test can. Multiple indicators—such as tests, products, media, and self-assessments—can make up a portfolio and contribute to a deeper understanding of an adult's learning. Portfolios can be an effective means of reflection and assessment for an adult's personal goals as they mesh with course goals in programs ranging from the vocational to the professional (J. O. Brown, 2002). The contents of a portfolio and the assessment criteria used to evaluate it will differ depending on the portfolio's purpose. In this book, the portfolio is not discussed as a vehicle for prior learning assessment. The following are some of the ways a portfolio can be used (Wiggins, 1998):

As a display of the learner's best work, as chosen by the learner, the instructor, or both

As a display of the learner's interests and goals

As a display of the learner's growth or progress

As documentation of self-assessment, self-adjustment, self-direction, and learning

As evidence for professional assessment of learner performance

A *process folio* (Gardner, 1993) goes beyond a conventional portfolio: it layers elements of the entire learning experience so that learners are able to document and reflect on challenges and understandings that emerge over time. The process folio documents three primary considerations: the content of learning (what is being learned), the context of learning (how what is being learned fits into a larger framework, possibly the learner's life, experiences, and culture), and perceptions of the process of learning (perceptions about various influences on the adult's learning and ways in which learning was enhanced). This type of portfolio is a powerful tool for responding to the interests and concerns of diverse learners (Wlodkowski and Ginsberg, 1995).

The following outline offers some guidelines for instructors and learners when working with portfolios:

1. Involve learners in the composition and selection of the portfolio's contents.

   a. Learners may want to explore different aspects of a particular discipline. In a research course, for example, the learner might design an ethnographic study and an experimental study for her portfolio.

   b. Learners may choose among different categories, such as most difficult problem, best work, most valued work, most improved work, and a spiritual experience.

2. Include information in the portfolio that shows learner's self-reflection and self-assessment.

   a. Learners may include a rationale for their selections.

   b. Learners may create a guide for their portfolio offering interpretations, commentary, critique, and matters of contextual importance.

   c. Learners may include self- and peer assessments indicating strengths, areas for improvement, and relationships between earlier and later works.

3. Be clear about the purpose of the portfolio.

   a. Learners should be able to relate their goals for learning to the contents of the portfolios.

   b. Learners should be able to provide a fair representation of their work.

   c. Rubrics and models for assessing portfolio contents should be clearly understood and available (see Strategy 53).

4. Exploit the portfolio as a process to show learner growth.

a. Learners may submit the original, the improved, and the final copy or draft of their creation or performance.

b. Using specific works, learners may make a history of their "movement" along certain dimensions in their growth.

c. Learners may include feedback from outside experts or descriptions of outside activities that reflect the growth illustrated in the portfolio.

5. Teach learners how to create and use portfolios.

a. Offer models of excellent portfolios for learners to examine but stress that each portfolio is an individual creation.

b. Review portfolios regularly and give feedback to learners about them, especially early in the term or year, when learners are initially constructing their portfolios.

Overall assessment of the content of a portfolio is usually a combination of applied checklists, rating scales, and rubrics with a particular sensitivity to learning improvement and progress. For example, an apprentice carpenter's early work displays inferior routing skills but his later products exhibit strong proficiency in these skills. His most recent creations would receive greater or maximum weight for an evaluation. Although there is less quantitative precision, portfolios are likely to obtain a richer and more meaningful understanding of what adults have learned.

• *Projects.* We often use the term *project* to describe the major undertakings of businesses and institutions ("We're working on a new project," or, perhaps more critically, "This thing is turning into a project"). In education and training, magnitude and complexity are what give something the status of a project. From community service to dramatic presentations, projects offer the multiple challenges, meanings, and creative resolutions that make learning motivating and capable of embracing cultural diversity. Because of their size and duration, projects provide the opportunity for active immersion across disciplines and the use of a wide range of intelligences. Projects can connect new concepts and skills with the real lives of adults, fostering the growth of more intricate neural circuitry through deeper and more complex motivated learning.

The investigation conducted by Daniel Solorzano (1989) and his students is a classic example of a collaborative project carried out with critical consciousness. In the late 1970s, Solorzano offered a sociology course at East Los Angeles College. Beginning with a discussion about the negative stereotypes of ethnic Mexicans in Hollywood gang movies, Solorzano and his students arrived at two questions: Why are ethnic Mexicans portrayed negatively in the mass media? and Whose interests are served by these negative portrayals?

To conduct extensive research on these queries, the class divided itself into three groups: (1) a library group to research contemporary and historical images of ethnic Mexicans in the media, (2) a group to research public information data on youth gangs in East Los Angeles, and (3) a group to research the film industry. After analyzing and discussing their research, the learners more clearly understood how film companies were exploiting ethnic Mexican (then referred to as Chicano) stereotypes. Consequently, they organized a boycott against these films. Collaborating with outside organizations for assistance, they founded the ad hoc Gang Exploitation Committee. Solorzano reports that no new Chicano youth gang movies appeared in the decade after this class. Student learning was extensive, and the students succeeded in doing something they considered important: using research and personal action to understand and to limit an unjust representation of ethnic Mexican youth in movies.

In the similar vein, the investigation of learning styles designed and executed by Yolanda Scott-Machado (see Strategy 23 in Chapter Six) is a fine representation of an individual project. Following are some guidelines to keep in mind for creating and carrying out projects:

- Learners should be involved in the conception and planning, whether the project is individual or collaborative.

- Consider goal setting (see Strategy 23 in Chapter Six) or some of its elements as a means to explore and plan the project.

- Request an outline of the project that includes some schedule of agreed-on documentation and a completion date.

- Arrange for the presentation of the project to a relevant audience who can offer authentic acknowledgment and feedback.

- Assess the project from numerous perspectives, including the learner's self-assessment (see Strategy 54). Overall, assessment may involve the quality of project planning, execution, and presentation; the challenge level; creativity and originality; the employment of resources; and what was learned. It may also incorporate the evaluation of other learners and knowledgeable people outside the course or training.

Strategy 53: When Using Rubrics, Make Sure They Assess the Essential Features of Performance and Are Fair, Valid, and Sufficiently Clear So That Learners Can Accurately Self-Assess

When it comes to assessment, rubrics are "where the rubber meets the road." That is because rubrics often mean more than assessment; they mean evaluation. Assessment describes or compares, but evaluation makes a value judgment. In evaluation, we fix passing scores or criteria that determine how acceptable or unacceptable a given performance is. Grades or scores may be assigned and recorded according to the rubric. Evaluations often significantly affect an adult's promotion to or qualification for particular programs or positions.

Although many adult instructors do not use rubrics formally, they do use them on an intuitive basis. They make evaluations of a learner's work based on experience and knowledge, but often without explicit language. For example, an instructor might say, "This writing is excellent, insightful, and entertaining"—without specifically saying why or what makes the writing so. Barbara Walvoord's definition speaks well to a rubric's advantage and limitation: "A rubric articulates in writing the various criteria and standards" that an instructor "uses to evaluate" a learner's work (2004, p. 19). "It translates informed professional judgment into numerical ratings on a scale. Something is always lost in the translation, but the advantage is that these ratings can now be communicated and compared" (2004, p. 19).

As a set of scoring guidelines for evaluating a learner's work, a rubric strongly directs learning. Neurologically, that can be a good thing. A rubric is like a blueprint. It guides frontal-lobe executive function so that learners can manage their learning knowing what literally counts the most (Koechlin and others, 1999). To perform this service proficiently, a rubric should answer the following questions (Wiggins, 1998, p. 154):

By what criteria should performance be judged?

What should we look for to judge performance success?

What does the range in quality of performance look like?

How do we determine validly, reliably, and fairly what score should be given and what that score should mean?

How should the different levels of quality be described and distinguished from one another?

I've been carefully and cautiously using rubrics for about ten years, and they can be deceptive even though they do not appear that way at first glance. They're like a wall whose cracks you can't see until you get very close. Baseball averages afford a good example of the complexity and elusiveness of rubrics. A rubric comprises a scale of possible points along a continuum of quality. Batting average is a rubric in the sense that we evaluate how good batters are by their percentage of hits for times at bat. The higher the average, the better the player. But is a .300 hitter a good hitter? Well, that depends: How many times has the player been to bat? Does she get extra base hits? How does she hit when players are on base? At night? With two strikes? When the team is behind? Against left-handed pitching? As many managers know, you don't use batting average alone to evaluate a player—not even to judge only hitting. And that's how it is with rubrics: they may seem concrete, specific, and telling, but life's contexts and complexity can make the simplest performance a puzzle.

Yet rubrics answer a question that counts for many adults: What are you going to use to judge me? If rubrics are fair, clear, reliable, and valid and get at the essentials of performance, and if learners can self-assess with them to improve before performance is evaluated, rubrics enhance motivation because they significantly increase the probability of learners' achieving competence. However, rubrics need models and indicators to make each level of quality concretely understandable. And they need to be created or revised with input from learners if they are to be culturally sensitive. For example, if we use *smiles frequently* as one indicator for *very good* presentation style, we penalize someone who tends to be droll or someone from a culture where smiling frequently is more an indication of anxiety than of ease. Excellent rubrics are valuable but flawed assistants in making judgments about learning—flawed because language at best renders, but never duplicates, experience.

Let's look at two straightforward rubrics: one for judging the clear expression of a main idea in an essay (Table 8.3) and the other (Table 8.4) for evaluating the recognition of alternative points of view in the same essay. (Other rubrics would be necessary

Table 8.3.   A Rubric for Expressing an Idea Clearly

Rating	Descriptor with Indicators
Exemplary = 4	Clearly communicates the main idea or theme and provides support that contains rich, vivid, and powerful detail.
Competent = 3	Clearly communicates the main idea or theme and provides suitable support and detail.
Acceptable with flaws = 2	Clearly communicates the main idea or theme, but support is sketchy or vague.
Needs revision = 1	The main idea or theme is not discernible.

for evaluating other dimensions of performance in the essay, such as critical thinking or writing skills.) These rubrics will give us examples to understand Grant Wiggins's guidelines (1998) for creating effective rubrics. In this case, the guidelines are adjusted to apply to the rubrics in Table 8.3 and Table 8.4.

An instructor evaluating a set of essays with the rubrics in Tables 8.3 and 8.4 (and a model, such as an essay from a previous class, with an exemplar for the descriptor of each performance level) would follow these guidelines:

- Use each rubric to discriminate accurately the essential features of performance *within each essay* for *expressing an idea clearly* and for *recognizing alternative points of view*. This makes each rubric valid.

- Rely on each rubric's descriptive language (what the quality or its absence looks like), as opposed to relying on vague evaluative language to make the discrimination. For example, it is preferable to say, "The personal experiences you use to illustrate the concept of

Table 8.4.   A Rubric for Recognizing Alternative Points of View

Rating	Descriptor with Indicators
Exemplary = 4	Acknowledges at least two alternative points of view expressed in the required readings. Summarizes them thoroughly, and reasonably indicates why he has chosen his point of view in preference to the others.
Competent = 3	Acknowledges at least one alternative point of view expressed in the required readings. Summarizes it thoroughly, and reasonably indicates why he prefers his point of view.
Acceptable with flaws = 2	Acknowledges at least one alternative point of view expressed in the required readings. Summarizes it well, but does not indicate or unreasonably indicates why he prefers his point of view.
Needs revision = 1	Does not acknowledge any alternative points of view in the required readings. Or if he does, they are summarized poorly and he does not indicate or unreasonably indicates why he prefers his point of view.

Source: Adapted from Walvoord, 2004, p. 89.

authenticity are rich, vivid, and powerful," rather than "Your writing in this paragraph is excellent."

- Use each rubric to consistently make fine discriminations across four levels of performance. When a rubric can be repeatedly used to make the same discriminations within the same sample of performances, it is reliable. (To maintain reliability, rubrics seldom have more than six levels of performance.)

- Make sure learners can accurately use these same rubrics and their descriptors (and the models) for each level of performance to self-assess and self-correct their work.

- See that each rubric is parallel to the others. Each descriptor generally matches the others in terms of criteria language used.

- See that each rubric is coherent. It should focus on the same criteria throughout.

- See that each rubric is continuous. The degree of difference between each descriptor (level of performance) should be as similar as possible.

There are many books in higher education and training about how to write rubrics. I find most of these books quite linear and not culturally sensitive. However, I do find them helpful for understanding the creative variety of rubrics that is possible and for deepening my critical awareness about the uses, value, and possible harm of rubrics. The Advanced Learning Technologies Project (ALTEC) offers a helpful Web-based tool for creating rubrics in Spanish or English (http://altec.org). If you develop rubrics for evaluation of adult performance, please keep Strategy 49 in mind as a general guide for a more culturally responsive approach to their construction.

Strategy 54: Use Self-Assessment Methods to Improve Learning and to Provide Learners with the Opportunity to Construct Relevant Insights and Connections

In addition to the type of self-assessment in which learners compare their work against rubrics and make self-adjustments, there are reflective assessment methods that enable adults to understand themselves more comprehensively as learners, knowers, and participants in a complex world. These methods help learners weave relationships and meanings between academic and technical information and their personal histories and experiences. These forms of self-assessment allow adults to explore their surprises, puzzlement, and hunches, to explore the tension they feel when they experience something that does not fit with what they know. Because integration of learning with identity and values is essential to adult motivation, this kind of self-assessment is a key process for deepening adult learners' feelings of competence: it can create the bridge that unites formal learning with learners' subjective world.

Neurologically, we create an idea, act on it, evaluate the consequences, and re-create the idea, followed by another action and another evaluation (Zull, 2002). That is how we evolve our knowledge and skills—every moment of every day. Sensitive self-assessment can powerfully contribute to this personal evolution, covering the spectrum from how important a new idea may be to our family's welfare to how valuable a new skill may be for use at work. Self-assessment not only makes us more aware of what we learn, but it also gives us greater control over what we learn.

In general, learners appreciate clearly knowing what to focus on (and what might possibly be learned) in the process of self-assessment. It's a good idea to explain how we as instructors will respond to or evaluate self-assessments. Our interest and timely feedback may encourage learners to concentrate more deeply on their work. Not everything needs to be read or commented on, but many learners are more likely to strengthen their reflective skills if they expect to receive supportive and specific feedback from us (or other learners). This is probably more so in the beginning phases of any self-assessment process. However, if my knowledge of the learners' self-assessment seems invasive or controlling, especially when the learning is personal or their culture is more private about revealing personal thoughts, I respect their confidentiality.

346 ENHANCING ADULT MOTIVATION TO LEARN

Jean MacGregor (1994) advises instructors to build self-assessment into longer learning situations as an ongoing activity. If we choose this approach, there are several types of self-assessments we can use throughout a learning experience and then summarize from a longer perspective. Among them, I have found journals, post-writes, closure techniques, and the Critical Incident Questionnaire to be very beneficial. (With the exception of journals, I have also found these techniques effective for shorter learning situations such as workshops and training seminars.)

• *Journals.* Journals can take a number of forms. For example, a journal in a science course can be used to synthesize lab notes, address the quality of the work, examine the processes on which work is based, and address emerging interests and concerns. Journals document risk, experimentation with ideas, and self-expression. They are an informative complement to more conventional forms of assessment.

To increase their sensitivity to cultural differences and their critical awareness of the origins and meanings of subject-specific knowledge, learners can use journals to address the following questions: From whose viewpoint am I seeing or reading or hearing? From what angle or perspective? How do I know what I know? What is the evidence, and how reliable is it? Whose purposes are served by this information?

Journals can address interests, ideas, and issues related to course material and processes, recurring problems, responses to questions from the instructor, responses to questions generated by the learner, and important connections that the learner is making. These important connections may be the learner's observations in the classroom, but optimally they are meanings that emerge as the learner applies course work to past, present, and future life experiences.

If we wish to promote this level of reflection, then we must make the classroom a place where this can happen. Providing time in class for learners to respond in their journals to readings, discussions, and significant questions builds community around the journal process and sends yet another message that the classroom is a place in which the skills of insight and personal meaning are valued.

Journals require time and effort. Initially, it may be best for learners to pay less attention to the mechanics, organization, and logic of their writing; they should simply try to get their thoughts and feelings down on paper where they can learn from them. Having sufficiently incubated, this material can be reorganized and summarized later.

- *Post-writes.* Post-writes are reflections that encourage learners to analyze a particular piece of work, how they created it, and what it may mean to them (Allen and Roswell, 1989). For example, we might say, "Now that you have finished your essay, please answer the following questions. There are no right or wrong answers. We are interested in your analysis of your experience writing this essay." The post-write could be a response to one or more of the following questions:

What problems did you face in the writing of this essay?

What solutions did you find for these problems?

Imagine you had more time to write this essay. What would you do if you were to continue working on it?

Has your thinking changed in any way as a result of writing this essay? If so, briefly describe.

It is easy to imagine ways in which this technique could be applied across disciplines. Consider, for example, slightly redesigning the previous questions to allow learners in math or science to identify and reflect on a problem that posed a particular challenge.

- *Closure techniques*. Closure activities are opportunities for learners to synthesize—to examine general or specific aspects of what they have learned, to identify emerging thoughts or feelings, to discern themes, to construct meaning, to relate learning to real-life experiences, to decide what learning to use, and so forth. Essentially, learners articulate their subjective relationship with the course or training material. For example, at the end of a workshop, we might ask participants to formulate an action plan to apply what they have learned. Closure, then, becomes a way of building coherence between what people have learned in the workshop and their personal experience beyond the workshop. Another example of this might be to ask participants to identify one particular obstacle they must still overcome to be more proficient with what they have learned. Here are three examples of positive and constructive closure activities:

- "Head, Heart, Hand" is a closure activity that allows learners to integrate different dimensions of a learning experience. After learners have had a short time for reflection, the activity may be conducted as a small- or large-group experience in which all learners have a chance to hear each other's voices. Learners may report out one or more of the following possibilities. For "Head," learners identify something they will continue to think about as a consequence of the learning experience. For "Heart," learners identify a feeling that has emerged as a result of the learning experience. For "Hand," learners identify a desired action they will take that has been stimulated by the learning experience.

- "Note-Taking Pairs" can be used intermittently during a lecture or as a culminating activity (Johnson, Johnson, and Smith, 1991). Either way, two learners work together to review and modify their notes. This is an opportunity to cooperatively reflect on a lesson, review major concepts and pertinent information, and illuminate unresolved issues or concerns. Many adults, including but certainly not limited to English-language learners, benefit by summarizing their lecture notes to another person or vice versa. Students might also prompt each other with questions: What have you got in your notes about this particular item? What are three key points made by the instructor? What is the most surprising thing the instructor said today? What is something that you are feeling uncertain about?

- "Summarizing Questions" enable learners to reflect on an entire course or training program. The following are examples from *Embracing Contraries: Explorations in Learning and Teaching* by Peter Elbow (1986) and *Discussion as a Way of Teaching* by Stephen Brookfield and Stephen Preskill (2005):

  Which assumption of yours was most challenged by what you learned in this course? Has it changed and how?

  What have you accomplished in this course that you are proud of?

  How do your accomplishments compare with what you had hoped for and expected at the start?

  What is the most important thing you did during this program?

  What were five or six important moments from this learning period: your best moments or turning points. Describe each in a sentence or two.

  Who is the person you studied whom you cared the most about? Be that person and write that person's letter to you, telling you whatever it is they have to tell you.

Which idea or skill was hardest to really "get"? What crucial idea or skill came naturally?

If this course were a journey, where did it take you? What was the terrain like? Was it a complete trip or part of a longer one?

You learned something crucial that you won't discover for a while. Guess it now.

What are a few ways you could have done a better job?

What advice would some friends in the course give you if they spoke with 100 percent honesty and caring? What advice do you have for yourself?

As a realization from this course, what do you have to work on most?

What perspectives different from your own did you gain from this course that you now appreciate?

As a result of this program, is there any way that you will act differently? If so, describe it.

What would you most like to say about being in this course?

• *Critical Incident Questionnaire.* I have adapted this self-assessment approach from the work of Stephen Brookfield (1995, p. 115). In training and teaching, it allows me to be more responsive as an instructor and helps learners to be more reflective about their significant experiences.

The Critical Incident Questionnaire has five questions, each of which asks learners to write details about important events that took place while they were learning (see Exhibit 8.1). For college courses, Brookfield and Preskill (2005) report they use it at the end of the last class of each week. For intensive workshops and seminars, I have found value in using it at the end of each session (four hours or longer). The questions are printed on a form, with space below each question for the learner's response. Learners complete the questions anonymously and retain a copy of their answers for their own benefit.

Exhibit 8.1   The Critical Incident Questionnaire

1. At what moment in this workshop did you feel most engaged with what was happening?

2. At what moment in this workshop did you feel most distanced from what was happening?

3. What action that anyone (instructor or learner) took in the workshop did you find most affirming and helpful?

4. What action that anyone (instructor or learner) took in the workshop did you find most puzzling or confusing?

5. What about the workshop surprised you the most? (This could be something about your own reactions to what went on, or something that someone did, or anything else that occurs to you.)

I explore the questionnaire forms looking for themes, patterns, and, in general, learners' concerns or confusions that need my response or adjustments. I also look for the part of our learning and instruction that has been affirmed. I find hints and suggestions for areas to probe or deepen. Most important, in my experience this questionnaire gives me a more sensitive reading of the emotional reactions of learners and of areas that may create controversy or conflict. However, I do realize that for some students, writing may inhibit their responses, and I publicly acknowledge this shortcoming of the process.

At the beginning of the session that immediately follows the distribution of the questionnaire, I outline the results in short phrases on an overhead projection and have a dialogue with the learners about these responses. This tends to build trust, further communication, and deepen learning. What I like most is that this form of self-assessment can be so fluidly used to build community. Brookfield (2004) has also developed the Critical Practice Audit, which uses a self-assessment format to judge the development of critical thinking in students preparing for professions such as teaching and nursing.

Some Thoughts about Grades, Assessment, and Motivation

Although they serve no legitimate teaching purpose and do not accurately predict educational or occupational achievement, grades receive very high status in U.S. society (Wlodkowski and Ginsberg, 1995). For most adults, low grades, because they are threatening and stigmatizing, do more to decrease motivation to learn than they do to enhance it.

Nationally, at the policy level in higher education, there is more concern about grades being too high, and although grade inflation continues to be debated, the inflationary trend probably spans several decades (Young, 2003). No matter what the outcome of this argument, B is the average grade in college (Rojstaczur, 2002).

I have a skeptical attitude toward grades but I cannot discount them. They determine too much for the future of adult learners—potential promotions, jobs, and graduate school opportunities. Yet I also agree with the observation made by Ohmer Milton, Howard Pollio, and James Eison in 1986: "A grade is . . . a true salmagundi. Translated, this means a given grade can reflect the level of information, attitudes, procrastination, errors or misconceptions, cheating, and mixtures of all of these plus other ingredients; all of this was noted in the literature over 50 years ago as well as today and is well known but ignored. The lone letter symbol is a conglomerate which specifies none of its contents" (p. 212).

At a university where I taught, faculty were concerned about grade inflation in the undergraduate adult education programs. The average GPA of the adult students (3.5) was higher than the average GPA of the younger students in the traditional college (3.2) of the same university. At a small international conference for adult educators (Wlodkowski, 2000), we generated possible reasons for this difference. Thirty-four colleges were represented and there was unanimous agreement that, if investigated, the average GPA of adult students in their schools probably would be higher than the average GPA of their traditional college students. The following reasons received the strongest agreement (this isn't rigorous research but I think these findings are insightful and realistic):

- Adults are more likely to regard grades as a reflection of their capabilities than younger traditional students are, and they pressure faculty for higher grades.

- Employers use grade averages to determine tuition support. Higher grades mean a higher percentage of financial support. This influences faculty grading.

- Adjunct faculty, the majority of instructors for many adult programs, don't see grades as reflective of true performance and are more casual about determining grades.

- Traditional faculty use more multiple choice and other typical test-like measures, which leads to lower grades in traditional courses.

- Faculty in adult programs use more projects and collaborative activities as the basis for their grading, which leads to higher grades because the work reflects the best thinking of the group and there is a chance to revise the work before it is graded.

- Faculty in adult programs identify more with their students and experience more anxiety in giving lower grades.

As instructors, we have to keep in mind that the "meaning of a grade is socially determined" (Walvoord and Anderson, 1998, p. 102). It is interpreted in the society we inhabit, and more specifically in the college and department in which we teach. Those standards are relative. Talking with our colleagues will give us a perspective. From there it is a professional decision that we negotiate with our students. The lack of validity of grades is the real national problem. To the extent that it exists, grade inflation is a symptom of this deeper issue.

Nonetheless, many of us still have to give grades. No matter what the scale (for example, A to C or A to F), they should be clearly specified and based on reasonable standards that students can use to guide their learning and receive feedback without penalty. Not surprisingly, at the top of my list, grades should also sustain and encourage intrinsic motivation to learn. There may be more approaches to meeting these goals than I am aware of, but, thus far, I have found two acceptable approaches to use with adults: contracts and rubrics.

Because contracts allow for mutual understanding and agreement and a dialogue about the content, process, criteria, and outcomes of learning, I have found them very helpful as a means for grading (see Chapter Six, Strategy 24). Using rubrics as the basis for grades has worked well when I have had models of former students' graded work available and have made sure to take time to talk with students about the criteria and given each of them an opportunity to discuss and have input for the final criteria. I make this judgment about contracts and rubrics based on (1) the overall quality of student work, (2) the climate and trust among us that follows this grading discussion, and (3) the supportive evaluations I receive at the end of the course regarding these approaches.

In general, the assessment strategies described in this chapter and the contracts described in Chapter Six, Strategy 24, can be used in various combinations to arrive eventually at the given grade. As a set of interdependent practices, they align with the guiding principles for assessment of adult learning offered by Kasworm and Marienau (1997). In general, adults become more competent, feel more confident, and look forward to assessment when assessment procedures have these characteristics:

Related to goals they understand, find relevant, and want to accomplish

Reflective of growth in learning

Indicative of clear ways to improve learning without penalty

Expected

Returned promptly

Permeated with instructor and peer comments that are informative and supportive

Used to encourage new challenges in learning

Fostering Transfer of Learning to Engender Competence

Within the last decade, a few studies have indicated that when people are motivated to use their learning, learning is enhanced and more likely to transfer as much as a year after training (Pugh and Bergin, 2006). In my experience, adults who begin a learning experience with sincere intentions to transfer what they learn to their work have stronger and more persistent motivation than do adults who adopt a "wait-and-see" attitude. In general, I believe fostering an *intention* and a *means* to transfer learning to adults' workplaces or communities significantly enhances their motivation to learn, their competence for what they learn, and their use of it after the course or training is completed.

In many instances, fostering transfer of learning is not a high priority in adult instruction. We know we "should" do it. Transfer is the justification for much of the human and financial investment in education (Barnett and Ceci, 2002). However, as Strategy 55 reveals, transfer is a complex, political, and time consuming process. In my opinion, it's well worth it, and it is an area of challenging professional growth for my own work.

Transfer of learning is how people apply what they have learned in an educational or training setting to their life, community, or workplace. Adults who intend to transfer their learning will want to deeply process what they are learning, try to understand rather than simply memorize, and use personal strategies to connect their knowledge to relevant real-world applications (Pugh and Bergin, 2006). Quite importantly, they are probably more willing to review and practice as well.

One of the challenges of transferring learning is that recalling complex learning is difficult (Schacter, 2001). There is not only erosion and pruning of unused neural circuits, but there is confusion and distortion. Review and practice of complex learning or skill is a must for transfer. Ask any musician. Better yet, ask any effective instructor. There are things that I have taught over twenty times, but unless I review them every time, I will not be able to proficiently teach them. A couple that easily come to mind are cognitive developmental stages and the application of each of the multiple intelligences as assessment processes. But the real issue here is *practice and review in the beginning of new learning*. We don't sustain what we didn't competently learn in the first place.

When I first learned clinical hypnosis as a psychologist, I diligently practiced it because I really wanted to be good at it and use it in my professional work. This attitude is not exceptional for adults who value what they are learning and believe they will apply it in the future. Although a challenge to accomplish, the following strategy can make such a disposition possible.

Strategy 55: Foster the Intention and Capacity to Transfer Learning

There are a number of conceptions of transfer (Pugh and Bergin, 2006). In the methods and example for this strategy, I will present situations where transfer is to contexts which are moderately different from the original learning environment—for example, transferring learning the process of scaffolding (Strategy 15, Chapter Six) in a graduate course on adult instruction to using scaffolding in an adult basic education course for non-traditional learners. Or for a non-academic example, transferring learning to shift gears and drive a car to learning to shift gears and drive a mid-size truck.

From her experience and review of the literature, Rosemary Caffarella (2002) has developed a comprehensive framework and typology of key factors influencing the transfer of learning. I have found her work very helpful for engendering competence and motivation to transfer new learning. What follows is a distilled adaptation of this approach; it includes her perspective on how these factors can work as enhancers and techniques to encourage and support transfer (2002, pp. 210–217).

In order to offer a realistic example of how this strategy can be applied, I present an actual case from my experience.

A number of years ago, I was asked to conduct a professional development program for the British Columbia Institute of Technology (BCIT) in peer coaching. The immediate goal was for a group of instructors (approximately twenty volunteer faculty) to learn how to effectively use the coaching process with their peers. At that time the student population at BCIT was undergoing a significant shift. Nearly half of the students were immigrants or children of immigrants, most of whom were from China and Southeast Asia. The vast majority of the instructors were from Euro-Canadian ethnic groups. The main purposes for learning the peer coaching process were these:

1. Provide the assistance, support, and encouragement each instructor needs to improve in the use of culturally responsive teaching practices.

2. Serve as an informal support group for sharing, letting off steam, and discussing problems connected with implementing culturally responsive teaching practices.

3. Serve as a base for faculty experienced in the use of culturally responsive teaching practices to teach others how to use these approaches.

The following factors enhance the intention and capacity to transfer learning and were used at BCIT.

1. *Program participants or learners* bring their culture, experiences, attitudes, and values, which all influence what they learn and whether they want to apply the new learning to their personal, work, or public lives. They may have the following characteristics:

- useful prior knowledge to connect to new learning

- a willingness to cooperate

- a prior attitude to learn and apply the new knowledge or skills

- authority or informal leadership skills

- cultural differences to add informative perspectives

For fostering transfer, I benefited greatly from the first group of participants at BCIT. Like many volunteers for a new professional development program, they had expertise, a positive attitude, and leadership characteristics coming into the program. They believed there needed to be some instructional changes to more effectively teach their students before I arrived. What I didn't anticipate was that most of them were also first-generation college graduates themselves and many were immigrants or children of immigrants as well. This history contributed to their compassion for their students. My good fortune in having such participants doesn't mean everything went smoothly for our program, but it was a significant advantage that lasted the entire time we learned together.

2. *Instructional design and execution* include learning activities that have methods or strategies for the transfer of learning:

- Authentic application exercises

- Approximating the learning environment to the real context for transfer

- Self-assessment to understand what learners can apply from new learning to the real context

- Direct transfer-of-learning strategies such as an action plan or developing a support group to maintain transfer in the workplace

For fostering transfer, I created exercises, with the assistance of the professional development staff, that were based on the courses the faculty actually taught. We did many role plays and simulations. Faculty taught partial lessons (revised to be more culturally responsive) from their courses to their peer coaching group. These faculty were then coached by colleagues from their peer coaching group, who were observed by the whole group while they practiced coaching. The practicing coaches received feedback and support from the observers based on the standards and techniques of cognitive coaching (Costa and Garmston, 2002). Thus, every member of the peer coaches went through a cycle of teaching, receiving coaching, practicing coaching, and receiving feedback on their coaching. The peer coaches informally self-assessed their progress. We kept the mood light and affirmative. We used videotape to model and critique techniques. Early on we decided to create a BCIT faculty coaching association with regular meetings, informal dinners, and an agenda to support and promote peer coaching across both campuses. The professional development team developed a calendar to extend coaching teams and visits through the next semester.

3. *Content* is the knowledge, skills, and values learned. Content is most likely to transfer when it is:

- Relevant and practical

- Connected with the prior knowledge, experience, and orientation to learning

- Competently learned

- Practiced in relevant contexts

For fostering transfer, all coaching practice was based on the courses that the peer coaches taught. This was a very hands-on group with a strong need for practical application. Because of the videotaping and the cycle of teaching to receiving coaching feedback, they saw that practice definitely helped them learn the techniques of cognitive coaching. After three cycles of practice, we created teams and moved the coaching process to the participants' classrooms. The professional development staff and I were careful to make the practice in coaching in the professional development program a very efficient next step to the practice in coaching in a real course, with feedback and debriefing as close to immediate as possible. Seeing what a difference practice made in terms of developing competence for coaching, we structured two coaching visits per instructor to actual courses as soon as possible. Just about everyone agreed that receiving coaching from their peers for more culturally responsive teaching in their actual courses was the cement that made new learning about how to coach really stick.

4. *Changes necessary to transfer learning* often include accommodations or conversions by people, professional practices, organizations, and communities to apply the new learning and endure the consequences of that learning and change. For this transfer to

succeed, there has to be preparation and responsibility to assure the following for the change process:

- It is doable and realistic.
- It is allotted enough time to develop.
- It is integrated into the roles of the people using the new learning.
- It is integrated into the roles of the people experiencing the con- sequences of the new learning.

For fostering transfer, it was agreed that all instructors completing the professional development program would visit another instructor's course as a coach at least twice a month and receive coaching at least twice a month. The instructors created teams of four among themselves to carry out this goal. This process would be conducted for a full semester and then revised as needed. The professional development staff agreed to survey the instructors and the students in their courses to assess the possible effects of peer coaching.

5. *Organizational context and support* are the people, structures, and cultural and political milieu of an organization that facilitate and sustain the transfer of learning:

- Key leaders, staff, and colleagues who view the transfer as positive and beneficial to the organization or community
- Appropriate financial and resource support
- Incentives and rewards that support the transfer of learning
- Structural adjustments to accommodate the transfer of learning

For fostering transfer, at the completion of the professional devel- opment program, the vice president for academics addressed the group and expressed his appreciation for their instructional lead- ership. Each of the faculty received a small BCIT pin as a token of appreciation from the institution. The BCIT Faculty Coaching

Association was inaugurated with the goal of recruiting other faculty to participate in the next professional development program for peer coaching. Among the professional development staff, a director volunteered to co-lead the next coaching program with me.

6. *Community and societal forces* are social, economic, and political conditions that can influence transfer of learning:

• Favorable economic and political conditions

• Continuing support from key leaders

• Continuing cultural adaptation

• Development of organizational norms to sustain transfer

To foster transfer, the professional development staff conducted the third coaching faculty professional development program with my assistance almost entirely long distance. Because the program remained voluntary, received faculty support, and was assigned a permanent staff developer, it continued for a number of years. Surveys indicated that more than two thirds of the instructors who had participated in the program reported an improved attitude toward their role as a teacher as well as toward their students and colleagues (Wlodkowski, 1992). Executive leadership at BCIT saw it as an important part of an overall plan to develop more culturally responsive teaching and a professional culture to support instruction.

As this example shows, the strategy to *foster the intention and capacity to transfer learning* is a coordinated system of actions both complex and political. I think that's what it takes to make significant new learning transferable. Otherwise, most adult learners see it as another "new flavor of the month" without the resources, appropriate learning, leadership, and will to make it happen and last.

This example and its six associated factors describe learning transfer in professional development or training for an institution, an organization, a business, or a community. A helpful instrument for diagnosing the learning-transfer process in such situations is the Learning Transfer Systems Inventory (Holton, Bates, and

Ruona, 2000). To encourage and support transfer of learning from a course in college to an individual student's uses, the first three factors—the learners, the instructional design and execution, and the content—are the most influential.

Although the BCIT example occurred in the 1990s, it was a five-year program and one of the times where I felt "we got it right." Planning for and utilizing these six factors made a difference. They are a valuable checklist. When adults see them in operation, they foster the realization that what is being learned will be used. If adults value that learning and endorse it, their motivation emerges *as an intention to transfer*, enabling new learning and competence in a powerful and lasting way.

Communicating and Rewarding to Engender Competence

The rest of the motivational strategies in this chapter also enhance competence but are frequently used apart from assessment or transfer. Often they are communications or rewards given as the situation merits.

Strategy 56: When Necessary, Use Constructive Criticism

Constructive criticism is similar to feedback but has a few more qualifications. It does emphasize errors and deficiencies in learning, but unlike ordinary criticism, it does not connote disapproval, disgust, or rejection. In general, criticism does not have to be used as often as we may think. Instructors may overuse criticism if they do not know how to use feedback properly or are working with learners who do not have entry-level skills for the learning task they are *required* to perform. The latter condition is best alleviated through more appropriate selection and guidance procedures, such as pretesting and interviews. However, constructive criticism may be a necessary strategy for engendering competence in circumstances such as these:

When the learning process is so costly or involves such a threat to human safety that mistakes cannot be afforded (examples are training with a dangerous machine, weapon, chemical, or medical procedure)

When the learning performance is so poor that to emphasize success or improvement would be ridiculous or patronizing

When the learning performance has significant errors and there are few remaining chances for improvement in the training or course

When a learner directly requests criticism

Constructive criticism may be a helpful and motivating way to deal with these situations. Like feedback, constructive criticism is informational, based on performance criteria, behavior specific, corrective, and prompt, and when possible, it provides efficient opportunities for improvement. Unless an emergency exists, it is given privately. Constructive criticism has the following additional characteristics:

- It helps the learner see performance in the context of overall progress and not as an isolated failure—for example, "Your science exam indicates that 70 percent of the concepts are still unclear to you. I hope you keep in mind that you've already progressed through four units, and although this one may seem difficult, that's a pretty good indication you can more fully understand these ideas. Let's go over the material."

- It respectfully informs the learner of the conditions that lead to the emphasis on mistakes or deficiencies—for example, "This machine can be quite dangerous. For your own safety, before you get another chance to operate it, I think we'd better take a look at any mistakes you might have made." Or "You've got only one more chance to practice before you meet with the review committee. I think the best use of our time would be to check your performance on the last case study and to concentrate on any parts that may need improvement."

- It acknowledges the learner's effort—for example, "There's no doubt you've put a great deal of work into this report. Just the number of references you cite testifies to the effort and comprehensive research that went into this project. Yet it seems to need more organization. There's no unifying theme that ties all this evidence together. What generalization could you think of that might serve this purpose?"

- It provides emotional support—for example, "At the end of your last session, your client stated he felt frustrated as he left. Do you think you may have been trying too hard? You sounded a bit strident and didn't respond to the client's stated needs. We can analyze the videotape to see just where this happened. However, you did very well with the other two clients you worked with. Since you have only one more chance to practice in this seminar, can I help you figure out what might not have worked so well? It's obvious you want to do your best, and I feel confident you'll learn from this situation."

When you are giving feedback and constructive criticism, adults benefit from knowing when more effort on their part or another learning strategy could significantly contribute to their learning. Strategy 18 (in Chapter Six) explains how to help learners make these attributions.

Strategy 57: Effectively Praise and Reward Learning

In this book, the term *praise* has the same meaning it usually has in conventional usage: "to commend the worth of or to express approval or admiration" (Brophy, 1981). It is an intense response from an instructor, one that goes beyond positive feedback to include such emotions as surprise, delight, or excitement as well as sincere appreciation for the learner's accomplishment. ("That's a remarkable answer! It's comprehensive, insightful, and extremely precise.")

As a strategy, the use of praise has had a controversial history. Some scholars have opposed praise and rewards on principle, viewing them as bribes for doing something that is often in the learners' best interest or in the best interest of society (Kohn, 1993). Others are critical of praise because it may contribute to a hierarchical relationship between learners and instructors: instructors distribute praise because they are the judges and experts who deem learners as praiseworthy. The critics see this kind of social exchange as being likely to diminish the chances for colearning and for a more egalitarian relationship with adult learners.

Although praise can enhance learners' motivation, there is considerable research to show it often does not serve this purpose (Kohn, 1993; Larrivee, 2002). Although most of these studies have been done with youth, they only strengthen the case for the need to be careful praising adults because of its potential to be misconstrued. Neurological research indicates the brain's pathways for rewards are complex, involving elements of anticipation, perception, goal orientation, memory, pleasure, and organizing structures (Schultz, 2000). How praise or rewards for complex behavior are processed is not well understood.

Praise is frequently ineffective because it is not related to exemplary achievement, it lacks specificity (the learner does not know exactly why it was given), it is not credible, or it is communicated as patronizing. For example, sometimes we may give praise because learners show us work about which they seem enthusiastic and we do not know what else to say (*awkward-moment praise*). Other times we may give it because we feel sorry for learners who are having difficulty and use it to boost their morale (*mercy praise*).

Many competent adults do not want or expect praise. They want clear, informative feedback about their progress and may experience praise as annoying or condescending (*snob praise*). Furthermore, praise given too frequently and indiscriminately may begin to seem perfunctory and predictable to learners, encouraging them to interpret it as a form of instructor small talk or flattery (*jabber praise*). Focusing on form rather than substance can cause a problem as well. Praise for turning in an assignment or for responses that agree with instructor values may seem controlling and manipulative (*puppet praise*). In some instances, instructors have even used praise to *end* contact with a learner. Perhaps a discussion initiated by a learner has, in our opinion, gone on a bit too long; to provide pleasant closure, we toss out a compliment about what has been said and move on to something else (*terminator praise*).

In general, to praise effectively we need to praise *well* rather than necessarily *often*. The same could be said about rewarding effectively. In fact, praise is often considered to be a verbal reward (Pittman, Boggiano, and Ruble, 1983). Whether the reward is verbal (praise), tangible (money, promotions, privileges), or symbolic (grades, trophies, awards), there are guidelines that can ensure the positive effects of rewards on learner motivation. The six suggestions that follow are based on a continuing analysis by Jere Brophy (2004), which has used research done largely with children and adolescents. However, this material is congruous with findings from studies focused on young adults (Morgan, 1984) and on adults learning in the workplace (Keller and Litchfield, 2002). Effective praise and rewards share these six characteristics:

1. *Given with sincerity, spontaneity, variety, and other signs of credibility.* These characteristics may be more pertinent for praise than for other rewards. Rewards are often known ahead of time and given with more uniformity of procedure. However, the affect with which a reward is given is critical to its impact on the learner. An insincerely given reward or statement of praise is an insult to an adult. (A personal note: I have conducted hundreds of workshops in which I have asked instructors to volunteer the guidelines for effective praise. Without exception, sincerity has been listed as the number one guideline.)

2. *Based on the attainment of specific performance criteria.* This means that the learner has achieved a standard and clearly understands what particular personal behaviors are being acknowledged. This approach not only makes the reward or praise informational but also significantly increases the person's chances of learning exactly which behaviors are important. For example, "Nice job" written on a paper is not as helpful as "This paper does not have a single spelling, grammar, or syntax error. I appreciate the meticulous editing it so obviously reflects."

3. *Adapted in sufficiency, quantity, and intensity to the accomplishments achieved.* Rewards that are less than what is merited can be insulting and demeaning. Rewards that are too much for what has been accomplished are excessive and disturbing. In fact, we have clichés to reflect adult embarrassment in response to inadequate or undeserved praise: "damning with faint praise" (too little praise) and "gushing over trivia" (too much praise).

4. *Given to attribute success to the apparent combination of the personal effort, knowledge, and capabilities of the learner.* Emphasizing these attributes increases the learner's sense of responsibility and implies the learner can continue such

accomplishments in the future—for example, "Your design of this model is exceptional. It meets all the criteria for strength, durability, and esthetics. Would you mind sharing how you created it with the rest of the team? I think we could all learn from your approach."

5. *Given contingent on success at a challenging task.* This makes the learner's task *praiseworthy* and testifies to the competence of the learner. The praise implies that the learner overcame real difficulty and deserves the recognition. If the task were not challenging, then the praise or the reward would be seen as indiscriminate.

6. *Adapted to the preference of the individual.* Again, this characteristic may be more applicable to praise than to other rewards. Rewards are often given in a ritualistic manner, as in award ceremonies. However, when possible, rewards should be attractive and appropriate to the learner's cultural preferences. For example, in more collectivist cultures such as many Asian societies, adults may prefer to receive praise indirectly as a member of a social group which is recognized, rather than directly as an individual (Plaut and Markus, 2005). One study found that Chinese adults did not want to be used as "good examples for others," whereas the adults from the United States found that to be quite acceptable (Jones, Rozelle, and Chang, 1990). When in doubt, it is probably best to give praise and other rewards privately.

There is a mnemonic device for remembering these six guidelines: 3 S-3P, which stands for Sincere, Specific, Sufficient, Properly attributed, Praiseworthy, and Preferred. The mnemonic can be stated this way in a sentence: praise (or other rewards) should be Sincere, Specific, Sufficient, and Properly attributed for genuinely Praiseworthy behavior, in a manner Preferred by the learner.

In general, it is important to remember that the subjective viewpoint of the learner and the context in which praise and other rewards are given will immensely influence their effect. As of now, there are no ways to accurately prescribe these conditions, except to encourage instructors to remain continually sensitive to their impact.

Strategy 58: Use Incentives to Develop and Maintain Adult Motivation in Learning Activities That Are Initially Unappealing but Personally Valued

Peters and Waterman (1982) offer the insight that positive rewards are an excellent means to help people move in directions they are already headed. Positive reinforcement can be a gentle and precise way to develop and maintain adult motivation for learning that is personally valued but not initially appealing.

An *incentive* may be defined as an anticipated reward. It serves as a goal we expect to achieve as a result of some specific behavior. Incentives take many forms, such as recognition, money, relationships, and privileges. Incentives are frequently used in the workplace (Herzberg, 2003; Ryan and Deci, 2000). However, this book discusses incentives only as they can be understood to support intrinsic motivation and individual autonomy and reason while learning (Brookfield, 2005). Incentives should be used as a means to assist adults in becoming more effective at what they personally value rather than as a means to manipulate them. As instructors and trainers, we can construct incentive systems with this critical perspective in mind.

Adults' lives are filled with incentives. We frequently use rewards for performing activities we value but find tedious, difficult, or perhaps even painful—exercising easily comes to mind, but there's also dieting, studying, budgeting, cleaning, and practicing just about anything from dance steps to golf swings. We reward ourselves at certain points for performing these activities. The reward may be a piece of chocolate, a massage, a movie, a long-distance call, or a walk outside. Knowing these kinds of incentives are coming at the end of our task makes the tedium or effort a little more bearable.

Regardless of how many times I tell myself it's great to get my heart rate up and sweat like a steam whistle, seeing my favorite cold drink at the end of the workout is a far more fetching notion to keep me working out. But please keep in mind that I chose the activity, I value the activity, and I want to be competent at it. I'm using a reward to help me sustain an activity I'm intrinsically motivated to perform. And make no mistake about it: in my mind, the reward makes the whole experience better. Used in this manner, the reward does not undermine my intrinsic motivation (Brophy, 2004). In fact, it supports it.

There are at least two situations in which incentives may be an effective and inviting means to encourage adult participation in a valued learning activity:

1. *The adult has had little or no experience with the learning activity.* Maybe the training or instructional program is very new or unique. Lack of experience can prevent the learner from enjoying or valuing what he is learning or cause him to feel cautious and apprehensive. Or perhaps he is learning how to use a new machine or how to apply a different auditing process or how to work with innovative technology. In this case, the learner anticipates the value of the activity but has not yet realized that value. Under such circumstances, incentives could actually contribute to an awakening of intrinsic motivation in the learner because there is no prior negative experience to lead the learner to believe that the incentive is being used as compensation for participation in an unpleasant learning task (Lepper and Greene, 1978). The learner is more likely to see the incentive as a reward for "trying out" or becoming competent in a new learning opportunity.

2. *The adult has to develop a level of competence before the learning activity can become enjoyable or interesting.* Some sports, such as tennis and swimming, are good examples of this situation, as are learning to speak a foreign language or use a personal computer or play the trumpet. There are so many things that are valuable to learn but just not that appealing to do until the learner has achieved at least a moderate level of competence. In such situations, incentives may be the only positive means to sustain effort until the necessary level of proficiency provides its own pleasure and satisfaction. That is why parents applaud vigorously and unashamedly for their children at those, to say the least, imperfect music recitals and why an instructor might have to give extra attention and recognition to a struggling student in an adult basic education course.

When it comes to intrinsic motivation and incentives, the paramount issues to consider are the learners' value for the activity or for what it leads to, the probability of increasing competence through the activity, the learners' view of the overall process, and, always, the cultural context.

Promoting Natural Consequences and Positive Endings

The concept of natural consequences comes out of reinforcement theory (Vargas, 1977). Natural consequences are changes in a person resulting from learning. Reading a book may have the natural consequence of producing new insights and expanded awareness in an adult. When working with natural consequences, we emphasize the result of learning (insights) more than the process of learning (reading) or its context (the book and where it was read).

Constructs from sociocultural theory (Mezirow and Associates, 2000), situated cognition (Fenwick, 2003), and neuroscience

(Caine and Caine, 2006) mutually support the perspective that all of these elements are intimately related and cannot be arbitrarily divided. For example, a person is motivated to solve a problem by the pleasure of analyzing it (process), the materials and instruments he uses (context), and the satisfaction of arriving at a solution (natural consequence). In other words, it's the trip, the vehicle, and the destination that are motivating. Yet emphasizing natural consequences is an effective motivational strategy, because like a good tour guide, it helps adults more vividly understand the importance of their destination.

Strategy 59: When Learning Has Natural Consequences, Help Learners to Be Aware of Them and of Their Impact

One can see that natural consequences and feedback go hand in hand. However, because using natural consequences as a strategy includes *every* consequence that an adult can perceive as a result of learning, it encourages instructors to *make learning active as soon as possible* so that adults can quickly have natural consequences to increase and maintain their motivation. The remarkably successful Suzuki violin method does this for children, but so might any instructor of adults teaching any skill, ranging from sailing to surfing the Internet.

Many learning activities have natural consequences for adults that are not included in the performance criteria. To miss these would be a shame. It would be like serving a cake without the frosting. People often do not realize some of the consequences of their learning. In these situations, instructors can act as mirrors or magnifying glasses to reveal relevant consequences not readily apparent. The guiding question is, As a result of this learning activity, what else does the learner know or what else can the learner do that is important to understand? Suppose, for example, that an adult takes a course in technical report writing. The standard of performance is based on a readability index that is precise and provides excellent informational feedback. The adult achieves the standard of performance and successfully completes the course. It is also possible that because of the learning in this course, the adult is more confident as a writer, enjoys writing in general more than ever before, can more clearly communicate verbally, sees improvement in personal letter writing, and will now pursue a career in which writing is a requisite skill. When the instructor takes some time at the end of this course to discuss with the learners what other outcomes they may have achieved, they are likely to deepen their motivation and broaden their transfer of learning.

Discussion is not the only means of making natural consequences more conspicuous. Authentic performance tasks and simulations often reveal more than the specific expected learning. Using self-assessment methods (Strategy 54) as well as videotapes and audiotapes to record progress and demonstrate before-and-after effects, we can highlight a variety of natural consequences. There is also the possibility of using examples in which a given skill or concept is applied outside the expected context, such as asking how a communication skill might be used with a learner's family as well as on the job.

Strategy 60: Provide Positive Closure at the End of Significant Units of Learning

A significant unit of learning can be determined by length or importance. In terms of length, when any course, seminar, or training program is terminating, a significant unit of learning has occurred. In longer courses segments based on particular content or skills may also have a clearly delineated beginning and ending. For example, a course in marketing might be divided into units on promotion, sales, and contracts.

In terms of importance, a significant unit of learning is any segment of learning that has some characteristic that makes it special: the level of difficulty, cohesiveness, or creativity; the type of learning situation, structure, or process (special equipment, materials, location, grouping, or task); or the presence of prominent individuals such as an esteemed audience or lecturer.

In all these cases, something notable is coming to an end. Positive closure enhances learners' motivation because it affirms the entire process, verifies the value of the experience, directly or indirectly acknowledges competence, increases cohesiveness within the group, and encourages the surfacing of inspiration and other beneficial emotions in the learners themselves. Positive closure can be a small gesture, such as thanking learners for their cooperation, or something much more extravagant, such as an awards ceremony. Celebrations, acknowledgments, and sharing are some of the ways to achieve positive closure.

- *Celebrations.* For people all over the world, festivals and holidays are a joyous means of acknowledging the ending of seasons, religious observations, and harvests. There is no valid reason to avoid celebrations in learning. Savor with learners their moment of triumph and accomplishment. This can be a pleasurable discussion, a party, a round of applause, sitting back and recalling special moments, or offering congratulations. But let the moment linger and enjoy it together. It is a happy occasion, not to be taken for granted. Celebrations are a wonderfully inclusive metaphor. They allow people to feel pleasure for whatever they personally accomplished or valued during the entire learning experience.

- *Acknowledgments.* These can be simple statements of gratitude and appreciation or more formal and ritualized awards. The goal is to recognize noteworthy learner contributions or achievements during the span of the learning event. Depending on the situation, acknowledgments can be given by the instructor, the learners, or both.

- *Sharing.* Sharing is anything the instructor and learners might do to show their caring and sensitivity to the special quality of the learning experience and those involved in it. Some have cooked dinner for their class. Some have told stories that reflect their special feelings or insights. Others have brought in personal collections or demonstrated their musical talents. More frequently, this type of sharing takes the form of a poignant final statement that may include an eloquent poem or an inspirational quotation. When something has gone well, it deserves a fitting form of closure.

9

Building Motivational Strategies
into Instructional Designs

When it is very good, instruction is technical excellence under the command of artistic expression. For no matter how many fixed rules, precise definitions, and logical strategies we establish in learning, the process remains embedded in a human context that is open ended, subjective, unique, and constantly changing. For this reason, instruction remains a science within an art, more akin to communication than to engineering. In fact, instruction may never be a sure thing, because what makes people learn is beyond guarantee or total prediction. Therefore, it will always need the timeliness, sensitivity, and vision that any effective relationship contributing to human growth demands. Among the many important aspects of instruction, none seem more deserving of this perspective than those that deal with motivation.

At our current level of understanding, human motivation in learning is too complex and indomitable to lend itself to easy panaceas. But we can plan for it. A logical and seductive assumption is that if instruction itself is well planned and efficient, motivation for what is being learned should neatly and nicely come along as well. In some instances this is true, especially when adults feel respected and know that what they are learning is relevant and when the instructional process increases their effectiveness. However, the longer the instructional sequence or the more complicated the human factors within it, the easier it is for motivation to diminish—which it seems to do with regularity. If this were not so, motivation would not be the epidemic concern it is for instructors.

Industry and business are filled with well-designed, efficient instructional programs that are not very motivating. Part of the problem is efficiency itself. Motivation takes people-to-people skills and time. Like a good conversation, it cannot be rushed. The best way to see a motivational strategy is as an investment. It pays dividends but often not immediately. Also, because what motivates people is often beyond the inherent structure of the knowledge or skill they are learning, instructors have to plan for motivation in its own right. It cannot be taken for granted. If we look at the motivational conditions and strategies described in the other chapters, most of them address cultural and internal human influences in learning, such as inclusion, attitude, meaning, and competence. Many instructional design formats for adults do not address these influences (King, 2005; Kasworm and Londoner, 2000). Yet they are essential to motivated learning, and planning for them, at the very least, seems sensible.

The Motivational Framework for Culturally Responsive Teaching can be used for instructional planning and design. It is a systemic structure for applying motivational strategies and learning activities throughout a learning sequence. Instruction is a complex network of influences and interactions whose results are produced by the total system of such influences, not by its individual parts (Wlodkowski and Ginsberg, 1995). With this motivational framework we can design instruction so that the development and enhancement of learners' *intrinsic motivation* is an essential part of the plan. The framework and its related strategies enable us to programmatically combine a series of learning activities from the beginning to the end of an instructional sequence so that they create a network of mutually supportive motivational conditions. These conditions—inclusion, attitude, meaning, and competence—work in concert to elicit adult motivation for learning for the entire learning sequence. It may be helpful to review Chapter Four's discussion of this framework before reading further sections of this chapter.

Increasing Motivational Self-Awareness

In preparation for our effective use of the Motivational Framework for Culturally Responsive Teaching, a few considerations may increase our sensitivity to how the framework can be most beneficial to our work. The first is to conduct an analysis of our roles as instructors, our assumptions about the motivation of adults, and our instructional situation relative to motivation. Such an inquiry will help us to understand how well this approach fits our philosophy, style, and professional environment. Exhibit 9.1 lists three areas significantly related to an instructor's approach to learner motivation. Please reflect upon them before you apply the framework.

Exhibit 9.1 Instructor Self-Assessment for Applying the Motivational Framework

Reflecting on the three areas listed here can help you be more aware of the extent to which the motivational approach offered in this book can be of use to you. Take a few minutes to answer the questions and to reflect on your responses. Writing them out may clarify your thoughts and make this self-assessment a deeper experience.

1. Your Perception of Your Role as an Instructor

This approach to instruction is generally incompatible with roles that are authoritarian and directive but very effective with those that are collaborative, egalitarian, and consultative. How appropriate and natural does it feel for you to be a colearner among adults? What generally have been your reactions to your experiences when you are a guide and facilitator of adult learning rather than a director or lecturer? How comfortable are you with respecting the perspectives of others as you teach? Are you open to learning the values and practices of other people to promote intercultural understanding? Are you self-reflective about personal attitudes and beliefs that might hinder the expression of learner opinions that differ from your own? Are you committed to continuing your professional growth and self-awareness as a culturally responsive instructor? What are three things you most often do to enhance learner motivation? What do these habits tell you about the kind of role you prefer as an instructor?

2. Your Assumptions about the Motivation of the Adults You Teach or Train

From your perspective, what motivates the adults you teach or train? How do you understand the relationship between how these adults have been socialized and their motivation to learn? What are your thoughts about the importance of teaching or training in ways that engage the motivation of *all* learners? The motivational approach set forth in this book respects cultural diversity and assumes that learning situations for adults should model equitable learning environments and promote an understanding of how what is learned relates to a more equitable society. What is your thinking on these matters? How important are they to you?

3. Your Perceptions of Your Instructional Situation

When you consider the organization you work for, what are its highest priorities for your instruction? How are these compatible with your goals and the goals of the instructional approach in this book? What adjustments may be necessary to apply the Motivational Framework for Culturally Responsive Teaching? What are the areas in which you have the most freedom to be flexible and self-directed? Are there parts of your instructional program that need a change? Has any of the information in the previous chapters helped in this regard?

If so, how? Where would be the best place to begin to make a few changes? And just as important, what material in this book has affirmed your teaching or training? In what ways do you think your learners would complete the following sentence: My instructor helps me feel motivated because he or she . . .?

Having reflected on the three points in Exhibit 9.1, you may wish to review all the strategies discussed in this book before proceeding to the instructional planning section of this chapter. Table 9.1 is a summary of the motivational strategies contained in the four previous chapters. It includes the four major motivational conditions and a listing of specific related strategies and the purposes they serve.

For instructional planning, which tends to be linear, you may want to assign these strategies to the time phase of the course or training suggested in Table 9.1. My experience and the experiences of the numerous instructors who have corresponded with me indicate that these strategies usually have their maximum impact when timed in this way. However, my experience has also told me that the creativity and complexity of teaching and learning make these strategies useful in any phase of a course. Depending on the situation, they may be a positive motivational influence at any moment, hour, or day.

Reviewing the list of strategies in Table 9.1 has three purposes. First, it will give you a more immediate sensitivity to all the possible strategies that can be used for instructional planning. Second, you can use the table as a checklist of all the strategies you are currently employing. Many instructors are not aware of all the things they do to enhance adult motivation for learning. This kind of inventory may give you a more concrete awareness of your repertoire of current motivational strategies. Third, the table also probably lists strategies which you might want to include in your instructional efforts. If you find more than a few motivational strategies that you would like to initiate, rank these strategies in terms of their

Table 9.1. Summary of Motivational Strategies

Major Motivational Condition	Motivational Purpose	Motivational Strategy
Inclusion (beginning learning activities)	To engender an awareness and feeling of connection among adults	1. Allow for introductions. 2. Provide an opportunity for multidimensional sharing. 3. Concretely indicate your cooperative intentions to help adults learn. 4. Share something of value with your adult learners. 5. Use collaborative and cooperative learning. 6. Clearly identify the learning objectives and goals for instruction. 7. Emphasize the human purpose of what is being learned and its relationship to the learners' personal lives and current situations.
	To create a climate of respect among adults	8. Assess learners' current expectations, needs, goals, and previous experience as it relates to your course or training. 9. Explicitly introduce important norms and participation guidelines. 10. When issuing mandatory assignments or training requirements, give your rationale for them. 11. Acknowledge different ways of knowing, different languages, and different levels of knowledge or skill among learners.
Attitude (beginning learning activities)	To build a positive attitude toward the subject	12. Eliminate or minimize any negative conditions that surround the subject. 13. Positively confront the erroneous beliefs, expectations, and assumptions that may underlie a negative learner attitude. 14. Use differentiated instruction to enhance successful learning of new content. 15. Use assisted learning to scaffold complex learning.

	To develop self-efficacy for learning	16. Promote learners' personal control of learning.
		17. Help learners effectively attribute their success to their capability, effort, and knowledge.
		18. Help learners understand that reasonable effort and knowledge can help them avoid failure at learning tasks that suit their capability.
		19. Use relevant models to demonstrate expected learning.
		20. Encourage the learners.
	To establish challenging and attainable learning goals	21. Make the criteria of assessment as fair and clear as possible.
		22. Help learners understand and plan for the amount of time needed for successful learning.
		23. Use goal-setting methods.
		24. Use learning contracts.
	To create relevant learning experiences	25. Use the entry points suggested by multiple intelligences theory as ways of learning about a topic or concept.
		26. Make the learning activity an irresistible invitation to learn.
		27. Use the K-W-L strategy to introduce new topics and concepts.
Meaning (during learning activities)	To maintain learners' attention	28. Provide frequent response opportunities to all learners on an equitable basis.
		29. Help learners realize their accountability for what they are learning.
		30. Provide variety in personal presentation style, modes of instruction, and learning materials.
		31. Introduce, connect, and end learning activities attractively and clearly.
		32. Selectively use breaks, settling time, and physical exercises.

(Continued)

Table 9.1. *(Continued)*

Major Motivational Condition	Motivational Purpose	Motivational Strategy
	To evoke and sustain learners' interest	33. Relate learning to individual interests, concerns, and values.
		34. When possible, clearly state or demonstrate the benefits that will result from the learning activity.
		35. While instructing, use humor liberally and frequently.
		36. Selectively induce parapathic emotions.
		37. Selectively use examples, analogies, metaphors, and stories.
		38. Use uncertainty, anticipation, and prediction to the degree that learners enjoy them with a sense of security.
	To deepen learners' engagement and challenge	39. Use concept maps to develop and link interesting ideas and information.
		40. Use critical questions to stimulate engaging and challenging reflection and discussion.
		41. Use relevant problems, research, and inquiry to facilitate learning.
		42. Use intriguing problems and questions to make initially irrelevant material more meaningful.
		43. Use case study methods to enhance meaning.
	To enhance learners' engagement, challenge, and adaptive decision making	44. Use role playing to embody meaning and new learning within a more realistic and dynamic context.
		45. Use simulations and games to embody the learning of multiple concepts and skills that require a real-life context and practice to be learned.

Competence (ending learning activities)	46. Use visits, internships, and service learning to raise awareness, provide practice, and embody the learning of concepts and skills in authentic settings. 47. Use invention, artistry, imagination, and enactment to render deeper meaning and emotion in learning.
To engender competence with assessment	48. Provide effective feedback. 49. Avoid cultural bias and promote equity in assessment procedures. 50. Make assessment tasks and criteria clearly known to learners prior to their use. 51. Use authentic performance tasks to deepen new learning and help learners proficiently apply this learning to their real lives. 52. Provide opportunities for adults to demonstrate their learning in ways that reflect their strengths and multiple sources of knowing. 53. When using rubrics, make sure they assess the essential features of performance and are fair, valid, and sufficiently clear so that learners can accurately self-assess. 54. Use self-assessment methods to improve learning and to provide learners with the opportunity to construct relevant insights and connections.
To engender competence with transfer	55. Foster the intention and capacity to transfer learning.
To engender competence with communication and rewards	56. When necessary, use constructive criticism. 57. Effectively praise and reward learning. 58. Use incentives to develop and maintain adult motivation in learning activities that are initially unappealing but personally valued. 59. When learning has natural consequences, help learners to be aware of them and of their impact. 60. Provide positive closure at the end of significant units of learning.

personal value to you as well as their probability of being successful. Using these criteria for selection will increase the chances that the new strategies you finally choose will be effective and adaptable to your instructional situation.

Designing an Instructional Plan

After reviewing the sixty strategies listed in Table 9.1, consider how to use the Motivational Framework for Culturally Responsive Teaching to design an instructional plan. These methods can be adapted to more prescriptive approaches to instructional design such as those used for online learning.

The first step is to clarify the learning objective. A clear understanding of the proposed learning outcome will suggest the sequence of instruction and its relationship to a larger instructional unit (if there is one). If prior assessments such as interviews or interest inventories are used to develop learning objectives, they can be either a prior step or part of the first step in this planning.

Once the learning objective is well understood, the next step is to determine the amount of time available to help learners accomplish it. The length of time will have a strong influence on the kind and number of motivational strategies chosen. For example, because processing a lengthy case study takes much longer than conducting a short role play, a role play may have to be selected for the instructional plan.

The third step is to analyze the inherent structure of the material, knowledge, or skill to be learned. This structure may determine the order of content or the sequence of steps needed to adequately learn the material, as is often the case in math or a foreign language.

In addition to analyzing the structure of the material, we need to consider the assessment process. Often we mentally have to go back and forth between the flow of the content and the type of assessment we will use in order to plan the appropriate sequence of learning activities. The instructional plan should provide sufficient engagement and practice followed by an assessment that establishes and verifies the competence of the learners. We may also want to include elements in the design that lead to optimal transfer (Strategy 55 in Chapter Eight).

There is no one way to sequence learning. For example, should learning activities make content flow from the general to the specific, or vice versa? Or should we begin with a concrete experience of the content, move to reflective observation, then to abstract conceptualization, and, finally, to active experimentation, as David Kolb (1984) has proposed? Or we might problem-pose the content and codevelop the sequence with learners, as Paulo Freire (1970) has espoused. Another approach that is very popular in adult education today is the examination of incidents in our lives through various forms of critical reflection (Mezirow and Associates, 2000; Brookfield, 2005).

In this book, I advocate following a motivational framework to teach content in a way that evokes intrinsic motivation to learn among diverse adults. I suggest teaching any significant learning objective in a course or training program with activities based on motivational strategies to establish the conditions of inclusion, attitude, meaning, and competence. Although concepts from critical consciousness, transformative learning, and critical reflection inform a number of these strategies and the tenor of this book, planning strategies according to the four conditions of the framework is very important. However, once learning has started, it may be an experience much more like playing jazz than playing classical music, with many unexpected but desired twists and turns. Then we can use the strategies for each of the four motivational conditions in a less linear order, on an "as-wanted" basis.

Nonetheless, some of us may be concerned about ordering content per se, relatively independent of pedagogical theory. If so, we can consider the following more technical guidelines from the field of instructional design (Tracey, 1992, p. 242; Dick, Carey, and Carey, 2004):

- Start the sequence with materials that are familiar to the learners and then proceed to new materials (integrating the familiar with the new).

- Give learners a context or framework to use in organizing what they are to learn.

- Place easily learned tasks early in the sequence.

- Introduce broad concepts and technical terms that have application throughout the instructional process early in the sequence.

- Place practical application of concepts and principles close to the point of the initial discussion of the concepts and principles.

- Place prerequisite knowledge and skills in the sequence before they must be combined with subsequent knowledge and skills.

- Provide for practice and review of skills and knowledge that are essential parts of tasks to be introduced later in the activity.

- Introduce a concept or a skill in the task in which it is most frequently used.

- Structure learning objectives in closely related, self-contained groups.

- Avoid overloading any task with elements that are difficult to learn.

- Place complex or cumulative skills late in the sequence.

- Provide support or coaching for practice of required skills, concepts, and principles in areas where transfer is likely to occur (see Strategy 55 for an expanded and deeper understanding of this guideline).

When it comes to the assessment component of instructional planning, I have a bias. Because of my experience and understanding of adult motivation, *I plan for some kind of authentic performance task as soon as possible.* I believe that competence is such a high priority and so motivating for adults that the sooner they experience it, the deeper their learning and motivation will be. Therefore, once I have ascertained the learning objective and the content, I begin imagining what kind of performance task could creatively and clearly reveal to learners that they are becoming more effective at what they value. Once I settle on the performance task, I go back to sequence the course content so that it can lead learners to successful accomplishment of the task.

For example, in a research course, one learning objective is to critique a research article effectively. The performance task is pretty straightforward: learners choose a relevant research article to critique. Now I'm back to content; I have to ask myself, What must learners know to make a basic critique, and in what order must they know it? The concepts of reliability and validity come to mind (teach reliability before validity). Now I return to the performance task to consider what the criteria and indicators should be. Once this is settled, I can begin to select motivational strategies to teach reliability and validity. And so it goes.

In this scheme, using assessment to enhance learning and motivation, especially as it affects learners' self-efficacy through their realization of competence, is on an equal footing with using assessment to audit learning. Therefore, it is very important to make the learning objective something that can be assessed in measurable terms by the learner. Accuracy is always important, but comprehensiveness may have to wait for a later, more summative assessment.

In motivation workshops, for example, I often give participants an instructional scenario to critique for teaching errors. They are requested to find the possible errors and indicate why these actions might be motivational errors. But the participants are not requested to modify the teacher's behavior. They haven't had a chance to learn the content to do this. However, in finding and explaining the errors, the participants discover that their learning about motivation is measurably increasing. This so deepens their motivation that I have made working with this scenario a standard practice.

Superimposing the Motivational Framework on an Existing Instructional Plan

For instructors who are more experienced and possess well-developed instructional plans or who are instructional designers and follow a strictly defined sequence for learning, the best way to use the motivational framework may be to *superimpose* it on an existing instructional plan. This approach uses the four conditions from the Motivational Framework for Culturally Responsive Teaching as a template, together with a previously completed instructional plan.

Exhibit 9.2 turns the four conditions into questions for the template. By asking these questions *with close attention to the diversity of the learners* as we peruse our instructional plan, we can estimate where our instructional activities fulfill the conditions of the motivational framework and where they do not. For those questions that are not adequately answered, we can develop learning activities based on the strategies related to the relevant motivational condition (see Table 9.1). The two main criteria for successful instructional planning based on the motivational framework are (1) the establishment of all four of the motivational conditions and (2) activities in each phase (beginning, during, and ending) of instruction to elicit significant motivation among learners.

One of the problems with instructional planning is the struggle to deal in a two-dimensional format with the complexity and

Exhibit 9.2   The Four Questions for Instructional Planning

1. Establishing inclusion. *How does this learning sequence create or affirm a learning atmosphere in which we feel respected by and* connected *to one another?* (Emphasis on beginning activities)

2. Developing attitude. *How does this learning sequence make use of personal relevance and learner volition to create or affirm a favorable disposition toward learning?* (Emphasis on beginning activities)

3. Enhancing meaning. *Are there* engaging *and* challenging *learning experiences that include learners' perspectives and values in this learning sequence?* (Emphasis on main activities during the instructional plan)

4. Engendering competence. *How does this learning sequence create or affirm an understanding that learners have* effectively learned something they value and perceive as authentic *to their real world?* (Emphasis on ending activities)

nuance of real, live teaching. In this struggle, it helps to remember that most of the sixty strategies are applicable *throughout* a teaching or training experience. For example, we might begin an instructional plan with an authentic performance task to estimate learners' competence for the skill to be taught, or we might start a course with a role play to evoke emotional relevance. The most important aspect of this approach is establishing the four motivational conditions as we instruct. The strategies are a means to this essential goal.

You may also be wondering about the specific calibration for each time phase. When does the "beginning phase" end and the "during phase" begin? When does the "during phase" end and the "ending phase" begin? Beyond individual judgment, there is no precise way of determining this because of the diversity in learners, content, learning situations, and learning objectives. In this respect, the time phases are analogous to the broad way in which we divide a day—morning, afternoon, and evening—imprecise segments of time that give order to our day and help us understand that some activities are more appropriate at certain times than at others.

The length of any instructional phase can be a few minutes or a few days, depending on the situation. For example, the beginning phase for a particular learning objective with a group of highly motivated and self-directed adult learners may be very short. However, for a group of restless and resistant adult learners, the beginning phase for the same objective may have to be quite a bit longer to develop positive attitudes toward learning.

My experience with conventional instructional design formats is that the beginning phase is frequently too short, so the motivational condition of inclusion is only slightly developed. Creating a climate of respect and connection with a group of diverse adults takes some time. For the courses and training I've conducted, establishing inclusion has taken, on the average, about 20 percent of total instruction time. The benefits are well worth the time. The quality of the dialogue and the depth of the thinking, the sincerity and realism of people's perspectives, the connections made, and the awareness that we're a community of learners in which our respect is deep and mutual—all have made the learning vital and the future hopeful.

Using the Motivational Framework as a Source for Instructional Planning

Another approach is to begin with intrinsic motivation as the *origin* for instructional planning. We will still have to respect the parameters of the learning objective, the structure of the content to be learned, and the time available, but we can focus on instructional planning in which motivation and culture are essential.

The learning objective remains a top priority because without it, the motivation of the learners has no direction. However, once we understand the objective, we then reflect on the learners, their culture, and their expected motivation regarding the learning objective. Next, we review the motivational purposes (listed in the second column of Table 9.1) to select motivational strategies to guide our choice of learning activities that will fit the learning objective and the learners' culture and expected motivation as well as the structure of the content and the time available for learning. In this manner, we do not merely add on or blend in motivational strategies but use them as the source for learning activities that fulfill the four motivational conditions and accomplish the learning objective.

Having selected the most relevant strategies for each phase (beginning, during, and ending), we then reflect on what learning activity will carry out the essence of each strategy. Because instructional design is a creative process and an act of composing, ideas for activities will sometimes emerge before we select strategies, in which case the strategies can be suitable afterthoughts that confirm the motivational intent of the activities. In fact, having conducted hundreds of workshops for the source approach has taught me that the creativity of teachers and trainers can justifiably obliterate any set method of instructional planning. Creating an instructional plan from the framework and its related motivational strategies can be as idiosyncratic a process as writing a story. However conceived, the plan should respect the cultural, structural, and temporal considerations for learning, establish the four motivational conditions, and accomplish the learning objective with an understanding of how it will be assessed or transferred or both.

Examples of Instructional Planning Using the Motivational Framework

Whether developed from the Motivational Framework using the superimposed method or the source method, an instructional plan contains an alignment of motivational purposes with motivational strategies and related learning activities or instructor behaviors in a time frame. The examples of instructional plans that follow begin with simple and short units of learning and move toward longer and more complex units of learning. (Note that in all the examples, the numbers of the motivational strategies correspond to those used in Table 9.1 and in Chapters Five through Eight.)

Example 1

An instructor is conducting a three-hour class session in the School for Professional Studies, a division of the university that serves primarily adult learners. This is a general education course titled the Modern American Novel. The topic for the evening is Alice Walker and her novel *The Color Purple*. The learners have been requested to complete the reading of this novel prior to this course session.

Type and number of learners: twenty men and women ranging in age from twenty-one to fifty-nine. There is considerable diversity of age, ethnicity, and race among the students in the class. Most of them have had at least a few general education courses before this one.

Learning objective: learners will communicate their perspective and understanding of the novel through participation in discussion and a short written critique. (Writing samples and related rubrics were passed out and discussed at the first class session.)

The instructional plan for Example 1 is shown in Table 9.2. This example contains at least one motivational purpose for each of the four major motivational conditions. In this example, the instructor used nine motivational strategies out of a possible sixty. Because this example is only illustrative, it is conceivable that more or fewer strategies could be used. The particular learning activities or instructor behaviors are what the instructor would do to carry out the motivational strategies. Note that it is common for one activity to carry out more than one strategy—as one does in this example, carrying out Strategies 5 and 26. In fact, one elaborate activity might represent as many as ten strategies.

Notice also that Strategy 5 (collaborative and cooperative learning) is used for the purpose of creating relevant learning

Table 9.2. Instructional Plan for Example 1

Condition— Timing	Motivational Purpose	Motivational Strategy	Learning Activity or Instructor Behavior
Inclusion— beginning	To engender an awareness and feeling of connection	4. Share something of value with your adult learners.	Share reactions when first reading the novel over 20 years ago: discomfort with the roles of the men but attraction to the idea of redemptive love.
	To create a climate of respect	11. Acknowledge different ways of knowing, different languages, and different levels of knowledge or skill among the learners.	Acknowledge Alice Walker's radical feminist perspective and the controversial issues dealt with in the novel: abuse, incest, violence, racism, and its vision of the liberation of women from men—areas where different ways of knowing, strong feelings, and new learning may emerge.
Attitude— beginning	To create relevant learning experiences	5. Use collaborative and cooperative learning. 26. Make the learning activity an irresistible invitation to learn.	Divide the learners into small groups to share (to the extent they are comfortable) any situations in the novel that they relate to their personal experiences— areas that have a resonance with their own reality.

(Continued)

Table 9.2. (*Continued*)

Condition—Timing	Motivational Purpose	Motivational Strategy	Learning Activity or Instructor Behavior
Meaning—during	To deepen learners' engagement and challenge	40. Use critical questions to stimulate learner engagement and challenge.	Conduct a whole-group discussion with the following questions: *Probe for assumptions:* Based on your reading, what do you think are Alice Walker's assumptions about the relations between men and women? Women and women? Men and men? Please offer evidence from the book for each of these assessments. *Compare and contrast:* What are some of the similarities and differences between this book's perspective of humanity and what we've read by Flannery O'Connor? *Critically assess:* A hundred years from now, will this book remain a classic? In this regard, what are its strengths and weaknesses?
	To maintain learners' attention	29. Help learners realize their accountability for what they are learning.	To encourage equitable responding, at times randomly select students, but only on those occasions when you have initially used *think-pair-share* to process the question.

Competence—ending	To engender competence with assessment	51: Use authentic performance tasks to enable adults to know new learning and to know that they can proficiently apply this learning to their real lives.	Request learners to write a short critique of the novel as they might for a newspaper or newsmagazine.
		48. Provide effective feedback.	After learners have finished writing their critiques, pass out copies of the actual reviews of the novel from the *New York Times* and *Newsweek* in 1982.
		54. Use self-assessment methods to improve learning and to provide learners with the opportunity to construct relevant insights and connections.	Ask learners to compare the reviews to their critiques, then to select one review and write answers to the following questions: How has this review informed my thinking? And how might my critique have informed this reviewer?
		48. Provide effective feedback.	Collect learner critiques and self-assessments. Return with feedback at the next class meeting.

experiences in the instructional plan. Its location apart from motivational purpose of engendering connection illustrates that many of the strategies can be used for purposes not indicated in the summary (Table 9.1). The initial alignment of strategies in the summary with particular motivational purposes is theoretically sensible but not permanent. Many of the strategies are quite useful at any time and for multiple purposes.

Finally, a strategy can appear more than once in an instructional plan, as Strategy 48 (provide effective feedback) does twice in this short plan.

Example 2

An instructor for the distance learning department of a college is conducting a two-hour program for an accessibility workshop for faculty who are designing online courses. She is teaching them how to write alternative text (alt text) descriptions for Web pages. *Alt text* is a text description of a graphic embedded inside the Web-page code to be read by a screen reader. It explains the graphic in detail for those who cannot see it such as online students who are blind or visually impaired.

Type and number of learners: ten faculty members, men and women ranging in age from thirty to fifty (each is seated at a personal computer). Most of the learners are Euro-Americans with professional experience in business, accounting, and law. They have a basic understanding of online course development.

Learning objective: learners will write lucid alt-text descriptions that produce the same understanding as graphics. (The graphics have been self-selected from their courses.)

The instructional plan for Example 2 is illustrated in Table 9.3. (This example is adapted from the instructional plan of Sally Cordrey, multimedia specialist with Regis University.) This example contains at least one motivational purpose for every major motivational condition. Example 2 also illustrates in a number of

Table 9.3. Instructional Plan for Example 2

Condition—Timing	Motivational Purpose	Motivational Strategy	Learning Activity or Instructor Behavior
Inclusion—beginning	To engender an awareness and feeling of connection	7. Emphasize the human purpose of what is being learned and its relationship to the learners' personal lives and contemporary situations.	Provide a short overview of the Americans with Disabilities Act and how it relates to accommodation throughout the university to provide accessibility to buildings, courses, and online technology.
		6. Clearly identify the learning objectives and goals for instruction.	Introduce the learning objective for the program with a clear example of a Web page with a graphic, its alt text, and a demonstration of how a screen reader works with this example.
	To create a climate of respect	8. Assess learners' current expectations, needs, goals, and previous experience as it relates to your course or training.	*Pretest:* Learners make a first attempt to write alt text for a graphic from one of their courses. With a light touch and humor the learners share their initial writing.

(Continued)

Table 9.3. *(Continued)*

Condition—Timing	Motivational Purpose	Motivational Strategy	Learning Activity or Instructor Behavior
Attitude—beginning	To build a positive attitude toward the subject	15. Use assisted learning to scaffold complex learning.	Having estimated the learners' zone of proximal development from their pretest and sharing, project a prototypical example of a graphic and its alt text on a computer screen. Then project an inadequate example. As a group, learners analyze and critique it. They identify features that define best examples of graphics and their alt text. They create a check list of quality criteria for alt text and then individually practice completing alt text for given graphics using their checklist.
Meaning—during	To deepen engagement and challenge	38. Use uncertainty, anticipation, and prediction to the degree that learners enjoy them with a sense of security. 42. Use an intriguing problem to make instructional material more meaningful.	Two volunteers sit back to back. One verbally describes a graphic (observable to the rest of the group), and the other tries to reproduce the graphic. The group can coach them. Practice up to three rounds.

		5. Use collaborative and cooperative learning. 41. Use relevant problems, research, and inquiry to facilitate learning.	The learners as a collaborative group write the best possible alt text for a graphic projected on the computer screen by the instructor. The instructor provides feedback.
Competence—ending	To engender competence with assessment	51. Use authentic performance tasks to enable adults to know that they can proficiently apply what they are learning to their real lives. 54. Use self-assessment methods to improve learning and to provide learners with the opportunity to construct relevant insights and connections. 48. Provide effective feedback.	*Posttest:* Learners now rewrite alt text for the graphic they brought from their course. They compare to their pretest and note differences and improvements using the checklist they created earlier. The instructor mingles among them, providing feedback as appropriate. The program ends with a large-group discussion about what has been learned and how it will be applied.

instances the combination of two or more motivational strategies to fulfill a single motivational purpose, such as Strategies 6 and 7 for the purpose of engendering an awareness and feeling of connection.

The scaffolding strategy (Strategy 15) has a number of sequenced activities aligned with it, which demonstrates that several learning activities can together carry out a single motivational strategy. *Instructors need not concern themselves that every instructional behavior or learning activity in a learning sequence has listed next to it every possible motivational strategy corresponding to it.* Creating too specific a breakdown in instructional planning can become confusing and unnecessarily labor intensive (Gronlund, 1985). The instructional plan should be sufficient and effective if we have listed the most important strategies and related activities, and the necessary structural components of the concept or skill are evident and linked in the sequence of learning activities.

The instructor "peppers" this plan with abundant opportunities for learners to practice writing alt texts. But notice that the practice is always imbedded in a motivational strategy (Strategies 15, 41, 42, and 51). There's no doubt that learning certain skills or concepts requires considerable practice. The strategies offer appealing ways for adults to have the practice they need to learn something proficiently.

Another thing to notice is that Strategy 5 (collaborative and cooperative learning) is used in this instance for developing deeper engagement in the *during phase* of the instructional plan. Its location again illustrates that many of the strategies can be used for times and purposes not indicated in the summary (Table 9.1).

Also note one more purpose of this example: although the skill learned is fairly technical, most of the activities are socially constructed learning experiences that elicit learners' perspectives, collaboration, interaction, and colearning.

Example 3

An instructor is conducting a three-hour class session for a community college developmental math course. This instructional plan is for the third class in a sequence of fifteen once-a-week classes. Students normally work in four-person teams with each team having a mix of math skill levels ranging from above the class average to below it. Team-building activities have occurred in the two prior class sessions.

Type and number of learners: twenty-one students ranging in age from seventeen to forty-eight. A few of the students are Haitian and Mexican immigrants. The other students are Mexican-American and Euro-American. The class is nearly 50 percent women and 50 percent men. Most of these students have been required to take this course as a result of their placement on an entrance exam.

Learning objective: students will learn a five-part strategy to solve math word problems. After learning this strategy, they will create word problems with correct solutions that are authentic to their own lives.

The instructional plan for Example 3 is illustrated in Table 9.4. (This example is adapted from the instructional plan of Janet Rivera, an instructor at Pueblo Community College in Colorado.) This example contains at least one motivational purpose for every major motivational condition. In this example, the instructor has four activities for the condition of Inclusion. Two main reasons for this emphasis are the diversity of the students and the need to increase their comfort for team work, a constant in this instructor's approach to learning.

Looking at the entire instructional plan, it is obvious that this instructor uses motivational strategies to overcome what could easily be tedious practice with more compelling activities. Using collaborative learning and intriguing word problems throughout her instructional plan, she exploits the logic and potential trickery of math to make learning more appealing. Yet her instructional

Table 9.4. Instructional Plan for Example 3

Condition— Timing	Motivational Purpose	Motivational Strategy	Learning Activity or Instructor Behavior
Inclusion— beginning	To engender an awareness and feeling of connection	5. Use collaborative and cooperative learning. 42. Use an intriguing problem to make initially irrelevant instructional material more meaningful.	Post the problem: "If the day before the day before yesterday is Tuesday, what is the day after the day after tomorrow?" Ask students to solve this problem individually, using any method they prefer including diagrams. After a reasonable amount of time, they meet in their regular teams to "persuade" other members of their answer and to arrive at a team answer. Eventually the whole group discusses the team answers.
		7. Emphasize the human purpose of what is being learned and its relationship to the learners' personal lives and contemporary situations.	Remind the class of the first class session when the majority indicated a desire to become better at solving math word problems. Relate math word problems to real-life situations that include examples from carpentry, cooking, and shopping.

	To create a climate of respect	8. Assess learners' current expectations, needs, goals, and previous experience as it relates to your course or training.	In their teams, students share their experiences and feelings about math word problems. They cover (1) previous experiences, both good and bad, (2) how they cope when they don't know how to solve a real-life math problem, and (3) what is the most difficult part of math word problems for them to do. Each team gives a summary of their discussion to the whole group.
	To engender an awareness and feeling of connection	4. Share something of value with your adult learners.	Share former frustrations with word problems. Indicate there are key strategies for solving math word problems that have been personally helpful.
Attitude—beginning	To develop self-efficacy for learning	17. Help learners effectively attribute their success to their capability, effort, and knowledge.	*Order the Numbers Activity.* Within 60 seconds, students try to circle numbers in sequential order (1,2,3, and so forth) within a large group of numbers that seem randomly scrambled across an entire page. After their first attempt, show how a clockwise pattern of selecting makes the task more efficient and understandable. Then have students do the activity again with this strategy. Their success will be evident. Offer a knowledge attribution for using this strategy and align it with the "five-step" strategy that is coming next.
Meaning—during	To maintain learners' attention	31. Introduce, connect, and end learning activities attractively and clearly.	Give a short lecture on the "Five Steps for Solving Word Problems." Pass out a handout with the steps clearly summarized.

(Continued)

Table 9.4. *(Continued)*

Condition—Timing	Motivational Purpose	Motivational Strategy	Learning Activity or Instructor Behavior
	To evoke and sustain learners' interest	29. Help learners realize their accountability for what they are learning. 38. Use uncertainty, anticipation, and prediction to the degree that learners enjoy them with a sense of security.	Introduce Step One: *Find the Question*. Students survey 10 relevant word problems to identify only "what they are being asked to find." For example, What is the worker's hourly wage? Each student writes the ten questions they have inferred from the problems and compares them with a peer. Then they compare their questions to a projected answer key. Discussion follows to increase clarification.
	To deepen engagement and challenge	5. Use collaborative and cooperative learning. 42. Use an intriguing problem to make instructional material more meaningful.	Introduce Step Two: *Choose the Right Numbers*. Students again work on 10 relevant word problems. However, each problem has numbers within it that are irrelevant to the solution such as a person's height in a problem about hourly wages. Students work on these problems with a partner. The goal is only to identify the numbers that are relevant to each problem but not to solve the problems. Partners return to their teams to come up with a team answer for each problem. After this collaboration, the correct numbers are projected on a screen and discussion follows to clarify. The team with the most correct numbers receives a round of applause.

	Introduce Step Three: *Recognize the Key Words*. Every word problem has key words like *total*, *difference*, *increase*, and *partition* that signal whether to add, subtract, multiply, or divide. With two volunteers at the whiteboard, the rest of the group imagines as many words as they can for each of the arithmetic operations they represent. These words are recorded on the board and copied by each student into their notes. Volunteers read 10 word problems. After each problem is read, students hold up colored cards indicating the arithmetic operations indicated in the problem. As the instructor assesses their understanding, she gives appropriate feedback and clarification.
47. Use invention, artistry, imagination, and enactment to render deeper meaning and emotion in learning.	
48. Provide effective feedback.	
5. Use collaborative and cooperative learning. 19. Use relevant models to demonstrate expected learning.	Introduce Step Four: *Calculate the Answer*. Ten more relevant word problems are distributed. Students individually solve the problems two at a time. After they have solved the assigned two problems they look up, have their work checked by the instructor, and are assigned to assist those students still working. They use the first three steps—find the question, choose the right numbers, and recognize the key words—as a guide to coaching their peers. After an appropriate time, the instructor requests a variety of students to demonstrate their solutions at the board.

(Continued)

Table 9.4. (Continued)

Condition—Timing	Motivational Purpose	Motivational Strategy	Learning Activity or Instructor Behavior
		5. Use collaborative and cooperative learning. 42. Use an intriguing problem to make instructional material more meaningful.	Introduce Step Five: *Check your Answer*. Five relevant "mystery" problems are distributed. (For example, A young teacher is lost on a large ranch. He is searching for a group of children from his school who were separated from him in a dust storm. He finds ….) At the end of each problem are two answers. Working with partners, students use the four previous steps to arrive at the correct answer. End with a whole-group discussion.
Competence—ending	To engender competence with communication and rewards	59. When learning has natural consequences, help learners to be aware of them and of their impact.	Individually or with a partner, students compose a word problem and its solution. Their goal is to make it as mysterious and challenging as possible. After an appropriate amount of time, these problems are exchanged and solved within each team. Each team nominates one problem for the class to solve. For the next class, each student is requested to compose three more word problems with mystery and/or humor as part of their narrative.

plan is cohesive with each activity flowing into the next and reinforcing prior learning.

Example 4

A faculty development specialist is conducting a seven-hour workshop on the management of strong emotions during classroom controversy.

Type and number of learners: fifteen faculty members ranging in age from thirty to sixty. Six of the faculty are women, and five are people of color. All participants have had at least three years of college teaching experience.

Learning objective: faculty will identify and practice teaching and communication methods that support learners' emotions in a manner that allows for both individual expression and continuing mutual respect.

The instructional plan for Example 4 is illustrated in Table 9.5. In this example, the beginning of the workshop has three consecutive small-group activities with intermittent whole-group discussions. Starting the *during phase* with a minilecture and overheads may be a welcome change of pace.

The activities for Strategies 41 (journaling responses to the video) and 44 (role playing) obviously include feedback during the related discussions and develop learner competence. I emphasize this relationship to point out that frequently in instructional planning, a learning activity corresponding to one major motivational condition (in this case, meaning) will contain elements for developing another major motivational condition (in this case, competence). Thus we see that a learning activity can comprise characteristics that simultaneously engender more than one motivational condition (in this case, meaning and competence). We can safely generalize that such activities are relatively strong sources of motivational influence because they have multiple positive effects. For purposes of planning, we should consider the flow of content

Table 9.5. Instructional Plan for Example 4

Condition— Timing	Motivational Purpose	Motivational Strategy	Learning Activity or Instructor Behavior
Inclusion— beginning	To engender an awareness and feeling of connection	1. Allow for introductions.	Ask people to briefly introduce themselves.
		6. Clearly identify learning goals.	Describe learning goals for workshop.
		2. Provide an opportunity for multidimensional sharing.	Participants form small groups to share a topic or skill they value teaching that also elicits strong emotions in them because of their cultural or social background.
	To create a climate of respect	5. Use collaborative and cooperative learning.	In the same groups, participants brainstorm particular student words, actions, triggers, or incidents they find very challenging to manage. Groups report out and the specialist records these items on a flip chart.
		8. Assess learners' current expectations and needs and their previous experience as it relates to your course or training.	

Attitude—beginning	To create relevant learning experiences	26. Make the learning activity an irresistible invitation to learn. 27. Use the K-W-L strategy to introduce new topics and concepts.	Participants form triads and volunteer methods each has used effectively to respond to one or more of the challenges listed on the flip chart. Triads report out and indicate their methods for responding to the listed challenges. The specialist surveys the group about which methods are familiar and which of the methods they would like to learn more in depth. Two of the highest rated are added to the workshop content. The specialist invites participants to continue to share their insights and experience throughout the workshop.
Meaning—during	To maintain learners' attention and to deepen engagement and challenge	30. Provide variety in personal presentation style, modes of instruction, and learning materials. 31. Introduce, connect, and end learning activities attractively and clearly. 40. Use critical questions to stimulate engaging and challenging reflection and discussion.	With a projection of participation guidelines (Strategy 9) on a screen, discuss their application and use. Ask participants to think of the perspectives and language of their students and to revise or add to the participation guidelines to make them more understandable and culturally respectful for personal application.

(Continued)

Table 9.5. (*Continued*)

Condition— Timing	Motivational Purpose	Motivational Strategy	Learning Activity or Instructor Behavior
	To enhance learners' engagement, challenge, and adaptive decision making	45. Use simulations and games to embody the learning of multiple concepts and skills which require a real-life context and practice to be learned.	Use controversial quotations and aphorisms to simulate a discussion where strong but differing opinions are likely in order to practice the think-pair-share strategy.
		41. Use relevant problems, research, and inquiry to facilitate learning.	Show a video of students at different points in an argument and ask participants to journal possible responses if they were the teacher. Afterward discuss the various responses as a whole group. Indicate possible consequences and, where appropriate, provide feedback.
		44. Use role playing to embody meaning and new learning within a more realistic and dynamic context.	Participants role-play a learning group in conflict over a controversial court decision involving race. Participants take turns practicing methods to lessen conflict in this group while maintaining communication and mutual respect. Activity concludes with a whole-group discussion of the role play.

Competence—ending	To engender competence with assessment	51. Use authentic performance tasks to enable adults to know that they can proficiently apply what they are learning to their real lives. 52. Provide opportunities for adults to demonstrate their learning in ways that reflect their strengths and multiple sources of knowing. 48. Provide effective feedback.	In small groups, participants respond to a case study in which a faculty member loses control of a culturally diverse class in conflict over a recent campus incident. Participants conceptualize what might have been done in the moment as well as what might have been done to prevent this incident.
	To engender competence with communication and rewards	59. When learning has natural consequences, help learners to be aware of them and of their impact. 60. Provide positive closure at the end of significant units of learning.	Participants compare their responses to the case study with the suggestions of three faculty members (not present) who are experienced multicultural educators. The workshop concludes with participants writing and posting action plans for their courses based on learning from the workshop. The specialist and participants visit the posters, in carousel fashion, to offer supportive comments and suggestions.

and the primary motivational condition we wish to establish and use this relationship as a guide to selecting and placing activities that may have multiple motivational influences. We should be aware of these additional influences but not restricted or burdened by them.

Example 5

A trainer is conducting a two-day job-search workshop for displaced workers in Denver.

Type and number of learners: twelve men and women ranging in age from twenty-eight to fifty-six. There is considerable diversity of occupation, socioeconomic status, ethnicity, and race among the trainees.

Learning objective: by the end of the workshop, participants will (1) understand a selected body of knowledge to more effectively manage their transition to another job; (2) develop introduction, interviewing, and resume writing skills to transfer to their job search; and (3) write their first draft of an informative and professionally suitable résumé. (In the ensuing weeks, consultation with the trainer or a follow-up workshop is available for participants to refine and advance the skills they learned in this workshop.)

The instructional plan for the two days in Example 5 is illustrated in Table 9.6. (This example is adapted from the instructional plan of René DeAnda, at the time an agency trainer for the Mayor's Office of Employment and Training.) In this example, the trainer clearly wants the participants to transfer the skills they learn in the workshop to their job searches. She plans to establish an *intention to transfer* (Strategy 55) as a beginning strategy for each day. She also plans to develop the *capacity to transfer* in the ending phase of the first day (see first half of Table 9.6) and the *during phase* of the second day (see second half of Table 9.6). Among the six elements to foster transfer, she concentrates on *content* (relevant, practical, connected to prior knowledge, practiced, competently learned) and *changes necessary* (doable, realistic, integrated into the professional roles of the learners).

Table 9.6. Instructional Plan for Example 5

		Day One (Six Hours)	
Condition— Timing	Motivational Purpose	Motivational Strategy	Learning Activity or Instructor Behavior
Inclusion— beginning	To engender feelings of connection and a climate of respect	1. Introductions.	Everyone introduces themselves and mentions one thing they like about living in the Denver area.
		2. Opportunity for multidimensional sharing. 8. Assess expectations, needs, goals, and experience as it relates to training.	Group divides into triads. Using a Venn diagram to highlight common ground among them, group members share jobs they've held since high school, places they've lived, the type of work they are interested in, and their expectations for the workshop. The expectations are reported out and listed by the trainer on an overhead screen.
		6. Identify learning goals. 3. Indicate your cooperative intentions. 55. Foster the intention to transfer learning.	Describe learning goals for workshop, relate them to expectations on the screen, and describe your experience as a displaced worker. Express your enthusiasm for the workshop and give brief histories of some of the people who have found satisfying work after completing this workshop.

(Continued)

Table 9.6. *(Continued)*

Condition— Timing	Motivational Purpose	Motivational Strategy	Learning Activity or Instructor Behavior
		11. Acknowledge different ways of knowing, different languages, and different levels of knowledge or skill.	Note the diversity in the room and discuss how there may be a variety of experiences, skill levels, and perspectives for dealing with the content in the workshop: "What we can learn from each other and with each other is a real benefit."
Attitude— beginning	To build a positive attitude toward the subject	13. Positively confront erroneous beliefs.	Introduce workforce data showing how in the last decade new jobs have increased but have shifted to consulting, service, health care, technology, and education rather than manufacturing.
	To develop self-efficacy	17. Help learners attribute success to capability, effort, and knowledge.	Emphasize how most of the workshop content is about strategies (that succeed) for finding satisfying work: networking, résumé writing, and so on.
Meaning— during	To sustain interest and deepen engagement and challenge	5. Use collaborative learning. 33. Relate learning to adult concerns. 40. Use critical questions to stimulate engagement and challenge.	Give a minilecture on possible reactions to loss such as disbelief, anger, hope, and so forth. Then divide participants into small collaborative groups to review this material with a few critical questions and to apply this understanding to their own lives—for example, What might someone do who was in a state of disbelief? What are the implications? How do these possible reactions relate to your situation?

		43. Use case study methods.	Introduce the stages of transition for change and give the participants a case study to discuss in small groups. Their goal is to identify the stages of transition in the case and to suggest how some of the reactions to loss might serve to facilitate the worker's progress from one stage to another—for example, transferring anger into action.
Competence—ending	To engender competence with assessment	54. Use self-assessment methods.	Participants conduct a self-assessment with a short learning-styles inventory. They discuss with a partner how the results of this assessment make sense to them.
		52. Provide opportunities to demonstrate learning in ways that reflect strengths and multiple sources of knowing.	Participants create action plans to apply to their families, to their educational futures, or to their job searches based on the information and learning in today's workshop.
		55. Foster the capacity to transfer learning.	The day concludes with volunteers sharing one important aspect of their action plan.

(Continued)

Table 9.6. (*Continued*)

Condition— Timing	Motivational Purpose	Motivational Strategy	Learning Activity or Instructor Behavior
		Day Two (Six Hours)	
Inclusion— beginning	To engender a feeling of connection	2. Provide opportunity for multidimensional sharing.	Participants introduce themselves again and do one cycle of "Head, Heart, Hand" regarding a thought, feeling, or action from yesterday's workshop that left a strong impression.
		6. Identify learning goals. 55. Foster the intention to transfer learning.	Review learning goals and how some were met by yesterday's work.
Meaning— during	To enhance engagement, challenge, and adaptive decision making	41. Use a relevant problem. 45. Use a simulation. 55. Foster the capacity to transfer learning.	Discuss needing a thirty-second introduction for networking and interviewing. Participants offer views about what might be essential to such a brief introduction. Most think some version of where you've been, what you did, and where you're going might suffice. Each participant writes out a personal version of this introduction and practices it with three other participants in a classroom *walkabout*. Activity concludes with participants privately giving each other feedback.

37. Use a story.
44. Use a role play.

Introduce the *short story technique* for interviews—a way to give evidence of one's competence by tying a skill to the place where it was used and the successful results that occurred. This information is delivered as a very short story. Demonstrate with a couple of stories from your own professional history. After conceptualizing two such stories, participants practice them in a role-playing format and receive feedback from the interviewer and observer.

30. Provide variety in instruction.
35. Use humor.
15. Scaffold learning.
19. Use relevant models.

Participants view and discuss a humorous video on the how, what, and why of networking.

With an exemplary model of a résumé on the overhead screen, review its format and think out loud through anticipated difficult areas. Provide a checklist of ten steps for writing an excellent résumé. Also provide examples of professionally done résumés from former participants of this workshop who have found satisfying work.

(*Continued*)

Table 9.6. *(Continued)*

Condition— Timing	Motivational Purpose	Motivational Strategy	Learning Activity or Instructor Behavior
Competence— ending	To engender competence with assessment	51. Use authentic performance tasks. 53. Use rubrics. 48. Provide feedback.	Participants write the first draft of their résumé. In addition to the ten-step checklist for writing the résumé, they have a handout describing and exemplifying the qualities of an excellent résumé. When finished with the draft, they find a partner. Each reads the other's draft and provides feedback based on the qualities highlighted in the handout. At this point they can make revisions or bring their draft to the trainer for another round of feedback or do both.
	To engender competence with communication and rewards	60. Provide positive closure.	Participants gather their chairs in a circle with the trainer and have the opportunity to briefly share one thing they are genuinely glad they've learned and will use in their job searches. They also can extend an appreciation to the group or any member of it. It is well understood that it is certainly agreeable for any member to pass on either opportunity.

Please note how short the beginning phase of the second day is. There is a goal review with an intent to transfer and one multidimensional sharing activity to renew a feeling of connection in the group; then it's on to new content. There are no activities to establish attitude because that appears to have been well done on the first day. When the activities for meaning and competence are collaborative and engaging, the need for strategies to sustain inclusion and attitude is oftentimes considerably less.

Also note that with the exception of the activities, which need a longer narrative to exemplify their tone and context, I've shortened the strategies and combined the purposes. This is to model what I've seen in the field: *most instructors develop a shorthand of phraseology for the various purposes, strategies, and learning activities so as to increase their efficiency in planning.*

On day two, the trainer uses a self-assessment strategy activity ("Head, Heart, Hand") to sustain inclusion, and she uses the scaffolding strategy, originally aligned with building a positive attitude, to enhance meaning. This flexible placement of the strategies and activities again illustrates the numerous motivational purposes they can serve.

Example 5 is the last of the examples of motivation planning in this book. I treated each example as a learning sequence that is a complete unit with beginning, during, and ending time phases so that it could exemplify as many aspects of the Motivational Framework for Culturally Responsive Teaching as possible. A complete learning unit can comprise minutes, hours, days, or weeks. The time and qualitative differences between a short presentation and a long-term course are immense. However, even in the latter instance, there will be separate units that can be planned. No matter what the length of a particular learning unit, we will need to apply strategies with a sense of timing if we are to establish the four motivational conditions and evoke continuing intrinsic motivation among diverse adults.

These examples are meant to show what might be possible and what is structurally necessary for instructional planning. They are not intended as precise models to follow. It is quite possible that better and more creative means could be found to approach adult motivation and learning for each of the learning objectives.

There is a practice effect to planning with the framework. The more often it is done, the more familiar the motivational conditions and their related strategies become. Practice significantly lessens the time required for instructional planning and makes the process more fluid. In my experience, most instructors need to practice applying the framework about *six times* before their planning with it becomes more intuitive and automatic.

For Review

The lists that follow summarize the basic steps for the two types of planning with this motivational framework.

Superimposed Method

1. Consider who the learners will be, paying particular attention to their experience and diversity.
2. Clarify the learning objective(s) with diligent regard for the learners and the learning situation.
3. Estimate the amount of time available for instruction.
4. Consider the inherent structure of the content or skill to be learned.
5. Examine the established curricular or instructional design to be followed for the learning unit.
6. Superimpose the four questions for instructional planning based on the Motivational Framework for Culturally Responsive Teaching (see Exhibit 9.2) onto the predetermined format of instruction to see where its instructional activities positively respond to these questions and where they do not.

7. For any of the four questions that are inadequately answered, select appropriate motivational strategies from Table 9.1 and develop related learning activities or instructor behaviors. (Because the total time allowed for instruction may limit these selections, it may be necessary to reduce or revise other predetermined learning activities.)

8. The ultimate criteria are that (1) the instructional plan establishes all four of the motivational conditions and (2) each time phase (beginning, during, and ending) has activities in its sequence of instruction to elicit significant motivation among learners.

Source Method

1. Consider who the learners will be, paying particular attention to their experience and diversity.

2. Clarify the learning objective(s) with diligent regard for the learners and the learning situation.

3. Estimate the amount of time available for instruction.

4. Consider the inherent structure of the content or skill to be learned and its relationship to intended assessment or transfer activities.

5. Review the motivational purposes listed in Table 9.1 as they align with the four motivational conditions and select motivational strategies to guide the development of learning activities.

6. Use the selected motivational strategies to choose or create learning activities that fit the flow of content or skill development and their assessment or transfer or both. Be reasonably certain this instructional plan can be carried out in the time available.

7. The ultimate criteria are that (1) the instructional plan establishes all four of the motivational conditions and (2) each

time phase (beginning, during, and ending) has activities in its sequence of instruction to elicit significant motivation among learners.

When either method is used effectively, the adult's response while learning is likely to be as follows:

1. I am a member of a learning community in which I feel a mutual sense of care and respect.
2. I am successfully learning something I find relevant and desirable.
3. I am engaged in challenging learning where my experience and perspective can inform as well as be informed.
4. I am becoming more effective in something I value.

These four statements represent what is possible when adults learn in a situation where the four motivational conditions— inclusion, attitude, meaning, and competence—are fully present. If adults can honestly make these statements, they will be motivated to learn and to continue learning. This does not mean adults bear no responsibility for their own motivation for learning. It does mean that we as instructors have optimally exercised our professional skill to respect adults as they are at that moment and to make instruction an experience that enhances their motivational resources.

Motivation is dynamic. As an emotional state (Izard, 1993), it grows or diminishes as learners engage in learning and are influenced by instruction. Like communication, motivation works reciprocally, and instructors are the lead communicators. Our responsibility is to maximally support and nourish the motivational capacities adults bring with them to the learning experience. Just as a dinner host provides the best setting possible to elicit conversation among all guests, we provide the best possible learning situation to evoke motivation among all learners. Having done so, we can reasonably expect adults to do what adults have done naturally under these circumstances for centuries—willfully learn what they value.

Assessing Learner Motivation

We have done our planning. We have a comprehensive, motivating instructional sequence from the beginning to the end of the learning unit. We are carrying it out. Now, how do we know if and when learners are motivated? Of all the questions in this book, this is one of the most challenging. Although using exams and other indicators of *learning accomplishment* as evidence of learner motivation makes sense, we have to be careful. Intuitively we may think, "If students are motivated, they will learn." However, learning achievement is strongly influenced by capability and opportunity (instructional quality, suitability of materials, time available, and so forth) as well as motivation. At best, learning is an indirect and only partial indicator of motivation.

Among the possible means of evaluating learner motivation are self-report instruments—questionnaires, rating scales, checklists, and the like—that elicit the learners' assessment of their own behavior, beliefs, or perceptions. A standardized self-report measure of motivation to learn is the Motivated Strategies for Learning Questionnaire, commonly known as the MSLQ (Pintrich and others, 1993; Garcia Duncan and McKeachie, 2005). It represents a social cognitive view of motivation, regarding it as dynamic and contextually bound. This instrument has been widely used in postsecondary education. The MSLQ is considered a reliable measure for getting feedback on student learning strategies and self-efficacy as well as for guiding decisions for course adjustments. Its scale for measuring Intrinsic Goal Orientation has been used in studies of adult learners (Bye, Pushkar, and Conway, 2007).

Self-reports can be very helpful as estimating and feedback devices. However, they have disadvantages. One is that learners may bias their responses for reasons that range from social desirability to grades they received, and another is that learners are not always aware of their motives or how to explain them. Whether standardized or instructor-developed, when well constructed and used with other indicators of motivation, such as observation ratings, self-reports can be informative (Assor and Connell, 1992). I often ask learners to complete the self-report shown here to give me their perceptions of how well the course or workshop is fulfilling the four motivational conditions of the framework. (Learners rate each of the following items on a four-point scale from strongly disagree to strongly agree.)

1. The workshop climate is friendly and respectful. (Inclusion)
2. This workshop is relevant to my personal or professional goals. (Attitude)
3. This workshop is challenging me to think. (Meaning)
4. This workshop contributes to helping me to be effective at what I value. (Competence)
5. The instructor respects learners' opinions and ideas. (Inclusion)
6. In this workshop, I can use my experience and ways of knowing to support my learning. (Attitude)
7. Most of the time during this workshop I feel engaged in what is going on. (Meaning)
8. I can actually use the information or skills I am learning in this workshop. (Competence)

Probably the best moment-to-moment method of assessing learner motivation is personal observation. This too is an imperfect method. Our biases and mood can contaminate what we perceive as well as what we select to perceive. (Focusing on one resistant adult learner seems to make the whole classroom look bleak.) It is also difficult to be totally sure that what we see is a real indicator of motivation. For example, it is possible that signs of learners' intensity might be nothing more than their obvious reactions to physical or mental discomfort. Understanding and assessing effort are also very tricky. Culturally speaking, when tasks become difficult, some people are socialized to be calm and contemplative rather than to become intense and more active. Looking for vigor to assess motivation in learners can be deceptive. That's why, especially over time, I prefer to use persistence as an indicator of motivation. Even though the kind of behaviors may vary, do learners continue to engage in actions aimed at accomplishing the learning task? Other observable indicators of motivation (Stipek, 2002) to consider are when learners:

Begin learning activities without resistance

Prefer the challenging aspects of tasks

Spontaneously relate learning to outside interests

Ask questions to expand their understanding beyond the learning at hand

Go beyond required work

Find joy in the process of learning—the studying, writing, reading, and so forth

Are proud of their learning and its consequences

Stay focused

Become reluctant to stop when engaged

I also pay very close attention to learners' physical energy. Most adults are capable of being in a state of flow when their activity level ranges between relaxed and alert and excited and involved (Csikszentmihalyi, 1997).

By keenly and continually observing to assess these indicators of motivation, we can adjust our teaching or training to enhance learner motivation. Also, as discussed in Chapter Seven, I believe we need minimum standards for the quality of motivation we observe in our courses and training. These standards may include the percentage of people who willingly begin a learning task, the percentage of people who persist to overcome a learning obstacle, and the percentage of people who appear relaxed and alert while learning. Possessing such standards enables us to be both aware and responsive, to steer a course while teaching that brings to life the instructional plan we so carefully designed.

Margery Ginsberg (Ginsberg and Wlodkowski, 2000) has developed an observation guide to assess how an instructor has established the four motivational conditions from the Motivational Framework for Culturally Responsive Teaching. Using this "Observation Guide for Culturally Responsive Teaching and Learning," one can locate evidence of specific norms and behaviors that indicate the presence of each condition during a learning experience. This information can inform future instruction and planning as well as point out motivational conditions that may need more development. The version of this guide for adult learners is reproduced in the Appendix.

In the future, brain measurement technology will probably provide a more accurate assessment of motivation to learn. Currently, the electroencephalogram (EEG) can indicate parts of the brain that are actively engaged in processing information (Bear, Connors, and Paradiso, 2007). However, like all forms of assessment, we will still need wisdom and compassion to use this technology well.

Continuing Adult Motivation and Lifelong Learning

In an increasingly complex technological society, where both adults work in 85 percent of all partnered or married households (Kessler-Harris, 2007), the need for continuous education and training during one's lifetime is an unavoidable reality. For such a culture, fostering the willingness of adults to learn may be of greater consequence than ensuring that they have learned some specific thing at a certain point in time. People who eventually find reading, writing, calculating, communicating, and expanding their knowledge and skills a satisfying way of being are usually considered lifelong learners and a source of human capital by their government.

The Commission for a Nation of Lifelong Learners (1997) recommended making the adoption of a programmatic approach to lifelong learning a national priority. Its recommendations include recognizing the connection between lifelong learning and global economic success, creating equity of access, use of technologies such as online learning, reshaping educational delivery, and establishing resources for lifelong learning sufficient to its need (Maehl, 2000).

However, the merits of lifelong learning are not without potential for exploitation. As Merriam, Caffarella, and Baumgartner point out, "Because lifelong learning is so pervasive throughout society, knowledge becomes a commodity that is produced, packaged, and sold to the consumer. Crass commercialism begins to define lifelong learning" (2007, p. 49). Lifelong learning has become a new market, a form of "vocationalism" where people learn "to work harder, faster, and smarter" to help their employer compete without awareness or commitment to the common good (Boshier, 2005, p. 375). How can one argue against the need to be competitive in a market-driven economy? Under the guise of staying competitive, it is easy to ignore the questions, How are the skills and technology used? Who has accessibility? Who profits the most? and What happens to the environment as a result?

I believe these criticisms are reasonable. That's why the use of instructional planning and the motivation framework has to have a value context and a critical consciousness. If it becomes subject to indiscriminate application without critical reflection, something as enriching and crucial to social cohesion and democracy as lifelong learning can become a kind of merchandise, more harmful to our humanity than generative of our highest goals.

There are a number of ideas for fostering lifelong learning. We know that lifelong learning can be informal and self-directed as well as formal, such as higher education and professional development. In order to develop lifelong learners, some scholars have advocated that learning processes in higher education should be designed to increase the capacity for self-directed learning, teach metacognitive skills to effectively guide learning, and foster a personal value for continuing learning over a lifetime (Dunlap and Grabinger, 2003).

Edward Deci and Richard Ryan (1991), who have spent most of their lives studying the phenomenon of intrinsic motivation, believe the key to acquiring this value—to finding the act of learning worthwhile—is feeling free enough to accept it as one's own. People who embrace this value and can be described as lifelong learners are deeply aware that the fundamental aspects of learning fit who they are. They read, reflect, and purposely seek to deepen their awareness and knowledge. Essentially, they possess a broad *intrinsic goal orientation* to learning that continues throughout their lives; they find new learning to be challenging, interesting, and worth mastering. They are able to learn autonomously, knowing how to use self-initiated exploratory strategies to guide new learning (Pintrich and others, 1991). In both attitude and skills, they have a continuing motivation to learn. Recent literature on aging indicates significant physical, mental, and social benefits for older adults who have a positive attitude toward learning and continue to learn (Purdie and Boulton-Lewis, 2003).

For teaching and training, the Motivational Framework for Culturally Responsive Teaching is ideally suited to encourage continuing adult motivation to learn. Beginning with a plan, we create, as a community of learners, compelling experiences to attain relevant learning with learner autonomy intact. Although the design is situational, love of learning is at its core. The goal is always to create an intrinsically motivating learning experience that contributes to and sustains a *lifelong motivation to learn*. The theories of self directed learning and self-regulation have something more to say about attaining this goal. Let's take a look.

Self-Directed Learning and Self-Regulation

Self-directed learning (SDL) is a mainstay and well-researched idea in adult education (Merriam, Caffarella, and Baumgartner, 2007). With no widely accepted definition and numerous interpretations, it has been a magnet for controversy in the field. Critiques range from whether it is a goal or a characteristic of adult learners to dissatisfaction with its individualistic, white middle-class male orientation. Linda Leach ends her essay on SDL in the *International Encyclopedia of Adult Education* with the following words, "Clearly, self-directed learning is contested. There is no agreement in the literature about what it is, to whom it applies, or how it might be implemented in practice, particularly in formal education. Rather, we each have to decide how we understand it and how it will play out in our practice" (2005, p. 568). In this respect, I have chosen elements from self-directed learning that are congruent with and parallel to self-regulation, a well researched theory in educational psychology.

Self-regulation is a process by which learners control their behavior, feelings, and thoughts to attain academic goals. In self-regulation theory, "learning is viewed as an activity that students do for themselves in a *proactive* [italics added] way rather than as a covert event that happens to them in reaction to teaching" (Zimmerman, 2002, p. 65). Distinct within this theory are the concepts of metacognition and social cognition. *Metacognition* is being aware and knowledgeable about one's own thinking—for example, reflecting on the steps one took to solve a math problem. *Social cognition* is the way in which social influences such as peers and coaches affect internal processes such as goal setting and self-evaluation.

Although most of the early research in self-regulation theory was done with children and traditional college students, the number of studies with community college students and adults is growing (Zimmerman and Kitsantas, 2005). At the theory level, there is considerable overlap between Garrison's model (1997) of SDL and conventional self-regulation theory. Both include self-management, self-monitoring, self-motivation, and abundant use of metacognitive processes.

My experience with adult learners is that most who exhibit continuing motivation to learn, such as spontaneous interest and value for a wide range of learning topics, already possess many metacognitive skills to self-regulate their learning. They fluidly decide their learning goals; they reflect on the strategies they use to learn; and they are conscious of their motivation and how to sustain it. From a motivational perspective, the adults for whom I more often need to be available and ready to assist are those who exhibit *ineffective effort*: when they want to learn, they often have difficulty deciding on a topic to learn, how to guide their learning, and how to sustain it (Trawick and Corno, 1995). Some examples of this phenomenon are churning through topics but remaining vaguely dissatisfied with any selection, setting unrealistic deadlines, or becoming so anxious when trying to learn something that distraction and frustration eventually diminish motivation.

Studies in self-regulation have demonstrated that people who want to learn but lack the metacognitive skills to sustain their motivation and learning can be directly taught these processes, which enables them to deal with distractions, increase their self-confidence, focus their attention, and control negative emotions about subjects from math to writing (Trawick and Corno, 1995; Zimmerman and Kitsantas, 2005).

Most people attain these skills without direct instruction. For example, with rare exceptions, expert writers use metacognition and effective writing strategies without someone teaching them how to think (Murray, 2004). We learn these skills socioculturally through familial practices, teacher modeling, collaborating with peers, and immersing ourselves in various subjects. In most instances, the strategies included in the Motivational Framework for Culturally Responsive Teaching do not directly teach self-regulation skills, but many do model them and support their use. The strategies aligned with the motivational purposes of developing self-efficacy (Strategies 16 through 20), establishing learning goals (Strategies 21 through 23), and engendering competence with assessment (Strategies 48 and 50 through 54)—when initiated and used by the learner—are commonly identified as methods of self-regulating learning (Zimmerman and Campillo, 2003).

There are other models that employ a self-regulation approach to learning and instruction. One that has been used in Europe with all age groups is the CLIA Model (De Corte, Verschaffel, and Masui, 2004). Essential to self-regulation is helping learners to talk to themselves about their learning so that they get into the habit of having an ongoing internal conversation about their own learning. A practical day-to-day approach to teaching self-regulation strategies is to assess how adults currently use the strategies by sensitively asking direct questions—for example, What steps did you take to learn this (Strategy 23, goal setting)? What did you tell yourself when you realized this might have been a mistake (Strategy 18, attributions to effort and knowledge)? What are you telling yourself to sustain your motivation (Strategy 20, encouragement)? Here is an example of how we might work with this last question.

> *Introduce the strategy and explain its usefulness*—for example, "Sometimes it helps to talk to yourself about your own motivation, to let yourself realize why this is important to you. When we remind ourselves we're likely to get a bit more energy for the work. What are some things you might reflect on that would encourage you to do this work?"

Use guided practice, reminders, and hints, coach a bit, and gently withdraw—for example, "You've been doing so well with self-motivation, I don't think any questions I might ask would be of any real assistance. It's a pleasure to see you taking charge of your learning."

In this way we help learners to be self-conscious—in the best sense of this expression—about their learning, to realize they have the power to employ their own motivational skills. Although there is a bridge between the motivational framework and how adults guide their own learning, there is also a limit. With the framework instructors can give opportunity, support, modeling, and a compelling lesson compassionately and creatively conceived. Yet much of learning occurs while we're alone—the studying, the reading, the writing, and the practicing. And, to be realistic, at such times anyone can bog down. In such moments, going forward is often a matter of the wisdom of knowing what to tell ourselves.

Epilogue

Ethical Considerations for an Instructor of Adults

> *In recognizing the humanity of our fellow beings, we*
> *pay ourselves the highest tribute.*
>
> Thurgood Marshall

It is probably only fair that what works so well for the learner works just as well for the instructor. To experience our jobs as intrinsically satisfying, we need to feel respected where we work, to believe what we do is relevant, and to have a sense that we can effectively accomplish the challenges we value. If these conditions are met, we live a professional life in which we breathe the air of vital meaning. In reality, we need the same conditions adults need to optimally learn.

Yet this book has sought something more than self-satisfaction for the instructor. As in the last edition, there is an emphasis on the value of respect for cultural diversity among the adults we teach and train and the belief that a learning environment should be a model of equitable opportunity where learning is connected to an encompassing ethical purpose beyond successful achievement.

Given the events of 9/11 and the devastation of the war in Iraq, I am more aware now that how I reveal myself as an instructor, how I use my authority, how I handle frustration or conflict is a reflection on aggression and power and their influence on human beings. I know that seeing adults compassionately overcome anger in others or themselves is one of the truest connections I have to a source of strength for peace within myself.

Fear is an overpowering emotion—for a person, a group, or a nation—and is only a split second away. When present, it is exceedingly difficult to overcome and can undermine our most cherished values and ideals. We need to be aware of it, name it quickly, and realize that when someone senses fear in us, their own fear is usually imminent. When an instructor can remain calm, respectful, and magnanimous in the face of conflict, it enables those present to retain their composure and gain a better chance to address the issue with reason and compassion.

Part of being an effective instructor is being a leader. Learners still look to us to be above the fray, possessed of at least a modicum of wisdom. When I consider our influence, I think leading by example continues to hold the greatest weight. I believe this responsibility requires some form of committed action on our part for social change. Not that we even mention it in our work, but that we live this experience so that it continues to inform us and humble us by revealing the true challenge involved in any consequential achievement of equity or justice.

Today teaching and training adults is an enormous global enterprise. In the United States well over 40 percent of all students in postsecondary education are adults, and the money spent for training adults in business and industry exceeds the total spent for all of higher education. Training and professional development clearly make a difference in securing success for any company or organization. However, with this growth has come a diffusion of the initial purpose of adult education—the advocacy and action for social and personal transformation. My personal observation in higher education is that this voice has become quieter, often muted by the need to regard adults as a market for increasing enrollments and sustaining profits. I think there is a necessary tension between the ideals of the discipline and the economic basics of running an institution. Keeping this relationship appropriately balanced is fundamental to the integrity of adult education.

The degree to which we enable *all* adults to learn well is a criterion essential to maintaining this balance. Our effectiveness as individuals and institutions in creating educational access and sustaining degree completion for low-income adults should be a standard for judging whether we are living up to the ideals of our discipline. I believe this is the greatest challenge for our field. As we continue to make progress toward this goal, we are obliged to consider more carefully the consequences of what we teach or train others to do.

Our work distinctly serves an age-old question: What is worth knowing and perpetuating? Our craft carries the responsibility to wrestle with this question just as medical doctors carry the obligation to know what life is and when it is worth saving. This duty does not lessen the joy of being an instructor. It is what gives our profession a soul.

When Charles Garfield (1986) studied older peak performers— adults who were sixty or older and loved their work and in the eyes of their peers were excellent at what they did, whatever the occupation—they had one thing in common. They saw their work as part of something greater than themselves. Garfield called this quality a sense of mission, a belief that one's work contributes to something transcendent. For some it was connected to a spiritual belief, for others to a social contribution or to the beauty of the work itself. To have this perception of ourselves as instructors, we need to realize and question the worth of what we teach or train, to inform our faith with doubt as well as reason.

The purpose of this book is to provide a useful means for creating unity among worth, meaning, and joy in adult learning. It offers a path to this goal through motivationally sound instruction. How much of this is science, or art, or intuition? As in the previous edition, I'm still not sure. But when it flows, when learning between instructor and learner is reciprocal and respectful, it is an inspired dimension of being—not something one practices or performs, but something one enters and lives.

Appendix

Observation Guide for Culturally Responsive Teaching and Learning (Adult Version)

Margery B. Ginsberg

This guide is organized to identify elements that support intrinsic motivation. It is not an assessment tool but an instrument to promote dialogue about instruction and to affirm what is working to foster the four motivational conditions.

Establishing Inclusion

*How does the learning experience contribute
to developing a community of learners who feel
respected and connected to one another?*

_____ Course procedures and norms help everyone to feel they belong.

_____ Learners and instructor have opportunities to learn about each other.

_____ Course agreements are negotiated.

_____ All learners equitably and actively participate.

_____ Instructor directs attention equitably.

_____ Instructor interacts respectfully with all learners.

_____ Learners talk to and with partners or small groups.

_____ Learners know what to do, especially when making choices.

_____ Learners help each other.

_____ Instructor and learners discuss perspectives, opinions, or ideas that differ from their own.

Evidence:

Developing a Positive Attitude

How does this learning experience offer meaningful choices or goals and promote personal relevance?

_____ Learners' experiences, concerns, and interests are used to develop course content.

_____ Learners' experiences, concerns, and interests are addressed in responses to questions.

_____ Learners' prior knowledge and learning experiences are explicitly linked to course content and questions.

_____ Instructor encourages learners to understand, develop, and express different points of view.

_____ Instructor encourages learners to clarify their interests and set goals.

_____ Instructor maintains flexibility in pursuit of emerging interests.

_____ Instructor and learners exhibit a *critical consciousness* about positionality, knowledge construction, or the consequences of what is learned.

Evidence:

*Instructor encourages learners to make
real choices or to affirm their
participation regarding:*

_____ How to learn (multiple intelligences)

_____ What to learn

_____ Where to learn

_____ When a learning experience will be considered to be complete

_____ How learning will be assessed

_____ With whom to learn

_____ How to solve emerging problems

Evidence:

Enhancing Meaning

*How does this learning experience
engage participants in challenging learning?*

_____ Instructor in concert with learners creates opportunities for inquiry, investigation, and projects.

_____ Instructor provides opportunities for learners to actively participate in challenging ways.

_____ Instructor asks higher-order questions of all learners throughout instruction.

_____ Instructor elicits or probes for high-quality responses from all learners.

_____ Instructor uses multiple *safety nets* to ensure learners' engagement and risk taking (for example, not grading all assignments and allowing learners to work with partners).

_____ Instructor and learners use problems, role-playing, simulations, enactment, or art to deepen learning and engagement.

Evidence:

Engendering Competence

How does this learning experience help learners to understand that they are becoming more effective in learning that they value and perceive as authentic to their real-world experience?

_____ There is information, consequence, or product that supports learners in valuing and identifying their learning.

_____ The purpose of the lesson is clearly communicated.

_____ The criteria for assessing outcomes is clearly communicated.

_____ There are opportunities for a diversity of competencies to be demonstrated in a variety of ways.

_____ Instructor helps all learners identify accomplishments.

_____ There are options for assessment.

_____ Learners receive feedback from the instructor about their individual learning.

_____ There are opportunities for learners to make explicit connections between new learning and prior knowledge.

_____ There are opportunities for learners to make explicit connections between their learning and the real world.

_____ There are opportunities for learners to self-assess their learning and to adjust or revise.

_____ There are elements such as planning and transfer-of-learning strategies to facilitate transfer of new learning to the community, family, or workplace.

_____ There are opportunities for learners to give each other feedback about perspectives, ideas, or learning.

Evidence:

References

Abercombrie, H. C., Kalin, N. H., Thurow, M. E., Rosencranz, M. A., and Davidson, R. J. "Cortisol Variation in Humans Affects Memory for Emotionally Laden and Neutral Information." *Behavioral Neuroscience*, 2003, *117*(3), 505–516.

Adams, M., Bell, L. A., and Griffin, P., eds. *Teaching for Diversity and Social Justice*. (2nd ed.) New York: Routledge, 2007.

Adams, M., Jones, J., and Tatum, B. D. "Knowing Our Students." In M. Adams, L. A. Bell, and P. Griffin (eds.), *Teaching for Diversity and Social Justice*, 2nd ed. New York: Routledge, 2007.

Adams, M., and Marchesani, L. S. "Curricular Innovations: Social Diversity as Course Content." In M. Adams (ed.), *Promoting Diversity in College Classrooms: Innovative Responses for the Curriculum, Faculty, and Institutions*. New Directions for Teaching and Learning, no. 52. San Francisco: Jossey-Bass, 1992.

Ahissar, E., Vaadia, E., Ahissar, M., Bergman, H., Arieli, A., and Abeles, M. "Dependence of Cortical Plasticity on Correlated Activity of Single Neurons and on Behavioral Context." *Science*, 1992, *257*(5075), 1412–1415.

Aldrich, C. *Learning by Doing: A Comprehensive Guide to Simulations, Computer Games, and Pedagogy in e-Learning and Other Education Experiences*. Hoboken, NJ: Wiley, 2005.

445

Alfred, M. V. "Linking the Personal and the Social for a More Critical Democratic Adult Education." In M. V. Alfred (ed.), *Learning and Sociocultural Contexts: Implications for Adults, Community, and Workplace Education.* New Directions for Adult and Continuing Education, no. 96. San Francisco: Jossey-Bass, 2002.

Allen, M. S., and Roswell, B. S. "Self-Evaluation as Holistic Assessment." Paper presented at the annual meeting of the Conference on College Composition and Communication, Mar. 1989. (ED 303 809)

Ancis, J. R., and Ali, R. "Multicultural Counseling Training Approaches: Implications for Pedagogy." In C. Z. Enns and A. L. Sinacore (eds.), *Teaching and Social Justice: Integrating Multicultural and Feminist Theories in the Classroom.* Washington, DC: American Psychological Association, 2005.

Andersen, P. A. "The Cognitive Valence Theory of Intimate Communication." In M. T. Palmer and G. A. Barnett (eds.), *Progress in Communication Sciences: Vol. 14. Mutual Influence in Interpersonal Communication: Theory and Research in Cognition, Affect, and Behavior.* Stamford, CT: Ablex, 1998.

Andersen, P. A. *Nonverbal Communication: Forms and Functions.* Mountain View, CA: Mayfield, 1999.

Andersen, P. A., and Bowman, L. "Positions of Power: Nonverbal Influence in Organizational Communication." In L. K. Guerrero, J. A. DeVito, and M. L. Hecht (eds.), *The Nonverbal Reader.* Prospect Heights, IL: Waveland Press, 1999.

Andersen, P. A., Hecht, M. L., Hoobler, G. D., and Smallwood, M. "Nonverbal Communication across Culture." In B. Gudykunst and B. Mody (eds.), *Handbook of International and Intercultural Communication.* Thousand Oaks, CA: Sage, 2002.

Andersen, P. A., and Wang, H. "Unraveling Cultural Cues: Dimensions of Nonverbal Communication across Cultures." In L. A. Samovar, R. E. Porter, and E. R. McDaniel (eds.), *Intercultural Communication,* 11th ed. Belmont, CA: Thomson Wadsworth, 2006.

Anderson, L. W., and Krathwohl, D. R., eds. *A Taxonomy for Learning, Teaching, and Assessing: A Revision of Bloom's Taxonomy of Educational Objectives.* New York: Longman, 2001.

Angelo, T. A., and Cross, K. P. *Classroom Assessment Techniques: A Handbook for College Teachers*. San Francisco: Jossey-Bass, 1993.

Apter, M. J. *The Experience of Motivation*. Orlando, FL: Academic Press, 1982.

Aslanian, C. B. *Adult Students Today*. New York: The College Board, 2001.

Association for Supervision and Curriculum Development. "Effective Teaching Redux." *ASCD Update*, 1990, *32*(6), 5.

Assor, A., and Connell, J. P. "The Validity of Students' Self-Reports as Measures of Performance Affecting Self-Appraisals." In D. H. Schunk and J. L. Meece (eds.), *Student Perceptions in the Classroom*. Hillsdale, NJ: Erlbaum, 1992.

Bailey, T. R., and Alfonso, M. *Paths to Persistence: An Analysis of Research on Program Effectiveness at Community Colleges*. Indianapolis: Lumina Foundation for Education, 2005.

Bandura, A. "Self-Efficacy Mechanism in Human Agency." *American Psychologist*, 1982, *37*(2), 122–147.

Bandura, A. *Self-Efficacy: The Exercise of Control*. New York: Freeman, 1997.

Barkley, E. F., Cross, K. P., and Major, C. H. *Collaborative Learning Techniques: A Handbook for College Faculty*. San Francisco: Jossey-Bass, 2005.

Barnett, M. S., and Ceci, S. J. "When and Where Do We Apply What We Learn? A Taxonomy for Far Transfer." *Psychological Bulletin*, 2002, *128*, 612–637.

Barret, L. F. "Feeling Is Perceiving: Core Affect and Conceptualization in the Experience of Emotion." In L. F. Barret, P. M. Niedenthal, and P. Winkielman (eds.), *Emotion and Consciousness*. New York: Guilford, 2005.

Bear, M. R., Connors, B. W., and Paradiso, M. A. *Neuroscience: Exploring the Brain*. Baltimore: Lippincott Williams and Wilkins, 2007.

Bee, H. L., and Bjorkland, B. R. *The Journey of Adulthood*, 5th ed. Englewood Cliffs, NJ: Prentice Hall, 2004.

Belenky, M., Clinchy, B., Goldberger, N., and Tarule, J. *Women's Ways of Knowing: The Development of Self, Voice, and Mind.* New York: Basic Books, 1986.

Bellah, R. N., Madsen, R., Sullivan, W. M., Swidler, A., and Tipton, S. *Habits of the Heart: Individualism and Commitment in American Life.* New York: HarperCollins, 1985.

Belzer, A., and St. Clair, R. "Back to the Future: Implications of the Neopositivist Research Agenda for Adult Education." *Teachers College Record,* 2005, *107*(6), 1393–1411.

Benseman, J. "Participation." In L. English (ed.), *International Encyclopedia of Adult Education.* New York: Palgrave Macmillan, 2005.

Berg, B. L. *Qualitative Research Methods for the Social Sciences,* 6th ed. Boston: Pearson, 2007.

Berger, N. O., Caffarella, R. S., and O'Donnell, J. M. "Learning Contracts." In M. W. Galbraith (ed.), *Adult Learning Methods: A Guide for Effective Instruction,* 3rd ed. Malabar, FL: Krieger, 2004.

Berliner, D. "But Do They Understand?" In V. Richardson-Koehler (ed.), *Educators' Handbook: A Research Perspective.* New York: Longman, 1987.

Berliner, D. "The Development of Expertise in Pedagogy." Charles W. Hunt Memorial Lecture. American Association of Colleges for Teacher Education, New Orleans, Feb. 17, 1988.

Beyer, B. K. *Practical Strategies for the Teaching of Thinking.* Needham Heights, MA: Allyn & Bacon, 1987.

Bloom, F., Nelson, C. A., and Lazerson, A. *Brain, Mind, and Behavior,* 3rd ed. London: Worth, 2001.

Blunt, A. "Attitudes." In L. M. English (ed.), *International Encyclopedia of Adult Education.* New York: Palgrave Macmillan, 2005.

Bong, M., and Skaalvik, E. "Academic Self-Concept and Self-Efficacy: How Different Are They Really?" *Educational Psychology Review,* 2003, *15*, 1–40.

Boshier, R. "Lifelong Learning." In L. M. English (ed.), *International Encyclopedia of Adult Education*. New York: Palgrave Macmillan, 2005.

Brock, T., and LeBlanc, A. *Promoting Student Success in Community College and Beyond*. New York: MDRC, 2005.

Brookfield, S. D. *Understanding and Facilitating Adult Learning: A Comprehensive Analysis of Principles and Effective Practices*. San Francisco: Jossey-Bass, 1986.

Brookfield, S. D. "Using Critical Incidents to Explore Learners' Assumptions." In J. Mezirow and Associates (eds.), *Fostering Critical Reflection in Adulthood: A Guide to Transformative and Emancipatory Learning*. San Francisco: Jossey-Bass, 1990.

Brookfield, S. "Self-Directed Learning, Political Clarity, and the Critical Practice of Adult Education." *Adult Education Quarterly*, 1993, 43(4), 227–242.

Brookfield, S. D. *Becoming a Critically Reflective Teacher*. San Francisco: Jossey-Bass, 1995.

Brookfield, S. D. "Adult Learning: An Overview." In A. C. Tuijnman (ed.), *International Encyclopedia of Adult Education and Training*, 2nd ed. New York: Pergamon, 1996.

Brookfield, S. D. "Assessing Critical Thinking." In A. D. Rose and M. A. Leahy (eds.), *Assessing Adult Learning in Diverse Settings: Current Issues and Approaches*. New Directions for Adult and Continuing Education, no. 75. San Francisco: Jossey-Bass, 1997.

Brookfield, S. D. "Critical Thinking Techniques." In M. W. Galbraith (ed.), *Adult Learning Methods: A Guide for Effective Instruction*, 3rd ed. Malabar, FL: Krieger, 2004.

Brookfield, S. D. *The Power of Critical Theory: Liberating Adult Learning and Teaching*. San Francisco: Jossey-Bass, 2005.

Brookfield, S. D., and Preskill, S. *Discussion as a Way of Teaching: Tools and Techniques for Democratic Classrooms*. San Francisco: Jossey-Bass, 2005.

Brooks, J. G., and Brooks, M. G. *The Case for Constructivist Classrooms.* Alexandria, VA: Association for Supervision and Curriculum Development, 1993.

Brophy, J. "Teacher Praise: A Functional Analysis." *Review of Educational Research,* 1981, *51*(1), 5–32.

Brophy, J. *Motivating Students to Learn,* 2nd ed. Mahwah, NJ: Erlbaum, 2004.

Brothers, L. "The Social Brain: A Project for Integrating Primate Behavior and Neurophysiology in a New Domain." In J. Cacioppo and others (eds.), *Foundations in Social Neuroscience.* Cambridge, MA: MIT Press, 2000.

Brown, J. O. "Know Thyself: The Impact of Portfolio Development on Adult Learning." *Adult Education Quarterly,* 2002, *52*(3), 228–245.

Brown, J. S. "The Social Life of Learning: How Can Continuing Education by Reconfigured in the Future?" *Continuing Higher Education Review,* 2002, 66, 50–69.

Bruffee, K. A. "Sharing Our Toys: Cooperative Learning Versus Collaborative Learning." *Change,* 1995, *27*(1), 12–18.

Bruning, R. H., Schraw, G. J., Norby, M. M., and Ronning, R. R. *Cognitive Psychology and Instruction,* 4th ed. Columbus, OH: Merrill, 2004.

Burton, E. M. "Distance Learning and Service-Learning in the Accelerated Format." In R. J. Wlodkowski and C. E. Kasworm (eds.), *Accelerated Learning for Adults: The Promise and Practice of Intensive Educational Formats.* New Directions for Adult and Continuing Education, no. 97, San Francisco: Jossey-Bass, 2003.

Butin, D. W. *Service Learning in Higher Education: Critical Issues and Directions.* New York: Palgrave Macmillan, 2005.

Butler, J. E. "Toward a Pedagogy of Everywoman's Studies." In M. Culley and C. Portuges (eds.), *Gendered Subjects: The Dynamics of Feminist Teaching.* Boston: Routledge and Kegan Paul, 1985.

Butler, J. E. "Transforming the Curriculum: Teaching about Women of Color."
In J. A. Banks and C.A.M. Banks (eds.), *Multicultural Education: Issues and
Perspectives*, 4th ed. New York: Wiley, 2000.

Buzan, T. *Use Both Sides of Your Brain*. New York: Dutton, 1979.

Bye, D., Pushkar, D., and Conway, M. "Motivation, Interest, and Positive Affect
in Traditional and Nontraditional Undergraduate Students." *Adult Education
Quarterly*, 2007, 57, 141–158.

Caffarella, R. S. *Planning Programs for Adult Learners: A Practical Guide for
Educators, Trainers, and Staff Developers*, 2nd ed. San Francisco:
Jossey-Bass, 2002.

Caine, G., and Caine, R. N. "Meaningful Learning and the Executive Func-
tions of the Brain." In S. Johnson and K. Taylor (eds.), *The Neuroscience of Adult
Learning*. New Directions for Adult and Continuing Education, no. 110, San
Francisco: Jossey-Bass, 2006.

Campbell, B. "Age Matters: The Cognitive Strategies and Benefits of Learning
among College-Degreed Older Adults." Unpublished doctoral dissertation, Ph.D.
Leadership & Change Program, Antioch University, 2006.

Campbell, D. P., and Hansen, J.I.C. *Manual for the SVIB-SCII*. Stanford, CA:
Stanford University Press, 1981.

Campbell, L., Campbell, B., and Dickinson, D. *Teaching and Learning through
Multiple Intelligences*, 3rd ed. Boston: Pearson, 2004.

Carnevale, A. P., and Desrochers, D. M. *Getting Down to Business: Matching
Welfare Recipients' Skills to Jobs That Train*. Princeton, NJ: Educational Testing
Service, 1999.

Carnevale, A. P., and Desrochers, D. M. "Benefits and Barriers to College for
Low-Income Adults." In B. Cook and J. E. King, *Low-Income Adults in Profile:
Improving Lives through Higher Education*. Washington, DC: American Council
on Education, 2004.

Checkley, K. "The First Seven . . . and the Eighth: A Conversation with Howard
Gardner." *Educational Leadership*, 1997, 55(1), 8–13.

Chi, M.T.H., Glaser, R., and Farr, M. J., eds. *The Nature of Expertise*. Hillsdale, NJ: Erlbaum, 1988.

Chirkov, V., Kim, Y., Ryan, R. M., and Kaplan, U. "Differentiating Autonomy from Individualism and Independence: A Self-Determination Theory Perspective on Internalization of Cultural Orientations and Well-Being." *Journal of Personality and Social Psychology*, 2003, 84, 97–110.

Chiu, C., and Hong, Y. "Cultural Competence: Dynamic Processes." In A. J. Elliot and C. S. Dweck (eds.), *Handbook of Competence and Motivation*. New York: Guilford, 2005.

Choitz, V., and Widom, R. *Money Matters: How Financial Aid Affects Nontraditional Students in Community Colleges*. New York: MDRC, 2003.

Christianson, S., ed. *The Handbook of Emotion and Memory: Research and Theory*. Hillsdale, NJ: Erlbaum, 1992.

Chularut, P., and DeBacker, T. K. "The Influence of Concept Mapping on Achievement, Self-Regulation, and Self-Efficacy in Students of English as a Second Language." *Contemporary Educational Psychology*, 2004, 29, 248–263.

Commission for a Nation of Lifelong Learners. *A Nation Learning: Vision for the 21st Century*. Albany, NY: Commission for a Nation of Lifelong Learners (www.regents.edu), 1997.

Compton, R. J. "The Interface between Emotion and Attention: A Review of Evidence from Psychology and Neuroscience." *Behavioral and Cognitive Neuroscience Review*, 2003, 2(2), 115–129.

Constitutional Rights Foundation. *Current Issues of Immigration, 2006*. Los Angeles: CRF Publications, 2006.

Cook, B., and King, J. E. *Low-Income Adults in Profile: Improving Lives through Higher Education*. Washington, DC: American Council on Education, 2004.

Cook, B., and King, J. E. *Improving Lives through Higher Education: Campus Programs and Policies for Low-Income Adults*. Washington, DC: American Council on Education, 2005.

Cooperrider, D. L. "Positive Image, Positive Action: The Affirmative Basis of Organizing." In S. Srivastva, R. E. Fry, and D. L. Cooperrider (eds.), *Appreciative Management and Leadership: The Power of Positive Thought and Action in Organizations*. San Francisco: Jossey-Bass, 1990.

Costa, A. L., and Garmston, R. J. *Cognitive Coaching: A Foundation for Renaissance Schools*. Norwood, MA: Christopher-Gordon, 2002.

Courtney, S. *Why Adults Learn: Toward a Theory of Participation in Adult Education*. New York: Routledge, 1991.

Coyle, D. "How to Grow a Super Athlete." *New York Times Play*, March 2007, pp. 36–41, 76–80.

Cozolino, L., and Sprokay, S. "Neuroscience and Adult Learning." In S. Johnson and K. Taylor (eds.), *The Neuroscience of Adult Learning*. New Directions for Adult and Continuing Education, no. 110. San Francisco: Jossey-Bass, 2006.

Cranton, P. "Types of Group Learning." In S. Imel (ed.), *Learning in Groups: Fundamental Principles, New Uses, and Emerging Opportunities*. New Directions for Adult and Continuing Education, no. 71. San Francisco: Jossey-Bass, 1996.

Cross, K. P. *Adults as Learners: Increasing Participation and Facilitating Learning*. San Francisco: Jossey-Bass, 1981.

Cross, K. P. *Learning Is about Making Connections*. Mission Viejo, CA: League for Innovation in the Community College, 1999.

Cruickshank, D. R., and others. *Teaching Is Tough*. Upper Saddle River, NJ: Prentice Hall, 1980.

Csikszentmihalyi, M. *Finding Flow: The Psychology of Engagement with Everyday Life*. New York: Basic Books, 1997.

Csikszentmihalyi, M., and Csikszentmihalyi, I. S. *Optimal Experience: Psychological Studies of Flow in Consciousness*. New York: Cambridge University Press, 1988.

Damasio, A. *The Feeling of What Happens: Body and Emotion in the Making of Consciousness*. Orlando: Harcourt Brace, 1999.

Davies, D. R., Shackleton, V. J., and Parasuraman, R. "Monotony and Boredom." In R. Hockey (ed.), *Stress and Fatigue in Human Performance.* New York: Wiley, 1983.

Day, H. I., ed. *Advances in Intrinsic Motivation and Aesthetics.* New York: Plenum, 1981.

De Corte, E., Verschaffel, L., and Masui, C. "The CLIA Model: A Framework for Designing Powerful Learning Environments for Thinking and Problem Solving." *European Journal of Psychology of Education,* 2004, *19*(4), 365–384.

Deci, E. L., and Moller, A. C. "The Concept of Competence: A Starting Place for Understanding Intrinsic Motivation and Self-Determined Extrinsic Motivation." In A. J. Elliot and C. S. Dweck (eds.), *Handbook of Competence and Motivation.* New York: Guilford Press, 2005.

Deci, E. L., and Ryan, R. M. "A Motivational Approach to Self: Integration in Personality." In R. Dienstbier (ed.), *Nebraska Symposium on Motivation, Vol. 38: Perspectives on Motivators.* Lincoln: University of Nebraska Press, 1991.

Delahaye, B. L., and Smith, B. J. *How to Be an Effective Trainer: Skills for Managers and New Trainers,* 3rd ed. Hoboken, NJ: Wiley, 1998.

Deshler, D. "Metaphor Analysis: Exorcising Social Ghosts." In J. Mezirow and Associates (eds.), *Fostering Critical Reflection in Adulthood: A Guide to Transformative and Emancipatory Learning.* San Francisco: Jossey-Bass, 1990.

Deshler, D. "Participation: Role of Motivation." In A. C. Tuijnman (ed.), *International Encyclopedia of Adult Education and Training,* 2nd ed. New York: Pergamon Press, 1996.

Dewey, J. *How We Think.* (Rev. ed.) Lexington, MA: Heath, 1933.

Diamond, M. *Good News about the Aging Brain.* San Francisco: American Society on Aging, 2001.

Diamond, M., and Hopson, J. *Magic Trees of the Mind.* New York: Penguin-Dutton, 1998.

Dick, W. O., Carey, L., and Carey, J. O. *The Systematic Design of Instruction*, 6th ed. Boston: Allyn and Bacon, 2004.

Donaldson, J. F. "A Model of College Outcomes for Adults." *Adult Education Quarterly*, 1999, 50, 24–40.

Donovan, M. S., Bransford, J. D., and Pellegrino, J. W. *How People Learn: Bridging Research and Practice*. Washington, DC: National Academy Press, 1999.

Driscoll, M. P. *Psychology of Learning for Instruction*, 3rd ed. Boston: Allyn and Bacon, 2005.

Dunlap, J., and Grabinger,, S. "Preparing Students for Lifelong Learning: A Review of Instructional Features and Teaching Methodologies." *Performance Improvement Quarterly*, 2003, 16(2), 6–25.

Eisner, E. W. *The Educational Imagination*, 2nd ed. Old Tappan, NJ: Macmillan, 1985.

Eisner, E. W. "The Uses and Limits of Performance Assessments." *Phi Delta Kappan*, 1999, 80, 658–660.

Elbow, P. *Embracing Contraries: Explorations in Learning and Teaching*. New York: Oxford University Press, 1986.

Elliot, A. J., and Dweck, C. S., eds. *Handbook of Competence and Motivation*. New York: Guilford, 2005.

Ellis, A. "Rational-Emotive Therapy." In R. J. Corsini and D. Wedding (eds.), *Current Psychotherapies*. Itasca, IL: Peacock, 1989.

English, L. M. "Problem-Based Learning." In L. M. English (ed.), *International Encyclopedia of Adult Education*. New York: Palgrave Macmillan, 2005.

Ericsson, K. A. "The Influence of Experience and Deliberate Practice on the Development of Superior Expert Performance." In K. A. Ericsson, N. Charness, R. R. Hoffman, and P. J. Feltovich (eds.), *The Cambridge Handbook of Expertise and Expert Performance*. New York: Cambridge University Press, 2006.

Feldman, K. A. "Identifying Exemplary Teachers and Teaching: Evidence from Student Ratings." In R. P. Perry and J. C. Smart (eds.), *Effective Teaching in Higher Education: Research and Practice*. New York: Agathon Press, 1997.

Fenwick, T. J., and Parsons, J. *The Art of Evaluation: A Handbook for Educators and Trainers*. Toronto: Thompson Educational, 2000.

Fenwick, T. *Learning through Experience: Troubling Orthodoxies and Intersecting Questions*. Malabar, FL: Krieger, 2003.

Fischer, K. W., and others. "Why Mind, Brain, and Education? Why Now?" *Mind, Brain, and Education*, 2007, *1*(1), 1–2.

Flint, T. A., and Associates. *Best Practices in Adult Learning: A CAEL/APQC Benchmarking Study*. Chicago: Council for Adult and Experiential Learning, 1999.

Flint, T. A., Zakos, P., and Frey, R. *Best Practices in Adult Learning: A Self-Evaluation Workbook for Colleges and Universities*. Dubuque, IA: Kendall/Hunt, 2002.

Fong, M. "The Nexus of Language, Communication, and Culture." In L. A. Samovar, R. E. Porter, and E. R. McDaniel (eds.), *Intercultural Communication*, 11th ed. Belmont, CA: Thomson Wadsworth, 2006.

Ford, M. *Motivating Humans: Goals, Emotions, and Personal Agency Beliefs*. Thousand Oaks, CA: Sage, 1992.

Frederick, P. "Diversity Dimensions." *Professional and Organizational Development Network in Higher Education News*, Dec. 1997, p. 2.

Freire, P. *Pedagogy of the Oppressed*. New York: Seabury Press, 1970.

Freud, S. "Letter to C. G. Jung, December 6, 1906." In E. Jones, *Life and Work of Sigmund Freud. Vol. 2: Years of Maturity, 1901–1919*. New York: Basic Books, 1955.

Friedman, T. *The World Is Flat: A Brief History of the Twenty-First Century*. New York: Farrar, Straus, and Giroux, 2005.

Gabriel, T. "Gen Xers of Color." In J. Black and K. Haywood (eds.), *Gen Xers Return to College*. Washington, DC: American Association of Collegiate Registrars and Admission Officers, 2003.

Gage, N. L. "The Generality of Dimensions of Teaching." In P. O. Peterson and H. J. Walberg (eds.), *Research and Teaching: Concepts, Findings, and Implications*. Berkeley, CA: McCutchan, 1979.

Gage, N. L., and Berliner, D. C. *Educational Psychology*, 6th ed. Boston: Houghton Mifflin, 1998.

Garcia Duncan, T., and McKeachie, W. J. "The Making of the Motivation Strategies for Learning Questionnaire." *Educational Psychologist*, 2005, 40(2), 117–128.

Gardner, H. *Multiple Intelligences: The Theory in Practice*. New York: Basic Books, 1993.

Gardner, H. *Multiple Intelligences: New Horizons*. New York: Basic Books, 2006.

Gardner, H., and Hatch, T. "Multiple Intelligences Go to School." *Education Researcher*, 1989, 1(8), 4–10.

Gardner, H., and Moran, S. "The Science of Multiple Intelligences Theory: A Response to Lynn Waterhouse." *Educational Psychologist*, 2006, 41(4), 227–232.

Gardner, J. W. *On Leadership*. New York: Free Press, 1990.

Garfield, C. *Peak Performers*. New York: Morrow, 1986.

Garrison, D. R. "Self-Directed Learning: Toward a Comprehensive Model." *Adult Education Quarterly*, 1997, 48(1), 18–33.

Gay, G. *Culturally Responsive Teaching*. New York: Teachers College Press, 2000.

Gephart, W. J., Strother, D. B., and Duckett, W. R., eds. "Instructional Clarity." *Practical Applications of Research*, 1981, 3(3), 1–4.

Gergen, K. J., Gulerce, A., Lock, A., and Misra, G. "Psychological Science in Cultural Context." *American Psychologist*, 1996, 51(5), 496–503.

Gilligan, C. *In a Different Voice: Psychological Theory and Women's Development.* Cambridge, MA: Harvard University Press, 1982.

Ginsberg, M. B. "Lessons at the Kitchen Table." *Educational Leadership,* 2007, 64(6), 56–61.

Ginsberg, M. B., and Wlodkowski, R. J. *Creating Highly Motivating Classrooms for All Students: A Schoolwide Approach to Powerful Teaching with Diverse Learners.* San Francisco: Jossey-Bass, 2000.

Glanz, J. "Action Research." *Journal of Staff Development,* 1999, 20(3), 22–23.

Gogtay, N., and others. "Dynamic Mapping of Human Cortical Development during Childhood and through Early Adulthood." *Proceedings of the National Academy of Sciences,* May 25, 2004, 101(21), 8174–8179.

Goldberg, E. *The Executive Brain: Frontal Lobes and the Civilized Mind.* New York: Oxford University Press, 2001.

Goldin-Meadow, S. *Hearing Gestures.* Cambridge, MA: Belknap Press of Harvard University, 2003.

Goleman, D. *Emotional Intelligence.* New York: Bantam, 1995.

Goleman, D. *Social Intelligence.* New York: Bantam, 2007.

Good, T., and Brophy, J. *Looking in Classrooms,* 9th ed. Boston: Allyn and Bacon, 2003.

Goodman, J. "Humor, Creativity, and Magic: Tools for Teaching and Living." Unpublished manuscript, Sagamore Institute, Saratoga Springs, NY, 1981.

Griffin, P. "Facilitating Social Justice Education Courses." In M. Adams, L. A. Bell, and P. Griffin (eds.), *Teaching for Diversity and Social Justice: A Sourcebook.* New York: Routledge, 1997a.

Griffin, P. "Introductory Module for Single Issue Courses." In M. Adams, L. A. Bell, and P. Griffin (eds.), *Teaching for Diversity and Social Justice: A Sourcebook.* New York: Routledge, 1997b.

Gronlund, N. E. *Stating Objectives for Classroom Instruction*, 3rd ed. Old Tappan, NJ: Macmillan, 1985.

Grotzer, T. A., and Perkins, D. N. "Teaching Intelligence: A Performance Conception." In R. J. Sternberg (ed.), *Handbook of Intelligence*. New York: Cambridge University Press, 2000.

Grubb, W. N., and Associates. *Honored but Invisible: An Inside Look at Teaching in Community Colleges*. New York: Routledge, 1999.

Gudykunst, W. B., and Kim, Y. Y. *Communicating with Strangers: An Approach to Intercultural Communication*. New York: Random House, 1992.

Gurin, P., Dey, E. L., Hurtado, S., and Gurin, G. "Diversity and Higher Education: Theory and Impact on Educational Outcomes." *Harvard Educational Review*, 2002, *72*(3), 330–366.

Guy, T. "Culturally Relevant Adult Education." In L. English (ed.), *International Encyclopedia of Adult Education*. New York: Palgrave Macmillan, 2005.

Guyer, B., Freedman, M. A., Strobino, D. M., and Sondik, E. J. "Annual Summary of Vital Statistics: Trends in the Health of Americans during the 20th Century." *Pediatrics*, 2000, *106*(6), 1307–1317.

Hall, E. T. "A System of the Notation of Proxemic Behavior." *American Anthropologist*, 1966, *65*, 1003–1026.

Hall, E. T. *Beyond Culture*. Garden City, NY: Anchor, 1976.

Hall, E. T. *The Dance of Life: The Other Dimension of Time*. Garden City, NY: Anchor, 1984.

Harkins, S., White, P., and Utman, C. "The Role of Internal and External Sources of Evaluation in Motivating Task Performance." *Personality and Social Psychology Bulletin*, 2000, *26*, 100–117.

Hattie, J., and Timperley, H. "The Power of Feedback." *Review of Educational Research*, 2007, *77*(1), 81–112.

Hattie, J., Marsh, H. W., Neill, J. T., and Richards, G. E. "Adventure Education and Outward Bound: Out-of-Class Experiences That Make a Lasting Difference." *Review of Educational Research*, 1997, 67(1), 43–87.

Hays, P. A. *Addressing Cultural Complexities in Practice: A Framework for Clinicians and Counselors*. Washington, DC: American Psychological Association, 2001.

Hecht, M. L., Andersen, P. A., and Ribeau, S. A. "The Cultural Dimensions of Nonverbal Communication." In M. K. Asante and W. B. Gudykunst (eds.), *Handbook of International and Intercultural Communication*. Thousand Oaks, CA: Sage, 1989.

Heine, S. J., Lehman, D. R., Ide, E., Leung, C., Kitayama, S., Takata, T., and others. "Divergent Consequences of Success and Failure in Japan and North America: An Investigation of Self-Improving Medications and Malleable Selves." *Journal of Personality and Social Psychology*, 2001, 81(4), 599–615.

Herzberg, F. "One More Time: How Do You Motivate Employees?" *Harvard Business Review*, 2003, 1, 3–11.

Hidi, S., and Renninger, K. A. "The Four-Phase Model of Interest Development." *Educational Psychologist*, 2006, 41(2), 111–127.

Highwater, J. "Imagination as a Political Force." General session address given at the annual conference of the Association for Supervision and Curriculum Development, Chicago, Mar. 1994.

Hill, C. E. *Helping Skills: Facilitating Exploration, Insight, and Action*, 2nd ed. Washington, DC: American Psychological Association, 2004.

Hillman, J. *The Force of Character and the Lasting Life*. New York: Random House, 1999.

Hmelo-Silver, C. E. "Problem-Based Learning: What and How Do Students Learn?" *Educational Psychology Review*, 2004, 16, 235–266.

Hofstede, G. *Culture's Consequences*, abr. ed. Beverly Hills, CA: Sage, 1980.

Holton III, E. F., Bates, R. A., and Ruona, W.E.A. "Development of a Generalized Learning Transfer System." *Human Resource Development Quarterly*, 2000, *11*(4), 333–360.

Hoyer, W. J., and Roodin, P. A. *Adult Development and Aging*, 5th ed. New York: McGraw-Hill, 2003.

Hsee, C. K., Hatfield, E., Carlson, J. G., and Chemtob, C. "The Effect of Power on Susceptibility to Emotional Contagion." *Cognition and Emotion*, 1990, *4*, 227–340.

Hurt, H. T., Scott, M. D., and McCroskey, J. C. *Communication in the Classroom*. Reading, MA: Addison-Wesley, 1978.

Hutchings, P. *Using Cases to Improve College Teaching: A Guide to More Reflective Practice*. Washington, DC: American Association for Higher Education, 1993.

Hutchinson, W. D., and others. "Pain-Related Neurons in the Human Cingulate Cortex." *Nature-Neuroscience*, 1999, *2*, 403–405.

Hyerle, D. *Visual Tools for Constructing Knowledge*. Alexandria, VA: Association for Supervision and Curriculum Development, 1996.

Izard, C. E. *The Psychology of Emotions*. New York: Plenum, 1993.

Izard, C. E., and Ackerman, B. P. "Motivational, Organizational, and Regulatory Functions of Discrete Emotions." In M. Lewis and J. M. Haviland-Jones (eds.), *Handbook of Emotions*, 2nd ed. New York: Guilford, 2000.

Jacobs, B., Schall, M., and Scheibel, A. "A Quantitative Dendritic Analysis of Wernicke's Area in Humans. II. Gender, Hemispheric and Environmental Factors." *Journal of Comparative Neurology*, 1993, *327*, 97–111.

Jensen, E. *Teaching with the Brain in Mind*, 2nd ed. Alexandria, VA: Association for Supervision and Curriculum Development, 2005.

Jensen, E. *Enriching the Brain: How to Maximize Every Learner's Potential*. San Francisco: Jossey-Bass, 2006.

Johnson, D. W. "Social Interdependence: The Interrelationships among Theory, Research, and Practice." *American Psychologist*, 2003, *58*, 931–945.

Johnson, D. W., and Johnson, F. P. *Joining Together: Group Theory and Group Skills*, 9th ed. Boston: Allyn and Bacon, 2006.

Johnson, D. W., and Johnson, R. T. *Cooperative, Competitive, and Individualistic Procedures for Educating Adults: A Comparative Analysis*. Minneapolis: Cooperative Learning Center, University of Minnesota, 1995.

Johnson, D. W., Johnson, R. T., and Smith, K. A. *Active Learning: Cooperation in the College Classroom*. Edina, MN: Interaction, 1991.

Johnson, S., and Taylor, K., eds. *The Neuroscience of Adult Learning*. New Directions for Adult and Continuing Education, no. 110. San Francisco: Jossey-Bass, 2006.

Johnson-Bailey, J., and Cervero, R. M. "Negotiating Power Dynamics in Workshops." In J. Anderson Fleming (ed.), *New Perspectives on Designing and Implementing Effective Workshops*. New Directions for Adult and Continuing Education, no. 76. San Francisco: Jossey-Bass, 1997.

Jones, A. P., Rozelle, R. M., and Chang, W. "Perceived Punishment and Reward Values of Supervisor Actions in a Chinese Sample." *Psychological Studies*, 1990, *35*, 1–10.

Jones, S. E. *The Right Touch: Understanding and Using the Language of Physical Contact*. Cresshill, NJ: Hampton Press, 1994.

Jourard, S. *The Transparent Self*. New York: Van Nostrand Reinhold, 1964.

Kasworm, C. E., and Londoner, C. A. "Adult Learning and Technology." In A. L. Wilson and E. R. Hayes (eds.), *Handbook of Adult and Continuing Education*. San Francisco: Jossey-Bass, 2000.

Kasworm, C. E., and Marienau, C. A. "Principles of Assessment for Adult Learning." In A. D. Rose and M. A. Leahy (eds.), *Assessing Adult Learning in Diverse Settings: Current Issues and Approaches*. New Directions for Adult and Continuing Education, no. 75. San Francisco: Jossey-Bass, 1997.

Kaye, J., and Castillo, D. *Flash MX for Interactive Simulations: How to Construct and Use Device Simulations.* Clifton Park, NY: Delmar Learning, 2003.

Keeton, M. T., Sheckley, B. G., and Griggs, J. K. *Effectiveness and Efficiency in Higher Education for Adults: A Guide for Fostering Learning.* Dubuque, IA: Kendall Hunt, 2002.

Keller, J. "Killing Me Microsoftly." *Chicago Tribune,* January 5, 2003, p. 9.

Keller, J. M., and Litchfield, B. C. "Motivation and Performance." In R. A. Reiser and J. V. Dempsey (eds.), *Trends and Issues in Instructional Design and Technology.* Columbus, OH: Merrill Prentice Hall, 2002.

Kerman, S. "Teacher Expectation and Student Achievement." *Phi Delta Kappan,* 1979, 60, 716–718.

Kessler-Harris, A. "The Rocky Road to Economic Citizenship." Lecture presented at the University of Washington-Seattle Graduate School. Seattle, April 18, 2007.

King, A. "Inquiry as a Tool in Critical Thinking." In D. F. Halpern and Associates (eds.), *Changing College Classrooms: New Teaching and Learning Strategies for an Increasingly Complex World.* San Francisco: Jossey-Bass, 1994.

King, A. "Structuring Peer Interaction to Promote High-Level Cognitive Processing." *Theory into Practice,* 2002, 41(1), 33–39.

King, K. P. "Distance Education." In L. M. English (ed.), *International Encyclopedia of Adult Education.* New York: Palgrave Macmillan, 2005.

Kinsella, K. "Instructional Strategies Which Promote Participation and Learning for Non-Native Speakers of English in University Classes." *Exchanges,* 1993, 5(1), 12.

Kitayama, S., and Markus, H. R., eds. *Emotion and Culture: Empirical Studies of Mutual Influence.* Washington, DC: American Psychological Association, 1994.

Knowles, M. S. *The Modern Practice of Adult Education: From Pedagogy to Andragogy,* rev. ed. Chicago: Follett, 1980.

Knowles, M. S. *The Making of an Adult Educator: An Autobiographical Journey.* San Francisco: Jossey-Bass, 1989.

Knox, A. B. *Adult Development and Learning: A Handbook on Individual Growth and Competence in the Adult Years.* San Francisco: Jossey-Bass, 1977.

Koechlin, E., and others. "Relational Memory by Cross-Curriculum." *Nature,* 1999, 399(6732), 148–151.

Kohn, A. *The Brighter Side of Human Nature: Altruism and Empathy in Everyday Life.* New York: Basic Books, 1990.

Kohn, A. *Punished by Rewards.* Boston: Houghton Mifflin, 1993.

Kolb, D. A. *Experiential Learning: Experience as the Source of Learning and Development.* Englewood Cliffs, NJ: Prentice Hall, 1984.

Kopp, B., and Wolff, M. "Brain Mechanisms of Selective Learning: Event-Related Potentials Provide Evidence for Error-Driven Learning in Humans." *Biological Psychology,* 2000, 51(2–3), 223–246.

Kornhaber, M. L. "Assessment, Standards, and Equity." In J. A. Banks and C.A.M. Banks (eds.), *Handbook on Research in Multicultural Education,* 2nd ed. San Francisco: Jossey-Bass, 2004.

Kuh, G. D., Kinzie, J., Schuh, J. H., Whitt, E. J., and Associates. *Student Success in College: Creating Conditions That Matter.* San Francisco: Jossey-Bass, 2005.

Laden, B. V., ed. *Serving Minority Populations.* New Directions for Community Colleges, no. 127. San Francisco: Jossey-Bass, 2004.

Lambert, N. M., and McCombs, B. L. "Introduction: Learner-Centered Schools and Classrooms as a Direction for School Reform." In N. M. Lambert and B. L. McCombs (eds.), *How Students Learn: Reforming Schools through Learner-Centered Education.* Washington, DC: American Psychological Association, 1998.

Land, M. L. "Vagueness and Clarity." In M. Dunkin (ed.), *The International Encyclopedia of Teaching and Teacher Education.* New York: Pergamon, 1987.

Langer, S. *Philosophy in a New Key*. Cambridge, MA: Harvard University Press, 1942.

Larkins, A. G., McKinney, C. W., Oldham-Buss, S., and Gilmore, A. C. *Teacher Enthusiasm: A Critical Review*. Hattiesburg, MS: Education and Psychological Research, 1985.

Larrivee, B. "The Potential Perils of Praise in a Democratic Interactive Classroom." *Action in Teacher Education*, 2002, *23*(4), 77–88.

Lather, P. *Getting Smart: Feminist Research and Pedagogy within the Post Modern*. New York: Routledge, 1991.

Lave, J. "The Culture of Acquisition and the Practice of Understanding." In D. Kirshner and J. A. Whitson (eds.), *Situated Cognition: Social, Semiotic, and Psychological Perspectives*. Mahwah, NJ: Erlbaum, 1997.

Leach, L. "Self-Directed Learning." In L. M. English (ed.), *International Encyclopedia of Adult Education*. New York: Palgrave Macmillan, 2005.

LeDoux, J. *The Emotional Brain*. New York: Simon & Schuster, 1996.

Lemieux, C. M. "Learning Contracts in the Classroom: Tools for Empowerment and Accountability." *Social Work Education*, 2001, *20*(2), 263–276.

Lepper, M. R., and Greene, D., eds. *The Hidden Costs of Reward*. Hillsdale, NJ: Erlbaum, 1978.

Light, R. *Explorations with Students and Faculty about Teaching, Learning, and Student Life*. Vol. *1*. Cambridge, MA: Harvard University Press, 1990.

Lleras-Muney, A. *The Relationship between Education and Adult Mortality in the United States*. Working Paper 8986. Cambridge, MA: National Bureau of Economic Research, 2002.

Lochner, L., and Moretti, E. *The Effect of Education on Crime: Evidence from Prison Inmates, Arrests, and Self-Reports*. Working Paper 8605. Cambridge, MA: National Bureau of Economic Research, 2001.

Locke, E., and Latham, G. "Building a Practically Useful Theory of Goal Setting and Task Motivation." *American Psychologist*, 2002, *57*, 705–717.

Loden, M., and Rosener, J. B. *Workforce America! Managing Employee Diversity as a Vital Resource.* Homewood, IL: Business One Irwin, 1991.

Lohman, M. C. "Cultivating Problem-Solving Skills through Problem-Based Approaches to Professional Development." *Human Resource Development Quarterly*, 2002, *13*(3), 243–261.

Lowe, J. "Time, Leisure, and Adult Education." In A. C. Tuijnman (ed.), *International Encyclopedia of Adult Education and Training*, 2nd ed. New York: Pergamon, 1996.

Lustig, M. L., and Koester, J. *Intercultural Competence: Interpersonal Communication across Culture.* New York: HarperCollins, 1999.

MacGregor, J. "Learning Self-Evaluation: Challenges for Students." In J. MacGregor (ed.), *Student Self-Evaluation: Fostering Reflective Learning.* New Directions for Teaching and Learning, no. 56. San Francisco: Jossey-Bass, 1994.

Maehl, W. H. *Lifelong Learning at Its Best: Innovative Practices in Adult Credit Programs.* San Francisco: Jossey-Bass, 2000.

Mager, R. F. *Developing Attitude toward Learning.* Belmont, CA: Fearon, 1968.

Manheimer, R. J. *Older Adult Education in the United States: Trends and Predictions.* Asheville, NC: North Carolina Center for Creative Retirement, 2002.

Marsick, V. J. "Case Study." In M. W. Galbraith (ed.), *Adult Learning Methods: A Guide for Effective Instruction*, 3rd ed. Malabar, FL: Krieger, 2004.

Maslow, A. H. *Motivation and Personality*, 2nd ed. New York: HarperCollins, 1970.

Massimini, F., Csikszentmihalyi, M., and Delle Fave, A. "Flow and Biocultural Evolution." In M. Csikszentmihalyi and I. S. Csikszentmihalyi (eds.), *Optimal Experience: Psychological Studies of Flow in Consciousness.* New York: Cambridge University Press, 1988.

McCombs, B. L., and Whisler, J. S. *The Learner-Centered Classroom and School: Strategies for Increasing Student Motivation and Achievement.* San Francisco: Jossey-Bass, 1997.

McDaniel, E. R., and Andersen, P. A. "Intercultural Variations in Tactile Communication." *Journal of Nonverbal Communication,* 1998, *22,* 59–75.

McEnrue, M. P., and Groves, K. "Choosing among Tests of Emotional Intelligence: What Is the Evidence?" *Human Resource Development Quarterly,* 2006, *17*(1), 9–42.

McKeachie, W. J. "Good Teaching Makes a Difference—And We Know What It Is." In R. P. Perry and J. C. Smart (eds.), *Effective Teaching in Higher Education: Research and Practice.* New York: Agathon Press, 1997.

Mehrotra, C. M. "In Defense of Offering Educational Programs for Older Adults." *Educational Gerontology,* 2003, *29*(8), 645–655.

Merriam, S. B., Caffarella, R. S., and Baumgartner, L. M. *Learning in Adulthood: A Comprehensive Guide,* 3rd ed. San Francisco: Jossey-Bass, 2007.

Meyers, C., and Jones, T. B. *Promoting Active Learning: Strategies for the College Classroom.* San Francisco: Jossey-Bass, 1993.

Mezirow, J. "Transformative Learning: Theory to Practice." In P. Cranton (ed.), *Transformative Learning in Action: Insights from Practice.* New Directions for Adult and Continuing Education, no. 74. San Francisco: Jossey-Bass, 1997.

Mezirow, J. "Learning to Think Like an Adult: Core Concepts of Transformation Theory." In Jack Mezirow and Associates. *Learning as Transformation: Critical Perspectives on a Theory in Progress.* San Francisco: Jossey-Bass, 2000.

Mezirow, J., and Associates. *Fostering Critical Reflection in Adulthood: A Guide to Transformative and Emancipatory Learning.* San Francisco: Jossey-Bass, 1990.

Mezirow, J., and Associates. *Learning as Transformation.* San Francisco: Jossey-Bass, 2000.

Michelson, E. "Multicultural Approaches to Portfolio Assessment." In A. D. Rose and M. A. Leahy (eds.), *Assessing Adult Learning in Diverse Settings: Current*

Issues and Approaches. New Directions for Adult and Continuing Education, no. 75. San Francisco: Jossey-Bass, 1997.

Mills, R. C. *Realizing Mental Health.* New York: Sulzburger and Graham, 1995.

Milton, O., Pollio, H. R., and Eison, J. *Making Sense of College Grades.* San Francisco: Jossey-Bass, 1986.

Moll, L. C., Amanti, C., Neff, D., and Gonzalez, N. "Funds of Knowledge for Teaching: Using a Qualitative Approach to Connect Homes and Classrooms." *Theory into Practice,* 1992, *31,* 132–141.

Mordkowitz, E. R., and Ginsburg, H. P. "The Academic Socialization of Successful Asian-American College Students." *Quarterly Journal of Laboratory of Comparative Human Cognition,* 1987, *9,* 85–91.

Morgan, M. "Reward-Induced Decrements and Increments in Intrinsic Motivation." *Review of Educational Research,* 1984, *54*(1), 5–30.

Morrison, G. R., Ross, S. M., and Kemp, J. E. *Designing Effective Instruction,* 5th ed. Indianapolis: Wiley, 2006.

Mortenson, T. G. "Undergraduate Degree Completion by Age 25 to 29 for Those Who Enter College 1947 to 2002." *Postsecondary Education Opportunity,* no. 137, Nov. 2003.

Mott, V. W. "Is Adult Education an Agent for Change or Instrument of the Status Quo?" In S. B. Merriam, B. C. Courtenay, and R. M. Cervero (eds.), *Global Issues and Adult Education: Perspectives from Latin America, Southern Africa, and the United States.* San Francisco: Jossey-Bass, 2006.

Murray, D. M. *Write to Learn,* 8th ed. Belmont, CA: Heinle, 2004.

Murray, I., and Savin-Baden, M. "Staff Development in Problem-Based Learning." *Teaching in Higher Education,* 2000, *5*(1), 107–126.

Nah, Y. "Can a Self-Directed Learner Be Independent, Autonomous, and Interdependent? Implications for Practice." *Adult Learning,* 2000, *18,* 18–19, 25.

Nakamura, J., and Csikszentmihalyi, M. "The Construction of Meaning through Vital Engagement." In C. Keyes and J. Haidt (eds.), *Flourishing: Positive Psychology and the Life Well-Lived*. Washington, DC: American Psychological Association, 2003.

Nasir, N. S., and Hand, V. M. "Exploring Sociocultural Perspectives on Race, Culture, and Learning." *Review of Education Research*, 2006, 76(4), 449–475.

National Center for Education Statistics. "Total Fall Enrollment in Degree-Granting Institutions by Attendance, Status, Sex, and Age: 1970 to 2011." [http://nces.ed.gov//pubs2002/digest2001/tables/dt174.asp]. 2001.

National Center for Education Statistics, U.S. Department of Education. *Digest of Education Statistics: 2002*. Washington, DC, 2002.

National Survey of Student Engagement. 2006 Annual Report: *Engaged Learning: Fostering Success for All Students*. [http://nsse.iub.edu/ NSSE_2006_Annual_Report/index.cfm]. Jan. 2007.

Nesbit, J. C., and Adesope, O. O. "Learning with Concept and Knowledge Maps: A Meta-Analysis." *Review of Educational Research*, 2006, 76(3), 413–448.

New England Adult Research Network. *Factors Influencing Adult Student Persistence in Undergraduate Degree Programs*. Amherst, MA: Victoria Dowling, University of Massachusetts, 1999.

Niedenthal, P. M., Barsalou, L. W., Ric, F., and Krauth-Gruber, S. "Embodiment in the Acquisition and Use of Emotion Knowledge." In L. F. Barrett, P. M. Niedenthal, and P. Winkielman (eds.), *Emotion and Consciousness*. New York: Guilford, 2005.

Nietzsche, F. W. *The Antichrist*. New York: Knopf, 1920.

O'Donnell, K. *Tabular Summary of Adult Education for Work Related Reasons: 2002–03*. U.S. Department of Education, National Center for Education Statistics. Washington, DC: U.S. Government Printing Office, 2005.

Ogle, D. "The K-W-L: A Teaching Model That Develops Active Reading of Expository Text." *The Reading Teacher*, 1986, 39, 564–576.

Oldfather, P. "Epistemological Empowerment: A Constructivist Concept of Motivation for Literary Learning," Paper presented at the National Reading Conference, San Antonio, TX, Dec. 1992.

Paley, V. G. *The Boy Who Would Be a Helicopter: The Uses of Storytelling in the Classroom.* Cambridge, MA: Harvard University Press, 1990.

Patterson, M. L. *Nonverbal Behavior: A Functional Perspective.* New York: Springer-Verlag, 1983.

Paul, R. "Socratic Questioning." In R. Paul (ed.), *Critical Thinking: What Every Person Needs to Survive in a Rapidly Changing World.* Rohnert Park, CA: Center for Critical Thinking and Moral Critique, Sonoma State University, 1990.

Paulson, K., and Boeke, M. *Adult Learners in the United States: A National Profile.* Washington, DC: American Council on Education, 2006.

Pearlman, M. "Trends in Women's Total Score and Item Performance on Verbal Measures." Paper presented at the annual meeting of the American Educational Research Association, Washington, DC, Apr. 1987.

Perkins, D. N., Allen, R., and Hafner, J. "Differences in Everyday Reasoning." In W. Maxwell (ed.), *Thinking: The Frontier Expands.* Hillsdale, NJ: Erlbaum, 1983.

Perry, B. D. "Fear and Learning: Trauma-Related Factors in the Adult Education Process." In S. Johnson and K. Taylor (eds.), *The Neuroscience of Adult Learning.* New Directions for Adult and Continuing Education, no. 110. San Francisco: Jossey-Bass, 2006.

Perry, W. G. *Forms of Ethical and Intellectual Development in the College Years: A Scheme.* San Francisco: Jossey-Bass, 1998.

Pesce, C., Guidetti, L., Baldari, C., Tessitore, A., and Capranica, L. "Effects of Aging on Visual Attention Focusing." *Gerontology,* 2005, *51*(4), 266–276.

Peters, T. J., and Waterman, R. H., Jr. *In Search of Excellence: Lessons from America's Best Run Companies.* New York: HarperCollins, 1982.

Phuntsog, N. "The Magic of Culturally Responsive Pedagogy: In Search of the Genie's Lamp in Multicultural Education." *Teacher Education Quarterly,* [http://www.teqjournal.org/sample_issue/article_6.htm]. Summer 1999.

Pintrich, P. R., ed. "Current Issues and New Directions in Motivational Theory and Research." *Education Psychologist,* 1991, *26,* 384.

Pintrich, P. R., and Schunk, D. H. *Motivation in Education: Theory, Research, and Applications.* Columbus, OH: Merrill, 1996.

Pintrich, P. R., Smith, D. A. F., Garcia, T., and McKeachie, W. J. A *Manual for the Use of the Motivated Strategies for Learning Questionnaire (MSLQ).* Ann Arbor: University of Michigan, National Center for Research to Improve Postsecondary Teaching and Learning, 1991.

Pintrich, P. R., Smith, D. A. F., Garcia T., and McKeachie, W. J. "Reliability and Predictive Validity of the Motivated Strategies for Learning Questionnaire (MSLQ)." *Educational and Psychological Measurement,* 1993, *53,* 801–813.

Pittman, T. S., Boggiano, A. K., and Ruble, D. N. "Intrinsic and Extrinsic Motivational Orientations: Limiting Conditions on the Undermining and Enhancing Effects of Reward on Intrinsic Motivation." In J. M. Levine and M. C. Wang (eds.), *Teacher and Student Perceptions: Implications for Learning.* Hillsdale, NJ: Erlbaum, 1983.

Plaut, V. C., and Markus, H. R. "The 'Inside' Story: A Cultural-Historical Analysis of Being Smart and Motivated, American Style." In *Handbook of Competence of Competence and Motivation.* New York: Guilford, 2005.

Poldrack, R. A., and others. "Interactive Memory Systems in the Human Brain." *Nature,* Nov. 29, 2001, *414,* 546–550.

Poplin, M., and Weeres, J. "Listening at the Learner's Level." *The Executive Educator,* 1992, *15*(4), 14–19.

Prenzel, M. "The Selective Persistence of Interest." In K. A. Renninger, S. Hidi, and A. Krapp. (eds.), *The Role of Interest in Learning and Development.* Hillsdale, NJ: Erlbaum, 1992.

Prickaerts, J., Koopmans, G., Blokland, A., and Scheepens, A. "Learning and Adult Neurogenesis: Survival with or without Proliferation." *Neurobiology of Learning and Memory*, 2004, *81*, 1–11.

Pugh, K. J., and Bergin, D. A. "Motivational Influences on Transfer." *Educational Psychologist*, 2006, *41*(3), 147–160.

Purdie, N., and Boulton-Lewis, G. "The Learning Needs of Older Adults." *Educational Gerontology*, 2003, *29*(2), 129–149.

Purnell, R., and Blank, S. *Support Success: Services That May Help Low-Income Students Succeed in Community College*. New York: MDRC, 2004.

Rangachari, P. K. "Twenty-Up: Problem-Based Learning with a Large Group." In L. Wilkerson and W. H. Gijselaers (eds.), *Bringing Problem-Based Learning to Higher Education: Theory and Practice*. New Directions for Teaching and Learning, no. 68. San Francisco: Jossey-Bass, 1996.

Ratey, J. J. *A User's Guide to the Brain: Perception, Attention, and the Four Theaters of the Brain*. New York: Pantheon, 2001.

Reason, P. "Cooperative Inquiry." In K. Taylor, C. Mariennau, and M. Fiddler (eds.), *Developing Adult Learners: Strategies for Teachers and Trainers*. San Francisco: Jossey-Bass, 2000.

Remland, M. S. *Nonverbal Communication in Everyday Life*. Boston: Houghton Mifflin, 2000.

Rendon, L. "Validating Culturally Diverse Students: Toward a New Model of Learning and Student Development." *Innovative Higher Education*, 1994, *9*(1), 33–52.

Renninger, K. A., and Shumar, W. "Community Building with and for Teachers: The Math Forum as a Resource for Teacher Professional Development." In K. A. Renninger and W. Shumar (eds.), *Building Virtual Communities: Learning and Change in Cyberspace*. New York: Cambridge University Press, 2002.

Renninger, K. A., Hidi, S., and Krapp, A., eds. *The Role of Interest in Learning and Development*. Hillsdale, NJ: Erlbaum, 1992.

Reuter-Lorenz, P., and Lustig, C. "Brain Aging: Reorganizing Discoveries about the Aging Mind." *Current Opinion in Neurobiology*, 2005, *15*(2), 245–251.

Rich, A. Lecture given at Scripps College, Claremont, CA, on the 164th anniversary of Susan B. Anthony's birthday, Feb. 15, 1984.

Rogers, C. R. *Freedom to Learn.* Columbus, OH: Merrill, 1969.

Rogoff, B., and Chavajay, P. "What's Become of Research on the Cultural Basis of Cognitive Development?" *American Psychologist*, 1995, *50*, 859–877.

Rojstaczur, S. "Grade Inflation at American Colleges and Universities." [http://gradeinflation.com/]. 2002.

Rossiter, M. "Radical Mutuality and Self-Other Relationship in Adult Education." In S. B. Merriam, B. C. Courtenay, and R. M. Cervero (eds.), *Global Issues and Adult Education: Perspectives from Latin America, Southern Africa, and the United States.* San Francisco: Jossey-Bass, 2006.

Ryan, R. M., and Deci, E. L. "When Rewards Compete with Nature: The Undermining of Intrinsic Motivation and Self-Regulation." In C. Sansone and J. M. Harackiewicz (eds.), *Intrinsic and Extrinsic Motivation: The Search for Optimal Motivation and Performance.* San Diego, CA: Academic Press, 2000.

Saint-Exupéry, A. de. *The Little Prince.* (K. Woods, trans.) Orlando, FL: Harcourt Brace, 1943.

Salovey, P., and Mayer, J. D. "Emotional Intelligence." *Imagination, Cognition and Personality*, 1990, *9*(3), 185–211.

Samovar, L. A., and Porter, R. E. "Approaches to Understanding Intercultural Communication." In L. A. Samovar, R. E. Porter, and E. R. McDaniel (eds.), *Intercultural Communication: A Reader.* 11th ed. New York: Wadsworth, 2005.

Samovar, L. A., Porter, R. E., and McDaniel, E. R., eds. *Intercultural Communication: A Reader*, 11th ed. New York: Wadsworth, 2005.

Sanes, J., and Lichtman, J. "Induction, Assembly, Maturation, and Maintenance of a Postsynaptic Apparatus." *Nature Reviews Neuroscience*, 2001, *2*(11), 791–805.

Sansone, C., and Smith, J. L. "Interest and Self-Regulation: The Relation between Having To and Wanting To." In C. Sansone and J. M. Harackiewicz (eds.), *Intrinsic and Extrinsic Motivation: The Search for Optimal Motivation and Performance*. New York: Academic, 2000.

Sapolsky, R. *Why Zebras Don't Get Ulcers: The Acclaimed Guide to Stress, Stress-Related Diseases, and Coping*, 3rd ed. New York: Holt, 2004.

Sarason, I. G., ed. *Test Anxiety: Theory, Research and Application*. Hillsdale, NJ: Erlbaum, 1980.

Savin-Baden, M. *Facilitating Problem-Based Learning*. Berkshire, England: Open University Press, 2003.

Schacter, D. L. "Understanding Implicit Memory." *American Psychologist*, 1992, 47(4), 559–569.

Schacter, D. L. *The Seven Sins of Memory*. New York: Houghton Mifflin, 2001.

Schaie, K. W. *Developmental Influences on Adult Intelligence: The Seattle Longitudinal Study*. New York: Oxford University Press, 2005.

Schaie, K. W., and Willis, S. L. *Adult Development and Aging*, 5th ed. Englewood Cliffs, NJ: Prentice Hall, 2002.

Scherer, K. R. "Unconscious Processes in Emotion: The Bulk of the Iceberg." In L. S. Barrett, P. M. Niedenthal, and P. Winkielman (eds.), *Emotion and Consciousness*. New York: Guilford, 2005.

Schied, F. M. "In the Belly of the Beast: Globalization and Adult Education in the United States." In S. B. Merriam, B. C. Courtenay, and R. M. Cervero (eds.), *Global Issues and Adult Education: Perspectives from Latin America, Southern Africa, and the United States*. San Francisco: Jossey-Bass, 2006.

Schön, D. A. *Educating the Reflective Practitioner: Toward a New Design for Teaching and Learning in the Professions*. San Francisco: Jossey-Bass, 1987.

Schultz, W. "Multiple Reward Signals in the Brain." *Nature Reviews Neuroscience*, 2000, 1(3), 199–207.

Schultz, W., and Dickinson, A. "Neuronal Coding of Prediction Errors." *Annual Review of Neuroscience*, 2000, 23, 473–500.

Scott, J. P. "A Time to Learn." *Psychology Today*, 1969, 2(10), 46–48, 66–67.

Seligman, M. *Helplessness*. San Francisco: Freeman, 1975.

Serious Games Initiative. Home page. [http://www.seriousgames.org/index2.html]. March 4, 2007.

Sheckley, B. G., and Bell, S. "Experience, Consciousness, and Learning: Implications for Instruction." In S. Johnson and K. Taylor (eds.), *The Neuroscience of Adult Learning*. New Directions for Adult and Continuing Education, no. 110. San Francisco: Jossey-Bass, 2006.

Shimamura, A. "Relational Binding Theory and the Role of Consolidation." In L. Squire and D. Schacter (eds.), *Neuropsychology of Memory* (pp. 61–72). New York: Guilford, 2002.

Shor, I. "Education in Politics: Paulo Freire's Critical Pedagogy." In P. McLaren and P. Leonard (eds.), *Paulo Freire: A Critical Encounter*. New York: Routledge, 1993.

Shor, I. *Empowering Education: Critical Teaching for Social Change*. Chicago: University of Chicago Press, 1992.

Shulman, L. S. "Knowledge and Teaching: Foundations of the New Reform." *Harvard Educational Review*, 1987, 57(1), 1–22.

Silvia, P. J. "Interest and Interests: The Psychology of Constructive Capriciousness." *Review of General Psychology*, 2001, 5, 270–290.

Sinacore, A. L., and Enns, C. Z. "Diversity Feminisms: Postmodern, Women-of-Color, Antiracist, Lesbian, Third-Wave, and Global Perspectives." In C. Z. Enns and A. L. Sinacore (eds.), *Teaching and Social Justice: Integrating Multicultural and Feminist Theories in the Classroom*. Washington, DC: American Psychological Association, 2005.

Skinner, B. F. *Verbal Behavior*. Englewood Cliffs, NJ: Appleton-Century-Crofts, 1957.

Smith, P. L., and Ragan, T. J. *Instructional Design*, 3rd ed. San Francisco: Jossey-Bass, 2004.

Smith, R. M. *Learning How to Learn*. Chicago: Follett, 1982.

Smolak, L. *Adult Development*. Upper Saddle River, NJ: Prentice Hall, 1993.

Solorzano, D. "Teaching and Social Change: Reflections on a Freirean Approach in a College Classroom." *Teaching Sociology*, 1989, *17*, 218–225.

Sousa, D. A. *How the Brain Learns*, 3rd ed. Thousand Oaks, CA: Corwin, 2006.

Squire, I. R., and Kandel, E. R. *Memory from Mind to Molecules*. New York: Scientific American Library, 2000.

Sternberg, R. J. *Successful Intelligence*. New York: Plume, 1997.

Sternberg, R. J., and others. *Practical Intelligence in Everyday Life*. New York: Cambridge University Press, 2000.

Stickgold, R., James, L., and Hobson, J. "Visual Discrimination Requires Sleep after Training." *Nature Neuroscience*, 2000, *3*, 1237–1238.

Stipek, D. *Motivation to Learn: From Theory to Practice*, 4th ed. Boston: Allyn and Bacon, 2002.

Svinicki, M. D. *Learning and Motivation in the Postsecondary Classroom*. Bolton, MA: Anker, 2004.

Sweller, J., van Merrienboer, J. J. G., and Paas, F.G.W.C. "Cognitive Architecture and Instructional Design." *Educational Psychology Review*, 1998, *10*, 251–296.

Tappan, M. B. "Sociocultural Psychology and Caring Pedagogy: Exploring Vygotsky's 'Hidden Curriculum.'" *Educational Psychologist*, 1998, *33*(1), 23–33.

Tatum, B. D. "Talking about Race, Learning about Racism: The Application of Racial Identity Development Theory in the Classroom." *Harvard Educational Review*, 1992, *62*(1), 1–24.

Tatum, B. D. *Why Are All the Black Kids Sitting Together in the Cafeteria? And Other Conversations about Race.* New York: Basic Books, 2003.

Taylor, K., Marienau, C., and Fiddler, M. *Developing Adult Learners: Strategies for Teachers and Trainers.* San Francisco: Jossey-Bass, 2000.

Tennant, M. "Practical Intelligence." In L. M. English (ed.), *International Encyclopedia of Adult Education.* New York: Palgrave Macmillan, 2005.

Tennant, M., and Pogson, P. *Learning and Change in the Adult Years: A Developmental Perspective.* San Francisco: Jossey-Bass, 1995.

Tharp, R., and Gallimore, R. *Rousing Minds to Life: Teaching, Learning, and Schooling in Social Context.* Cambridge, England: Cambridge University Press, 1988.

Tinto, V. "Colleges as Communities: Taking Research on Student Persistence Seriously." *Review of Higher Education,* 1998, *21*(2), 167–177.

Tisdell, E. J. "Poststructural Feminist Pedagogies: The Possibilities and Limitations of Feminist Emancipatory Adult Learning and Practice." *Adult Education Quarterly,* 1998, *48*(3), 139–156.

Tisdell, E. J. *Exploring Spirituality and Culture in Adult and Higher Education.* San Francisco: Jossey-Bass, 2003.

Tobias, S. "Interest, Prior Knowledge, and Learning." *Review of Educational Research,* 1994, *64,* 37–54.

Tobin, K. "Role of Wait Time in Higher Cognitive Level Learning." *Review of Educational Research,* 1987, *57*(1), 69–95.

Tomlinson, C. A. *How to Differentiate Instruction in Mixed Ability Classrooms,* 2nd ed. Alexandria, VA: Association for Supervision and Curriculum Development, 2001.

Tomlinson, C. A. "Differentiating Instruction." *Theory into Practice,* 2005, *44*(3), 262–269.

Tracey, W. R. *Designing Training and Development Systems*, 3rd ed. New York: AMACOM, 1992.

Trawick, L., and Corno, L. "Expanding the Volitional Resources of Urban Community College Students." In P. R. Pintrich (ed.), *Understanding Self-Regulated Learning*. New Directions for Teaching and Learning, no. 63. San Francisco: Jossey-Bass, 1995.

Tsang, H. Wh., Paterson, M., and Packer, T. "Self-Directed Learning in Fieldwork Education with Learning Contracts." *British Journal of Therapy and Rehabilitation*, 2002, 9(5), 184–189.

Uguroglu, M., and Walberg, H. J. "Motivation and Achievement: A Quantitative Synthesis." *American Educational Research Journal*, 1979, 16, 375–389.

U.S. Census Bureau. Annual Demographic Supplement to the March 2002 Current Population Survey: "People: Aging." [http://factfinder.census.gov/jsp/saff/SAFFInfo.jsp?_pageId=tp2_aging]. October 2006.

U.S. Department of Education, National Center for Education Statistics. *The Condition of Education*. Washington, DC: U.S. Government Printing Office, 1998.

U.S. Department of Health and Human Services. *A Profile of Older Americans: 2003*. Washington, DC: Administration on Aging, 2003.

U.S. Department of Labor, Bureau of Labor Statistics. *A Profile of the Working Poor*. Report No. 968. Washington, DC: U.S. Government Printing Office, 2003.

Varella, F. J., Thompson, E., and Rosch, E. *The Embodied Mind: Cognitive Science and Human Experience*. Cambridge, MA: MIT Press, 1995.

Vargas, J. S. *Behavioral Psychology for Teachers*. New York: HarperCollins, 1977.

Vaughan, M. S. *The End of Training: How Simulations Are Reshaping Business Training*. Golden, CO: Keystone Business Press, 2006.

Viens, J., and Kallenbach, S. *Multiple Intelligences and Adult Literacy: A Sourcebook for Practitioners*. New York: Teachers College Press, 2004.

Voss, J. F. "Problem Solving and the Educational Process." In A. Lesgold and R. Glaser (eds.), *Foundations for a Psychology of Education*. Hillsdale, NJ: Erlbaum, 1989.

Vygotsky, L. S. *Mind in Society: The Development of Higher Psychological Processes*. Cambridge, Mass.: Harvard University Press, 1978.

Walberg, H. J., and Uguroglu, M. "Motivation and Educational Productivity: Theories, Results, and Implications." In L. J. Fyans Jr. (ed.), *Achievement Motivation: Recent Trends in Theory and Research*. New York: Plenum, 1980.

Wallis, J. D., Anderson, K. C., and Miller, E. K. "Single Neurons in Pre-Frontal Cortex Encode Abstract Rules." *Nature*, 2001, *411*, 953–956.

Walvoord, B. E. *Assessment Clear and Simple: A Practical Guide for Institutions, Departments, and General Education*. San Francisco: Jossey-Bass, 2004.

Walvoord, B. E., and Anderson, V. J. *Effective Grading: A Tool for Learning and Assessment*. San Francisco: Jossey-Bass, 1998.

Watkins, J. M., and Mohr, B. J. *Appreciative Inquiry: Change at the Speed of Imagination*. San Francisco: Jossey-Bass/Pfeiffer, 2001.

Watson, J. S., and Ramey, C. G. "Reactions to Response Contingent Stimulation in Early Infancy." *Merrill Palmer Quarterly*, 1972, *18*, 219–228.

Weiner, B. *Human Motivation: Metaphors, Theories, and Research*. Thousand Oaks, CA: Sage, 1992.

Weiner, B. "Interpersonal and Intrapersonal Theories of Motivation from an Attributional Perspective." *Educational Psychology Review*, 2000, *12*, 1–14.

Wertsch, J. V. *Voices of the Mind: A Sociocultural Approach to Mediated Action*. Cambridge, MA: Harvard University Press, 1991.

Whaba, M. A., and Bridwell, L. G. "Maslow Reconsidered: A Review of Research on the Need Hierarchy Theory." *Organizational Behavior and Human Performance*, 1976, *15*, 212–240.

White, R. W. "Motivation Reconsidered: The Concept of Competence." *Psychological Review*, 1959, 66, 297–333.

Wiggins, G. P. *Educative Assessment: Designing Assessments to Inform and Improve Student Performance.* San Francisco: Jossey-Bass, 1998.

Willis, J. *Research-Based Strategies to Ignite Student Learning.* Alexandria, VA: Association for Supervision and Curriculum Development, 2006.

Winkielman, P., Berridge, K. C., and Wilbarger, J. L. "Emotion, Behavior, and Conscious Experience: Once More without Feeling." In L. S. Barrett, P. M. Niedenthal, and P. Winkielman (eds.), *Emotion and Consciousness.* New York: Guilford, 2005.

Wlodkowski, R. J. "An Analysis of the History, Status, and Impact of Peer Coaching at the British Columbia Institute of Technology." Report to the Learning Skills Center of the British Columbia Institute of Technology, Vancouver, 1992.

Wlodkowski, R. J. "Brainstorming: Reasons for Grade Inflation." New Ventures' Partner School Conference, Puerto Rico, July 19, 2000.

Wlodkowski, R. J. "Fostering Motivation in Professional Development Programs." In K. P. King and P. A. Lawler (eds.), *New Perspective on Designing and Implementing Professional Development of Teachers and Adults.* New Directions for Adult and Continuing Education, no. 98. San Francisco: Jossey-Bass, 2003.

Wlodkowski, R. J., and Ginsberg, M. B. *Diversity and Motivation: Culturally Responsive Teaching.* San Francisco: Jossey-Bass, 1995.

Wlodkowski, R. J., and Kasworm, C. K., eds. *Accelerated Learning for Adults: The Promise and Practice of Intensive Educational Formats.* New Directions for Adult and Continuing Education, no. 97. San Francisco: Jossey-Bass, 2003.

Wlodkowski, R. J., and Stiller, J. *Accelerated Learning Online Research Project: Phase 1.* Denver: Center for the Study of Accelerated Learning, Regis University, 2005.

Wlodkowski, R. J., Mauldin, J. E., and Campbell, S. "Early Exit: Understanding Adult Attrition in Accelerated and Traditional Postsecondary Programs." *Synopsis*, July 2002, Indianapolis: Lumina Foundation for Education, 1–12.

Wlodkowski, R. J., Mauldin, J. E., and Gahn, S. W. *Learning in the Fast Lane: Adult Learners' Persistence and Success in Accelerated College Programs.* Indianapolis: Lumina Foundation for Education, 2001.

Wolfe, B., and Zuvekas, S. *Nonmarket Outcomes of Schooling.* Discussion Paper No. 1065–95. Madison, WI: Institute for Research on Poverty, 1995.

Woolfolk, A. *Educational Psychology*, 10th ed. Boston: Pearson, 2007.

Young, C. "Grade Inflation in Higher Education." *ERIC Digest*, ED482558, ERIC Clearinghouse on Higher Education [http://www.ericdigests.org/2005-1/grade.htm]. 2003.

Zimmerman, B. J. "Becoming a Self-Regulated Learner: An Overview." *Theory into Practice*, 2002, *41*(2), 64–70.

Zimmerman, B. J., and Campillo, M. "Motivating Self-Regulated Problem Solvers." In J. E. Davison and R. J. Sternberg (eds.), *The Nature of Problem Solving*. New York: Cambridge University Press, 2003.

Zimmerman, B. J., and Kitsantas, A. "Acquiring Writing Revision Skill: Shifting from Process to Outcome Self-Regulatory Goals." *Journal of Educational Psychology*, 1999, *91*, 241–250.

Zimmerman, B. J., and Kitsantas, A. "The Hidden Dimension of Personal Competence: Self-Regulated Learning and Practice." In A. J. Elliot and C. S. Dweck (eds.), *Handbook of Competence and Motivation*. New York: Guilford, 2005.

Zull, J. E. *The Art of Changing the Brain: Enriching the Practice of Teaching by Exploring the Biology of Learning*. Sterling, VA: Stylus, 2002.

Zull, J. E. "Key Aspects of How the Brain Learns." In S. Johnson and K. Taylor (eds.), *The Neuroscience of Adult Learning*. New Directions for Adult and Continuing Education, no. 110. San Francisco: Jossey-Bass, 2006.

Name Index

Suject Index

something beneficial for adults as,
50–52; pairing with enthusiasm,
71–72; as thorough knowledge of
topic, 52–54

F

Failure, 76, 195–196
Fear: dealing with, 436; minimizing
conditions stimulating, 177–178;
reducing for participation,
236–237; test anxiety, 313
Feedback: flow experiences and, 267;
instruction plans incorporating, 41,
397, 401; learning and, 19–20;
prompt, 191–192; providing
effective, 314–322, 397, 398,
407; requesting on instructional
clarity, 83–84, 85–86;
self-adjustment from, 316, 397;
using constructive criticism as,
363–366
Feeling connected. *See* Inclusion
Feelings: accepting expression of,
253–254; conceptualizing to focus,
252; considering learners'
perspectives and, 66–68. *See also*
Emotion
Five hanging pendula, 283–285
Flash MX for Interactive Simulation
(Kaye and Castillo), 297
Flow: characteristics of, 267–269;
description of, 22–23, 266–267;
engagement and, 232–234; as sign
of learner motivation, 427
FMRI (functional magnetic resonance
imaging), 13
Formative assessments, 183, 324
Foundational entry point, 216, 218
Foundational exit point, 219
Four questions for instructional
planning, 390, 391, 422–423
Framework for culturally responsive
teaching. *See* Motivational
Framework for Culturally
Responsive Teaching, The
Free writing, 288
Frontal lobe, 14

Frustration, 178
Funds of knowledge, 232

G

Games: developing to explain
learning concepts, 305;
instructional plans using, 412; using
in adult education, 301–302. *See
also* Simulations
Gender: avoiding bias toward,
322–323; orientation in cultures,
131–132
Generativity, 310
Gerontological Society of America, 34
Goals: committing to, 209;
establishing confidence by
completing, 206; establishing
relevant learning, 118, 119;
expressive outcomes, 157–158; flow
experiences and, 267; focusing
attention on, 207–208; identifying
learning, 152–160, 399, 410, 415,
418; learning contracts as,
210–214; learning with clearly
defined, 153–155; making
challenging and attainable,
200–202; making schedule for,
209–210; measuring progress
toward, 206–207; positive
interdependence of, 143–144;
preplanning to achieve, 208;
problem-solving, 155, 157, 158;
setting, 204–210; understanding
learners', 59–65
Goethe, J. W., 186
Grades: about motivation,
assessments, and, 352–355;
authenticity of, 312–314; GPAs,
353; learning contracts as aid for,
354–355
Group Embedded Figures Test, 205
Group feedback, 321–322
Guidelines: assisted learning, 185;
group participation, 164–166, 251;
introducing cooperative learning,
162–166; portfolio, 336–337;
rubrics, 342–344

400, 404, 406, 408; essential conditions of, 114; establishing inclusion, 113, 114, 116, 118, 399; example instructional plan 1, 394–398; example instructional plan 2, 398–402; example instructional plan 3, 403–409; example instructional plan 4, 409–414; example instructional plan 5, 414–421; examples, analogies, metaphors, and stories in instruction, 257–259, 419; facilitating learning with relevant activities, 275–283, 401, 404, 418, 419; fostering lifelong learning, 430–431; four questions for instructional planning, 390, 391, 422–423; frequent response opportunities for learners, 235–239; giving effective feedback, 314–322, 397, 398, 401, 407, 413; goal-setting methods, 204–210; helping learners avoid failure, 195–196; helping learners recognize natural consequences of learning, 373–374, 408, 413; humor in instruction, 255–257, 419; identifying learning objectives and goals, 152–160, 399, 410, 415, 418; illustrated, 113; incentives to maintain motivation, 370–372; indicating intention to help adults learn, 138–139, 415; inducing parapathic emotions, 257; instructional design using, 377–378; instructional planning using, 421–422; internships and other methods for authenticating learning, 302–303; introducing new topics with K-W-L strategy, 222–223, 411; introducing norms and participation guidelines, 162–166; invention and artistry in deepening meaning and emotion, 303–306, 407; knowledge of culturally different groups, 92; learning activity as invitation to

learn, 220–222, 395, 411; learning contracts, 210–214; methods of self-assessment, 344–352, 417; modeling expected learning, 196–198, 407; observation guide for, 428, 439–444; outlining benefits of learning activity, 254–255; overview of, 112–114; planning time for successful learning, 203–204; praising and rewarding learning, 366–370; promoting control of learning, 189–192; providing learners chance to demonstrate strengths and knowledge, 329, 332–339, 413, 417; providing rationale for course requirements, 166–167, 175; purpose of, 101–102; realizing learner's accountability for learning, 239–241, 396, 406; relating learning to individual, 249–255, 416; scaffolding complex learning, 183–186, 189, 400, 402, 419; self-assessment for applying, 379–381, 401; self-understanding in, 92; sharing something of value with learners, 139–140, 175, 395, 405; significance of, 122–123; simulations and games in learning, 296–302, 412, 418; as source for instruction plans, 392–393, 423–424; structuring learning activities clearly, 244–247, 405; summary of strategies, 382–385; superimposing on existing instruction plans, 390–392, 422–423; support for self-regulation skills in, 433–434; uncertainty, anticipation, and prediction, 259–263, 400, 406; using and reviewing, 381, 386; using Multiple Intelligences Theory to learn topic or concept, 215–220; variety in learning, 241–244, 411, 419
Motivational plans: effective use of, 115; including with instruction plans, 47

Rewards: maintaining motivation with incentives, 370–372; motivating competence with, 366–370
Role playing: embodying new learning with, 294–296; instructional plans using, 409, 412, 419
Roles: of instructor in collaborative learning, 140–141; positive interdependence of, 144; reciprocal learning, 186
Rubrics: as aid for grading, 354–355; defined, 340; designing, 339–344, 420; example, 342, 343; guidelines for, 342–344

S

Satiation, 75
Scaffolding complex learning, 183–186, 189, 400, 402, 419
Security: maintaining learner, 263; role playing to protect sense of, 296
Self-assessments: for applying motivational framework, 118, 119, 379–381, 401; closure techniques for, 348–350; Critical Incident Questionnaire, 350–352; estimating learners motivation with, 425–426; feedback as, 316, 397; "Head, Heart, Hand" closure activity for, 348, 421; helping learners recognize natural consequences, 373–374, 408, 413; journals and, 346–347; methods of, 344–352, 417; note-taking pairs for, 348–349; post-writes, 347; respecting confidentiality of, 345; "Summarizing Questions" activity for, 349–350; using, 190
Self-determination, 158
Self-directed competence, 311–312
Self-directed learning (SDL), 431
Self-education, 93
Self-efficacy: acquiring, 188–189; defined, 187; developing, 172, 173, 186–189; effort attribution and,

192–195, 405, 416; establishing challenging and attainable goals, 200–202; helping learners avoid failure, 195–196; making fair and clear criteria for assessments, 202–203; modeling expected learning, 196–198, 407
Self-regulation, 431–434
Sense of mission, 437
Septum, 16
Serious Games Initiative, 302
Service learning, 302–303
Service Learning in Higher Education (Buntin), 303
Settling time, 248
Shared expectations, 162–163
Sharing: providing opportunities for, 136–138, 415, 418; something of value, 139–140, 175, 395, 405
Silence, 252–253
Simulations, 296–302; defined, 296–297; elements of example, 297–299; instructional plans using, 412, 418; sample description of, 299–301; uses for, 297; using games in adult education, 301–302
Situational interest, 229–230
Skills: adapting instruction to learners', 65–66; expertise as ability to demonstrate, 52–53
Smart models, 301
Social cognition, 431
Social skills facilitating cooperative learning, 146–147
SSIPP acronym, 220–222
Stereotyping, 323
Stories in instruction, 257–259, 419
Stress, 76
Structuring learning activities: breaks, settling time, and physical exercises for, 248; connecting, 245–247; ending activities, 247, 290–291; instructional plans, 411; introductions, 245
Study groups for problem-based learning, 278